Füsilier-Regiment von Alt-Loßberg
Chef, Se. Excell. Gen. Lieut. v. Loßberg

FACING *Washington's* CROSSING

The Hessians AND THE Battle of Trenton

STEVEN BIER

WESTHOLME
Yardley

Facing title page: Carl, J.H., "Fusilier Regiment von Alt-Lossberg" (1784). (*Anne S.K. Brown Military Collection, Brown University Library*)

Maps by Tracy Dungan

Westholme Publishing, LLC
904 Edgewood Road
Yardley, Pennsylvania 19067
Visit our Web site at www.westholmepublishing.com

ISBN: 978-1-59416-443-9
Also available as an eBook.
Printed in the United States of America.

Contents

PART III. *WAR*

PART IV. *NEW JERSEY*

PART V. *TRENTON*

PART VI. *AFTERMATH*

Illustrations

MAPS

A gallery of images appears after page 124.

Preface

Emanuel Leutze's painting *Washington Crossing the Delaware* hangs from steel beams embedded into the wall of the American Wing of the Museum of Modern Art in New York City. Displayed in the museum for more than a century, reprinted in textbooks, parodied in political cartoons with George Washington represented by a spectrum of characters from Snoopy to President Barack Obama, and reproduced on American paraphernalia from postcards to belt buckles, the painting is one of the nation's most enduring icons. Groups of schoolchildren still visit the gallery, gazing up at the image of General George Washington leading a surprise attack across the Delaware River on Christmas night 1776. He stands at the boat's bow, staring into the distance toward an unseen enemy on the other side of the river. His red-lined cape flaps in the wind. His boat is crowded with soldiers who strain against the ice-laden current with wooden oars. One soldier deflects ice away with a pole, while another at the back of the boat crudely steers using an oar as a paddle. James Monroe stands next to Washington. The twenty-two-year-old Monroe clutches a flag against the wind as he, like Washington, stares into the distance.[1]

But there is something different in the appearance of the two future presidents. Monroe is leaning to one side, wide-eyed, perhaps worrying about the fragility of their wooden boat or perhaps anxious that the enemy has detected them. Washington stands erect. His left foot rests nonchalantly on the side of the boat. He stares straight ahead in defiance, gazing into the light of dawn toward the unforeseen enemy that waits on the far shore. He and his men know all too well the enemy they hope to surprise: the Hessian garrison in Trenton.

Historically, this iconic work of art has been romanticized. However, Leutze painted a scene designed to evoke emotion and convey a message to its viewers. He succeeded, as the scene he created has served as a symbol of resolve and defiance since its public debut, helping to keep the story of Washington's crossing alive.

While many Americans are familiar with Washington's crossing of the Delaware, fewer understand who Washington was going to attack. Most textbooks offer little about the Hessians beyond casting them as convenient villains.

On his twelve-and-a-half by twenty-one-and-a-half foot canvas, Leutze has captured the desperation and firm resolution that enabled the Continental Army, a volunteer army of farmer-soldiers, to ultimately defeat the British Empire. While the painting has etched that cold Christmas night into American consciousness, it leaves unanswered questions about the Hessians encamped in the village of Trenton on the other side of the Delaware River. Who were these men? Why were they in Trenton? Their homeland, the Principality of Hessen-Kassel, lay about one hundred miles north of Frankfurt, Germany—about four thousand miles and a three-month ocean voyage from America. How did German soldiers from this distant land become Washington's most feared and despised enemy?

The Americans were British subjects fighting a British sovereign. Why would the Hessians embark on a perilous voyage across the Atlantic Ocean to fight against a people who were rebelling against someone else's king? The 2,700-square-mile region of Hessen-Kassel was smaller than Connecticut and had a population of only three hundred thousand in 1776. How did soldiers from this small feudal state end up at the crossroads of history on the banks of the Delaware River?

The Hessians were ruled by Frederick II, Landgrave of Hessen-Kassel, who had inherited the throne from his father, William VIII. Addressed by the title of "His Serene Highness," Frederick posed for portraits sporting military medals overlying his family coat of arms. He paraded about with a flag depicting a sword-wielding lion sticking out its tongue. Frederick's theatrical display seemed more befitting a comic opera, not the grand stage of history alongside figures such as George Washington and King George III.

Almost certainly unbeknownst to the Hessian soldiers that Christmas night was that competing political and philosophical ideas of eighteenth-century Europe had converged on their small land-locked principality. Frederick II had studied Enlightenment philosophy in Geneva. He was deeply moved by the works of the great philosophers of the Enlightenment and even corresponded with Voltaire. At the same time, Frederick despised the American rebels who revolted against their rightful sovereign, King George III, Fredericks's nephew. Tutored by followers of Voltaire but raised under the precepts of the militaristic Prussian Frederick the Great, the landgrave devised a plan for his subjects that was so ambitious and contradictory in its goals that by the end of 1776, the army of Hessen-Kassel would be both feared and then humiliated. Following a precedent established by his grandfather, Frederick decided to rent out his adult male subjects as soldiers to George III. The landgrave hoped that the money raised from fighting in this foreign war would lead to great benefits for the families of these soldiers. This plan resulted in one of the great ironies of the eighteenth century: Frederick II rented out his adult male subjects as soldier conscripts to bring the individualism, human rights, and liberties of the Enlightenment to their country.

The ideals of the American Revolution would, of course, prove irrepressible. The Hessians' reputation would soon be permanently tarnished, and most Americans would remember them only as "mercenaries" who attempted to crush George Washington and his fledgling revolution. Although colonial publications denounced them as "barbarians" who indulged in "rapine and bloodshed," the reality was more nuanced. Some of the cruelties attributed to the Hessians are undoubtedly true. The Hessian army was primarily composed of peasants who could be bigoted, misogynistic, and pitiless, particularly toward those who had rebelled against their king. However, for the most part, the Hessians followed eighteenth-century European rules of engagement, often showing more restraint than their British allies. Yet, it is the perception, not the reality, that has defined the Hessians' legacy.

The full story of the Hessians is complex. Most Hessian soldiers were forced to travel to a world they knew nothing about to fight in a war they did not understand. This book presents Washington's crossing from the Hessians' point of view. We will follow the opposing armies, and in particular three Hessian soldiers who fought Washington's troops at the Battle of Trenton: Private Johannes Reuber and Lieutenants Jakob Piel and Andreas Wiederhold.

The tale of the Hessians is just as fantastic as any adventure: terrifying sea voyages, survival in a land four thousand miles from home, ambivalent rulers, military conquests, and humiliating defeats. Throughout their ordeal, the Hessians grappled with a total misunderstanding of their American enemy and the democratic principles that they found themselves fighting against.

In Leutze's painting, one might follow Washington's gaze through the breaking dawn to envision the Hessian regiments asleep in the snow-covered village of Trenton, muskets at their sides, drowsy sentries on the town's dirt roads huddled against the icy rain, blissfully unaware that the same Enlightenment ideas motivating their landgrave to ship them to the New World were also inspiring the American rebels to march against them. By morning, their Teutonic world would be shattered. Most would find themselves prisoners of the Americans. Some of those prisoners would choose to remain in the New World after the war ended. Eventually, their descendants would become part of the foundation of the new American nation, and in a way neither they nor their landgrave could ever have imagined, they would ultimately benefit from the ideas of the Enlightenment as citizens of the new American republic. What would surely have been even more unbelievable to these Hessian soldiers was that one day, generations later, the descendants of Hessians who stayed in America would return to Europe, wading through the surf at the beaches of Normandy to confront the descendants of those who had remained in the fatherland.

FACING *Washington's* CROSSING

Prologue

Boston, April 1775

On April 19, 1775, British soldiers fired upon, or were fired upon by (depending on whose story is to be believed) colonists at Lexington and Concord, Massachusetts. The colonial response was immediate. American ships raced across the Atlantic with the rebels' account, reaching British newspapers before the government's own reports arrived. Messengers rode south through New York and New Jersey, ferried across the Delaware into Pennsylvania, and pressed on to Virginia and the Carolinas, reaching even to Kentucky's wilderness. Along the route, town committeemen were roused from sleep, signing for dispatches in their nightshirts before sending on fresh riders. Within days, talk of resistance and even rebellion spread along the entire Eastern Seaboard.[1]

In New England, the same scene was played over and over. On hearing the news, men went to their homes, collected their firearms, and joined neighbors on the road to Boston. Wives packed meat and bread, expecting them home in a few days to tend the crops. Women and children lined the routes, offering water to the passing columns. By nightfall, the men lay under blankets on the hills surrounding Boston, muskets at their sides.

Overnight, the largest army ever seen on the continent had spontaneously formed and taken up residence on the heights looking down on Boston. The speed with which the angry, determined men of New England had assembled astounded Patriot officers and alarmed British officials. By sunset on April 19, campfires ringed the city. Through the darkness, the British soldiers now trapped in the city heard drums, voices, and the steady tramp of arriving companies. While future generations would speak of the Spirit of 1776, the spirit of 1775 was undoubtedly just as, if not more, zealous. Volunteers poured in from New Hampshire, Connecticut, and Rhode Island. Within sixty days, ten companies of riflemen arrived from Virginia, Maryland, and Pennsylvania—some having marched eight hundred miles.[2]

The British were dumbfounded. General Thomas Gage, the commander in chief of His Majesty's Army in New England on April 18, was now hemmed in by this newborn army on April 19. He wrote with remarkable understatement that the Americans showed "an uncommon degree of zeal and enthusiasm." This growing rebel force threatened not just the British Army in Boston but Crown control of the entire Eastern Seaboard.[3]

But the Americans had serious problems too.

Their collection of militias lacked central leadership and military infrastructure. The Second Continental Congress, meeting in Philadelphia within three weeks, would need to address these deficiencies quickly. Unbeknownst to the Americans, the British high command had convinced the king that he needed to supplement his forces that had stretched thin across a global empire. After other European powers declined to lease soldiers to the British, King George began negotiations to hire highly trained professional soldiers from the Germanic state of Hessen-Kassel.

Hessen-Kassel represented the antithesis of the nation the colonists hoped to build. The Hessian military was steeped in tradition, having fought in nearly every major European conflict for a century. Its infrastructure was capable of equipping and fielding an army in weeks. But the average Hessian soldier, usually illiterate and devoutly Calvinist, had no concept of the American cause. His world was bounded by loyalty to the prince, honor, and tradition. Most Hessians had never seen the Atlantic Ocean, encountered a free Black person, or imagined a land where farmers owned their soil.[4]

The militia and volunteers surrounding Boston who rushed to join the American army brought passion but little military experience to their cause. Most owned farms or shops, and unlike the Hessians, most could read and write. Their backgrounds reflected colonial diversity: Anglican, Catholic, and Jewish; some owned slaves while others opposed slavery. Though their feelings toward King George remained mixed, they shared a deep resentment of Parliament.

The cultural differences between the Hessians and the Americans were vast, and soon, these differing cultures would clash to determine if the New World would continue to be ruled by the Old World or if a new self-governing nation would arise.

PART I

Hessen-Kassel

CHAPTER 1

A Village Goes to War

January–April 1776

DURING WINTER 1775–1776, Arctic winds swept across the North Sea, carrying British ships into Germanic ports. They brought to the tiny Principality of Hessen-Kassel, several hundred miles inland, news of revolution in America against King George III. For seventeen-year-old Johannes Reuber, this meant opportunity—a chance to serve his prince and go to war.

Two years earlier, Reuber had reported on his fifteenth birthday to his village council in Niedervellmar, as mandated, to register for the army. Local pastors verified recruitment lists against church records, drafting poor teenagers while exempting married men.[1]

Like most of Hessen-Kassel, the town of Niedervellmar, population 357, was impoverished, its economy stunted by a lack of natural resources. The rocky terrain was poorly suited for agriculture, cursed with infertile soil and a generally cold and rainy climate.[2] Thirteen years earlier, during the Seven Years' War, foreign troops had ravaged the countryside, destroying crops and stealing cattle, wrecking the nation's fragile economy. The principality had never fully recovered.

The teenagers of Hessen-Kassel knew they would be soldiers in the Hessian army. All young men were eligible for the draft if they were "strong and straight-limbed," aged sixteen to thirty, and not under five-foot-six-inches, or five-foot-four inches if still growing.[3] There was no escaping registration for military service. Hessian officers often marched potential army recruits, gangs of mostly foreigners and landless wanderers, through Niedervellmar on the way to Kassel, the capital of the principality. The great city was only a few miles away with castles and gardens. Still, here in Niedervellmar, there were no castles, just homes built by peasants, who, unable to obtain enough lumber in the war-denuded forests of Kassel, built half-timbered houses of widely spaced wooden beams stuffed with mud and branches. The wind seeped through cracks in the muddy walls, leaving the villagers perpetually cold.[4]

Unscrupulous recruiting agents tried to enlist any males they encountered. Though army doctors could grant exemptions, the list of qualifying conditions was small. Potential recruits stood against cold walls with pants dropped to their ankles as doctors roughly probed the men's groins, searching for causes of exemption, looking for hernias, signs of bubonic plague, or swollen lymph nodes.

The renting out of the Hessian army was a lucrative business, vital to the nation's economy. Still, it made little sense to undermine other essential enterprises, so the recruiting agents were under orders from the prince to exempt those men who were essential to the economy or hard to replace. This included the hangmen who conducted public executions, apprentices in all kinds of trades, men who hauled salt, cooking pot salesmen, students, those who performed public whippings of criminals, servants at the prince's court, liveried servants of noblemen, miners, property-owning farmers, married men with families, and high-income taxpayers. Noblemen, homeowners, sons of land-owning families, and the rare affluent businessman could receive an exemption from service by paying a contribution to the state or by paying an impoverished neighbor to serve in their place.[5] Of course, clergy could not be recruited. Jewish men were prohibited from military service, as the government believed their presence would "corrupt" other troops.[6]

A surprising number of men wanted to join the army. These were mostly men facing social and economic hardships: the poverty stricken, misfits, and deserters. Officials classified them as undesirable "riff-raff." Criminals were rejected if they bore visible signs of previous punishments from the police, such as cutoff ears and noses or branding scars. The one criterion for rejection that cut across all social barriers was bad teeth, for without teeth, a soldier couldn't bite open gunpowder cartridges in battle.[7]

On New Year's Day 1776, the regiment was ordered to join Major Johann Jost Matteus's company at Immenhausen. After a two-hour march along six miles of dreary rutted roads, Reuber and the other village soldiers reached Immenhausen. The next day, his group was put on the road again, marching three miles to the village of Grabenstein where they were quartered, equipped, and began training twice a day.[8] Throughout Hessen-Kassel—in tiny villages with ancient Germanic names—Ziegenhain, Wolfhagen, and Melsungen—men mustered arms. The principality of three hundred thousand souls prepared for war, though only a few men of power knew where they would fight.[9]

The next two months tested young Reuber severely. His battalion joined the Rall Grenadier Regiment under Colonel Johann Gottlieb Rall, a fifty-year-old veteran of thirty-six years of service. The army was his calling—he joined his father's regiment as a fourteen-year-old cadet in 1740, earning promotion to warrant officer within a year. His combat record was extraordinary: the War of Austrian Succession, Scotland's Jacobite Rising of 1745, the Seven Years' War, and service to Catherine the Great in Russia's Fourth Russo-Turkish War. Rall rose through the ranks, eventually taking command as colonel of an infantry regiment in 1771.[10]

Though Rall was well-liked by his men, his middle-class manners and earthy language grated on aristocratic Hessian officers. He showed no deference to superiors who lacked his combat experience, telling them exactly what he thought regardless of their noble birth. They resented his attitude and despised his uncouth demeanor, but they could not deny his fighting spirit.

His adjutant's diary revealed strengths and troubling weaknesses. While praising Rall as "magnanimous," "generous," and worthy of "the highest respect," he also described a man easily distracted: "His love of life was too great. A thought came to him, then another, so that he could not settle on a firm decision." Something was not quite right with Colonel Rall. This deficit of attention was manageable while he was under the command of experienced officers; but if he was ever given an independent command, his actions could prove catastrophic.[11]

***

For sixty grueling days, the regiment trained in bitter cold and deep snow until their skills matched the other seasoned units. They drilled on slippery ice, learning to keep their balance as they plunged bayonets into straw-filled dummies. In formation, they learned to keep two feet between each man in line, front and back, and two feet between soldiers on either side, their elbows nearly touching during firing drills. Since inexperienced soldiers tended to shoot too high, they practiced aiming for an enemy's belly, firing at wooden targets that splintered when hit. Daily parades dominated their routine—marching back and forth through town, shouldering muskets with hands numbed by cold.[12]

The regiment buzzed with terrifying rumors—none more unsettling than talk of sailing across the Atlantic to America. Though this made sense, as King George III was related by marriage to the landgrave and the king's colonies in America were in open revolt, most of the men had never seen the ocean, let alone imagined crossing it.[13]

The rumors solidified into reality on March 3, 1776, when orders arrived for the regiment to march to Kassel for inspection by the fifty-six-year-old Landgrave Frederick. As officers pried open barrels of musket balls and carefully unsealed gunpowder casks, huddling against the wind to protect the precious contents, enlisted men stuffed bread into linen pouches and sharpened bayonets on whetstones. Each crack of a barrel opening, each scrape of stone on steel brought them closer to war.[14]

"This is it," Reuber realized as officers confirmed the men's worst fears—they were bound for America. The regiment's mood turned sour. Reuber's friends grew despondent, bewildered by the prospect. He counseled them, and himself, to be patient.[15]

Around a warming campfire, the regiment's officers stamped their feet to keep warm, telling boastful stories as they sharpened, polished, and then carefully wrapped six-foot-long spears in cloth for the journey to America. Though spears had little value as weapons since the advent of artillery and muskets, officers still used the sharp tips to prod frightened soldiers back into formation on the battlefield. These seasoned officers believed the razor edge of their regiment's spears would be needed, as they feared the wilderness of America would break many new recruits' resolve. However, they had underestimated the ferocity of the Hessian soldiers.[16]

Leaving home, joining the Rall Grenadier Regiment, and parading for the landgrave were probably the highlights in Reuber's life to that point, but to forty-four-year-old Lieutenant Andreas Wiederhold of the Knyphausen Fusilier Regiment these were routine procedures. His family can be traced back to the thirteenth century to a single ancestor, Volland, who was a judge, though his people never reached the level of nobility. Most of his ancestors owned land, had civic roles, or served local lords. Born in Spangenberg, about a day's march from Kassel, Wiederhold had served his prince for twenty-four years. He was promoted to lieutenant in 1760 and two years later distinguished himself in an outpost fight defending Kassel during the Seven Years' War. Attentive to his men yet critical of commanders, which may explain his low rank after decades of service, Wiederhold competently handled responsibility. He still found time for recreation, fathering seven children—including one born out of wedlock.[17]

Wiederhold's regiment, the Knyphausen Regiment, was also mobilizing for war, drilling one final time on the main road to Kassel before entering the walled city to be inspected by the landgrave. Passing through arched stone gates, the soldiers' black boots echoed off the stone-paved streets as they marched past neat rows of government buildings.[18] They crossed the massive new town square, the *Friedrichsplatz*, and proceeded onto the landgrave's parade ground.[19] Around them, the architecture and sculptures of Kassel, the principality's capital and residence of their prince, reinforced the all-encompassing power of the state.

Frederick had created a large, magnificent parade ground, the *Paradeplatz*, in front of his palace by filling in a ditch and extending the grounds to the racetrack. This government work project, financed by Frederick, further endeared the prince to his subjects as it put money into the pockets of impoverished craftsmen.

Frederick's castle was on one side of the square, while on the opposite side, a semicircular colonnade opened toward the palace. In the center loomed an eighty-foot triumphal arch made of rectangular columns decorated with stone medallions and crowned by a sculpture of a female figure holding the landgrave's bust.[20]

Marching across the parade ground, the men passed statues exemplifying the regime's emphasis on masculinity: wrestlers, fencers, and Roman slingers. Near the castle reared two enormous sandstone horses with muscular flanks, their manes and tails flowing. They were flanked by sandstone warriors grasping the steeds' bridles in one hand and their billowing cloaks in the other.[21]

The men assembled on the racetrack's brown, snow-tinged grass, and stood stiffly, preparing to be reviewed by their prince, His Serene Highness

Landgrave Frederick II. From a towering wooden platform, Frederick surveyed the men. His elongated, egg-shaped head, topped by a powdered wig, bobbed up and down in approval as he strode along the platform with black boots that reached above the knees of his chubby legs. His luxurious potbelly parted his waistcoat.

Wiederhold looked approvingly at Frederick, as it was known in the officer corps that the landgrave had struck an excellent bargain for the country, receiving thirty gold crowns from King George III for each soldier sent to America.

After a decade without combat, the officers had grown restless with the monotony of garrison life. Peacetime brought with it a significant reduction in their salaries, barely enough to cover basic necessities. As officers, they bore the responsibility of maintaining their uniforms at their own expense. With their limited resources, it was not uncommon for officers to go to bed hungry during peacetime and even endure Hessen-Kassel's bitterly cold winters without firewood to warm their stoves.[22]

Most of the officers were already in their thirties or forties and some in their fifties. Unlike many other European armies, the officer corps was not predominantly aristocratic, as at least half the officers were commoners. As the soldiers unfurled the regimental colors, a large white-and-purple banner embroidered with the image of a sword-carrying lion sticking out its tongue, the officers embellished the years of peace with boastful tales of drinking. The officers displayed a paradoxical mixture of coarseness and culture. Some had studied academic subjects at the Collegium Carolinum, and some were of noble birth. All were proud, some were violent and racist against other ethnic and religious groups. They playfully argued about who had consumed the most liquor or who had the most dueling scars. Drunken romps of thrashing unsuspecting night watchmen and young apprentice lads made one a "fine fellow," and cheating a Jew was considered "genius." The landgrave hated their boorishness and had tried to refine them by introducing them to his court's French etiquette.[23]

As they formed their men into marching columns, the officers were aware of the tradition entrusted to them. Their grandfathers had been rented out by Frederick's grandfather to fight the French Catholics, and their fathers leased out by the landgrave's father to fight for the Hanoverians. The officers did not discuss the one irreconcilable moment twenty years earlier when six thousand Hessians were leased to King George II of England while another six thousand were sent to the opposing forces of Emperor Charles VII of Bavaria.[24]

The French had decimated Hessen-Kassel during the Seven Years' War—the first "world war," pitting Catholic France and its allies against Protestant Britain, Prussia, and their allies. The battles had spanned the globe from Hessen-Kassel to India to Manila to Quebec, and it was the eighteenth century's bloodiest war, resulting in almost one million deaths.[25]

The French army occupied Kassel and ravaged the countryside, burning villages in retaliation for partisan acts of violence, confiscating money, food, and supplies, exacerbating problems in the principality's fragile economy. Now, a decade later, treasury funds remained low, even as Frederick maintained over three hundred court staff. Desperate to crush the colonial rebellion, George III would pay in gold. English gold would replenish the government's cash reserves and bankroll everything from Frederick's social programs to the new opera house he had built.

After a decade of garrison duty, Wiederhold and his fellow officers were eager to serve their prince, but their motivation extended beyond mere loyalty: the promise of promotions and increased salaries that combat would bestow on them added to their fervor.

The general populace was less enthusiastic. They huddled at the racetrack's edge, a staging point for the departing troops. Allowed briefly to break ranks, the soldiers hugged their loved ones. Parents, wives, and children stood in the cold winter chill, embracing and kissing the infantrymen.[26]

Horns sounded the start of the princely review. Officers barked orders, the well-drilled troops stiffening to attention.

The soldiers had been mostly drawn from the country's poor, men deemed dispensable to the economy. This group included the unemployed, vagrants, and the nation's disinherited younger sons, as local law looked more favorably on the eldest sons, blessing them as the sole inheritors of family farms and exempting them from the military draft.[27] The average age of the soldiers was twenty-four, with some as young as sixteen. Most had at least four years of military experience. Over 90 percent were unmarried. Fewer than 10 percent were foreigners, and over 90 percent were Calvinists. About half the men had a trade. Carpenters were needed to build field works. Shoemakers, weavers, stocking makers, and tailors mended uniforms. Men with expertise in transportation—coach builders, wheelwrights, saddlers, harness makers—were vital. Butchers, bakers, and cooks fed the troops. Moreover, there were musicians, barbers, scribes, printers, needle makers, even tobacconists, all trades needed to keep an army on the march clothed, fed, and safe.[28]

The majority of the people saw Frederick's traditional, patriarchal, absolutist government as God ordained and were used to acquiescing to the prince and officials' dictates.[29] Few if any of the soldiers were aware of the revolution in America. Government-controlled newspapers had reported on colonial rebels firing on King George's brave troops near Boston, and there was talk among the small intellectual circle of Hessen-Kassel about the tyranny of kings, but this did not interest the mostly illiterate men now forming into regiments on the racetrack.[30]

Events were unfolding rapidly for Reuber and his fellow soldiers in the Rall regiment. The five-foot-one-inch Reuber (his town elders needed recruits and had ignored the army's height requirement of five-foot-four) was indistinguishable from the other skinny, undernourished soldiers standing in line.[31] This was the first war for most of Reuber's comrades. Many were frightened of combat; others, never having been apart from their families, were homesick. Some of his poorer, less-skilled friends, anticipating the usual three weeks of local militia service, had voluntarily enlisted for a small bounty, *hand geld*, and now the poor souls stood terrified at the prospect of being sent to fight in America.[32] Bewildered, they questioned the officers: Where is America? Why must we cross the ocean on ships? If Spain owns New Spain in the New World, why can't we march to Spain, cross into America by foot, and forget this madness about sailing across the oceans? One Hessian described the journey to America as adventurous as a trip to the moon.[33]

A young man stumbled onto the field, blood dripping from the stump of his index finger. He stood sobbing beside his father and told of the farm accident that had severed his finger, depriving him of the honor of serving his prince. The officers exchanged knowing smirks and summoned police to take the boy away. Under careful questioning at the police station, the young man confessed that his widower father had intentionally severed his finger in a desperate bid for exemption. Dishonored and disgraced, the boy was jailed and a few days later committed suicide.[34]

Frederick descended from the platform to inspect the troops. He had been landgrave for sixteen years, and he knew that his three hundred thousand subjects lived a hard life, the majority barely eking out an existence from the country's poor soil, so he was confident the discipline of military service would require little adjustment for the raw recruits.[35] Yet Frederick sensed some men were less than eager to fight. He had tried to act in their best interests, shrewdly opening negotiations with the British in winter 1774–1775, haggling over prices months before the Americans had officially started their revolution.[36] Originally, he hoped to rent out five thousand soldiers, but the British were desperate for manpower, and he could not resist the treaty's generous terms. So he pledged to send twelve thousand men. One out of every seven of his subjects was draftable, but that would not be enough to satisfy Britain's needs. George III wanted more. Frederick's recruiting agents had done a superb job, vigorously scouring the countryside, putting up recruitment posters, roaming highways, cajoling men in taverns across Hessen-Kassel, and spreading their efforts into neighboring principalities as far away as Switzerland.

The treaty would be an economic boon for Frederick, yet deep down he began to feel anxious. News had filtered in from America. The rebels had captured Montreal and were besieging Boston.[37] Had he miscalculated? He began to have doubts that the Americans were not the pushovers everyone anticipated.[38]

There were more than three hundred German principalities. Hessen-Kassel was a disjointed patchwork, the remnants of centuries of war, diplomacy, and inheritance that left Frederick ruling three noncontiguous sections. The largest contained the capital, Kassel. Another straddled the Rhine to the southwest. The smallest, in the north along the Weser River, was the Schaumberg, containing the old walled city of Rinteln. In total, the three areas equaled about a third of the modern-day German state of Hesse.[39]

Frederick was well aware that small neighboring principalities were also renting men to the British—Brunswick, Hessen-Hanau, Anspach-Bayreuth, and Waldeck had treaties to provide twelve thousand men combined. But none had secured as advantageous a deal as Hessen-Kassel's. Its troops would receive treatment that was equal to their British comrades, including pay, provisions, and medical care. British pay was high compared to standard Hessian wages and served as an incentive to recruitment. Frederick had even negotiated to receive £40,000 owed by England from the previous war.[40] He felt confident that he had out-negotiated them all, though he regretted one misstep: After announcing the pay scale for the expedition to America, he had decided to reduce the soldiers' monthly wages, pocketing the difference for himself. But he now tried to compensate for the pay cut by announcing that the wealthy rebels in America would be ripe for plunder.[41]

Frederick had confidence in his generals leading the expedition's two divisions. The 8,647 men of the 1st Division were under the command of sixty-year-old Lieutenant General Philip von Heister, a tough veteran of many wars. He was known to be brave, having been wounded often and lame in one leg. But he was not known to be a military genius. A British observer noted plans had to be clearly outlined for Heister. He tended to be vain about his military experience and expected to be treated with deference, an attitude that would cause friction with the British and his own subordinates. Heister took the liberty of reminding the prince of his advanced age, his many wounds, and his fear not of death itself but of making his wife an impoverished widow. Frederick assured Heister that he would personally pay off the old general's debts and grant his wife a pension. Assured, the prideful Heister declared Frederick would see what "this old head and these bones can do."[42]

The 2nd Division, consisting of 4,327 soldiers, was led by another seasoned veteran, Lieutenant General Wilhelm von Knyphausen. Educated in Prussia under his father, a colonel in the Prussian Army, Knyphausen had entered military service at eighteen and accumulated forty-two years of experience. Widely renowned in the Hessian army, he was described by the Loyalist Joseph Galloway as a "truly great and gallant officer." Knyphausen was known for his serious demeanor, maintaining impeccable posture, but he also possessed an eccentric quirk, regularly buttering his bread with his thumb. During the lengthy voyage to America, he inquired of the ship's captain if they had inadvertently sailed past their intended destination. Nonetheless, Knyphausen would prove himself as one of the landgrave's most exceptional officers. Similar to Heister, he requested and was granted an additional stipend for his family.[43]

The army consisted of three types of heavy infantry armed with muskets and bayonets: field, grenadier, and garrison.[44] The field regiments were made up of professional Hessian soldiers enrolled for twenty-four years. In theory, the members of the grenadier battalions were large powerful men, the best soldiers in the army. Still, many of the most elite soldiers had been taken by the landgrave for his personal guard and would not be going to America. In the previous century, the tallest and strongest men in a regiment had been organized as grenadiers, with the duty of throwing hand grenades at the enemy, but that practice had been mostly abandoned. The less-seasoned garrison regiments consisted of rural militia who drilled one month a year between planting and harvest. As part-time, nonprofessional soldiers, they stored their weapons in their villages and could be called on as local police for peacetime emergencies. While most of their men were young and healthy, during wartime the army's oldest and most infirm soldiers were added to their ranks since the regiments were usually stationed in Hessen-Kassel for home defense, but King George's desperation for troops compelled Frederick to deploy them overseas. In the weeks before leaving for America they drilled at every opportunity. Officers trained them at a frenzied pace to ensure they were fit for the journey and for the fighting that awaited them on the other side of the ocean.[45]

Within the Hessian army, "regiment" and "battalion" were synonymous, consisting of about 450 to 625 men. The regiments usually comprised five 125-man field or garrison companies and one 125-man grenadier company. For America, the grenadier companies detached to form battalions. The grenadier battalions had four 125-man companies for a battalion total of about 450 to 500 men.[46]

The army's light, mobile infantry was a special corps of a few hundred men known as Jägers. The Jägers were forest men, gamekeepers, and hunters, volunteers known for their skills in the countryside. They dressed in olive green coats with green triangular-shaped hats topped with feathers. Armed with rifles, these excellent marksmen were at home in the wilderness. In theory, they advanced ahead of the main army, leading the column, protecting flanks, reconnoitering, foraging, and skirmishing. They also covered retreats. By war's end they would suffer more casualties than any other Hessian unit.[47]

The expedition had three 150-man artillery companies that operated British-supplied artillery pieces. The companies did not operate together but were assigned in detachments to infantry units, generally two artillery pieces per regiment. The Hessians impressed the British with this innovative tactic of putting two guns on the firing line with an infantry unit, thus increasing the firepower of the troops. The British adopted this practice by the end of the war.[48]

The twelve thousand men of the 1st and 2nd Divisions consisted of twelve field infantry regiments, three garrison infantry regiments, four grenadier infantry regiments, two Jäger corps, and the artillery corps.[49] A typical regiment was led by a colonel, lieutenant colonel, and a major with a total of sixteen to twenty commissioned officers, forty-eight to sixty noncommissioned officers, and 420 to 525 privates. In addition, a wide range of specialists was assigned to each regiment: surgeons, chaplains, apothecaries, armorers, color bearers, provost marshals, clerks, drummers, woodwind players, oboists, drivers, baggage masters, judges, and quartermasters.[50]

As the 1st Division stood before their prince, a war college (Krieg Collegium) representative read the men the Articles of War, reminding them that "the true soldier bravely does his duty and is virtuous." The men cheered Frederick as they paraded through town. Their appearance had been shrewdly designed to instill fear and awe. Grenadiers, such as Reuber in the Rall Regiment, led the march. Fierce-looking mustaches blackened with shoe polish hung from their upper lips. Hair grown long, waxed shiny with beeswax, and gathered into a single pigtail swung behind them. Tall, cone-shaped hats with large metal plates in the front made their heads look large. Long, stiff, black collars stretched their necks and kept their chins and heads high. Bluecoats purposely cut short and tight, the sleeves ending well above the wrists, created the illusion of a massive body bursting the uniform's seams. Shiny metal buttons, polished and engraved belt buckles, and long black leggings added to their intimidating attire.[51]

Over two hundred women, either for practical reasons or unwilling to separate from their loved ones, accompanied the army. Trudging behind the soldiers, bundles and washbasins in hand, they were listed on the muster rolls as "Women and Baggage." Seven walked with the unmistakable gait of pregnancy. Many came on board with children. Most served as laundresses, but many had ideas of their own. America offered opportunities; there were unsettled lands for those bold enough to desert, with rum trading to be ventured, and clothing, jewelry, and furniture to be plundered.[52]

The army had been rented out more than thirty times during the previous century. The regiments had usually returned fairly intact, but every regiment had left behind soldiers buried on foreign soil. The last expedition—during the Seven Years' War—had been bloody and costly, but that had involved professional Prussian and French armies. Now the army would be fighting under the banner of King George III against American rebels. The women and their soldier husbands marching to the seacoast had no reason to believe that an excursion to America would be anything but profitable.

CHAPTER 2

Frederick: Despot or Enlightened Prince?

FREDERICK WATCHED his army parade across the racetrack, regiments striding toward town against the bite of icy wind. Thirty years prior, in 1745, the young Frederick had witnessed his father, Wilhelm VII, rent troops to the British, as his grandfather, Landgrave Karl, had first done nearly a century earlier in 1677—leasing 120 men to the Danes for 3,200 talers. Though nearly half never returned, Landgrave Karl launched Hessen-Kassel's most lucrative enterprise. By 1730, the nation received an average of four hundred thousand talers (approximately £300,000) a year from Britain for soldiers. The army had become the principality's most profitable export. Frederick's father called his army the nation's "Peru," a reference to Spain's riches derived from their South American gold and silver mines.[1]

Frederick understood that Karl had paid heavily for his foresight, losing two sons in battle. When 1,000 troops were sent to Venice against the Turks in 1687, only 191 returned. Many intellectuals labeled his grandfather a slave trader, but professors from the learning centers at Rostock and Württemberg wrote theses concluding that princes had the legal right to aid foreign allies. Rented soldiers were, by this legal definition, not mercenaries, but "auxiliaries" or, as the peasants would say, Hulfs-Volcker (helpers). Frederick knew there were grumblings against the treaty in certain small circles of the educated bourgeoisie, but even in these enlightened groups, there was no serious talk of opposing Frederick. As the columns of soldiers faded from his vision, he was confident that his subsidy treaties with England had the sanction of international law and custom.[2]

He felt the pressure of competing not only with the two great neighboring powers of Prussia and the Austrian hereditary dominions but also a jumble of more than three hundred surrounding electorates (land ruled by members of the electoral college of the Holy Roman Empire), duchies (dominions ruled by a duke of duchess), bishoprics (regions of the church headed by bishops), margraves (feudal-era military administrators), and free cities (self-governing city states). In addition, he had to navigate the political quagmire of the 1,400 estates of the Imperial Knights and their Holy Roman Empire that surrounded Hessen-Kassel; they forced him to be alert to the scheming and back stabbing that constituted German politics. He made the cornerstone of his foreign policy subsidy treaties and the fees they generated from renting his army to the Protestant English monarchs while simultaneously maintaining an alliance with Protestant Prussia, hoping that the income derived from foreign powers combined with strong alliances would keep his tiny principality safe from his powerful neighbors.[3]

Frederick was born on August 14, 1720, the only child of Landgrave Wilhelm VIII and his wife, Dorothea Wilhelmine von Sachsen-Zeitzwas. Wilhelm was thirty-eight when Frederick was born, and the age difference made it almost impossible for Wilhelm to be part of young Frederick's life. Frederick could barely remember his mother. The courts had declared her mentally ill and had taken her away when he was just five years old. Despite his princely status, he was a lonely child and played mostly with his sister. Seventeen of his aunts and uncles died. Then, his sister died. Frederick's childhood was a solitary one, with his principal companion being his tutor, Professor Jean-Pierre de Crousaz.[4]

De Crousaz was even older than Frederick's father, but he brought life to the dreary castle, expanding young Frederick's world with art, music, and philosophy, a stark contrast to his father's military tales.

The best years of Frederick's early life were spent traveling with de Crousaz to Switzerland and studying with the leading figures of the Swiss Enlightenment.[5] Geneva was a breath of fresh air to young Frederick. His royal carriage had brought him from the dreary Germanic countryside across the lush Swiss plateau into Geneva, a city bustling with European travelers. In tolerant Geneva, far from the rigid orthodoxies of German principalities, he enjoyed five years of university learning under the guidance of leading figures in the Swiss Enlightenment, something unprecedented for a Hessian prince. Frederick absorbed transformative concepts: religious tolerance, natural law, and the belief that human beings could discern right from wrong through reason based upon universal moral standards. His intellectual awakening deepened with exposure to radical ideas and concepts such as educational secularization, and separation of church and state-run schools.[6]

Frederick had never experienced such an open society before. Religious tolerance was not an accepted practice for a Hessian ruler. A few hundred French Huguenots had been allowed to settle in Hessen-Kassel, but that was more of an economic decision due to the entrepreneurial knowledge that the Huguenots brought and their ability to teach French to upper-class Hessian children.[7]

Could Frederick change the way his subjects, who were overwhelmingly Reformed Calvinists, treated other religions? Almost all Hessians viewed Jews as foreigners, even Jewish families who were legal Hessian citizens. The principality had historically mistreated them, sometimes brutally.[8] To reside in Hessen-Kassel, the Jewish population had to purchase a letter of protection from the state. Only affluent Jewish families were allowed to live in Hessen-Kassel, and only if they adhered to strict quotas that kept their numbers largely unchanged. They were banned from guilds and forbidden to buy property. Every few years, Frederick's father summoned Jewish leaders to Kassel so the government could levy special taxes on Hessian Jews based on an audit of their assets.[9]

Yet his teachers said a truly enlightened prince did not meddle in his subjects' religion. He should be promoting the arts and science, not telling people how to serve their lord.

He wrote to Voltaire and was shocked when the great Frenchman wrote back. Soon Voltaire was sending him poems, and they began a lifelong correspondence. "May you live on master of Literature," Frederick gushed in a letter, "for the profit of humanity."[10]

He visited Voltaire, and the philosopher returned the visit. It was a momentous day for Frederick, strolling the streets of Kassel with the greatest enlightened mind on the continent. He knew that no previous Hessian prince had ever taken such liberal ideas seriously.

The impressionable seventeen-year-old returned to Hessen-Kassel with an ambitious vision: to become his homeland's first truly enlightened prince. Yet a question lingered: Could such liberal notions take root in the traditional soil of Hessen-Kassel?

Frederick looked back with regret at his marriage in 1740 to Princess Mary, the daughter of England's King George II. Wilhelm had approved of his son marrying the Protestant girl. The couple had one child, William. Frederick thought married life would be stable—even predictable—but his studies had sparked a fascination with religions outside of his Protestant faith. He preferred the extravagances of Catholic ceremonies to the bland services of the Protestants. In a convoluted train of thought, he saw the Protestant policy of allowing commoners to study Scripture as a trap of blind faith.[11]

"The Protestants have erred to say that the Holy Scripture is so easy to understand and that human reason permits even the common man to study it," he wrote.[12]

To prove his point, he secretly converted to Catholicism. Frederick, heir of the Protestant and military-dominated Principality of Hessen-Kassel, was going to be a Catholic, liberal, enlightened prince.

Then his father learned of his secret conversion, and everything changed.

The nation was horrified. Their future ruler was now a Catholic. False rumors circulated that Frederick had a Catholic lover who promised that if he were "to surrender his soul to her, she would give him her body."[13] Princess Mary filed for divorce. Wilhelm restricted Frederick's ability to appoint Catholics to government positions and barred him from his Protestant wife and child. The nation was in such frenzy that all Hessians were mandated to swear an oath of allegiance to the Protestant cause.[14]

Threatening letters arrived from the countryside. Shunned by his father and court, a paranoid Frederick was convinced he would be executed. He tried fleeing to Austria but was betrayed and put under house arrest. He had been unprepared for the negative reactions of the people and stunned by their wrath.

"I don't believe everything the priests tell me," he pleaded. "Surely, on the Day of Judgment, the worthy man of all religions will be saved. And as for my change of religion, that's not a matter to make such a great noise about."[15]

But his pleas fell on deaf ears. Alone, he sank into melancholy. He missed his child. He worried about what people thought of him and was unable to make decisions. When someone entered his room, he talked incessantly, trying to please the visitor, hoping to win their approval. He needed acclaim. "I question whether the marvelous love of mankind does not derive more from vanity than good nature," he wrote. "I suspect the desire of being applauded and admired has a great share in it."[16]

In 1755, after his separation was formalized, Wilhelm sent him off to Berlin to study under the Prussian leader, Frederick the Great. Immersed in the Prussian army, thoughts of family and Enlightenment faded amid the excitement of war.[17]

In 1756, at the start of the Seven Years' War, Hessen-Kassel aligned with Prussia and Great Britain against Catholic France and Austria. Great Britain agreed to pay Hessen-Kassel an annual subsidy for renting its troops. Frederick the Great shrewdly made Prince Frederick a lieutenant general in the Prussian Army. This was accompanied by a trip to Berlin, during which the royal court received him in a friendly manner. All Hessian rulers needed military training, and now as a young, ambitious man desiring to travel outside the stuffy confines of Hessen-Kassel, and away from the threats of Protestant enemies, young Frederick found great satisfaction in the army of Frederick the Great. This would prove to be a turning point in his life.[18]

Many in the ruling class of Hessen-Kassel worried that their impressionable prince would fall under the spell of the charismatic Prussian leader, and to no one's surprise, he did.

Prussia was almost as much fun as Switzerland. The women of Berlin were beautiful and adventurous. Frederick had a general's star on his shoulder and women in his bedroom. In 1759, he was made general of the infantry and vice governor of the well-known fortress at Magdeburg.[19] The fort was not involved in any serious fighting, and Frederick's position held no real military responsibility, but the title and his interactions with the Prussian aristocracy in Magdeburg served to draw him into the world of Prussia's rigid, authoritarian, military style of thinking.[20]

He thought his father would be proud, but instead Wilhelm sent derogatory letters to Frederick the Great saying the young prince was capricious. A few years before, complained his father, Frederick wanted to bring the liberal ideas of the Enlightenment to the Hessian court, and now his fickle son was promoting the idea of incorporating authoritarian Prussian ideology into the court.

The Seven Years' War brought death, destruction, and poverty to Hessen-Kassel. Geographically caught between the French and the Prussians, the principality was occupied by both sides. Kassel changed hands four times, and the Catholic armies of France were harsh occupiers. But despite Frederick's belief in Catholicism, Hessen-Kassel fought alongside its Protestant Prussian allies.

Still, the Protestant rulers in Germany grew fearful when in 1760, Landgrave Wilhelm died and Prince Frederick assumed the throne. On hearing of Wilhelm's death, Duke Ferdinand of Brunswick, fearing that Frederick's Catholicism would sway him to surrender the city to the French, put his army on alert and increased the number of troops stationed in Kassel to protect the city from the French. Frederick the Great made an all-out effort to keep him in the Protestant camp through flattery and praise, even appointing the new landgrave field marshal general.[21]

Their fears were not without merit. Despite what an envoy accurately termed a "zealous admiration of everything that is Prussian," the landgrave resented Frederick the Great for numerous perceived slights and ridicule through the years. He recognized that Prussia's strength and proximity were a constant threat to Hessen-Kassel. At the same time, he felt alienated from his other Protestant ally, Great Britain, due to ill feelings over his failed marriage to King George II's sister. With all this in mind, Frederick contemplated how best to alleviate the plight of his subjects who were subjugated by the French forces occupying much of Hessen-Kassel. Unbeknownst to his allies, he secretly opened negotiations with the French court about renting the Hessian army to France.

This reckless proposition alarmed Frederick's ministers. They reminded him of his people's "undying hatred" toward their French and Austrian occupiers and the likely vengeance Prussia would wreak on the principality should he join forces with France. Moreover, they cautioned that England owed Hessen-Kassel substantial subsidy arrears—debts unlikely to be paid if Hessen-Kassel became France's ally. This subsidy money was vital for rebuilding the ravaged principality. Frederick swiftly grasped the potential adverse economic impact of switching allegiances. The idea was dropped.[22]

Instead, he reassured his Protestant subjects and foreign allies with a declaration:

"The national religion [Protestantism] must remain untouched, the slightest deviations lead to the saddest consequences for public peace."[23]

His critics calmed down when they saw that Frederick was keeping his promise that he would not violate the religious status and constitution of the Protestant state, and that the few Catholics in his country, who were allowed to pray publicly in only Kassel and Marburg, would not be given new rights.

Since converting to Catholicism, Frederick had been threatened and isolated, but his spirit was not broken. He was determined to be a benevolent, enlightened ruler. He publicly vowed what he would demand of himself as prince: love of order, humanity, and peace; reform of the Hessian criminal justice system, including abolition of torture; and promotion of the fine arts. He believed in the Enlightenment of Voltaire and also in the absolutism and militarism of Frederick the Great. He was determined to combine the two contradictory philosophies. He would reform the archaic Hessian government, improving the lives of his subjects, but would do it while retaining total power. He was going to be the world's most enlightened leader, while nonetheless holding absolute power. He had found his purpose in life.

CHAPTER 3

Marching to Their Destiny

March–April 1776

THE REGIMENTS' SILK FLAGS whipped in the breeze as the army circled the huge *Friedrichsplatz,* the town's magnificent square with its unfinished public museum. Reuber had never seen such a structure: a museum meant not for royalty but for common people like himself. No other people in Europe had such a privilege.[1]

Most of the town's eighteen thousand inhabitants lined the sidewalks. Some cheered, many watched somberly. Towering above them in the distance, the twenty-seven-foot copper statue of Hercules gazed down on the peasants from the peak of Bergpark (Mountain Park). Hercules was perched atop an obelisk crafted from volcanic rock, which in turn rested on an octagonal edifice. Water gushed from man-made waterfalls, cascading down the mountainside, carried along by meticulously designed colossal concrete steps. These waters were channeled through aqueducts and propelled by waterwheels, culminating in a dramatic aquatic performance as the waters crashed into Neptune's Basin, a wide pool where an imposing statue of the Roman sea god himself stood sentinel at the basin's edge.

Remarkably, this entire architectural marvel—the Hercules statue, the obelisk, the octagonal structure, and the intricate water display—served no utilitarian purpose. It had been built for the sole purpose of promoting the spirit of the landgrave's rule, radiating power and technological sophistication. The citizens of Kassel and visitors from across Europe would eagerly wait for an acoustic signal to announce the commencement of the water displays. The signal was produced when the water's force generated sufficient air pressure to elicit a deep, unworldly roar from the horns of the centaur statues, a sound that could be heard for miles around.[2]

The army passed the governmental buildings bestowed on the people by Landgrave Frederick. Pregnant whores leaned against the brick walls of the Foundling House orphanage. Frederick had built it to help reduce the nation's scandalous incidents of infanticide; these had accompanied a rising out-of-wedlock birthrate that began after the horrors of the Seven Years' War.[3]

The landgrave believed there was a causal relationship between poor health, poor productivity, and poor subjects. Thus, for the sake of the nation's health and economy, a charity hospital had been built. He shrewdly established a permanent source of revenue for the hospital by levying tax on three very incongruous things: dog ownership, butchered meat, and marriage.[4]

Down the street was the Work & Craft House, built by Frederick to educate beggar children and give employment to their parents. Begging had become a plague in postwar Hessen-Kassel.[5] To set a good example, Frederick listed the names of almsgivers prominently in the local gazette and let it be known that he was passing the poor box at his own church twice a week.[6]

But the coins that landed in the churches' collection plates could not keep pace with the nation's poverty. Highwaymen continued to rob travelers and burglarize farmhouses. The landgrave hoped the income from this new war in America and a newly enacted progressive income tax would ease the country's dire financial situation.

Reuber admired the landgrave. The fire insurance company the prince had formed was forcing city dwellers to replace the dangerous straw roofs that used to catch fire so easily. Families were buying leather fire buckets and learning not to smoke in their beds.[7]

A government officer carrying letters was stopping at each shop. It was all part of Frederick's ingenious plan to offer door-to-door mail delivery.[8]

During Frederick's reign, the city was filled with the sights and sounds of transformation—workers widening streets, laborers leaning their weight against crowbars to pry up cobblestones that had been in place for generations. Stonemasons swung hammers against chisels as they dismantled the town's weathered medieval walls. What stirred the hearts of Kassel's citizens most profoundly was their prince's unprecedented decision to place this work in the calloused hands of peasants. Defying tradition, Frederick had turned away from the powerful guilds with their jealously guarded privileges, awarding contracts instead to humble laborers whose families had known generations of poverty. Never before had these workers earned wages sufficient to provide meaningful support for their families.[9]

For most of the soldiers, this was likely their first glimpse of the new, modernized Kassel. With the walls leveled and thoroughfares widened, the once-congested city had shed its former constraints. Sunlight and fresh air now reached neighborhoods that had long been cramped and hemmed in. Commerce flourished on the open, navigable avenues. Merchants established markets along the broad thoroughfares, no longer restricted by claustrophobic alleys. Some of the marching soldiers had in the past participated in the time-honored practice of using the city's streets to drive cattle to and from countryside pastures, but this was now forbidden. The soldiers could see carriages carrying noble families sharing space along the promenades with working peasants returning home on foot. Financed largely by British subsidy money from the Seven Years' War, Kassel had become a modern European city. The presence of the Landgrave's court, Kassel's substantial garrison of troops, and the presence of numerous foreigners had brought unprecedented prosperity to Kassel's citizens.[10]

The army turned out of the Friedrichsplatz, past the empty space where Frederick had suggested a temple could be built for Jews. The ministry had quickly rejected that idea. Even someone as benevolent and powerful as Frederick sometimes had to bow to criticism arising from his governmental bureaucracy, and a highly visible Jewish house of worship remained unacceptable to his Protestant nation.[11]

Approaching the Leipzig Gate, the soldiers could hear the calls of the animals from the landgrave's menagerie, especially the bellowing of the crown's prized elephant echoing through the square. Outside the gate sat one of Frederick's anonymous wooden drop boxes where poor, unmarried women left newborns for his orphanage.[12] Beside it loomed a Drehhauser (revolving house), a wooden cubicle on a spinning platform into which an individual convicted for a misdemeanor was placed and whirled until they vomited. But the wooden cubicle now sat unused because Frederick had banned its use; under his rule no peasant would be spun to the point of nausea because of a minor infraction.[13]

The eight thousand men of the 1st Division departed town, beginning their 120-mile march to the North Sea, where ships would meet them for their journey to America. Among them were the Knyphausen Regiment with Andreas Wiederhold and the Rall Regiment with Johannes Reuber.

The army marched out of town with flags flying. Fahnenjunkers (flag-bearers) carried five silk flags for each regiment, each flag hanging from a metal-tipped spear. The flags had purposely been designed so the land-grave's symbol—a red-and-white-striped lion carrying a sword, sticking out his tongue, and looking over his shoulder—stared down at the men. Lest the men should still forget who their sovereign was, a wreath with the monogram F. L. (Frederick Landgrave) was painted in each corner of the flags.[14]

Many of the men did not seem happy. Under the watchful eye of their officers, they put on an air of mirth, but during unguarded moments they were depressed, even angry at the idea of risking their lives to save the British Empire. Provost marshals rode among the troops watching for deserters.[15]

Johannes Reuber thought the march across Germany to the sea would be an easy journey. The Lord had blessed the country with dry weather, and Prince Frederick had magnanimously ordered the officers to rest the army every third day. But soon Reuber may have wondered if the Lord was displeased. When the regiment reached the top of the hills above the Weser River, Reuber saw that the Weser had broken through its dam. Below him floodwaters covered the countryside; in some villages, only treetops and the thatched roofs of houses were visible. Broken remnants of bridges floated in the swirling river. The men heard the rush of water—melted snow—flowing down the Bavarian mountainsides. The flood water had turned the roads into muddy quagmires. The regiment had to be transported, some in wagons, some in boats, into the nearest city, Bremen.[16]

Neighborhood farmers came out to help. They rapidly loaded the soldiers' gear onto wagons and voluntarily pulled the wagons through the mud, offering to walk through puddles with the army's gear on their backs. To Reuber, their help seemed to be a charitable act of kindness. But the peasants were neither charitable nor fools. They were proud of their army, but on a more practical level, they knew that the troops were always hungry and the officers always on the lookout for more recruits. The sooner the blessed landgrave's troops passed through their locale, the better.

Some peasants waded through the floodwaters carrying gear and pulling wagons while others paddled small craft filled with soldiers. None of the peasants dared to complain. The cold mountain water soaked the soldiers' boots and trousers, chilling them as they trudged toward the sea. Some had never seen a large body of water before and needed the officers to explain that the roofs that jutted from the floodwaters were not ships at sea.[17]

The army crossed the dreary marshes of the Great Heath where there were only a few villages. For ten days the men marched through swampy ground and saw few people. They were cold, and most had to sleep outdoors.[18] The ground finally dried. The roads became dusty. Veterans jostled their way to the front of the marching columns. The newer recruits naively laughed at the veterans' sudden enthusiasm, but laughter soon turned to curses. The recruits, now forced to the rear of the marching column, choked on the dust clouds kicked up by the boots of the veterans marching in front of them.

The Lossberg Regiment, with Lieutenant Jakob Piel, was also marching with the 1st Division to the North Sea. Piel was born in 1742, in Bremen. He had fourteen years of military experience in the Hessian army, was literate, and had excellent mapmaking skills.[19] The regiment had left a few days earlier than the Rall Regiment from its home base, the city of Rinteln, a small walled city on the Weser River about a day's march from Kassel.[20] Jakob Piel could see ahead of him the Lossberg Regiment's flag. It was similar to the flags of other Hessian regiments, with a red-and-white-striped lion sticking out its tongue and carrying a sword. By contrast, the Lossberg flag was made of a unique bright orange silk that was easy to spot from a distance.[21]

Piel and his comrades had been marching for two days straight without incident. The soldiers were known to complain that the rhythm of marching was monotonous, as they would spend their days trudging forward, seeing nothing but the feet of the man ahead of them. But the regiment seemed to be at ease with its departure from home. Then a calamity struck.

The sun was setting when the army reached Rehburg-Loccum, one of several villages in the flatlands north of Rinteln. The little village was dominated by a five-hundred-year-old monastery, Kloster Loccum. Tomorrow, the regiment was promised, would be a "halting day," a day of rest. They knew that at least some of them could expect a warm night's rest in a peasant's home, whether the peasants wanted them to be there or not, while others would make do with tents pitched on the surrounding fields.

Soon, officers were knocking on the enormous wooden doors of the monastery, brushing past monks, and helping themselves to fashionable guestrooms and splendid chambers while outside the troops scrambled, looking for barns and straw-covered farmhouses with comfortable fireplaces. That night the men would sleep soundly.

They had scarcely been asleep for half an hour when screams awoke the regiment. The soldiers had been trained to quickly overcome fatigue. Grabbing guns, men ran coatless into the cold night and squinted into the darkness. A bedroom ceiling in the monastery, where Lieutenant Colonel Francis Scheffer and Major Ludwig von Hanstein were billeted, had collapsed onto them. They lay in the rubble, stunned and a bit bloodied, but miraculously unharmed. [22]

Soldiers like Piel and Reuber believed that the Lord ordained all things, so after the debris was cleared off the injured officers, the regiment prayed for the Lord's continued favor and expressed thanks for the generosity of the landgrave's order: He had made sure that all the regiments mobilized for war had an army surgeon and a chaplain on their staff.[23]

Piel was proud of his regiment. They had shown that they could respond well to an emergency. He and his comrades were no longer farmers. They were soldiers. The Hessians were confident that they could respond to any nighttime crisis.

History would prove him wrong.

As the army neared the port city of Bremerlehe, peasants began to walk alongside the marching columns. Officers like Andreas Wiederhold were suspicious of the extreme friendliness of the usually timid civilians. Peasants generally tried to stay clear of the army lest they be recruited into the ranks themselves, but these peasants were different. They offered food and drink at no charge and soon were joking with the soldiers and whispering into their ears.

The commander of the 1st Division, General Heister, had obtained "authentic information" that Prussian recruiting officers had promised to pay the local peasants five thalers, equivalent to about $1,000 in today's currency, for each Hessian soldier they enticed to desert to the Prussian army.[24]

Peasants were approaching Hessian soldiers asking, "Why do you march for the landgrave of Hessen-Kassel?" They promised that the king of Prussia would make them a much better offer, and they swore that he would lavish on them good food and good pay and even beautiful women.

At night, strangers circulated through the camp. They spoke quietly to the troops, carefully avoiding the Hessian officers. Wiederhold was experienced enough to know that they were around, even if he never saw them in the darkness. Reuber and Piel were loyal to their prince and almost certainly shunned these strangers.

One night, armed sentries rushed the camp and grabbed the intruders. They were identified as Prussian recruiting agents and placed under guard in a peasant's house. During the night, the Prussian captives mocked the Hessian guards and played musical instruments. The music and laughter of the Prussians drifted across the solemn camp, and some soldiers were undoubtedly tempted by the generosity and boldness of the Prussian army. Then the Hessian general's elite guard appeared. The Hessian camp soon heard the sound of metal and wood breaking. In the morning, the army awoke to find the wounded Prussians' bodies laid out on the stoop of the house; all the troops could see their bloody, beaten faces and their smashed musical instruments. The vision of the battered and whimpering Prussians with their bloodied shirts and their broken bones sprawled out on the ground served as a reminder that the power of the landgrave was absolute. Further emphasizing the prince's power was his standing order that any peasants turning in deserters would be rewarded with gold coins; and to the soldiers, the thought of being put in irons because of the greed of an illiterate peasant was terrifying. If a soldier deserted in a town, the landgrave could hold the townsfolk responsible and force them to pay for the deserter or even worse, force the town to substitute one of its sons for him.[25]

The soldiers knew that if they did their duty, there would be no trouble from either the peasants or the landgrave. Thus, for the rest of the trip, the men obeyed their officers and marched quietly into the port city of Bremerlehe. When King George III's commissary agent, Colonel William Faucitt, met them at the Bremerlehe docks, the officers ordered them to cheer. Without hesitation they cheered, "Long live the king!" as if they could not wait another minute to serve George. But what really had their attention were the ships at anchor in the harbor. These were the ships that would bring them to the New World, where they might become rich with plunder—or might die in a foreign land thousands of miles from home.

CHAPTER 4

Shopping for Soldiers

April 1776

NO MAN IN ENGLAND was as familiar with the armies of the various German states as King George's representative, Colonel William Faucitt. His piercing brown eyes, receding white hairline, thick but neat eyebrows, smooth skin, and ruddy cheeks gave him an air of authority and intelligence. He had fought alongside the Germans in the Netherlands during the War of Austrian Succession and again in western Germany during the Seven Years' War. Now he had to evaluate these German armies for King George.[1]

Faucitt knew all too well that his countrymen feared and hated military institutions and saw them as a threat to English democracy. They preferred an enlargement of the army in times of crisis with demobilization as soon as the crisis was resolved. Thus, at the outbreak of the American rebellion, the British Army had only 48,677 soldiers to defend England and its overseas empire. To make matters worse, this army was spread over the globe, from Minorca in the Mediterranean Sea to the West Indies. There were fewer than eight thousand British soldiers in North America. Faucitt had his work cut out for him. He needed to hire enough men to crush the American rebellion before the rebels overwhelmed the king's tiny army.[2]

After shopping and comparing, he had decided to rent the army of Hessen-Kassel. A draft treaty was drawn up on December 20, 1775, and sent to London for approval. By February, a final draft was agreed on. Faucitt understood how greedy the German princes could be, but even he was surprised when Frederick insisted that Faucitt backdate the February treaty to January 15 so the landgrave could receive an extra few weeks of rental payment from the British.[3]

There was no keeping Faucitt's mission secret; German newspapers reported his movements. Initially, he had sought Russian troops as auxiliaries, but he was rebuffed by Catherine the Great. He then approached the United Providences of Netherlands, but the Dutch parliament refused to allow their troops to fight outside of Europe. He then shopped around, comparing the prices and quality of the troops of the various German princes. Brunswick, Hanover, Waldeck, and several other of the small German states had men for sale. He rejected troops from Württemberg and Bavaria, whom he deemed of inferior quality.[4]

Faucitt did not bicker, nor was he particularly determined in negotiating over price. He even agreed to pay Frederick £41,820 for Hessian medical expenses from the previous war, though he knew the bill was being grossly padded.[5] What did it matter if he promised the landgrave large subsidies for each day the British rented his army? The British and Hessian armies were ruthless professionals, and they would be fighting Americans—farmers with little to no military training. Faucitt had enough experience to conclude that the war would be over in one campaign, perhaps two. He calculated that the army would spend more time on the ships sailing to America than actually fighting there.

Faucitt began requesting ships and sailors to transport the Hessian army to America, but the landgrave was sending men faster than either the Royal Navy or the rest of Europe could supply ships. Faucitt sent messages to Frederick telling him to slow the mobilization, but there was no stopping the landgrave. The Hessians kept coming.[6]

Faucitt recognized the delicate nature of his task. Navigating both the German and British military bureaucracies was within his capabilities, but misusing the king's funds on troop rentals was a misstep he couldn't afford. Vigilance was essential; unscrupulous recruiters often attempted to include men unsuitable for duty, such as idlers, defaulters, and domestic abusers. In Marburg, a cunning recruiter sought out dysfunctional families and resolved disputes by offering troublesome husbands and rebellious youths the opportunity to serve in America instead of a jail sentence. One baker's wife ran a family counseling service and would refer problem clients to recruiters. When a Hessian master cooper was sentenced to jail for beating his wife, the government let him know that if it happened again, he would go to North America as a conscript.[7]

Faucitt felt great apprehension when recruiting men in Hessen-Kassel for King George. The recruits were slippery creatures, always trying to swindle him. They would try to deny eligibility, fake sickness, and often try to run away. A disabled tailor from Kassel who joined the army admitted that he did not come to America to fight but to collect debts owed him by several officers. Faucitt had to teach his agents that rounding up men at taverns to serve their king was dangerous work. He constantly reminded his agents to wear sword and pistol when escorting a recruit and to never allow them to get too close. Faucitt warned his men that when transporting these "volunteers" they must also avoid walking through the man's hometown.[8]

But it was the nights that worried him most. His agents had to be careful at the inns they chose to sleep in. Many a recruit had slipped away by shimmying out a bedroom window while an unsuspecting agent slept. Faucitt tried to teach his agents to sleep with their recruits only at inns where the landlords were loyal to the landgrave. The more experienced agents knew to look for hidden weapons by stripping their recruits naked before retiring for the evening. Army manuals instructed the agents to give their clothes and the clothes of the recruit to the innkeeper lest the recruit try to sneak out wearing the agent's attire. Before sleeping naked next to the recruit, the more experienced agents gave all their weapons to a landlord and lit a large candle to burn through the night. In the morning, the landlord would return the agent's belongings. Only after the agent had dressed and reclaimed his weapons was the recruit allowed to have his clothes back.[9]

Faucitt understood that sometimes a disobedient recruit had to be killed. This was acceptable, as long as the appropriate paperwork was filled out, but there would be hell to pay if a recruit simply escaped. Many a bruised and beaten recruit was brought in holding up his pants after a quick-thinking agent had stopped him from running away by cutting away the suspenders and buttons of the reluctant soldier's breeches.[10]

His recruiters learned to be imaginative. Some marched through towns accompanied by a drummer, leading to the phrase "drumming up business."[11] Officers often used alcohol to facilitate the process. They employed "ladies of the evenings," using the talents of these delicious "fallen Venuses" for the good of the state. Many innocent tavern goers were tempted by peeks at sketches of naked women with promises of intimate contact after induction into the army.[12]

Despite these aggressive recruiting methods, at most, 5 percent of recruits ended up in the military by coercion or force. Frederick needed more troops. He filled his ranks with young inexperienced troops as well as older professional soldiers. He recruited outside his borders, and eventually foreigners made up a fifth of his army. The majority of the foreigners, about 87 percent, were from other German-speaking territories, but troops also came from other European countries, from Portugal to Norway and Ireland to Russia.[13]

After almost a year of work, Faucitt arrived in the little seaside town of Bremerlehe, where the Weser River flowed from Hessen-Kassel into the North Sea; he was waiting for the army he had purchased to arrive. He had placed his son on the Hessian General Staff to help expedite matters and now found himself frantically writing to him, asking to slow the Hessian mobilization until the navy could supply enough ships to take the army across the ocean to America.[14]

Nearly all the inhabitants of the town's three hundred houses came out to see the troops arrive. They crowded the roadway, some cheering, others watching apprehensively. Bremerlehe was not a very healthy town, and the local inhabitants appeared pale and gaunt. It had been struck the previous year by Rinderpest (cowpox). Standing with his staff along the road, Faucitt was uncomfortable. The air blowing in from the sea was so damp that by morning Faucitt's clothes were soaked.[15]

The Hessian troops appeared on the highway. The grenadiers led the way in their tall, metal-plated cone hats with waxed ponytails swinging behind them and their purposely undersized uniforms almost bursting at the seams. Shiny metal cartridge boxes decorated with the landgrave's family arms—a lion sticking its tongue out—and powder pouches made of animal hide hung from belts slung from their left shoulders to their right hips. Traditionally, the grenadier regiments consisted of the army's most powerful men, elite soldiers taken from other regiments' companies. Impressive and intimidating, the regiments used a straight-legged, high-stepping march the men called a "goose step" past the representatives of King George, the wooden causeway creaking under their black, polished boots.[16]

Faucitt saw that the men were robust, but his experienced eye spotted potential problems. The mustachioed men in the front and rear columns were large and fierce looking, but those in the middle were shorter and younger; these were likely new recruits the landgrave was trying to make less noticeable. Perhaps they would need more training? No, the Hessian officers assured him, they were already being trained at least twice a day. They informed Faucitt that veterans administered beatings to any new recruits who struggled to master their training, a practice they described as necessary encouragement for proper learning. And Faucitt conceded that even the young ones were "stout . . . and well put together." The Hessian officers were taciturn but confident, and he had to admit that the soldiers in their undersized uniforms with shining metal buckles were intimidating. He wrote the British War Office that this was a "fine body of men throughout, for Air, as well as Stature, and Strength; and all in the Prime of their Age."[17]

The Jägers made a strong impression on Faucitt when they marched past in their famous green coats that identified them with their hunting heritage. These coats had bright red cuffs and facings; many of the men sported three-cornered hats with a knot of ribbons and a feather sticking out. Faucet understood that these were Hessen-Kassel's elite unit of hunters, woodsmen, and game wardens. As explained to the British Lord Suffolk by a Hessian minister, "those employed in hunting and in the forest . . . a well esteemed class . . . what one calls a corps of distinction . . . [this corps] is by no means composed like the infantry of the lowest class of people"[18]

Most Hessian infantrymen relied on volley fire sent in the general direction of an enemy to do damage, but the Jägers were expected to be expert marksmen, capable of hitting targets at long range.

The weapon utilized by most of the army was a flintlock smoothbore musket and bayonet combination firing a one-ounce lead bullet, such as the .75-caliber Prussian musket. They were careless, sloppy weapons that during the chaos of battle had an effective range of less than one-hundred yards. Accuracy did not come anywhere near the level of modern armies, as no more than 5 to 10 percent of shots would hit their intended target. The musket balls they fired were much smaller than the diameter of the gun barrel so the balls tended to ricochet wildly down the barrel when the trigger was pulled. To compensate for their poor accuracy, the Hessian infantrymen were trained to deliver a volley into an area instead of at an individual.[19]

The Jägers' firing during battle was more accurate than the musket-carrying infantrymen's. The Jägers used a rifle that at that time was a technologically advanced weapon; it had a hexagonal grooved barrel that gave a bullet a spin as it exited. The spin gave the rifle greater accuracy, even at long distances. The spin kept the bullets on a true, straight course, allowing for an expert marksman to excel. Its long firing range made placement behind cover a safer, more effective alternative to simply standing in formation. But the rifles were short and lacked bayonets. The rifled grooves made loading the weapon more difficult, as ramming a bullet down a grooved barrel was tricky. At a distance, the Jägers were mobile, deadly sharpshooters, but the lack of bayonet and the rifle's slow rate of fire made them vulnerable in close action to bayonet charges and cavalry.[20] Because of this, the Jäger Corps would often carry *Blankwaffen*, or short swords, to fend off enemies in close quarters.[21]

Even a seasoned recruiter like Faucitt was impressed with the Jägers, stating that they were "a stout, active Body of Men, armed with Rifle-Barrel Guns, to the use of which they are thoroughly inured . . . and as they are commanded by skillful experienced Officers, They cannot fail."[22]

Faucitt knew that the Hessians maintained a company-level command and control that was superior to that of the British. The British usually had three officers assigned to a regiment, and often one would be absent from a battle performing staff duties. The Hessians usually used four officers. Thus they were better able to absorb the wounding or death of a single officer during a battle. Four officers also made the task of maneuvering a regiment through uneven terrain easier.

Faucitt even had to evaluate the Hessian army's drummer boys, as the drummers were the equivalent of a modern era signal corps. Under the command of a drum major, they transmitted orders using drums with extra taut drumheads that were loud enough to be heard over the din of battle. The British had one drummer per company, the Hessians had three.[23]

But not all observers agreed with Faucitt's optimistic conclusions. In order to reach the coast from landlocked Hessen-Kassel, the army had marched through Hanover, a neighboring ally ruled by King George III. The Hanoverian officers escorting the troops had praised the Hessian army. But two regiments of the 1st Division drew criticism, the Rall Regiment and the Lossberg Regiment, which Johannes Reuber and Jakob Piel belonged to respectively. The Hanoverians noted that the Lossberg Regiment, garrisoned during peacetime in the isolated enclave of Rinteln, was composed of many deserters from other countries. Of all the regiments, the Lossberg had the most deserters during the march, fifteen, while all the other regiments combined had only nine. Even on the morning of the embarkation, a desertion plot was discovered and thwarted, and three men imprisoned.[24]

While the problem of desertion raised concerns about Piel's comrades in the Lossberg Regiment, it was hoped that the discipline of the Hessian military would mitigate the problem. However, Faucitt could not ignore the potential problems in the Rall Regiment. Although it was labeled a grenadier regiment, and the men wore grenadier caps, it was not composed of elite soldiers taken from other regiments, as was the tradition for most grenadier regiments. Instead, the Rall Regiment contained many older men who were heads of households. The Hanoverian officers reported that they were the least impressive men of the 1st Division; the landgrave had taken the best for his own guards, and the regiment was now composed of mostly illiterate farmers. During peacetime, all the regiments typically had about a quarter of the soldiers on furlough at any one time. However, when mobilization started, the Rall Regiment had a higher number of men on furlough than any other regiment in the 1st Division. As a result, the regiment would necessitate more intensive training and discipline compared to the other units in the division.[25]

Faucitt worried that the Rall Regiment was inferior to the others because its men were smaller than the rest of the division and its peacetime training standards were laxer. He also worried about the high number of new recruits in the regiment. "Rall's Regiment is the worst of all I have seen," Faucitt wrote, "both in size and physical strength of the men."[26]

In the end, Faucitt was convinced that Hessian discipline and training would prevail. Despite the limitations that he saw in the Rall Regiment, Faucitt said he was confident it would do well "owing to the activity and cleverness of their Colonel [Rall], who is one of the best officers of his rank in the Landgrave's army." [27]

Faucitt was confident he had done well for his king. As the last of the troops boarded the transport, he muttered to himself, "*Mon Dieu! Quelle nation! On peut faire avec elle tout ce qu' on veut!*" ("My Lord! What a nation! What one can do with them!")

Unbeknownst to Faucitt, the Hessian officers standing near him spoke French and overhearing him, they smiled.

As the officers stood alongside Faucitt, watching the regiments march past, they never imagined that within the year, three of these very regiments would suffer defeat in battle, be taken as prisoners, endure humiliation across the colonies, and most distressingly, fall from grace in the eyes of their landgrave.

While the first regiments were arriving at the coast and being sworn into the British Army by Faucitt, the Hessian military continued to mobilize. Throughout Hessen-Kassel, messengers were riding on frozen dirt roads, carrying pouches filled with orders from the army. Arriving in village squares and taverns, they announced to the inhabitants that His Serene Highness, the Landgrave Frederick II, desired all soldiers on leave to return to their regiments. Most of the principality's men followed the orders; some snuck away. Most important, noncommissioned officers were requested to hurry back to their companies, thereby assuring the regiments had enough leadership for the journey to America.[28]

Lieutenant Andreas Wiederhold, like his fellow officers throughout the principality, had been working frantically for weeks on the mobilization. Oblivious to the cold of winter, Wiederhold began exercising his troops. His men in the Knyphausen Regiment shattered the quiet of the countryside, firing from an arsenal of nine thousand practice cartridges, improving their marksmanship while scaring the nearby farm animals. Some soldiers waited impatiently as Wiederhold scoured government documents, drawing up lists of men who owned property or were their family's only son. Those men, known as *Unabkommlich* (the indispensable), were exempt from foreign service and would instead remain as garrison troops. Wiederhold had to inform drummers, gunsmiths, doctors, and even a judge that they were required to serve by "the gracious command" of Frederick.[29]

The quartermasters of the Hessian Ordnance Department faced mounting pressures. They worked rapidly but methodically. They submitted requests to army headquarters for funds to compensate farmers for requisitioned food. Distributing cartridges, they meticulously documented each transaction. They secured vital medical supplies and assembled a competent medical team for field hospitals. The sick were ensured transportation to military hospitals. Additionally, they organized horses to transport officers to the embarkation ports, especially for those not bringing their own mounts to America.[30]

The Hessian military bureaucracy had been working at full speed and remarkably, during just the second week in April 1776, the landgrave's fifteen regiments, totaling 8,647 men, were embarking for England. An additional 1,247 men would be left behind because the Royal Navy lacked transport ships. The landgrave could boast that it was not his fault if the world's largest navy could not keep pace with the efficient Hessian military machine.[31]

Colonel Faucitt was quite pleased. His tallies showed that only twenty-four men had deserted, and the resulting vacancies were quickly filled from a group of waitlisted soldiers (supernumeraries) carried by all Hessian regiments.[32] The colonel believed the Hessians were well equipped to deal with recruits reluctant to serve their prince, as each regiment carried a supply of thumb screws, handcuffs, and large wooden canes. In order to prevent desertion, officers kept their troops away from local civilians as best they could. They closed bridges and stationed guards on the main roads. In towns along rivers, they had recruits sleep on local boats that were watched by guards on the piers.[33]

Now that Faucitt was satisfied with the quality of the men of the 1st Division, the soldiers were assembled and swore an oath of loyalty to King George III. A British officer read the oath in German in a loud voice. The soldiers held their muskets with their left hands. Officers removed their gloves, and everyone had to repeat the oath out loud while raising their right hands.[34] Legally, this was an important event, for the soldiers were now under the authority of a foreign king and subject to the laws of Great Britain, yet the moment had little impact on the men and was nonchalantly mentioned in soldiers' diaries and letters.

"Marched to Bremerlehe," Reuber wrote in his diary, "and were inspected by English delegates and had to pledge allegiance to the King of England. Then back . . . to our quarters."[35]

Colonel Faucitt, knowing the men would be homesick, enthusiastically suggested the Hessian soldiers mark the outside of their homebound letters "*Bureau General des Postes `a London.*" This would allow the Hessian soldiers free use of British mail routes. It would also enable the British to spy on the mail of their Hessian allies.[36]

CHAPTER 5

Can a Broken Nation be Fixed?

Messengers arrived at the landgrave's castle with welcome news: The first Hessian regiments were boarding transports for England. He could, at least for a while, feel satisfied. He had shown the British the professionalism and efficiency of the Hessian military by seamlessly mobilizing an army for an expedition to the other side of the world. In ninety days, Frederick had readied General Heister's 1st Division—more than eight thousand fighting men. With the British gold deposited and treaty signed, full mobilization could begin.

Frederick believed he served his nation's good. "A ruler should rule without bragging, and with deep effort search for manners to make his people happy," he had written in his *Various Thoughts of a Prince*, a book praised by Voltaire himself. Yet sending subjects to war pained him, even as he saw no alternative.[1]

The Seven Years' War had left Hessen-Kassel in ruins. French armies had invaded three times. In Marburg, beggars so crowded the gates that guards struggled to close them at nightfall. Officers rode through silent villages where only loose doors and shutters moved in the wind. Crop and livestock losses, in addition to food confiscated by the army, had starved peasants out of their homes. During the war, many had fled to the forests and humiliated the nation by begging food from enemy garrisons. Only undertakers prospered, as death rates tripled.[2]

The situation in the principality was so dire after the Seven Years' War that the soldiers in Kassel had the audacity to greet Frederick's return to the capital with a poem:

> *Here in horrid rubble from fallen walls lies the reward*
> *of long hard work,*
> *As for Kassel's splendor, the rapacious war with bold hands*
> *has turned the paradise there into empty deserts.*[3]

Even before the war, the principality was plagued by poverty and economic stagnation. Ninety percent of the people engaged in farming, but the country was not well suited for agriculture. The terrain was hilly, with thick forests, and the sections of land that were arable were of poor quality, with little sunlight and too much rain. A third of the peasants were cultivating plots of less than three acres. Even the lives of the nobility lacked the luxury of other European noblemen, as arable plots were small, scattered, and difficult to cultivate. The lack of private business opportunities compelled many nobles to seek government employment. The country's commercial and manufacturing infrastructure were undercapitalized and hampered by the poor weather and rough terrain that rendered the maintenance of roads difficult. The economy, the weather, and the postwar mood of the people were all dreary.[4]

Frederick felt it was his duty to put the country back on a proper economic footing. "A prince is naturally obliged to adopt as his main goal the good of his subjects," he wrote.[5]

He threw himself wholeheartedly into his work, involving himself and his government in almost every aspect of Hessian life. Whatever the war had destroyed, he would fix. Whatever was lacking, he would supply.

Much of the nation's forests had been despoiled, threatening the Hessian construction, fuel, and baking industries, so he imposed restrictions on cutting down timber, prohibited the export of wood, and even commanded that all new homes have their lower floor made of stone. This practice of conserving wood reached its peak when he closed private wood-burning baking ovens in favor of communal ovens.[6]

Fruit was in short supply, so fruit trees were planted on country roads and lanes. Frederick even ordered that newly married couples plant four fruit trees on the day of their wedding. On a trip to Paris, he noticed that the French had nice storefront signs, so upon his return to Kassel, he issued an ordinance to improve the aesthetics of storefront lettering.[7]

Critics claimed he was capricious. They said there were more military men in his court than civilians. He responded by enrolling seventy-two renowned ministers and professors into a Society of Agriculture to establish policy for the nation's lackluster farming industry. The society imported a new crop, potatoes, and ran a contest for the best essay about the benefits of the new food. They gave out prizes for the most imaginative ideas, though many were impractical, such as an attempt to grow silk from Asian silkworms and an essay on how to produce hats from goose feathers.[8]

But the society's most important goal was to teach modern farming techniques to the peasants, who were largely uneducated, superstitious, and inclined to cling to traditional customs. The society promoted progressive innovations that had been tried successfully in other countries, such as more-intensive cultivation of the soil and the use of animal husbandry.[9]

When crops failed in 1771 and grain prices rose 300 percent, the society froze prices and wages.[10] Frederick weighed in on the fight against inflation by repealing the nation's export tax and issuing a proclamation freezing interest rates at 5 percent. He issued fifteen coinage laws and removed debased currency from circulation without minting additional money. When these efforts to improve economic conditions were unsuccessful, he continued to work diligently until inflation was finally halted by opening the country's borders to cheap foreign goods.[11]

Antisemitism, always a stain on the region, flourished, as it often does during difficult economic times, with people looking for scapegoats. A governmental investigation in 1773 concluded that "a major reason for the deteriorating living conditions in the countryside" was the presence of Jewish families. The destruction of villages, pilfering of crops, and execution of Hessian partisans during the Seven Years' War by foreign invaders, notably the French Army, was forgotten; instead, the principality's most persecuted minority was blamed for the deteriorating economy. A Prussian adviser to Frederick publicly said what many in the government believed when stating bluntly that the principality's 7,500 Jews were the principal cause of poverty in Hessen-Kassel.[12]

The government made this antisemitic explanation official policy, concluding after a nine-month investigation that the presence of Jews in Hessian farming villages was "an extremely dangerous situation." The Jews, the government believed, were reluctant to farm Hesse's countryside and were more interested in commerce. Following this line of thought, the government investigators claimed that the presence of Jews "corrupted" the customary distinction that the government believed should be kept between business-oriented cities and agriculturally based countryside villages.[13]

The concept of religious tolerance taught to him by his Enlightenment tutors notwithstanding, Frederick approved the banishment of the nation's Jews from the countryside and, like so many European states, required that they live only in cities.

"Like all merchants," Frederick stated, "Jews belong in the cities, not in villages." Like many eighteenth-century ostensible adherents to the Enlightenment, Frederick found that practicing religious tolerance was far more difficult than preaching it.[14]

Hoping to bring successful foreign businesses and entrepreneurs to Hessen-Kassel, Frederick sent his ministers abroad to learn new agricultural and manufacturing skills. He wooed skilled artisans from abroad with twenty-year tax exemptions and free land. Hessian officials traveling abroad, whether they were academics, diplomats, or even ailing officials on medical leave, shamelessly tried to enlist entrepreneurs they met.[15]

Frederick tried to make life easier and fairer for his subjects. He abolished state-sanctioned torture, restricted the use of the death penalty—he would allow it to be used only twice during his reign. Free legal representation for peasants was established. While liberals and conservatives debated these measures, almost everyone applauded his imposition of fines against lawyers who submitted frivolous cases and his limiting of fees that lawyers could charge.[16]

The Hessian civil service was slow and corrupt. Frederick reformed it by enforcing an entrance examination, requiring university-level training, and making employment and promotions based on quality of work, not rank or political influence. He boosted workers' morale by ending the practice of paying civil servants up to nine months late, expanded a widows' and orphans' fund, and raised salaries. And most important, he continued the tradition by which commoners could use a distinguished career in the civil service as a steppingstone into the nobility.[17]

Lest anyone be idle in his realm, he put male prisoners to work producing chewing tobacco, repairing room clocks and pocket watches, preparing snuff, and grating stag horns for mounting on walls, and he compelled female prisoners to knit and sew. Beekeepers were encouraged to send two-thirds of their wax to candle factories. The cavalry was ordered to turn over its horses to peasants to alleviate the serious shortage of draft animals in the countryside. The nation lacked private investment capital, so Frederick sponsored capitalistic enterprises. Homebuilders were given land, subsidies, tax exemptions, and even precious military exemptions. Farmers were given free grain seed and a four-year moratorium on farm debts, and they were permitted to work the land on Sundays. Even the upper classes benefited from Frederick's largesse, as he shrewdly used his own money to assume debts, give out grants, and reduce taxes for the nobility. This policy gave him political leverage in pursuing his grand schemes. The reach of the Hessian government was massive, with an average of one new ordinance a week.[18]

But still Frederick worried. Three out of four of his subjects lived in the countryside, and much of their land had been damaged by the Seven Years' War, their fields left uncultivated, and more than half their cattle killed. The number of marriages dropped, as young men could not support a family and few prospective brides had any dowry to offer. The economic situation had gotten so bad in the district of Bauna that parents were not allowing their children to marry residents from there. Adding to peasants' woes were the compulsory and burdensome *Dienst* (services), such as building roads and hauling baggage trains, that state officials and local landlords imposed. The peasants were required not only to work but often to supply horses, carts, and materials for municipal building projects. Frederick then eased his citizens' burdens by limiting the amount of compulsory service that could be imposed on the peasants and establishing, for the first time, payment for such work. When a group of farmers protested enforced labor and their leaders were arrested, Frederick went so far as to pardon them.[19]

Yet for all his efforts, sometimes Frederick brooded; he was overcome with melancholy, believing that his people didn't appreciate him. When in the enclave of Schaumburg he facilitated the peasants' ability to buy their freedom from serfdom, lowering the cost to less than a single coin, Frederick was flabbergasted that the peasants did buy their freedom and promptly left Hessen-Kassel.[20]

But there were some gratifying successes. Under his tutelage, the quantity and quality of the nation's sheep and cattle improved, due to modernization of feeding methods. The textile industry boomed because of the army's need for uniforms and tents. He successfully established twelve new factories in one year. A massive reforestation program reseeded almost one hundred thousand acres of denuded forest. Damage to potato crops by wild boars was alleviated once he taught peasants to plant the potatoes away from the forests and closer to their villages.[21]

He won over the hearts of many peasants when he ended par force hunting. These were the royal hunts with the nobility mounted on powerful, swift horses surrounded by packs of dogs, which caused damage to farmlands and terrified the peasantry. The state's gun industry flourished, and Hessian muskets were shipped around the world, including to the British colonies in America, where they would soon be used to kill Hessian soldiers.[22]

The number of workers in the textile industry doubled. Linen production had been largely a cottage industry, pursued by farmers as a sideline income, especially during the winter, but it grew to become one of the most significant sources of wealth for Hessen-Kassel, yielding two million tons a year. But once again, Frederick's inclination for government control outweighed his Enlightenment dreams as he imposed quality-control regulations on an industry that operated out of peasants' cottages. In the village of Hersfeld, the flourishing linen trade provided "the country dwellers with . . . an unprecedented level of prosperity over the poor[er] valleys of the principality."

At each level of his regime, from his own to the lowest bureaucracy, people saw themselves as agents of a new age of enlightenment that was committed to improving the lives of the citizenry. Yet Frederick knew that despite his efforts, the lives of his subjects had only slightly improved. So meager was the state's economy that a fiscal expert on Frederick's staff wrote: "There is no industry in Hessen-Kassel. . . . All Hesse is a village. The towns and cities are merely villages enclosed with walls."[23]

Hessen-Kassel was surrounded by rivers, but only one waterway, the Weser River, was navigable to the North Sea. This waterway should have aided Hessen-Kassel's exports, but trade was hampered by two dozen tolls imposed by petty princes from neighboring principalities. Adding to the problem were boatmen from these foreign states who were prone to seizing Hessian goods that competed with their own industries.[24]

Frederick imported ten thousand grapevines from Switzerland and planted mulberry trees in an attempt to begin wine production and form a silk industry. Both failed, and his dream of ruling an enlightened kingdom began to clash with his Germanic autocratic upbringing. According to the prevailing mercantilism, money needed to stay within the borders of the country and circulate there. Gold and silver left the country for luxury items that Hessen-Kassel lacked, such as coffee and fine clothes. The government saw the purchase of foreign luxury goods as not only an economic threat but also an attack on public morality that promoted idleness and lethargy.[25]

Ignoring the wishes of his people, Frederick tried desperately to limit the import of these luxuries. With the prince's blessing, imports and exports were regulated by the state. Exporting raw materials was forbidden. Importing finished goods that could compete with domestic manufacturers was forbidden. Tailors who used imported luxury cloth in garments were threatened with imprisonment. The export of rabbit skins was also prohibited because they were needed for use in domestic hat factories. Rags and bones, the raw materials for the state-sponsored paper industry, could not be sold to foreign traders. Tobacco consumption was banned, but the ban was lifted following the building of a state-owned tobacco factory.

Coffee was a particularly sensitive topic as the government saw it not only as an import that drained domestic capital but as an unhealthy product that eighteenth-century physicians falsely believed caused male sterility, menstrual hemorrhaging, and miscarriages. Once again, ignoring his enlightened beliefs, Frederick unleashed government spies, known by the locals as "coffee sniffers," allowing them to peer into homes to weed out coffee drinkers. Government posters warned of the dangers of coffee and exhorted the benefits of Hessian-brewed beer, but despite the government's efforts, smugglers snuck in coffee by the barrelful. Hessians desperate for caffeine crossed the border to neighboring foreign coffeeshops.[26]

Conflicting priorities continued to arise as the government attempted to protect its citizens while simultaneously improving the economy, often with the disappointing result of antagonizing the populace and producing little economic benefit. In 1774, the government forbade the children of peasants from enrolling at universities unless the family could prove it could withstand the loss of labor. The government's efforts to improve education were now pitted against its efforts to protect the economy from the loss of teenage laborers. This conflict arose again when the government outlawed foreign lotteries, a form of gambling that threatened to impoverish the citizenry and the economy by exporting people's money. After speaking with a Polish diplomat, Frederick impulsively established his own state-run lottery. He justified the decision by explaining that the threat it posed to the financial integrity of the poor was outweighed by the hope it would inspire among a great number of people, the fortune it would afford a lucky few, and the additional income it would bring the state.[27]

The experiment was a disaster. Though an instant success with crowds flocking to Kassel for the biweekly drawing, it soon became apparent that workers were taking the day off to attend the drawings. Even worse, many poor people were investing everything they had into purchasing lottery tickets. In a telling decision, Frederick, ignoring the corrupting effect he knew gambling could have on his poorer citizens, allowed the lottery to continue, even expanding it to Marburg, and continued to collect a 12 percent profit on each ticket sold.[28]

It was an article of faith in the Hessian government, from the landgrave down to local officials, that poverty arose from man's inclination to hedonism and laziness. The Hessian nobility thought it was their responsibility to dissuade the peasants from excess consumption when times were good and discourage indebtedness during hard times. Therefore, Frederick, despite his resolve to rule benevolently, instructed local authorities to keep watch over the activities of workers and look for evidence of laziness. Local officials were given the authority to forbid festivals, music, or any form of entertainment they believed threatened to undermine worker productivity.[29]

Despite all efforts, the results were, on the whole, insignificant. The actions of the Hessian bureaucracy, which were meant to improve the economy, instead hindered the principality's finances.[30]

When he was a fifteen-year-old student tutored by Swiss Enlightenment philosophers, Frederick had written, "Let us live as Nature has taught us. . . . The nobility and the poor have the same origins." Now, as the ruler of a nation whose capital was flowing out for the purchase of frivolous goods, he disregarded what Voltaire had taught him, rejecting his own egalitarian concepts; instead, he gave his citizens rankings by social class from one to twelve. He allowed the classes one to six, the upper class, to import luxury goods such as gold-embroidered clothing, gold watches, cotton stockings, and coffee. Classes seven through twelve, which included all Jews, were ordered to wear domestic products and were forbidden to drink coffee. The system was so rigid that class regulations extended to funerals. The upper ranks were allowed the use of up to six horse-drawn carriages to accompany a hearse that itself could be drawn by four horses. Everyone else was allowed up to four horse-drawn carriages and two horses to pull the hearse.[31]

Every day, Frederick told himself he was working to improve the lives of his subjects, but as failures mounted, outweighing his meager successes, Frederick turned further away from the Enlightenment, embracing and even expanding the traditionally obtrusive, autocratic Hessian regime.

He felt trapped. The demographics of his country were unfavorable for prosperity. Their resources were limited, and the farmland was only mediocre. Much of the nobility along with the rest of the upper classes were privileged and unsympathetic to the plight of the working people.

He saw no other choice. The only adequate source of finance for his poor country was the soldier trade. He would continue to rent out his male citizens for war, use the profits to enrich the government's treasury, and one day, he hoped, use the money to create a more open, progressive, enlightened Hessen-Kassel.

CHAPTER 6

The First Time at Sea

North Sea, April–June 1776

On April 12, the Rall Regiment, including Johannes Reuber, boarded the ninety-two-foot-long HMS *Success Increase.* The people of Bremerlehe lined the shore and cheered as the men were rowed out to the transport ships. The soldiers in the rowboats sang Hessian marching songs. Spotting their commander, General Heister, in an adjacent rowboat, men began chanting, "It's true, is it not, Papa, that you will soon follow us!" The usually reserved general waved, and in response the soldiers fired their guns into the air.[1]

For most of the men it was their first time aboard a seafaring vessel. Reuber stood at the ship's railing and watched the fresh water of the Weser River flow into the salt water of the sea. Innocent to the symbolism of his observation, he wrote: "Now we looked back to the land. We noticed that the sweet water of the Weser disliked to join the salt water of the sea."[2]

The men waited on the *Success Increase* for a favorable wind. On the 18th, the wind shifted and the gentle flow of the waters became choppy and turbulent. The men were not accustomed to being at sea; for the first time in his life, Reuber felt the floor beneath him sway. He tried to ignore the motion, concentrating on the beauty of the seaport and the smell of the salt air. But the floor continued to move, and his stomach felt strange.[3]

About twenty-five wives from the regiment remained on shore, standing ankle deep in the water, washing laundry. Each regiment was allowed twenty-four to thirty women, but often, more women, and even children, snuck on board. When it had become known that the army was departing for North America, chaplains received many pleas for hastily arranged marriage ceremonies. Some newlywed brides accompanied their grooms for the voyage, others remained behind, many living in the local militia's now-empty barracks.[4]

Most of the 1st Division, including the Lossberg Regiment with Jakob Piel, had already sailed for England, but the Rall Regiment with Johannes Reuber, and two companies from the Knyphausen Regiment under the command of Andreas Wiederhold, were still stuck in the harbor due to a shortage of ships and poor winds.[5]

On the fateful day, after a week's delay awaiting a favorable wind, a signal gun had been fired, the anchors were raised to a great cheer, and the ships cast off—but the wind soon shifted south and the fleet stalled. The men muttered restlessly. Reuber assured his friends that the Lord was all knowing. If the Lord delayed them, it must be to protect them from storms lurking on their path.[6]

Lieutenant Wiederhold concerned himself more with personal matters than the Lord's will. He was a womanizer, in the vernacular of the day "a rake" who "played at courtship." Before departing, he wrote to a friend about how the sorrowful farewells of officers' wives had affected him: "I had armed myself with steadfastness [in saying goodbye to the ladies] in order to march out like a soldier and not shed a tear, but how weak I have become . . . over the melancholy in saying good-bye."[7]

In Bremerlehe he courted a "pretty landlady" but swore that he had not consummated the relationship since he was promised to a "Hessian Beauty" back home. But his fidelity proved shallow as he soon wrote that his "chastity went on a journey" with another landlady—a "very beautiful landlady."[8]

In another letter, Wiederhold addressed his primary concern: his illegitimate daughter in Hessen-Kassel. He asked his friend Georg Ernst von und zu Gilsa to forward a letter to the authorities: "It is the woman who has my child with her [that the letter is for]. I have chosen this opportunity because I consider it the safest." Wiederhold knew that by the time she received the letter, he would have already sailed for America. He would not allow his illegitimate child to spoil his chance to serve in the New World.[9]

The fleet remained stuck at the mouth of the Weser River for another seven days. The men stood at the ship's railings, staring at the townsfolk on shore, who stood staring back at them. On the seventh day, a shot echoed across the harbor, signaling to the sailors that a favorable wind was arising from the south. Anchors again lifted, and the fleet sailed farther out to sea. Some of the women were on shore doing yet more laundry, which was retrieved and placed on board, but those women who hadn't yet boarded were left behind to be brought to New York with the next fleet.[10]

The embarkation of the army took several weeks, from mid-March through June, as regiments arrived from all parts of Hessen-Kassel.* The plan was for the fleet to sail to Portsmouth, England, take on supplies, then sail to New York. Sailors told the Hessians the trip to England would be a pleasant three-day voyage. The men watched the sea beat against the fading shore. Seagulls circled the ships looking for food, but as the sun set, the sky soon darkened and a strong wind rose up. Reuber was mesmerized by mysterious lights that seemed to originate from the ocean.

"Something new for us appeared," he wrote in his diary. "The water seemed to originate a light, as if sparks were sprayed. . . . It seemed to be

---

*Departures of the Hessian Army to America:
1ST DIVISION. Lieutenant General Phillip von Heister: 8,647 men. Departed from Bremerlehe, mouth of Weser River, March–April 1776. Arrived New York August 12: Grenadier Battalions (Linsing, Block, Minnigerode); Field Regiments (Du Corps [also called Leib], Crown Prinz [Erb Prinz], Prinz Karl, Ditfurth, Donop, Lossberg, Knyphausen, Trumbach, Block, Linsingen); one Jäger company (128 men); Field Artillery Battery (242 men, two 3-pounders). Four ships with Colonel Block became separated and arrived four days earlier than the rest of the fleet. The following 1st Division troops were delayed due to lack of ships, and sailed April 17–19, 1776, but due to favorable winds, arrived in New York the same day as the rest of 1st Division: Major General Werner von Mirbach detachment consisting of the Rall Grenadier Regiment, Mirbach Regiment, 154 Knyphausen men under the command of Lieutenant Andreas Wiederhold (20 men of the Company Du Corps of the Knyphausen Regiment and 134 men of the Minnigerode Company of the Knyphausen Regiment), field artillery battery with four guns, and men from the Commissary Department.
2ND DIVISION. Lieutenant General Wilhelm Freiherr von Knyphausen: 4,327 men. Departed from Ritzebuttal, mouth of Elbe River, June 9, 1776. Arrived New York October 19: Grenadier Battalion (Koehler); Field Regiment (Von Wutginau); one Jäger company; Field Artillery Battery, two 3-pounders; Garrison Regiments (Stein, Wissenbach, Huyn, Bunau).
Sources: Atwood, *Hessians*, 37, 51, 55, 56; Schwab, *German Troops in the American Revolution*, 25; Bardeleben, "Diary Bardeleben," 50.

an electrical phenomenon, the light was much brighter and stronger where a large rope entered the water."[11]

The sailors told the Hessians that the strange lights foretold favorable winds. Later that day, favorable winds arose and the fleet entered the English Channel.[12]

The fleet crossed the English Channel to Portsmouth. Prince Frederick had ordered that no one go ashore. But he was far away, and officers snuck out to visit the English city while the enlisted men and wives remained on board. After ten days of living aboard ship with 250 men, the officers were invigorated by the tangy smell of gooseberries in the town's market. The Hessian officers walked as a group, in uniform, eyeing the ladies and bowing to the gentlemen. Smoke billowed from the tall chimneys of Portsmouth's red brick buildings. Freshly plucked ducks, geese, and chickens hung from the butcher stalls as English gentlemen strolled the market with "bouquets" of flowers pinned to their suits.[13]

The officers were surprised by the "fashionable dress" of the English women. Pretty housewives in red dresses scampered about the market squeezing cauliflowers and cabbages. Even maids wore dresses with headgear and sunbonnets as they swept the cobblestone streets. The officers found the women to be "well grown" in comparison to the shorter and poorly nourished females of Germany. The beauty of the English women and the neatness of the seaport "enamored" the Hessians. But for one group of officers the mood was soon broken.[14]

A young girl with a "dainty innocent face" stepped out from a doorway. The men removed their hats and stepped forward. She smiled at them, and despite themselves, the men snuck a peek below her hemline at her exposed feet. One man admitted that he felt a rush of passion in his loins. She had the "most beautifully formed feet and face," he thought.[15]

"Gentlemen, please to walk in," she cooed, but something was wrong. Boys ran up and thrust notes into their hands from a "country woman" offering to entertain them at her "country house." The men were confused until one of the veteran officers explained: "Whore!" The officer pointed and shook his finger accusingly at the innocent-looking woman. The men were crestfallen. One would later joke that the woman made his "good old Adam stir," but despite the temptation his "Hippocrates" said no. Up and down the street and from every doorway women beckoned. They had never seen so many "frivolous women" before. Proudly they boasted that no city in Germany had such a collection of "fallen Venuses"; although they had to admit, the whores of England were much better looking than their German counterparts.[16]

Whatever enticement remained was dashed as one of the officers snickered, "Let's make like puppies!" Contemptuously, the men unbuckled their pants, urinated on the wall of the brothel, and ran away laughing.[17]

The adventure gave the men a grand story to tell, but soon they returned to the transport ships and rested in their comfortable sixteen-by-eleven-foot officers' cabins. The British had designed these berths so every nook was put to use, with storage recesses and a bed in the wall. After an invigorating stroll around Portsmouth, the men would have no trouble falling asleep on their English straw mattresses.[18]

Three thousand miles away, word was spreading that North Carolina had become the first colony to officially call for independence from Britain. When news of this proclamation finally reached Europe, practically no one in the Hessian or British military believed this action would mark the beginning of a determined, violent change in the attitude of the Americans.

The enlisted men were not having as much fun as their officers. Stuck on their ships in Portsmouth Harbor as the fleet awaited favorable winds for the voyage to America, they amused themselves by watching horses being lifted onto the cavalry transport ships by means of broad leather bands strung under the animals' bellies. The horses swayed above the ship, their legs dangling as the bodies of the terrified animals trembled.[19]

On days when the sea was calm, Reuber and his comrades sat on the wooden deck eating zwieback with pork, peas, and raisins from a tin plate balanced on their knees. For dessert Reuber treated himself to suet, a fat-based pudding he scooped out of a linen bag. He washed the meal down with beer. Reuber enjoyed watching the shimmering reflection of the sun on the water as it set on the horizon. Occasionally, a cloud of cigarette smoke would rise from the deck. It was the only situation in which the men were allowed to smoke, and they made the most of the free time, jumping onto each other's backs, playing tag, and dancing to the music of the regimental band.[20]

The soldiers dreaded the approach of sunset. The ship was only ninety-two-feet long, and at night Reuber was crammed with more than 250 soldiers into a large room of bunk beds. Six men were assigned to each of the six-by-six-foot beds with six more men sleeping in the bunk above them.

The men were so tightly packed that they could not move, let alone turn over. When a group tired of lying on one side, the man on the end called out, "Everybody turn!," and they rolled over in unison.[21]

Mornings were no better. The men were awakened not by sunrise but by the smell of their comrades in the poorly ventilated room. The monotony was only broken by assignment to the cleaning detail. The soldiers would lug the bedding up the narrow staircases onto the deck to air out. Then they scrubbed and mopped the large sleeping quarters with vinegar. The sailors used hand pumps to ventilate the room, but when the weather was bad, they shut the air holds and worked in the hot, stuffy space, inhaling the smell of vinegar.[22]

Reuber explored his ship. He watched carpenters saw and hammer mysterious seafaring devices. Sailors tugged on ropes, fighting the winds as if their very lives depended on it—and for all Reuber knew, perhaps their lives did depend on the ropes he was constantly tripping over. Servants and busboys scampered up and down hatchways, carrying boxes, polishing metal, scrubbing anything that did not move. On the lowest deck he discovered mounds of food and barrels filled with river water from the Thames. The water sloshed inside the barrels, and throughout the trip the soldiers heard strange noises inside the sacks of foods. It seemed as if the ship was alive; still, the men tried to block out the thought of vermin and the possibility that some of the ship's occupants might have had more than two legs.

Finally on May 6, after they had been stuck in a windless Portsmouth Harbor for over a week, a north wind arose, filling the sails of the fleet. A signal gun was fired to the cheers of the men, anchors were raised, and the one hundred vessels of the English fleet—with fifty-two of the ships carrying Hessian soldiers—sailed toward the open ocean. On each ship, the ripping of envelopes could be seen; these were the classified sailing instructions from the fleet's commander, Commodore William Hotham, being torn open by the ships' captains. To no one's surprise, the fleet had been ordered to sail for America.[23]

As the tide pulled the fleet out to sea, the ship began to shake. The soldiers began vomiting. Men rushed onto the deck for fresh air. Reuber figured out that the center of the ship was the most stable place to be, so he held onto the middle mast. The British sailors laughed. What a voyage this would be! They had about four thousand miles to travel—the ship had not even reached the ocean and already the passengers were seasick.[24]

Reuber ignored their taunts and tried to concentrate on the other ships in the fleet. A vessel raced past, its corroded anchor chain broken, its sailors dipping hooks and nets into the water in a desperate attempt to recover the lost anchor. The sailors would be rewarded one-third of the anchor's value if they found it.[25]

Soon the *Success Increase* passed the anchorless ship and entered the wider sea. "As we set sail with our fifty ships the view was spectacular," wrote Reuber. "The bright moon was our friendly companion and lighted our way. Our hearts were full of thanks to God, who allowed us to undertake our trip under such wished for conditions. The command ship has struck out a lantern so that we could follow it. . . . During the night I got up and found to my great joy that the wind still remained so favorable. For this the soul was filled with thanks. . . . Now we are completely in the open sea where nothing is to be seen but the sky and water."

The ship's English captain then distributed a small allotment of liquor. For Reuber and his comrades, it was their first taste of rum. They drank the strange brew, but most did not like its sweet taste. They believed that beer was a nourishing beverage and were used to drinking it with at least one meal a day. On many of the ships, the soldiers did not understand the need to ration food; and during the first few days of the voyage, they drank all the beer on board. They were not happy to find that for the remainder of the voyage, they would be issued only the strange, sweet-tasting rum.[26]

"We accepted the reduction [in beer] against our will in order to make this beneficial drink last longer," wrote Lieutenant Johann von Bardeleben.[27]

From time immemorial, sailors had estimated the direction of the wind by noting the course of waves, holding up a wet finger, and listening for the noise of the wind in their ears. Now the sailors, probably to keep the Hessians busy on this long voyage, taught the Hessians nautical tricks for reading the wind. An easterly wind was good for travel, but the winds now came from the north, slowing their speed.

A sailor fell overboard. Reuber watched from the railing, helpless as the man thrashed about in the water. No Hessians who watched could swim. The man fought the waves and made his way to the side of the ship, while sailors lowered a rope. The man grabbed on as the sailors pulled violently. He reached the railing, and sailors rushed forward to bring him over. The Hessians would see several horrific instances of sailors and young cabin boys swept overboard by waves. Some sailors were saved; most were not.

The Hessians reacted to the losses with sadness, despondent at the futility of battling the sea.[28]

That night Reuber could not sleep. The creaking of the boat kept him awake. All he could think of was that only a few boards of wood and tar separated him from the ocean's depths.[29]

Jakob Piel was on the HMS *Union* with other soldiers from the Lossberg Regiment. The men's spirits were lifted when one of the sailors screamed out for a cock fight. The soldiers and sailors cheered their approval.

The ship's English captain and a Hessian Army captain brought out cages. The sea was calm, and the men crowded onto the deck. The sound of yelling in English and German reverberated through the ship. The fighting roosters charged from their owners' hands and began thrashing at each other. Feathers flew. The sharp claw of the German cock cut deep into the neck of the English bird. Blood dripped from the English cock, and soon the wounded bird was dying. Cursing his rooster, the English captain snapped its neck and threw his losing bird overboard. The men laughed, English pounds and German thalers changed hands, and the mood became festive.[30]

The first few days of the journey were wonderful. Piel described these days, saying "the sea was calm as a mirror" or "the sea became very dull" or simply "calm."[31]

Before breakfast, Reuber stood on deck of the *Success Increase* admiring the view.

"While on the deck of the ship, we see the sun in majestic splendor appear on the horizon," he wrote. "The sky, painted with beautiful colors, had an aurora, which, with its pleasant purple colour, announced the sun prior to its arrival. With such pleasant views and an empty stomach, our breakfast was gladly received."[32]

He quickly learned that the beauty of the ocean was an illusion; it was like a mirage, obscuring mortal danger.

Throughout the voyage, the same issue would plague all the ships: after a few pleasant days, clouds would appear, obscuring the stars and the moon. The air would become wet, soldiers would describe the humid air as seeming to be too "close" or "suffocating." Heavy rain would start, reducing visibility. The soldiers would describe the sea as "raging," "mountains of waves" with the water hitting so hard "that one could believe from the noise that we had hit a rock." The captains would order the ships' guns to be fired, bells rung, and drums beat as a signal to prevent collision with other ships in the fleet. The soldiers would be ordered belowdecks into the suffocatingly, damp, 250-man sleeping quarters. Wind and waves would violently pound the ship, and it would become necessary to extinguish the lamps to prevent the rolling ship from tipping over a lamp and starting a fire. Sailors would shut the vents and close the hatches to keep out water that covered the deck and cascaded down the air shafts, soaking the men huddled belowdecks. Soldiers would lay in the suffocating darkness, vomiting and praying for the lord to save them. Boxes, secured with ropes, would break loose, and even the soldiers' sleeping berths would be torn from the walls and sent crashing about the room.

With the air vents and the hatches closed, the men were left in darkness. They would fall to the ground, unable to stand in the dark room as the ship rocked to and fro. The ships would be carried to the peak of the monstrous waves and then crash down into the troughs. The waves towered above the vessels, sometimes higher than the mainmasts.[33]

If the ship was unable to escape the storm, the captains would order the sails drawn in and the rudder bound. The ship would be left to fate.[34]

The storms could rage for days. Then finally, the men would be awakened by silence. Rain would no longer beat the deck. The ship would slowly come to life. Sailors would carefully open hatches. The men would stumble above and feel the relief of cool, clear air with no wind. Eventually the bright rays of the sun would break through the clouds. Equipment would be brought on deck to dry. All assignments would be canceled, and the soldiers and sailors would sleep in the open air. The men could once again enjoy the sea breeze, but the ocean refused to let them forget its power: Days of water soaking the ship's wood and iron left a stench.[35]

Johannes Reuber, blocking out the horrors of his days at sea and appreciating how precious life was, thanked the Lord for protecting him. Above him red pennants fluttered from the top of the center masts. The pennants, flying just below the Union Jack, signified that these ships carried the army of Hessen-Kassel to protect the people of the New World who awaited them, those brave souls still loyal to the British monarch.

But neither Reuber nor his Hessian comrades appreciated the vastness of the Atlantic Ocean nor how much longer they would be at sea, how many more trials the Lord would impose, and how many soldiers and sailors would never again see their homeland.

PART II

America

CHAPTER 7

Hessians: Savage Mercenaries or Legal Auxiliaries?

It was 1776, and the American Revolution was now a year old. The colonies were in full rebellion. The English fleet traversing the Atlantic was filled with Hessian soldiers who believed the war in America would be a brief campaign against ill-trained settlers, a war of skirmishes in the wilderness followed by garrison duty after the rebel towns were liberated. But back in Hessen-Kassel, Frederick had started to receive ominous reports about the war.

Strolling through his English gardens, the landgrave could see towering 1,640 feet above the town the twenty-six-feet tall copper statue of Hercules standing proud atop its volcanic rock obelisk. Frederick could stand at the base of the statue and feel empowered by what it symbolized—strength, courage, and wisdom—but he felt more than Hercules' mythological potency. To him, the statue was a symbol of the triumph of art over nature and the omnipotence of human creativity. In the figure of Hercules he saw his own virtues as a ruler, the virtues that he believed made it possible for him to best the powerful King George in negotiations. [1]

The treaty between His Majesty King George III and Frederick II Landgrave of Hessen-Kassel had been written in French and signed four months earlier on January 15, 1776. The wording of the document—which seemed innocuous, although somewhat strange and grammatically awkward—had been shrewdly chosen by men who understood the subtleties and power of European diplomatic language. King George agreed to pay 360,000 crowns ($23.6 million in today's currency)[2] for twelve thousand fully equipped soldiers and an additional 450,000 crowns for each year he used the army. However, the treaty specifically stated that the landgrave was "full of attachment for" George and that Frederick "desires nothing more than to give him . . . proof of it . . . by virtue of this treaty . . . a strict friendship, and a sincere, firm, and constant union, in so much that the one shall consider the interests of the other as his own."[3]

These phrases had been carefully selected to show to the world that the landgrave had no desire to merely make a profit by leasing his soldiers to King George. By wording the treaty this way, Frederick was having things both ways. Technically he was not making money for renting out his soldiers, he was only charging George for the right to inspect and hire Hessian soldiers. George would pay the soldiers, who would swear an oath of allegiance to him; thus the Hessian soldiers were now, by international law, considered to be auxiliaries of the British Army rather than mercenaries. In other words, by following the strict, literal translation, Frederick was not selling his male citizens but simply allowing King George to "hire" them. And to make sure that no one missed the point, the treaty further specified that the landgrave's motives were not monetary and that he was only concerned with forming "a strict friendship" with Britain. Frederick even added a clause that if Hessen-Kassel was attacked, Britain would come to the assistance of the principality. In Frederick's way of thinking, this clause was additional proof that the treaty was a defensive alliance, not a business transaction, and that his men were not mercenaries. Frederick believed his reputation would be further enhanced because in the contract he did not demand a so-called blood money clause. This was a morbid though not uncommon feature of mercenary agreements, whereby the state renting out its soldiers was paid a bonus for each soldier killed, and three wounded soldiers were paid at the rate of one dead soldier.[4]

Frederick was comforted that the tainted label of "mercenary" had been legally removed, but much to his chagrin, he would soon learn that many world leaders and educators he admired were not impressed, nor were they fooled, by such legal niceties. Future generations would label him as a trader in mercenaries, a ruler who filled his coffers with gold obtained by sacrificing the lives of his citizens. Frederick would have been mortified, and probably a little confused, to learn his reputation would eventually be denigrated on both sides of the Atlantic.

Within weeks of the publication of the treaty, Frederick found himself being criticized for his soldier trade (Soldatenhandel). Nothing in his life had suggested such a strong negative reaction to the treaty. After all, this Anglo-Hessian treaty was the fifteenth of its kind since 1694. The renting of soldiers to foreign kings had not only been common practice in Europe, it had also been approved by some of Europe's most prestigious legal scholars and philosophers. Britain had hired foreign auxiliaries for some of its late-seventeenth century wars and all of its major eighteenth-century wars. Yet without warning, Frederick found himself being attacked by the European intelligentsia. He was severely criticized by German philosopher Immanuel Kant, French activist Comte de Mirabeau, and German writer Johann Wolfgang von Goethe—three men who were admired throughout Europe. He was denounced in the periodical *Deutsche Chronik*, a unique newspaper that reached not only twenty thousand readers in Germany, an enormous amount for the era, but was read across Europe.[5]

Mirabeau called the Hessians "mercenaries . . . packed together like cattle" on foreign ships, sent to fight a people "who had not done them any harm." The colonists, on the other hand, were defending their homeland from Hessian invaders who had been "spit out by the ocean" onto their shores.[6]

Frederick failed to grasp the transformation that Europe was undergoing. In previous centuries, a prince could sign a subsidy treaty without fear of reprimand, as scholars only distinguished between soldiers who fought as part of a military organization and those who did not. A soldier's service was considered legitimate as long as he was part of a regular state-controlled army, regardless of his origin or whether he was compensated for his actions. But the understanding of military service was changing. Many scholars were now conferring legitimacy on military service only when a soldier fought for his nation rather than for a foreign sovereign.[7]

Frederick did not understand that he had struck a nerve among Enlightenment philosophers. He was confused and embarrassed. In the past, Enlightenment thinkers had tolerated war as a necessary part of life, yet somehow the war in America was different. He did not expect that the enlightened elite he admired would see America as a model for the world they wished to eventually create in Europe and a paradigm for fixing Europe's flawed societies. Most embarrassing of all was the scorn heaped on him by his hero, Frederick the Great of Prussia.

Frederick was shrewd enough to know that the Prussian leader's criticism was both hypocritical and self-serving, but once again the landgrave had been humiliated by the ruler he most admired. In private correspondence, Frederick the Great had told the landgrave that he himself detested the American rebels and would gladly volunteer troops to suppress them; then in correspondence with Voltaire, the Prussian ruler accused the landgrave of selling "his subjects to the English as one sells cattle to be dragged to the slaughter."[8]

Frederick was mortified. His carefully crafted image of an enlightened ruler was in jeopardy. His public humiliation deepened when the army reported that a significant number of Hessian soldiers, more than initially estimated, had evaded deployment to America by either deserting or relocating to other countries.

Frederick soon learned that there were a multitude of reasons for the desertions: higher recruitment bonuses from the ruler of Hanover, fear of crossing the Atlantic, fear of the exaggerated perils of the American wilderness, and the long separation from their families while fighting a war on the other side of the world.[9]

Then reports began to arrive from America that things were not going as well for the British as had been expected. The Hessian army was already at sea when word trickled back to Europe that the British had abandoned Boston—the great American seaport was now in rebel hands.[10]

Frederick craved approval from his peers; instead, his hero, Frederick the Great, taunted him. Great Enlightenment figures like Voltaire seemed to be abandoning him. Some segments of his principality were deserting him; and most frightening of all, the Americans were beginning to look like they would not be beaten so quickly.

Everything he had worked for his entire life was now at stake as the English fleet carrying his precious army continued its voyage to America.

CHAPTER 8

The Atlantic Crossing

June–August 1776

LIEUTENANT WIEDERHOLD and his fellow officers of the Knyphausen Regiment had much to do. They were responsible for the regiment's 391 men, thirty-five servants, five sutlers, twenty women, eighteen children, and seven drivers. Before sailing, Frederick had issued "stringent orders" that while on the ships, the men must wash and shave each day. It was an order the men tried to ignore. They exercised and drilled, practicing the skills they would use to crush the American rebels. They pretended to march from Boston to Philadelphia on the less-than-ninety-foot wooden deck. Afterward, the soldiers tended to lounge about the deck in filthy, smelly clothes. The officers knew that sometimes men were no better behaved than children; now they would be treated like children.[1]

Every day the same scene would play out: The Hessian officers called to the English sailors to bring them water. The Hessian soldiers groaned and began to strip. Laughing, sailors dipped buckets into the ocean and hoisted them up with sea water splashing over the sides. Naked men were soon running about the deck throwing water and slipping on soapy bubbles. From the lower decks, sweating servants struggled to carry up casks of Thames River water for drinking. The sailors, who loved spinning tall tales at the expense of the innocent Hessians, would assure the soldiers that Thames water was well known for not turning rancid on long voyages. The now-clean, wet soldiers listened to the seamen and drank the warm, stored water, which was at least several weeks old. Smirking, the sailors quietly ducked into the corners of the ship and drank cool, fresh rainwater collected the night before in clean casks.[2]

The officers made sure each soldier received two-thirds of a pound of biscuit with peas and oatmeal. But unscrupulous vendors had supplied the navy with dough that had been made without salt and then baked so hard that the men were forced to hold the biscuits against the deck and beat them with their guns to break them up. The sailors told them not to despair of the bland, saltless taste; the seawater used for cooking would supply all the salt they could ever want. The cooks hauled large copper kettles on deck. As they started the coal fires, the men felt their stomachs churn hungrily as the aroma of boiling beef and pork filled the air. The men sat on deck eating from bowls and jars made of wood, as glass or porcelain vessels were too fragile to survive the ocean voyage. When the sea was rough, the soldiers would go belowdecks and eat sitting on the floor with one hand holding onto a table or bed. Pouring hot liquids became a dangerous adventure, so they would tie their coffee kettle to a rope that hung on a nail. As the waves tossed the ship, each man would gingerly approach the swinging kettle and fill his cup with trembling hands.[3]

The officers soon broke the news to the men that the supply of beer and tobacco had been exhausted.[4] Men went belowdecks and pulled straw from the mattresses. They rolled the straw in writing paper and soon the deck was covered in a haze of smoke, as the tobacco-deprived soldiers tried to satisfy their craving by smoking straw cigarettes.

At sunset, well-fed and washed, the soldiers relaxed on the decks of the transport ships as the sun dipped below the horizon turning the sky purple before plunging it into darkness. Stories and rumors circulated throughout the fleet. One such story—which was actually true—was that to amuse the men, the captain of the ship *Malaga* had thrown his dog and a broom into the ocean. Dumbfounded soldiers had watched nervously from the railings as the dog thrashed about in the water. It eventually fetched the broom and was drawn up with a rope to the cheers of the men. There was no denying to the Hessians that the dog was braver in the water than they were.[5]

But as so often happened at sea, the mood could change in an instant. On the *Judith*, a transport carrying parts of the Lossberg Regiment, a seaman took a depth sounding. He dropped a lead weight and called out "Four!" The Hessians thought he said "Fuer!" (fire!), at which point they panicked and raced for the lifeboats. Men who only moments before were the best of comrades now clawed and shoved at each other, trying to climb into the little boats. Lifeboats began to tear away from their moorings. English sailors tried to restore order, but they spoke no German, and the panic continued to spread. The sailors lost control of the ship, and it drifted into the path of a nearby transport. Helplessly, the soldiers watched as the sides of the ships rubbed against each other for an instant and there was the terrifying sound of wood scraping on wood. Then the vessels drifted apart. The sailors began screaming at the Hessians, chasing them away from the lifeboats and cursing them for their stupidity, until calm finally prevailed.[6]

Collisions, and near collisions, at sea were terrible events that occurred almost daily in both calm and foggy conditions.[7] Piel was on the deck of his vessel, the *Union*, enjoying a pleasant breeze when a large British ship suddenly turned into its path.

"It was a frightful moment as the ship came towards us," Piel recalled. He looked up and saw the rigging of their neighbor hovering over him, as the sails cast an ominous shadow across his face. The bow of the vessel rammed the middle of Piel's ship. The bowsprit of the intruding vessel slid over the *Union's* deck and struck its forward mast. Moments before, women on both ships had been relaxing on deck. Now Piel heard them shrieking as the broken mast threatened to crush them. Piel saw the soldiers from the adjacent ship, their eyes wide with fear, staring helplessly across the railings at him. Sailors shimmied up adjacent masts and pulled tightly on ropes, changing the angle of the sails and allowing the ships to separate. Remarkably, no one was hurt and peace was restored. Piel was impressed by the speed and professionalism of the Royal Navy sailors, as the damage was repaired within an hour.[8]

Wiederhold kept his men on a pleasant, uneventful schedule, but he could never quite relax himself. The Hessian officers were never sure from where the next problem would arise. And as they feared, the tranquility was often broken for the most unexpected reasons.

Dozens of wives were on the ships working as laundresses, seamstresses, and baggage carriers. Married couples were allowed to share a bed, but officers tried to "prevent misbehaviour" by placing their beds in conspicuous locations. Incredibly, on several occasions during the voyage, a soldier's wife announced she was about to give birth. The first of these women to go into labor was Maria Elisabeth Haemer. Following somewhat improvised procedures, a doctor was summoned and soldiers carried the expectant mother belowdecks. A bunk was cleared for her, the six soldiers who usually slept there were told to find room elsewhere on the already fully occupied ship, and some of the other wives hung sheets around the bunk for privacy. The officers left the details of the birth to the doctor and went back on deck where the husband had been left to wait nervously. The endless expanse of water seemed a godforsaken place for a new life to enter the world, but within a few hours, a healthy baby boy was born.[9] (On another occasion at a Hessian shipboard birth, the doctor came on deck and noiselessly eased his way to the railing, quietly passing the expectant father and his comrades. The men thought their hearts would stop as they watched the doctor throw a bloody package overboard. Stillborn! No, the doctor assured them, just the placenta. Mother and baby were fine belowdecks.)

Maria Elisabeth Haemer lay in the hot windowless room with her sweaty hair fanned out on the pillow. There was nothing that could be done to freshen the room or ease the heat. The father held the infant—a tiny pink baby in a large gray woolen army blanket. He awkwardly tried to balance the child in his huge hands while soldiers nursed the mother, gently tipping to her lips a cup of brandy and warm beer with pepper.[10]

She had given birth to a healthy boy, but the new arrival presented a religious problem. Twenty-five-year-old Chaplain Georg Christoph Coester, who had only five years of experience, was rowed over from another ship for the baptism. The army preferred to recruit young, recently graduated theologians who usually earned their livelihood tutoring. They were considered military personnel but were allowed to wear the native Hessian civilian dress worn by clergy. So Coester likely arrived wearing a black hat, a black coat, and black boots.[11]

The ship's captain was asked to be one of the godfathers. Embarrassed, he declined, claiming that since he was at sea, his duties made it impossible to fulfill his potential responsibilities. Afterward, he admitted he felt uncomfortable with the role as it was not a common practice in his Presbyterian Scottish homeland. The Hessian officers listened politely and said nothing. But they knew this was not good. A lot of tolerance would be needed to fight in an alliance comprising differing religions, especially in the hostile wilds of America.[12]

The winds were fluctuating during the last two weeks of May, and the fleet's progress was slower than had been hoped for. The officers wanted to know everything their soldiers were doing. They would report to their superiors, who would report to the landgrave anything that seemed amiss. But none of the officers noticed the occasional disappearance of Private Adam Koch and his wife, Maria, amid the crowded ship. Six months after landing, their baby, Wilhelm Philip, was born and baptized. At the ceremony, officers attending the service counted backward on their fingers and shook their heads in confused wonder as they contemplated the seemingly impossible privacy the couple had somehow found within the ship's cramped quarters.[13]

As the spring weather remained pleasant and the speed of the ship increased, schools of giant fish, some so large they formed a dark patch on the water, began circling the vessels. Sailors explained that the fish were porpoises. Reuber was astonished to see thousands of them "frolicking in the water." They were chasing schools of flying fish. The Germans lined the rail as the creatures sprang from the water in dazzling arcs. On the transport ship *Jenny*, one fish flew onto the deck and hit a sailor in the back of the head. Sailors spread stories through the ship that the porpoises were an ominous sign that a storm was coming and someone was going to die. The sailors baited a hook with four pounds of pork and lowered it into the water to trail the ship. A porpoise swam around it but did not bite, so the sailors stuck feathers on the bait and the animal, evidently mistaking it for a flying fish, snapped it up and was caught. The Hessian quartermaster on the *Molly* caught one with a harpoon, hoisted it on deck, and was shocked to see that the porpoise's face looked more like a swine than a fish. The sailors, with their seemingly never-ending supply of pseudoscientific stories and theories, told the soldiers to cook the carcass after carefully filling a pot with silver coins to draw out any poisonous copper, which the sailors claimed porpoises were known to ingest.[14]

In another case, a large fish the soldiers estimated to be at least eighteen feet long was trailing a ship carrying soldiers of the Lossberg Regiment. Sailors told the soldiers it was a shark. They explained that sharks were dangerous, but that Negroes knew better how to deal with them than white men. The soldiers listened in awe as the sailors explained that off the coast of America, the Negroes, who were a race of "expert swimmers," swam out into the ocean with daggers to do battle with the monstrous fishes. Since everyone knew that a shark must lie on its side to swallow, the sailors claimed, the Negroes would wait until the shark had flipped on its side and then dive under the fish to stab it. The Hessians were amazed. The ship's captain joined in to say that each year a shark grows a new row of teeth. Why, he himself had caught one beast in the West Indies that had thirty-five rows of molars.[15]

The sailors hung ropes with meat-laden metal hooks over the side. After a short while, a rope jerked, and the sailors lifted up an eight-foot shark. The hook had ripped open its mouth. The Hessians backed away as the fish landed on the deck and began thrashing about, its tail splintering the wooden deck and its blood flowing across it. The sailors killed it. Then they began to bicker over it, as the fish contained a large amount of precious fat, fresh meat, and a much-sought-after rough, hard skin that was used for shining metal. The soldiers' bickering quickly turned to fighting. Hessian officers tried to quell the conflict, hitting the sailors with short, heavy, wooden clubs, but soon a second fight broke out among the sailors. The Hessians, terrified that they would be knocked overboard by the fracas, hailed a man-of-war that was passing by. Officers from that ship quickly came on board and ended the fight with threats of punishment.[16]

May turned into June. The pleasant weather continued, and the men settled into a monotonous but relaxed routine. One afternoon, Piel watched as his ship was enveloped by a fog so thick he could not see the ocean. For two days, the fog teased the men, momentarily lifting to reveal sunlight and then descending again to plunge the ship into darkness. When the fog finally disappeared, Piel and his comrades were dumbfounded to see that the ship was surrounded by an enormous flock of seabirds that had evidently been using the ship to guide themselves through the fog.[17]

On the *Jenny*, Lieutenant von Bardeleben of the von Donop Regiment was eating lunch when the fog lifted.

"Someone came into the cabin," Bardeleben wrote, "and in a loud voice shouted, 'Look how many fish!' We hurried on deck. An innumerable great many fish completely surrounded our ship, as far as could be seen. A host of them were swimming among one another. We could not learn what they are called but they were very large, almost ten feet long. Above all the variety and number of marine animals is beyond belief and even the smallest species shows the greatness of the Creator."[18]

Reuber got along well with the sailors of the *Success Increase*, especially since he would trade his allotment of rum with them for bread. They taught him the right mixture of salt and "sweet" water (salt-free water such as rainwater) to use for cooking. They explained the sailor's habit of washing clothes in urine.[19]

The soldiers had learned to watch the floor for open hatchways, as the sailors often forgot to close the hatches and sometimes Hessians fell in, tumbling down the stairs to the deck below. The men looked forward to the calm nights seated on deck, liberated from the stuffiness of their sleeping quarters and watching the most beautiful moon they had ever seen. Outlined in the moonlight, members of the ships' crews jested with each other, making obnoxious noises with trumpets. The women came on deck and danced with their husbands. The unwed soldiers danced with each other to the music of the regimental band.[20]

An officer from the Mirbach Regiment wrote, "Lieutenant von Wurmb and I celebrated the Saints Day for people named Hendrich and Henrietta, with considerable pleasure. The health and long life of all our dear friends of these names were toasted by us, frequently, with the only bottle of red wine and a bottle of white wine. Towards evening our soldiers entertained with dancing on deck, and we were moved to do the same, but unfortunately without the company of Women."[21]

Throughout the voyage, Reuber was continuously awed by the vastness of the Atlantic Ocean. "Our souls and thoughts were perpetually occupied with the fact that we were in the open ocean where we saw nothing but sky and water," Reuber wrote in his diary.[22]

He soon began to appreciate that everything was amplified at sea: The sunrises were more inspiring, the moonlight more beautiful, and the stars more numerous. As the favorable wind died down, there was still no sign of land. It had been almost three months since they'd sailed from Germany. The Royal Navy had stocked the ships with a ninety-day supply of food. Reuber was about to learn that at sea, not only the good things were amplified—hunger was too.

Storms plagued all the ships transporting the Hessians. For Reuber, the first sign of trouble began on June 8, 1776. The air was damp and his joints ached. Pressed in his bunk bed between five comrades, he had fallen into a deep sleep but was awoken by screams. A sailor was running about, announcing that the end was near, the ship was breaking up, and it would not be able to hold back the ocean. On June 10, the sailors grew anxious as their superstitious beliefs in the magical power of porpoises seemed to come true when the sea suddenly grew rough and porpoises were seen chasing flying fish, confirming that a porpoise induced storm was coming.[23]

The storm hit so suddenly that Reuber was caught out on deck. The wind roared with a deafening howl. Bolts of lightning illuminated the sky.

"The crash of thunder was accompanied by the most terrible lightning so that it often seemed that fire, water, and ship were a single object," wrote Lieutenant Bardeleben.[24]

Reuber struggled to a hatch as the sailors fought the wind and were barely able to take down the sails. The sailors at the helm tied themselves to the mast with thick ropes. Water swept the deck, chasing everyone into the hatchway, and poured down the stairwells and into the sleeping quarters. Sailors battened down the hatches, sealing them with tar and nailing sailcloth over them. Screams echoed through the sleeping quarters as waves tossed the ship, the typically reserved soldiers overcome with terror.[25]

Reuber huddled with his five bedmates. The tossing of the ship made soldiers feel as if they were being rolled down a mountainside in a barrel. Cabinets burst open, and men were showered with bits of glass from cups and bottles. Canteens, chairs, and even smoking pipes slid wildly across the floor.[26]

None of the soldiers were immune to the paralyzing fear that the Atlantic storms aroused in them. Men lay down on their beds or on the floor and held onto the waists of the soldiers next to them. They were moaning, crying, and hunched over vomiting. Wine, tea, liqueurs, and other liquids released from shattered bottles mixed with seawater and vomit, filling the lower decks with an oddly sweet yet putrid aroma.

One soldier needed air. He left his bed and went onto the deck. A few sailors with experienced sea legs were working ropes. The ship began to roll, and a wave roared over the side onto the deck. The soldier's legs gave out. The wave carried him to the railing. His head hung over the edge as he stared into the foamy waters. Then the ship rolled him back onto the deck, and he scampered back to his bed.[27]

Jakob Piel's *Union* which had already been damaged in the collision mentioned earlier, was tossed about in a five-day storm. He lay in bed seasick, convinced the ship would soon be "smashed to pieces." A sailor came into the quarters and ordered everyone above. A neighboring ship, its deck unmanned, was sailing directly for them. The sailors, with the Hessians bringing up the rear, struggled to the deck, screamed in unison, and ran back down below. The crew on the other ship heard the yell and veered away.[28]

The Hessians, most of whom had never seen a body of water larger than a river, stayed curled up in their beds during storms, wondering what type of people these Americans were. How could they rebel against their king and cause so many people so much misfortune?

The storms at last abated, and during the first week of July, Wiederhold's vessel crossed the halfway point to America. On the *Greyhound*, the men celebrated with a "sailor's baptism." First, the sailors were given rum. Then a group of sailors on the deck formed what was known as a "human ship." They sat on the deck while their hands and feet were bound, and an oar stuck into their pants rubbed against their backsides. Their faces were painted red, black, and yellow, and the name *Greyhound* was painted on the first sailor to represent the bowsprit. Their shipmates poured buckets of water on them. The sailors then tore themselves loose and had a water fight, much to the amusement of the Hessians.[29]

On the *Success Increase*, the sailors celebrated the halfway point of the crossing by pranking Reuber and the other Hessian soldiers. They told them that the ship was in the Mediterranean. The hills on the horizon, the Azores, were presented to the Germans as Grenada.[30]

But not all the soldiers joined in the celebration. They had been at sea for too long, and there could be only one explanation for such a long sea journey: the ship must have sailed past its destination, America.[31]

No amount of pleading could dispel their fear—even some of the educated officers were unsure—and the mood on the ship turned ugly. The voyage slowed due to contrary winds. Soldiers claimed to see St. Elmo's fire, a supposedly fiery apparition, hovering at the tops of the masts. Word spread that a waterspout, capable of sucking a ship down, was seen and barely averted.[32]

On the *Unanimity,* Captain Graf von der Lippe's spaniel began to howl. The captain accused Lieutenant Carl August von Kleinschmidt of provoking the dog and challenged him to a duel. The lieutenant suggested that they fire pistols harmlessly in the air, thereby preserving their honor and their lives. But the captain stomped his foot, called Kleinschmidt "an old woman," and insisted they duel. The captain got his wish, and Kleinschmidt fatally wounded him.[33]

On his deathbed, the captain admitted he had been the instigator, and he forgave Kleinschmidt. His autopsy was performed the next day. It was determined that Kleinschmidt had acted properly. The captain's corpse was tipped overboard after being dressed in a uniform and wrapped in a linen cloth filled with heavy coal.

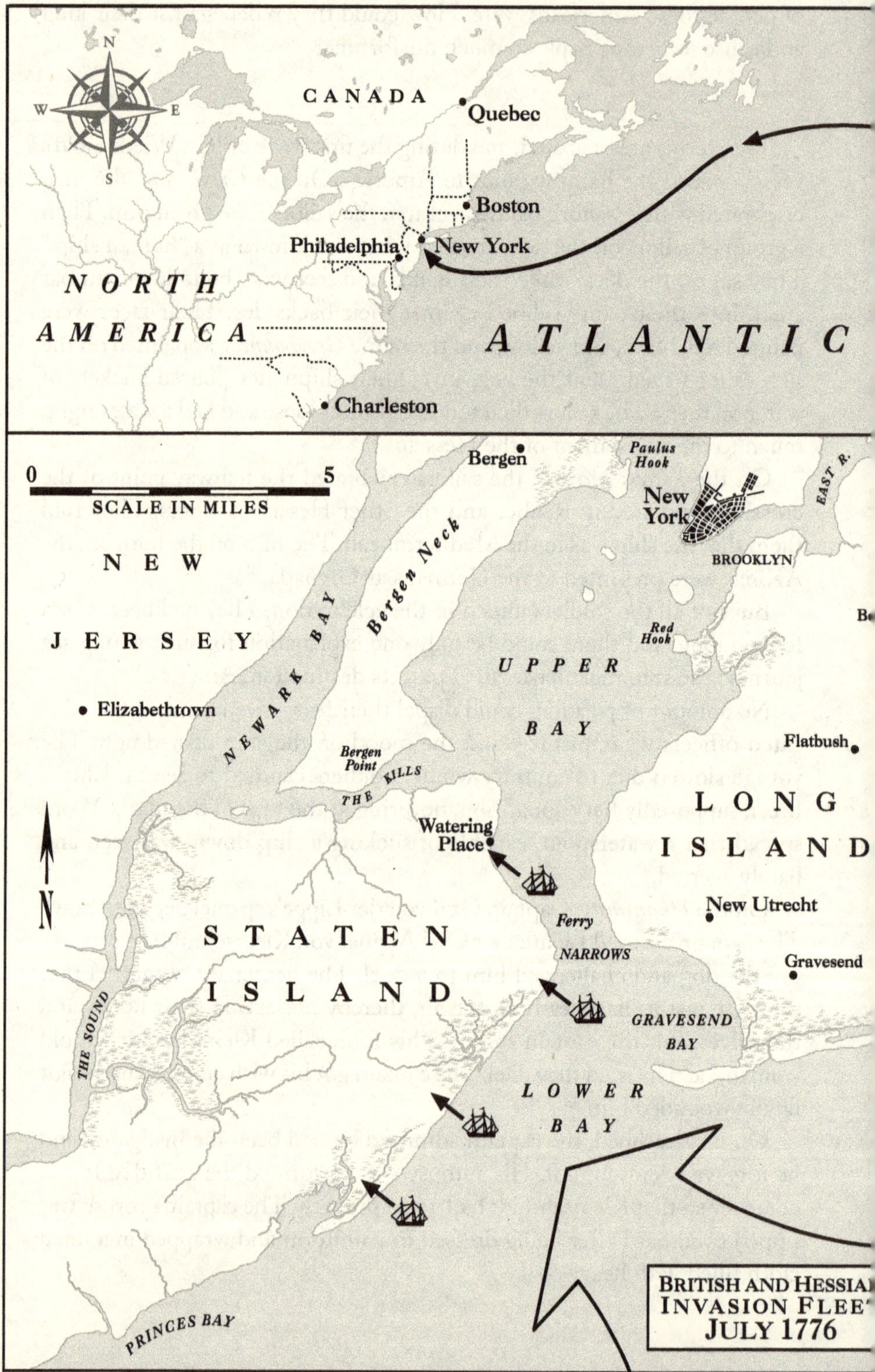

BRITISH AND HESSIA
INVASION FLEE
JULY 1776

THE ATLANTIC CROSSING OF HESSIAN FORCES
DEPARTURE: MARCH–MAY 1776
ARRIVAL: JUNE–AUGUST 1776
0
1000
SCALE IN MILES
Denmark
England
London
Portsmouth
German Kingdoms
Kassel
Rhine R.
La Harve
Saint Malo
EUROPE
France
BAY OF BISCAY
La Rochelle
Marseille
OCEAN
Spain
MEDITERRANEAN
NORTH SEA
April–May 1776
Kiel
HOLSTEIN
Bremerlehe
MECKLENBURG-SCHWERIN
Hamburg
Weser R.
HANOVER
ETHERLANDS
PRUSSIA
Hanover
Rintlen
Münster
MÜNSTER
Nieder-vellmar
Weser
Düsseldorf
Kassel
HESSEN
Katzein-Bogen
Wiesbaden
HESSEN-KASSEL 1776

The captain's funeral was not the only one held that week. The small amount of remaining food was turning rotten, and men began to die. Soldiers gathered at ships' railings as dead comrades were shoved overboard, their bloated corpses weighted down by sacks of rocks tied to their heads or wrapped around their feet. Peasants who, prior to this, had never even seen an ocean had now been given watery graves.[34]

Johannes Reuber sensed the mood of the trip shifting from pleasant monotony to fear. American pirates, privately owned ships sanctioned by the Continental Congress to capture British vessels, were spotted stalking the fleet, boldly sailing between English vessels. Their audacity provoked anxiety and indignation from the British sailors. In response, the number of nighttime lookouts was increased. Hessian soldiers and English sailors were soon standing on deck, armed with any weapon that was on board: pistols, rifles, sabers, and even long, curved, deadly Arabian scimitars. They stared out at a black sea in case the Americans attempted a surprise boarding. The men took turns manning the outlooks under star-filled skies, peering into the distance to distinguish enemy vessels from friendly ones, and trying to ignore their fear.[35]

As edible food became scarcer each day, the shipboard rats grew bolder. One night a sleeping soldier on the *Greyhound* felt a wetness between his legs and pulled back the covers to discover the nose of a rodent sniffing in his crotch. As sickness increased, the soldiers bled themselves in a futile attempt to prevent disease. Dolphins, whom the soldiers had previously been marveling at, began to be fair game for hunting.[36]

Soldiers, comfortable with using antisemitic theories to explain their hardships, blamed the lack of fresh meat, bread, and vegetables on lecherous British profiteers who, in the words of the men, had "made a Jewish profit." Zwieback and potatoes became the main fare, but soon even the potatoes were gone. The men began to live on dumplings and oatmeal; but even worse, the kegs of stored water, the supposedly imperishable Thames River water, smelled awful and had long green filaments floating on top of the casks. The summer heat hastened the contamination. Fresh water became so scarce that no one was allowed to wash their hands and feet, except with seawater. Some days belowdecks became so hot that bars of sealing wax melted. A joke made the rounds that the best source of meat were the worms in the bread. The bacon turned black on the edges and yellow in the middle.[37]

"Our provisions keep diminishing in quantity and become worse in quality," complained an officer of the Lossberg Regiment. "Instead of butter we receive stinking olive oil for melting. . . . There are worms in the bread and the water smells so bad that the most extreme thirst could not force us to drink it."[38]

The officers' personal provisions ran out, and they were forced to eat the same fare as the enlisted men. There was no more beer, wine, or sugar. Soldiers took to sweetening their coffee with raisins. "Whoever wants to know what it tastes like should try it," said one officer.[39]

Deprived of their culinary pleasures, soldiers fired their guns at porpoises and fished for turtles. The officers on General Heister's ship feasted on a sixty-four-pound turtle. So desperate were the officers for decent food that when a duck flew off the general's ship, a rope was tied around a sailor and he was lowered into the rough sea to retrieve the bird.[40]

Patience wore thin. On the transport *Perry*, a sailor threw burning coal at a Hessian sentry; there was an altercation, and the sailor was given fifteen strokes with a cane by a Hessian officer. When the English commodore complained of the incident to General Heister, he replied: "It is easy to understand that a people like the Hessians, tired of being imprisoned for four or nearly five months . . . and obliged to drink foul water and to eat moldy biscuit and meat salted right through, without beer, cheese, and butter, cannot be in a good humor."[41]

The hospital ships had been mostly empty during the early part of the trip, but as the water became foul, the sick bays of these vessels began to fill up. Scurvy, rashes, and fevers broke out. The doctors treated the men with bleedings for the fevers and salt water for scurvy.[42]

"An individual soon gets so vexed and impatient because of contrary winds," wrote one officer, "that he would rather die than remain at sea."[43]

Johannes Reuber refused to complain. Like most of his peasant comrades, he loved his king and had faith in the Lord. When he recorded his voyage, he contemplated the beauty of the sea, always taking note of the weather, omitting any discussion of hunger or scurvy, but the long voyage and the vastness of the ocean were beginning to fill him with doubts.

"We no longer believe there is land on the other side," he wrote. "There is still nothing to see but sky and water."[44]

He had grown accustomed to the vicissitudes of the ocean, the thin line between the sea's beauty and death. When rough waves tore loose a cannon, Reuber wrote casually that the cannon had "crashed into the sea." He was no longer moved by such dangerous incidents.[45]

A week later, his belief in the Lord and the landgrave was tested by another Atlantic storm. It began in the early morning with rain. The men stayed on deck; it was better to be wet than cooped up in the hot, smelly lower decks, but as noon approached, Reuber felt the sea grow restless. The ship began swaying. Suddenly a wave crashed on deck and carried a little cabin boy overboard. The men watched helplessly as the boy's body bobbed up and down. He had been carried too far away to reach with a rope, and the water was too rough to try a rescue.

"We watched him in sorrow, but could do nothing to help," Reuber wrote in his diary.[46]

Reuber noticed there was no more talk of punishing the disloyal Americans. The soldiers just wanted to land. Finally, on August 10, 1776, a fir tree floated past his ship and the men became excited. That night no one slept. Men lined the deck hoping for a glimpse of land in the impenetrable darkness.

By morning they could smell vegetation. The sailors retrieved the anchor line from storage so it would be ready when they needed it in a harbor. The captain began making depth soundings. Seagulls circled the ship, and for the first time in four months the smell of salt water was overpowered by the lush aroma of pine.[47]

During the evening, men not already on deck were awakened by a signal shot. Sleepy soldiers raced above but saw nothing. The sailors explained that the ship had found land but in the darkness had sailed so close to the shore that they were in danger of running aground, so the captain turned the ship about and weighed anchor. They would have to wait till daylight before they could proceed, yet now everyone was awake. They lined the deck and inhaled the sweet fragrance of an unseen land. Daybreak brought a spectacular sight. The fleet had sailed into a large harbor filled with ships, warships, and transports bobbing gently in the calm water. Tree-covered hills overlooked the harbor, with English soldiers and cannons lining it.[48]

"Imagine the finest kind of harbor with room for one thousand ships . . . all filled with men," wrote a Jäger officer. "[A]nd all these men ready for a task upon which hung the whole welfare of England."[49]

A grenadier quartermaster wrote: "I greatly doubt that Columbus could have had greater joy then we at his first view of the New World. . . . Everyone seemed to revive again. The sick had themselves brought up from between decks to convince themselves of this discovery."[50]

The Hessians had arrived in New York.

Just as the men began to cheer, their horrible trip finally over, another fleet was spotted. The sailors panicked: an enemy fleet! The Hessians who moments before were preparing to land amid the apple trees of Staten Island were now told to arm themselves.

The command ship peeled away and approached the enemy fleet while firing a cannon and raising an English flag. There was no response, no attempt by the strange vessels to identify themselves. The Hessians waited on deck, loading their muskets and preparing to be boarded.

For many this would be their first battle, and none, not even the veterans, had ever fought a conflict on board ship. Had they come so far and faced such hardship only to have their voyage climax in a fight between a boarding party and a rebel fleet? The command ship made a second signal and raised a white flag, but the unknown fleet still did not respond. Now the horizon was filled with sailing vessels. They were too large and numerous to be opposed. The command ship sailed forward a third time, turned, fired another cannon shot and raised an English flag on its highest mast. A massive, three-deck warship with eighty cannons sailed forth, fired, and raised an English flag.[51]

"Joy upon joy!" exclaimed Reuber, realizing that the mysterious fleet approaching them was actually the first group of Hessian soldiers that had sailed days ahead of them from Portsmouth. Storms and poor winds had prolonged their passage. They began to commence with a *feu de joie*, each soldier ceremoniously firing into the air in succession, striking a continuous rumble and a rising cloud of gun smoke. The English soldiers on Staten Island joined in until the harbor was filled with the sound of cannon fire and cheering men.

"Praise the name of the Lord!" shouted Reuber. Then he knelt and prayed, "May the Lord continue to shelter and protect us on the solid ground when we march against our enemies."[52]

Reuber had never seen an American and had only the vaguest notion what this war in America was even about. He was here only because his ruler needed money—still, he was already thinking of the Americans as his "enemies."

CHAPTER 9

The Hessians Are Coming!

May–July 1776

THREE MONTHS EARLIER, on May 20, 1776, a weary traveler arrived in Philadelphia and made his way to the London Coffee House near the city docks. The London Coffee House, which sold a wider selection of drinks than the name implied, was a hub of Philadelphia's mercantile exchange and social life, described as "the pulsating heart of excitement, enterprise, and patriotism" of the city. Inside, the smell of tobacco smoke and beer replaced the damp air of the shoreline.

The mood was volatile in spring 1776, as members of the Continental Congress drank alongside sailors, merchants, and mechanics. Men exchanged gossip and business news, but conversations were dominated by talk of whether the colonies should declare independence. For although the colonists had been fighting the British Army for the past year, most Americans still saw themselves as loyal British subjects, and many rebels still raised glasses to toast the king. Most saw their fight as one of restoring order, returning to the equilibrium of the past where their rights as Englishmen were protected by a just monarch; they were open to reconciling with their sovereign, who would in turn safeguard their liberties. Tonight, Josiah Bartlett, a congressional delegate from New Jersey, was drinking at the tavern when a traveler, George Merchant, walked in with papers that would end any hope of reconciliation with the king and Britain.[1]

Merchant had a harrowing tale to tell. He had been captured by the British in Quebec and transported back to England in chains. The lord mayor of London, John Sawbridge, a radical and friend of the colonists, secured Merchant's release and brought him to meet a group of colonial sympathizers who gave Merchant copies of the British-German Auxiliary Treaties. Merchant understood the explosive nature of these papers. King George was hiring mercenaries to crush the rebellion; once the colonists learned of these treaties, the rebels' resolve would stiffen, and the war would grow even bloodier. He concealed the papers in the waistband of his breeches and began the long journey back to America.

Merchant sailed first to Halifax and then made the voyage to New Hampshire on a small fishing schooner. During his trip, he was searched several times by British officials, but none of them discovered the hidden papers. Rebel sympathizers aided Merchant, surreptitiously transporting him through New England until finally he was presented to George Washington. After examining the documents, Washington sent the well-traveled courier on to Philadelphia.

The day after breaking bread with Josiah Bartlett, Merchant presented the Continental Congress with copies of the treaties negotiated between King George and the troop-supplying German states of Hessen-Kassel, Brunswick, and Hesse-Hanau. Members of Congress had been expecting the king to send peace commissioners to America but were horrified to learn that instead he had engaged the services of seventeen thousand mercenaries.[2]

In the colonies, public opinion was galvanized by news that King George was deploying a mercenary army. Up until then, Americans were by no means united in a desire to sever relations with England and declare independence. But news of the treaties silenced many voices of moderation and mobilized the radical factions seeking independence.

"What a scene of determined rapine and roguery do the German treaties present us," wrote congressional delegate Richard Lee of Virginia to his brother. A few days later, on June 7, 1776, he rose in Congress and moved that "these united colonies are, and of right ought to be, free and independent states." After debating the measure, Congress decided to postpone a vote so delegates could receive instructions from their home colonies.[3]

The response of the Pennsylvania Elk County militia was typical when it passed a resolution for independence since "all hopes of a reconciliation between Great Britain and these colonies are at an end." Culminating its list of grievances was "the employment of foreign troops for the express purpose of subjugating and enslaving us."[4]

The citizens of Boston gave their support and denounced the king for inviting "every barbarous nation whom he could hope to influence" to assist him in his "inhuman purpose."[5]

The citizens of Scituate, Massachusetts, wrote that George's deployment of foreign troops showed Britain's determination to "extirpate the Americans from the face of the earth."[6]

"The King of England delights in blood, yea, thirsts for the blood of America," wrote a patriot in Massachusetts. "Hessians, Hanoverians, Brunswickers . . . are invited to the carnage."[7]

The New Hampshire legislature stated that the "British Ministry . . . determined to reduce by fire and sword our bleeding country to their absolute obedience . . . have engaged foreign mercenaries . . . to ravage and plunder."[8]

Talbot County, Maryland, declared that the mercenaries planned to subdue Americans "or cut their throats."[9]

The *Norwich Packet* added that the Hessians' natural ferocity would cause "a scene of cruelty, death, and devastation, as will fill those of us who survive the carnage, with indignation and horror."[10]

Within a month of learning of the treaties, the colonies that had previously wavered on the question of independence voted unanimously to dissolve their relationship with England. Fear of the Hessians drove moderates into the radical camp. Near the end of the Declaration of Independence, one of the main grievances against the king was:

"He is at this time transporting large Armies of foreign Mercenaries to complete the works of death, desolation and tyranny, already begun with circumstances of Cruelty & perfidy scarcely paralleled in the most barbarous ages, and totally unworthy the Head of a civilized nation."

The British decision to hire mercenaries, even if they referred to them only as mere "auxiliaries," accelerated and strengthened the movement toward American independence. Without this, the two factions in Congress might never have been united; the fear and anger that the mercenaries provoked was a catalyst for rebellion. As the ships carrying the Hessians were traversing the blue waters of the Atlantic Ocean, American ministers stood at their pulpits spitting wrathful outrage at the mercenary army while their American congregants vigorously prayed for the destruction of the barbarian fleet. But despite the worst of the colonists' curses and damnations, the Hessians had arrived, disembarking from their ships, their polished black boots splashing through water. They had just stepped foot onto the coastline of New York Harbor.[11]

CHAPTER 10

Land of Milk and Honey—and Ungrateful Rebels

August 14, 1776

For the first time in months, Johannes Reuber could feel the security of solid ground beneath his feet as he waded through the tide onto the sandy beach of Staten Island.[1] Soldiers were running into the soft weeds that marked the edge of the small beach. Barges followed, smoothly floating up to the water's edge, depositing the regiment's gear onto the sand. Other ships were docking at piers, their decks jammed with cheering soldiers carrying their gear. Soldiers were hoisting equipment out of the barges and onto their backs. The cooks had already set up large metal field kettles in the brush. Soldiers were bending over the pots and lifting the lids. The men could smell the tangy aroma of steaming sauerkraut boiling inside. Smoke from roasting meat drifted from campfires. Dockside vendors were selling coffee, their voices rising above the din. The transactions were completed in a jumble of German and English.[2]

The troops could not ignore the dozens of stretchers being carried off the ships, each bearing a soldier felled by illness during the journey at sea. The faces of the infirmed were marred by the effects of scurvy: splotchy skin; swollen, blackened gums; itchy rashes from louse bites; and missing teeth.[3]

Able-bodied soldiers thanked the Lord for their own good health and beheld the beauty of land. Green meadows spread out from the beach. After months of living on cramped, smelly ships, the men now inhaled the sweet fragrance of woodlands: oak, pine, cedar, and chestnut trees.

A chaplain dropped to his knees. "I was unspeakably glad when I landed," he proclaimed. "I could hardly refrain from kissing mother earth."[4]

"In the woods," wrote a Hessian officer, "there are quantities of wild grapes, black walnuts, wild chestnuts, oaks and cedar trees." It was obvious to all that the rebel land must be fertile and the inhabitants prosperous.[5]

Looking out onto New York Harbor, Reuber could see the large British fleet filling the Verrazano Narrows between Staten Island and Long Island with white sails flying and colors on display. Guns fired in salute. The men on shore and those still on the ships shouted greetings to each other. There was not a single rebel soldier in sight.

But the nearly one hundred days at sea had left Reuber and his comrades wobbly.

"It did not clearly register that I was on solid ground," wrote a Hessian officer upon awakening from a nap. "I looked around, even walked around, and did this time and again, but still could not get adjusted to the idea. I could not believe that I was in America."[6]

As they stood on land for the first time in months, the men watched the spectacular sight of ships of the Royal Navy filling the harbor. The 120-vessel flotilla that had brought them here had been led by the frigate HMS *Thames* and followed by dozens of transport ships, with the eight thousand soldiers of the Hessian Army 1st Division crowding the rails, cheering when the flotilla cruised with the flood tide into New York Harbor. The ships had sailed through the Verrazano Narrows, carefully obeying the flag signals of the fleet's commander, Commodore William Hotham, and dropped anchors near the Staten Island shore, completing the almost-four-thousand-mile journey from Hessen-Kassel. There were now four hundred British ships in the harbor: warships, troop transporters, ammunition carriers, hospitals, horse transporters, and victualers. King George had committed almost half of the Royal Navy and two-thirds of the British Army to fighting the rebellion in North America.[7]

The guns of every warship saluted General Heister as he sailed to meet General William Howe. Once again, the flash and smoke of gunpowder and the sound of cannon shots reverberated around the harbor. The meeting of the two commanders was a promising and festive event for the soldiers. No one could foresee that soon their alliance would be tested and the commanders' trust in one another broken, much to the detriment of the king's army and the Royalist cause.[8]

After eating, Reuber's Rall Regiment formed up for the march inland. The men grumbled when they realized their British hosts had few horses or carts to help carry their supplies for the fifteen-mile trek to the regiment's campsite. The navy had transported critical equipment from England across the Atlantic, but for these final miles of the journey, Reuber and his comrades had to carry the tents, canteens, and field kettles—precious items that were needed to replace those left behind when Washington drove the British out of Boston.[9]

The Hessians gawked at the sights and forgot about the heavy gear they were dragging on their backs. Each abandoned rebel farm they passed was as huge as a German forest. Why would such people rebel against their sovereign? The smallest of the farms was larger than the largest in Hessen-Kassel. The houses were magnificent. They were one or two stories, built of wood and brick, and covered with shingles. They dwarfed the half-timbered, mud-and-stick-lined hovels of their homeland. In one abandoned house they found to their astonishment the walls were papered—a simple farmer's home lined with wallpaper! They encountered Loyalist families who welcomed them. Almost all of the rebel families had fled across the water to New Jersey or Manhattan. In one Loyalist home, the wood burning in the enormous fireplace to cook just one meal for one family was equivalent to the amount of wood a German family would use in a week. And the fat dripping into the fire tantalized and frustrated the men; this precious, wasted fat would have been used for making bowls of soup back home.[10]

They saw plots of land so large that the barns were more than a hundred feet from the house. Other homes had stables just for carriages. The farmers had their own transportation: carts, carriages, and red wagons pulled by little horses. And then there were cattle, huge oxen, and sheep roaming freely in the fields. Even the gnats were monstrous. The locals called them mosquitos, and the little flying beasts were sucking everyone's blood, leaving the regiment red and scratchy.[11]

British soldiers pointed out the names of the different local farmers, shrewdly showing the Hessians that the land was privately owned. Where were the king's lands? There were none—the rebels owned everything in sight. To the Hessians it appeared that the good king had permitted his ungrateful subjects to possess the richest acreage. Everywhere one looked was someone's personal property. Land for planting and water for fishing. Turkeys, geese, ducks, chicks, and hens ran about everywhere. There were turtles as big as a man's hand. There were no beggars, no petty government officials, and no army recruiting agents. Where were the savage Indians they had heard so much about? The water tasted coppery. Perhaps that explained the attitude of the people. Scientists back home had warned that the unhealthy American climate would cause life to deteriorate and men to degenerate. The Hessians wondered if perhaps it was the climate that made such people fight against a king who had made them all so prosperous.[12]

"The climate and type of soil are surely the finest, healthiest, and most agreeable in the world," a Jäger officer wrote home, "and one or more individuals could prepare a treasure for their posterity."[13]

Looking out at the rolling hills of Long Island on the other side of the expansive, white-capped bay, Reuber thought about this thing called "liberty" that the rebels were fighting for. He had heard much talk about it since sailing for America. Hessians saw liberty as just a form of order, like the assurance of order one felt from allegiance to a strong prince. To them, liberty was a privilege one earned from loyalty to one's sire. The officers explained that it was wealth that had made the people so insolent and greedy. The meanest man in Germany could become rich here. And so many different religions were tolerated! Such a nation must be faithless. Birthright, breeding, even honor meant nothing to these people. It was the idleness of pleasure that was causing all the trouble.[14]

Captain Wiederhold's opinion of the revolution echoed those of most of his comrades:

> An honest man's heart pounds in his body to see such a happy land and dwelling stripped by wicked and defiant rebels who are not satisfied with their undeserved blessings from heaven, and not true to God and the king—to see it ruined! However, God will give us luck and them regret, so that everything is not spoiled according to their misguided wishes.[15]

Off the ship, the men trudged with their gear along the dusty road under the glare of the hot August sun, breathing the humid air and getting soaked by occasional summer rains. They inhaled a strong scent of pine emanating from Staten Island's forests. The island was small, only fifty square miles, but the heat and the humidity wore out the men. They no longer resembled the sparkling clean, ramrod straight Hessian army who had paraded under the watchful eye of their prince when they started their journey to America. The voyage had weakened them. Now, most wore soiled uniforms crawling with vermin, and many of them were wrecked by the effects of scurvy and diarrhea.[16]

Red-coated British soldiers handed out the stimulant sassafras bark and the regiment's allotment of rum. The soldiers began to sing German folk tunes. The warmth of the sun felt intoxicating; today even the officers seemed relaxed. The men grabbed at apple trees, eating the unwashed fruits. Others were picking flowers. But soon the singing stopped. Men began a painful wailing. Soldiers were stumbling off the road. In view of everyone, they were hurriedly unbuttoning their pants. Diarrhea and foul wind poured out. The doctor ran down the line ordering the men not to eat the apples. He explained that after months of eating rotten ship food, their undernourished bodies were unable to withstand the assault of sugar and fiber. But it was too late. The men ran about the woods wiping their wet anuses with leaves until they collapsed from dehydration and cramps. Soldiers who had avoided the fruit helped carry some of the stricken into camp. By nightfall, many of the Hessians had swollen red hands and anuses—the British soldiers explained they had wiped themselves with poison ivy.[17]

The next few days saw civilian workers, British soldiers, and slaves hastily constructing fortifications and deploying artillery and trenches as a precaution against the unlikely chance that rebels would attack Staten Island. They noted the defensive fortifications being constructed at the Watering Place, a bountiful freshwater spring where ships could take on potable water and islanders could fill buckets to satisfy all their drinking and household needs.[18]

Hessian regimental quartermasters were in the fields planning the construction of campsites for the troops. The quartermasters were protected by elite Jäger marksmen. British officers explained that American reconnaissance detachments periodically infiltrated Staten Island and set up ambushes or small raids. Since there were only about a dozen qualified Hessian quartermasters, they had to be well protected, as their loss could be potentially disastrous.[19]

On August 15, Heister changed the regiments' alignments. The Colonel Rall Regiment was combined with the Lossberg Regiment and the Knyphausen Regiment to form a brigade under the command of General von Mirbach. Reuber didn't mind, and few of his comrades gave the new alignment much thought. Reuber was proud that the Rall Regiment was placed in the center of the brigade and granted the great honor of "protecting the [Hessian] flag." He didn't know that fate and George Washington would, before year's end, combine to turn this seemingly mundane reshuffling of troops into a source of great dishonor to himself and his noble prince.[20]

Walking along the island's shore, the Hessians, accustomed to living in a landlocked nation, were fascinated by all the boat and ferry docks, and the fishermen's weather-beaten wooden shacks. The land was sparsely occupied by just over two thousand farmers and fishermen, with about six hundred Black slaves and freemen. The Hessians were disappointed not to see any "savages," but the local Native Americans had been driven from the island many years before. The countryside was green and brown, dotted with regimental campsites with rows of tents looking like little islands of white against the lush, green fields. The soldiers passed horses so tame and plentiful that many roamed without confinement. Bundles of hay, derived from the tall salt grasses of the tidal marshes, were being bought by the quartermasters from the locals. Many of the cattle were gone, as local rebel farmers had withdrawn to New Jersey ahead of the approaching British troops driving their fat, bellowing herds ahead of them.[21]

The Hessian privates were beginning to appreciate what the English commanders already knew: Despite its grand size, King George's expeditionary force was short on transportation; carts and horses were to be treated as a more-precious commodity than the soldiers.

The quartermasters had picked out campsites and placed flags for tent locations. It was vital that the site plan of each regimental camp conformed exactly with the army's Order of Camp regulations, for if it did not, then messengers, particularly when arriving at night, might not find the appropriate officer; American raiders might pierce the camp's perimeter; deserters could slip away; and looters could slip in.[22]

The men arrived with the drummers beating a march. The noncommissioned officers barked out orders for the men to form into platoons, and a head count was taken. Pickets were sent out. The men piled their arms and were dismissed to erect their tents at their assigned spots. The regiment was resupplied with kettles and cloth and, most importantly, new paper cartridges for carrying gunpowder, as those cartridges that had made the ocean voyage had been spoiled by water or eaten by rats.[23]

The camp women collected clothing for a long-overdue washing. They boiled the clothing to kill lice. They scrubbed the garments in streams or in tubs of fresh water and hung them on clotheslines or draped them over their tents. Soon the clean smell of wind-dried clothing drifted across the camp. Once dry, they were collected for mending, with the women sewing rips and tears in the clothing and repairing holes caused by vermin.[24]

At night the Hessians sat around campfires singing religious hymns with great solemnity. Their British comrades tended to be less pious, and while the Hessians sang, the British soldiers played around, joking and cursing. British officers lectured the Hessians and explained how a small group of radical rebels were misleading the bulk of the good people of New York. If the people could see the Hessian army on display, see a proud loyal army—a real army, not a ragtag rebel mob—they would remember how glorious it was to be loyal to one's king, and they would end the tyranny of the revolution. It was obvious to the British soldiers that despite the debilitating Atlantic crossing, as well as the ravages of a deficient diet and the harshness of the hot, humid, American weather, the Hessians were still spoiling for a fight. The Americans' attitudes toward their king, notably their lack of gratitude, irked the Hessians.[25]

For the next week, the regiment rested at its campsite. Strict discipline was maintained, but the workload was light, and the men could bathe, eat, and relax. Each man received a duty assignment, and groups of soldiers were sent out to draw drinking water, chop firewood, and dig kitchen and sanitary pits. The regiment drilled twice a day. At night they listened to tales told by British soldiers. The rebels are barbarians, the British warned. They stuffed the bodies of prisoners with wood chips and burned them alive. It was the good, "quite too good" manner of living that had made the rebels "haughty." There were sixty thousand rebels, armed to the teeth, waiting to massacre the king's troops. (Actually, Washington's army had fewer than twelve thousand troops; almost none of them had bayonets, and some even lacked guns.) And worst of all, the British said, the poor peasants had been misled by the rebel leaders into believing they would be evicted from their homes and sold into slavery if the British continued to rule. It was best to give no quarter to such desperate men.[26]

And there were other dangers waiting for the unsuspecting. British soldiers recounted tales of the American monster known as a rattlesnake. The men listened horrified to how these beasts, some sixteen feet long, could charm a man into paralysis. The rattler, with a head as large as a dog, would perch in a tree, catch a helpless man's gaze so he would freeze, and bite off his legs, devouring the hypnotized soldier limb by limb. Reuber knew there were strange things here in this New World. The regiment had been awakened the first night by greenish lights flickering in the air. Their British comrades laughed and dismissed the lights as flying insects called fireflies, but the Hessians were skeptical. Although the men knew there were no witches in America—they existed only in Europe—the fireflies caused men to spread frightening tales of illuminating ghouls through the camp. [27]

A rally was planned to raise their spirits, and hundreds of Reuber's comrades gathered around a huge campfire. The fagots were lit and flames leaped up, lashing at four tarred-and-feathered effigies of rebel Generals Charles Lee, Israel Putnam, and George Washington, and Declaration of Independence signer and Princeton College President John Witherspoon.

The soldiers cursed and screamed at the dummies, but a thunderstorm broke out, sending the men scattering for shelter.

"No one could remember ever having had such a storm," wrote Lieutenant Bardeleben of the von Donop Regiment. "Lightning, thunderclaps, storms, and driving rain, all in extremes. My tent, surrounded by a constant fire, seemed to tremble with the ground at every thunder peal."[28]

After the storm abated, a soldier ran through camp with the frightening news that all the effigies had been burned except Washington's. Like the Lord's burning bush that summoned Moses, Washington was on fire but not consumed. The sight of the wet, unburned Washington, staring down at the soldiers and standing tall over the other ashen figures, sent the men into a fearful panic. Surely this was rebel magic, the same magic that had cursed the Hessian fleet with storms when crossing the Atlantic.

"Poppycock!," declared the officers who investigated the still-standing Washington. The Washington dummy had been tarred last, after the rain started, so the effigy was soaked and only the tar had burned, leaving the underlying figure unscathed. The officers tried to explain that the episode was the result of basic science, not magic, but superstitions ran deep in the Hessian population; even the minority of Hessians who were educated believed in the supernatural. Some of the officers even marked the days in their diaries with astrological signs: Tuesday: Mars ♂ ; Wednesday: Mercury ☿ ; Thursday: Jupiter ♃ ; and so on.[29]

The army spent less than a month in Staten Island, yet men would remember it decades later. They were overwhelmed by the richness of the land and confused by why anyone would be disenchanted living there. They were fundamentally unsympathetic to the rebels' enlightened philosophies and did not accept their concept of liberty. The Hessians were confident of victory and scared only by their own superstitions.

CHAPTER II

The Adversaries

Summer 1776

In May 1775, when the Second Continental Congress deliberated appointing a commander in chief of the new American army, forty-three-year-old George Washington, a head taller than most of those around him, strode into the hall wearing his old French and Indian War uniform. This made him the only person in the room dressed in military attire. The implication was clear, but, never uttering a word, he sat quietly as Congress unanimously elected him commander in chief of the new Continental Army.

His earlier life had prepared him to be a military leader.

He had been a surveyor, planter, politician, soldier, landowner, and, regrettably, slave owner. As a young man, he surveyed the wilderness, often sleeping under the stars and eating stale food cooked over a campfire.[1]

At twenty-three, commissioned as a major by the governor of Virginia, he led an expedition that battled the French over disputed land in Ohio. He surprised and captured a French force by attacking at dawn after advancing under the cover of darkness during a severe storm. The victory taught him the effectiveness of a dawn attack during bad weather, a lesson he would remember.[2]

He saw firsthand during the French and Indian War how vulnerable the British Army was when forced to fight in the American wilderness, unable to employ the open-field tactics of European armies. The Battle of Monongahela River was a disaster for the British Army, but Washington distinguished himself. Two horses were shot out from under him. A bullet pierced his hat, and three others cut through his uniform without injuring him. When at the Battle of Duquesne two Virginia units blundered into a skirmish mistaking each other for the enemy in the wilderness, Washington rode between the lines knocking down guns with his sword.[3]

He was appointed chief of Virginia's militia and wrestled with many of the same problems he would face during the American Revolution: a war that was unpopular with a significant portion of the population, rivalries between the colonies, and a scarcity of recruits and resources.

He tried to protect the Virginia border with a string of outposts. The tactic proved flawed, as Native Americans overran the isolated outposts. From this he would learn a valuable lesson: Military outposts that looked imposing could nevertheless be vulnerable due to their isolation.[4]

For the next sixteen years, he was a businessman. He was married to Martha Custis, and they lived with relatives, artisans, overseers, and eventually several hundred slaves on his plantation that grew to the size of a small town.

Although Washington was known for his poise and serenity, his success in the dangerous world of land speculation was a clue that there was another side to the future president: Besides being a supposed man of honor, he was also a risk taker and gambler—a quality that most of his colleagues, and particularly the British, failed to appreciate in him.[5]

After the Battles of Lexington and Concord, with a clear single-mindedness, he shifted his allegiance from Crown to Congress.[6]

He took command of the new Continental Army that had the British bottled up in Boston. He quickly realized that his army was no army at all, just a collection of angry, poorly armed citizens with little training and no discipline. He spent the next nine months trying to make an army of this mob.[7]

In March 1776, the British commander in Boston, General William Howe, learned that Washington planned to fortify Dorchester Heights, an imposing hill to the south of Boston. Placing rebel artillery on Dorchester Heights would make the town uninhabitable for the British, but the English officers did not believe digging was possible with the ground frozen solid so they did not occupy the heights.

On the evening of March 4, 1776, Washington had three-hundred ox wagons assembled to haul up the hill prefabricated fortifications, along with rock-filled barrels for rolling down on attackers. Washington had thousands of spades sharpened so the frozen earth could be dug up quickly. Five thousand rebels silently climbed the heights; as they worked by moonlight, the noise—the creaking wheels, the axes, the plodding of horses, and the rustling of men—was drowned out by Washington's artillery deceptively firing at the other end of the harbor.[8]

When the mist lifted in the morning, an amazing sight was revealed: a fully fortified hill. The British were stunned. One engineer blamed the accomplishment on "the genie belonging to Aladdin's wonderful lamp." The British, cowed by the cannons staring down from Dorchester Heights, decided it best to abandon Boston and they sailed away, north to Canada. [9]

Washington knew that the British Army's voyage to Canada would be temporary, just enough time for refitting; after that, the Royal Navy could land Howe's army anywhere along the Eastern Seaboard. With clear decisiveness, Washington concluded that New York would ultimately be Howe's goal.

Sometimes Howe didn't know why he was in America commanding the British Army. Life had been good back in Britain. His wife never got in the way of his gambling. Anyone of importance in London knew him, and he was able to walk into most clubs to enjoy a toss of dice and the pleasure of a woman. Now as he watched British and Hessian reinforcements march across the beach of Staten Island, all he could do was worry. The ships of the Royal Navy stretched across New York Harbor, covering the landscape with white canvas and Union Jacks. Warships sped by, their sails filled with wind. Large, creaky transports bobbed up and down, as the surprisingly strong current of the narrows tugged at their anchors. Hundreds of barges floated to the shore, unloading supplies. Soldiers splashed through the waves, their boots crunching the sandy coastline of Staten Island. There was not a rebel in sight; not even a single rebel vessel had ventured out to challenge the royal fleet. The enemy cowered in New York City across the bay, squeezed into a few square miles at the southern tip of Manhattan Island with no navy to oppose the British landing. On the opposite shore, Brooklyn sat green and lush and very quiet.[10]

Worried, Howe rubbed his large, bulging eyes. He watched the sturdy Hessian auxiliaries form into regiments on the beach. Over the next six weeks, throughout the hot, humid New York summer and extending into the cool of autumn, five-hundred transport and supply ships would arrive with even more soldiers, bringing his army's strength to over thirty thousand British and Hessian troops. More than two-thirds of the empire's army were in the colonies, supported by seventy British warships—half the Royal Navy's fighting strength.[11]

Though he was confident in the fighting ability of his men—his infantry averaged over nine years in experience while most rebels had only a few months of active duty—the logistics worried him. How would he feed an army with a population equal to that of New York City when England was over three thousand miles away? He would need an unprecedented naval supply line. This was the largest seaborne operation ever attempted by a European power. No matter how strong his army was it would always teeter at the end of a fragile, transatlantic umbilical cord.

Howe had spent most of his life in the military and in Parliament representing Nottingham. During the past decade, as tensions grew between England and the colonies, he had tried advocating a lenient policy toward the rebels—although he'd had to admit some of this was political posturing for his constituency in Nottingham since the region depended on trade with the colonies. Before sailing to America, he had advocated a limited war: a naval blockade of New England, occupation of New York, and offensives along the Hudson and Connecticut Rivers to isolate New England from the other colonies. He believed this plan was reasonable and would succeed.[12]

Publicly, he told his constituents that he would reject the chance to command the British forces in America. Privately, he let the government know he would be honored to accept command. His rationalization was that he had not sought the command, but the command had been thrust upon him by George III. The command of the king's forces in America would be the pinnacle of his career.

Howe had been born second cousin to George and had prospered from his relationship with the royal family. British Army commissions were sold to upper-class families, and, after he attended Eton College, his family purchased him a lieutenancy.[13]

Howe looked back on his life with little to no regret. Like Washington he had served in the Seven Years' War. He gained instant personal glory when he led the detachment that courageously scaled the Heights of Abraham to capture Quebec and win the war. He had fought the French again at Belle Island and enjoyed the amusing spectacle of the French commander attempting to disguise the weakness of his force by parading all the females of the garrison in soldiers' uniforms.[14]

Howe seemed to be the perfect man to lead the king's fight against the rebels. He had experience fighting in North America and had an unquestioned loyalty to the Crown.

But there was something not quite right about William Howe. Although the British public did not perceive it yet, he lacked a certain daring that Washington possessed. He even lacked Washington's muscular physical presence. Howe's shoulders were narrow, his belly bulging. He had a broad nose, bulging eyes, and a round face that flattened out into a weak chin. While Washington's experience in politics changed his life, he had learned to care for his country more than for his king; he had also absorbed revolutionary ideas, transforming himself from a man who sought wealth into a leader of a rebellion. Howe, on the other hand, had learned little. For the twenty-two years before the war, he, like Washington, had not only worked for the army but had also been a legislator. Yet unlike Washington, he hadn't given a major political speech or introduced a piece of legislation for twenty years. He had spent his free time betting on cards. His accumulated gambling debts likely influenced his decision to accept the lucrative job of crushing the rebellion in America.[15]

By the third week of August, the entire British Army was encamped in Staten Island while across the bay the Americans occupied Manhattan and Brooklyn. The geography of New York was a nightmare for Washington. The island of Manhattan was thirteen miles long. The settled portion—New York City—was crammed into the lower three miles of the island. The region was made up of three large islands—Staten Island, Long Island, and Manhattan Island—with dozens of surrounding smaller regional islands. Therefore, whoever controlled the waterways of New York would control the city.[16]

To oppose a British landing that could occur in any of a hundred different places in the region, Washington had nineteen thousand men, almost half of them poorly trained militia. About two thousand of the men had no weapons. The colonists had practically no cavalry, only a few pieces of artillery, and no navy.[17]

Washington clung to the belief that Howe would land in Brooklyn or Manhattan, so he split his forces, sending six thousand to Brooklyn and leaving a garrison of thirteen thousand in Manhattan. His army would be on two islands, separated by the three-quarters-of-a-mile-wide East River. In reality, he did not have any good options. He was trying to defend an island-based city against the world's largest navy *and* the British Army. He also believed that abandoning New York would be a political disaster for the revolution, perhaps even fatal to the fledgling republic.

The most logical place for the British general to land was on the northern tip of Manhattan, thereby trapping Washington on the island as British warships blockaded the coastline. Howe's forces were so large he could even split them and attack two regions at once.

While Washington worried that the Royal Navy could land the British Army anywhere Howe chose, Howe was asking himself: Where should one strike to subdue the rebellion? Where was the center of the revolution? Philadelphia, where Congress was housed? The hundreds of small towns that supplied men and goods to the Continental Army? The Continental Army itself? The uprising was spread across thirteen colonies, and each colony was split into counties and cities of varying degrees of loyalty to the Crown. The revolution was politically and economically fragmented. This left Howe with no single point of attack and no clear objective. There was no London or Paris or Vienna to capture. No one victory could break the insurgency since no one city or organization dominated it.

Howe and his superiors in England were not only ambivalent about how to fight but also how *hard* to fight against their rebellious subjects. "Here pity interposes," wrote a British general, "and we cannot forget when we strike, we wound a brother." Even King George, lately the very symbol of evil in the rebels' eyes, wrote, "Notes of triumph would not have been proper when the successes are against subjects not a foreign foe."[18]

Howe envisioned a policy that projected fear but also friendship to those willing to abandon the rebellion. Such a policy could work, but Howe knew the army had to be on its best behavior and constantly serve as a reminder to the people that security and prosperity could only be found through loyalty to the Crown. With such a policy in mind, Howe sent out orders reminding the troops not to plunder and to act with decorum.[19]

In the Hessian camp, the men were confused. Hadn't the landgrave promised them great plunder in the New World? Hadn't plundering been promised to them as the means sanctified by their prince for supplementing their low pay?

Howe wanted to start the campaign immediately, but the Hessian commander, General Heister, strongly urged him to give the Hessians time to recover from their three-month ocean voyage. Howe agreed to give them a week to rest.[20]

The Hessians rested for the week, and then Howe marched them from their camps to the coastline of the Verrazzano Narrows where the British fleet rocked gently in the water, waiting to carry them across the harbor to invade the rebel-held territory of Brooklyn. Howe had decided on the simplest strategic option: Capturing Brooklyn would not only give him a springboard for invading Manhattan, it would also liberate and aid the Loyalist farmers of Long Island and provide his army with crops and livestock.

The attack was set to begin on August 22, with Generals Henry Clinton and Charles Cornwallis leading a British advance guard of four thousand highly mobile troops, consisting of British chasseurs (light infantry), the Donop Brigade of Hessian grenadiers, and a twenty-man Jäger company. They would lead the invasion of Brooklyn by crossing the Verrazzano Narrows on specially constructed flatboats. This advance guard would secure beachheads, driving the rebels guarding the shore inland. They would be followed a few hours later by eleven thousand troops and two days later by five thousand Hessians.[21]

The invasion was so massive and so complex that it would take five days to deliver all the men and equipment from Staten Island to Brooklyn. The Hessians struck their camps, marched to the region of Howe's headquarters, about one mile from the shore, and set up new camps. The men were assured that their women and other "indispensable baggage" would follow on transport.

CHAPTER 12

Brooklyn: Invasion

August 19–25, 1776

FOR JOHANNES REUBER, things were happening fast. After months of living aboard a cramped ship, he had spent only a few days marching back and forth across the dusty roads of Staten Island before finding himself once again preparing to be loaded onto a vessel. For two days his regiment waited near the Staten Island coastline while the first wave of the expeditionary force began the invasion.

The night before the invasion, a violent thunderstorm raged for five hours with lightning strikes. The soldiers were soaked as the wind blew down tents and drenched equipment. Men worried that this was a sign of divine disapproval. Hymns and prayers were sung with great passion. The men on Staten Island knew their situation could be worse, as the soldiers who made up the advance guard of the invasion were already on transport ships and barges in the narrows, trapped in their vessels and at the mercy of the surging tide.[1]

Many soldiers assumed the amphibious operation would be canceled, but the morning of August 22 dawned clear. Reuber watched as British warships guarded the narrow strait between Staten Island and Brooklyn. Barges and transports, protected by the massive warships, carried the four thousand men and supplies of the first contingent across the water to Brooklyn's Denyse's Ferry and the five thousand men of the second contingent farther south to Gravesend Bay.

The next day, August 23, the remaining Hessian regiments on Staten Island struck camp and marched to the beach near the natural spring known as "The Watering Place." There, cold, fresh spring water flowed freely, cooling the air. Men filled their canteens, and even the stern-looking, mustachioed Hessians could not resist splashing their companions.

After setting up their tents, the men sat cross-legged on the ground making their final preparations for the coming battle. Their uniforms were damp from the frequent rains and getting more uncomfortable as the humid summer heat caused them to sweat. The soldiers meticulously cleaned and polished their muskets, clearing the firelocks of residue with a wet cloth and carefully brushing dirt from the firing mechanisms with a horsehair whisk. Then they inserted new flints and flushed their barrels with hot water to wash away powder deposits. The men were glad to get some cool air after sunset, but they had learned to resist the temptation of removing their uniforms and exposing their sweaty skin to mosquitos.[2]

On August 25, Reuber was awakened by the beat sound of reveille. Today was invasion day for the Rall Regiment. Men were washing their hands and faces, combing their tallowed hair, retying ponytails, and waxing mustaches. After roll call and inspection, they ate a cold breakfast as the sun rose and the air grew hot and damp.

Everyone filled their canteens with the day's allotment of rum mixed with fresh spring water. Men went to work breaking down the campsite, striking tents and tying them into neat bundles for transport, putting out campfires, and filling the latrines with dirt. Due to the army's shortage of horses, twelve soldiers, grunting and cursing, had to carry each of the heavy-wheeled cannons up and over ramps onto flatboats. A group of soldiers and sailors, under the watchful eye of senior officers, hoisted the gold-and-silver-filled Hessian war chest aboard Admiral Howe's flagship HMS *Eagle* for safekeeping.[3]

Because the ground was muddy from the heavy overnight rains, the soldiers moved slowly under the weight of their sixty-pound combat loads, which consisted of a backpack, cartridge pouch, small sword, canteen, and linen bread bag. With great care, the men had packed a three days' allotment of cold rations: three pounds of bread and two-and-a-half pounds of cooked pork. Lastly, they shouldered their muskets.

The final head counts and inspection were taken before their departure from the beaches where they had landed ten days earlier. Every third man carried a field kettle for his mess group. Hospital equipment was carried up ramps onto transport ships. The men who had brought wives and children said goodbye to them—though they were assured that their families would follow on transport ships once the circumstances were deemed safe.[4]

Naval subalterns, identified by blue jackets and white waistcoats, their uniforms blending in with the blue of the summer sky, directed the soldiers to their ships. Maintaining Hessian discipline and pomp, the men, under drum tattoo, marched two by two down a ravine to the beach, where a flotilla of flatboats awaited them. Each man strode up the ships' ramps and over the side, carefully stepping onto the deck. They soon stood shoulder to shoulder; there was no seating, the flat-bottomed boats having only one purpose: to carry soldiers and equipment. The Hessians had never participated in an amphibious operation. They felt defenseless, jammed together, and surrounded by open water.[5]

Speaking among themselves, the Hessians tended to hide their fears with euphemisms. The coming baptism by fire was referred to as "our breakfast" or "our pay-day," and no one dared mention dying, only "carrying away their booty." The Hessian regimental chaplain led the men in prayer. The Hessian soldiers begged the "Great Jehovah" to watch over the "rulers of the earth" whom the men acknowledged the Lord had "sent to rule over us." They prayed the Lord would take under his protection "the British King and the entire royal family," their own prince, including the "entire Hessian ruling house," the general staff, officers, and lastly the privates—themselves included.[6]

Twenty oarsmen propelled the boat, rowing in unison under the verbal commands of a Royal Navy coxswain at the tiller. Reuber undoubtedly joined in the singing of hymns as English commands mixed with the German melodies. Under the protection of massive Royal Navy warships, the eighty-eight flatboats crossed the narrows and ground to a halt on the Long Island beachhead.

After three horrific months at sea and ten days' rest in Staten Island, the Hessians were finally heading into battle.

PART III

War

CHAPTER 13

Brooklyn: *Cowardly Rebels, Cunning Rebels*

August 25–28, 1776

JOHANNES REUBER and the rest of the Rall Regiment dashed from the grounded barges onto a Brooklyn beach and quickly formed up with their muskets shouldered—but there was not a rebel in sight. Looking inland, Reuber could see pristine woods, fields, and dirt paths. In the distance, hidden by the surrounding woods, were a few scattered villages populated by descendants of Dutch farmers and still carrying their old Dutch names: New Utrecht, Flatbush, Gravesend. About ten miles to the north towered the 150-foot Guana Heights, a range of hills ten miles long, running east to west with steep, heavily wooded slopes.[1]

Like the first wave of troops that had landed days before, this landing had been executed with expert skill and no casualties. The rebels manning coastal outposts had fled, setting fire to crops. The invaders smelled smoke along with the sweet scent of burning stacks of hay and stalks of corn. Washington had ordered that the region's cattle be taken, lighthouses set on fire, and mills dismantled. Quartermasters had scouted ahead and with their color-bearers marked out previously selected campsites with sticks and flags near the village of Gravesend. After unloading its equipment, the regiment, accompanied by drums and lively martial music, marched about four miles to its assigned campsites near Gravesend. [2]

General Heister had expected horses to be available for him and his staff; instead, a fine carriage waited on the shore to carry him and General Howe. The army marched past homes more befitting royalty than farmers, plush houses with everything a man could want—bookcases, commodes, mahogany chairs—but there were no people. Some of the men were breaking ranks and plundering the furniture, but, unbeknownst to them, some of the homes had been assigned to serve as quarters for the generals. Heister was soon on the road with a security detail arresting the plunderers; even worse, he was threatening the regiments with harsh punishment if this happened again.[3]

"On this march," wrote Lieutenant von Bardeleben of the Donop Regiment, "signs of the enemy's mood were found everywhere. During their flight . . . they left behind burned out houses, grain standing in the fields, some of it in ashes, and the road was lined with dead cattle. Now and again old people, with sad glances, looked back at their homes, which the flames had destroyed and which appeared previously to have been a paradise standing in blooming abundance."[4]

That night Reuber and his comrades settled into camp. All was peaceful, and there was no sign of the rebels. British soldiers rested alongside them, spinning tales of Black people who were slaves like in the days of the pharaoh. The British swore that the Black slaves did all the work and made the rebel farmers rich; and if a slave was not satisfactory to his master, the slave owner could tell the slave he must find a new master for himself.[5]

Two rebel deserters reported that Washington planned to attack the Hessian camps. While this seemed doubtful, the Hessian commanders were taking no chances, and the soldiers were ordered to sleep in their uniforms. The night was hot and the men were sweaty, uncomfortable, and anxious.[6]

Heister and Howe had spent much of the day in meetings, analyzing intelligence reports, planning with Generals Clinton, James Grant, and Cornwallis, speaking with Brooklyn Loyalists, and poring over maps. All through the summer, British observers on Staten Island had peered through telescopes and stared out across the narrows to watch Continental soldiers, civilians, and slaves cutting trees and shoveling dirt; they were building a line of fortifications on the Heights of Brooklyn, the northernmost region of Brooklyn, near the East River and only a few miles from Manhattan. Just south of Brooklyn Heights was the even-larger Guana Heights, and Washington had troops on both prominences. Howe appreciated that this was a well-chosen location to stop an invasion of Manhattan from Brooklyn. He undoubtedly thought back to the year before and the disaster at Breed's (Bunker) Hill, the bloodiest day in the history of the British Army; he had led column after column of Redcoats in futile, bloody attacks against the rebel fortifications. His "victory" that day almost destroyed his army. He had seen again at Dorchester Heights how good the rebels were at building fortifications, erecting defenses in just one night. He would not make the same mistake. Having learned from his experiences, he listened to his staff, sometimes grudgingly, and devised a simple plan he believed would be effective in driving the rebels out of Brooklyn without incurring a great many British casualties.[7]

Howe saw that Guana Heights was ten miles long, running east to west and almost paralleling the East River. It towered 150 feet above the Brooklyn countryside with steep, heavily wooded slopes that would make any British charge against the fortifications a difficult proposition. It could be crossed at only four passes where country roads ran through it. Behind it, northward, was the second rebel defensive line of entrenchments on Brooklyn Heights, close to the East River. On paper, their formation seemed formidable, but the British, aided by locals loyal to the king, had found a flaw in Washington's plan. He had manned Guana Heights with troops commanded by General William Stirling, known as Lord Stirling, on the right, guarding the pass at Gowanus Road; troops commanded by General John Sullivan guarded the passes at Flatbush and Bedford Roads in the center. This positioning protected three of the four passes that crossed the Heights, but for reasons that remain unclear, Washington foolishly left the Americans' left flank unprotected—where Jamaica Road ran behind the heights. This gave the British an undefended route into the Americans' rear.

The British devised a simple but effective plan. They would march north from their camps in Gravesend toward the rebel line and make camp near the village of Flatbush, just before the Guana Heights. General Grant would lead a noisy demonstration against the rebels' right flank. General Heister would do the same with his Hessians in the center, and General

Clinton would lead the bulk of the army, ten thousand men, in a sweeping movement around the rebels' unprotected left flank at the Jamaica Road and attack them from behind. The Royal Navy would then sail into the East River, isolating the rebels in Brooklyn from the rebels in Manhattan. Thus Washington would not be able to retreat to Manhattan nor be reinforced from there. The rebels would be surrounded with no option but death or surrender. At least, that was Howe's design.[8]

While the invasion of Brooklyn was going well for the British, the Royal Navy had flawlessly executed the amphibious landing of twenty thousand troops onto the coastline of Brooklyn, and those troops were now on the march across the woodlands with no opposition. The American command was in disarray.

Washington's spies and intelligence gatherers had failed him. He did not know exactly where the enemy was. His lack of a cavalry hindered his army's ability to patrol and scout for the enemy, and without cavalry, he was unable to screen the front and flanks of his army. British light infantry and Jägers dominated the ground between the armies, screened the British positions, and freely probed the rebel positions.[9]

Washington's intelligence led him to believe that Howe's landing in southern Brooklyn was a diversion to mask an invasion of Manhattan. Thus Washington assigned about ten thousand men to Brooklyn, leaving a large portion of his army in Manhattan and a small portion in New Jersey. This was a tragic miscalculation.

Further aggravating the situation, his best general, Nathanael Greene, was ill with fever. Washington's choice to replace him, General John Sullivan, was unfamiliar with the terrain and with the positioning of their men. Washington then replaced Sullivan with General Israel Putnam. In the days before a major battle, the American army changed commanders three times. Adding to the confusion, Washington's headquarters tried to reshuffle regiments into brigades. This led to units being unsure of who their commanders were and what their positions would be. As the day of battle approached, Washington's army was scattered, poorly positioned, and lacking cavalry and reliable intelligence. The Americans were unaware that the British had found an unguarded road that would offer them the opportunity to encircle the American army in Brooklyn.[10]

***

The morning of August 26 started with wind and fog, but the sun soon shined through the haze. The Hessians broke camp and marched to the village of Flatbush. The men found the march across Brooklyn to be pleasant. The countryside was full of meadows, cornfields, and many varieties of fruit trees. The region was similar to the German countryside where the people lived on scattered farms.[11]

The men were vexed when they learned that the British wanted them to abandon their time-honored method of marching with closed ranks, each man fighting shoulder to shoulder with his comrades on both sides. The British insisted on trying something new in this heavily wooded terrain. No more marching in closed files in ranks three deep, but instead marching with the regiments divided into small groups. Green-coated Jägers, Hesse-Kassel's elite hunters, trappers, and forest men, would advance ahead of the army, flushing out the enemy. Some of these advance groups would carry a light cannon. The main body of troops would march in columns, two men abreast and rather far apart, as if lined up for someone to run the gauntlet.[12]

To common soldiers like Reuber, these tactics seemed strange, as the infantry always put its trust in close-order volleys and bayonet charges with the men bunched together, relying on the brute force of hails of bullets and the stab of sharpened bayonets—not marksmanship and mobility. As mentioned above, the Jägers used rifles with grooved barrels that gave the rifles greater accuracy than other guns, even at long distances.[13]

To leverage the strengths and mitigate the weaknesses of the swift-moving Jägers and the formidable yet slower grenadiers, Howe consolidated the two units. This departure from tradition caused much chagrin among Reuber and his fellow soldiers. Contrary to established practice, they were instructed to abandon closed formations and, instead, break up into smaller groups as they advanced through the dense woods of Brooklyn. Going into battle for the first time in his life, Reuber would not have the steadying comfort of marching in a well-disciplined line with a fellow soldier only two feet away.[14]

Communicating with the British was not easy for the Hessians. Almost none of the British spoke German. Most of the communication was done in French, broken English, and with hand signals. There had been no time for joint staff exercises or combined training maneuvers to meld the two disparate armies into a smoothly functioning allied command.[15]

But there were still more changes. The British officers were ripping off their stripes so as to be indistinguishable from the privates. Just as the Hessians

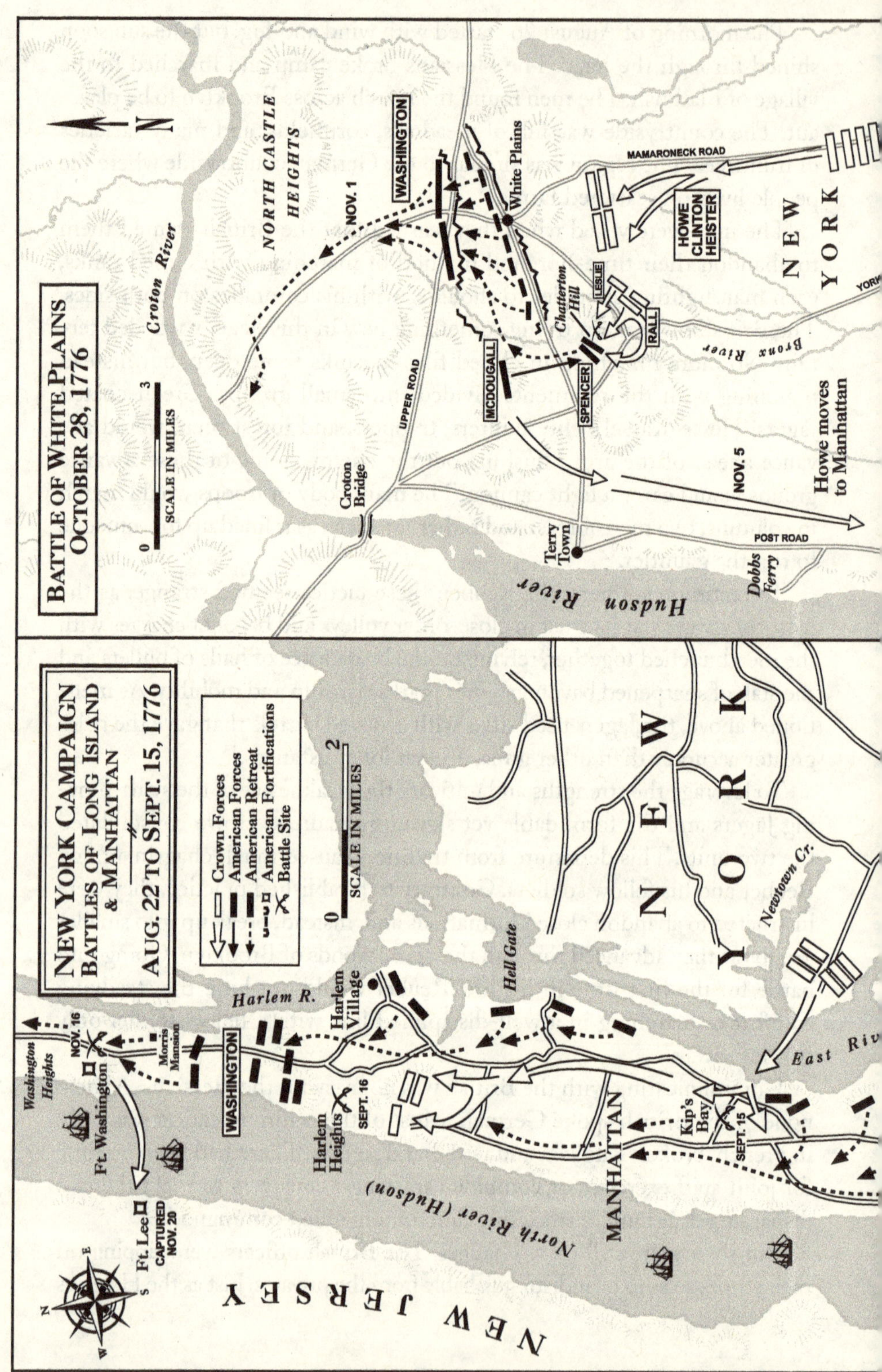
BATTLE OF WHITE PLAINS
OCTOBER 28, 1776
SCALE IN MILES
0
3
N
Croton River
NORTH CASTLE HEIGHTS
WASHINGTON
NOV. 1
White Plains
MAMARONECK ROAD
HOWE
CLINTON
HEISTER
NEW YORK
Chatterton Hill
LESLIE
RALL
Bronx River
MCDOUGALL
SPENCER
UPPER ROAD
Croton Bridge
Terry Town
NOV. 5
Howe moves to Manhattan
POST ROAD
Dobbs Ferry
Hudson River
NEW YORK CAMPAIGN
BATTLES OF LONG ISLAND & MANHATTAN
AUG. 22 TO SEPT. 15, 1776
Crown Forces
American Forces
American Retreat
American Fortifications
Battle Site
SCALE IN MILES
0
2
NEW YORK
Newtown Cr.
Hell Gate
Harlem Village
Harlem R.
NOV. 16
Washington Heights
Morris Mansion
WASHINGTON
Ft. Washington
Harlem Heights
SEPT. 16
Kip's Bay
SEPT. 15
East River
MANHATTAN
North River (Hudson)
Ft. Lee
CAPTURED NOV. 20
NEW JERSEY

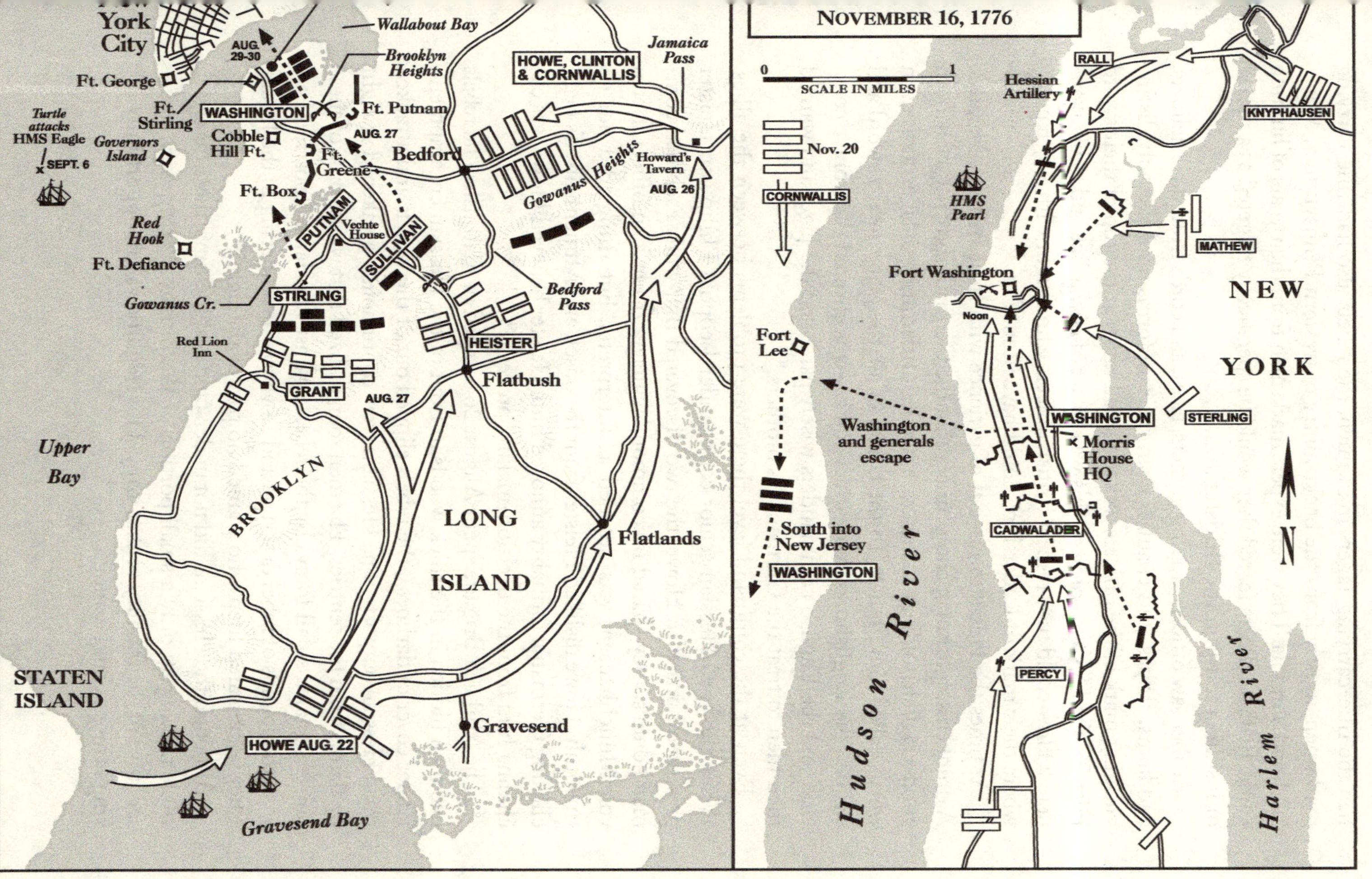
York City
AUG. 29-30
Wallabout Bay
Brooklyn Heights
Ft. George
Ft. Stirling
WASHINGTON
Ft. Putnam
HOWE, CLINTON & CORNWALLIS
Jamaica Pass
Turtle attacks HMS Eagle
SEPT. 6
Governors Island
Cobble Hill Ft.
AUG. 27
Ft. Greene
Bedford
Gowanus Heights
Howard's Tavern
AUG. 26
Ft. Box
PUTNAM
Vechte House
SULLIVAN
Red Hook
Ft. Defiance
Gowanus Cr.
STIRLING
Bedford Pass
Red Lion Inn
HEISTER
GRANT
Flatbush
AUG. 27
Upper Bay
BROOKLYN
LONG ISLAND
Flatlands
STATEN ISLAND
HOWE AUG. 22
Gravesend
Gravesend Bay
NOVEMBER 16, 1776
0
1
SCALE IN MILES
RALL
Hessian Artillery
KNYPHAUSEN
Nov. 20
CORNWALLIS
HMS Pearl
MATHEW
Fort Washington
Noon
NEW YORK
Fort Lee
WASHINGTON
STERLING
Washington and generals escape
Morris House HQ
South into New Jersey
WASHINGTON
CADWALADER
Hudson River
PERCY
Harlem River
N

had the rifle-carrying Jägers marksmen, the rebels also had rifle-carrying marksmen, mostly from the backcountry of western Pennsylvania, Maryland, and Virginia. They were expert marksmen from their years of hunting game. British officers feared they would be specifically targeted as a means of instilling terror in the British ranks.[16]

Reuber saw officers ripping gorgets, laces, and cords from their helmets, and knots, stripes, and epaulets from their uniforms until the only distinguishing mark of the officers was the small knots at the top of their sword hilts. To the Hessian soldiers, this was an act of cowardice and many wondered: How could they respect British officers who fought with a torn patch where their mark of leadership should have been?[17]

At times the Hessians ran out of patience with their British comrades. A drunken Englishman complaining that the Germans took pay away from good English soldiers made the mistake of damning a Jäger and, even worse, called him French. To the horror of all, the Jäger drew a sword and stabbed the Englishman to death. The Hessians cheered their brave comrade, and the English commanders wisely pardoned the Jäger and warned their men to treat the Germans "as brothers."[18]

Even at the command level there were problems between the allies. When the aged Hessian senior commander Leopold Philip von Heister presented himself to Howe, the two discovered that while each had command duties, they shared no common language. A Hessian officer, Levin von Münchhausen, was detailed as interpreter, but things did not go smoothly. Howe disliked Heister from the onset, and Münchhausen's heel-clicking Germanic formality annoyed him. Heister believed Howe was excluding him from the decision-making process.[19]

The Mirbach Brigade spent August 26 camped in Flatbush. The rebels had men hidden in the thick woods in front of the Hessian encampment. Under cover of darkness, the rebels slipped out of the woods and attacked small Hessian outposts. The Hessians were continuously awakened at night by alarms from the sentries. The men soon realized that while some of these noises signaled small forays by the rebels against Hessian outposts, others were the sounds of rebel deserters and Loyalists surrendering to the Jägers. They were scared men who wanted no part of the fight.[20]

Although the Hessians did not understand it at the time, these deserters, while making up only a small portion of Washington's army, were representative of the fragility of that army. This fragility was an opportunity the king's troops could exploit.

The morning of August 27 was warm and sunny. The brigade broke camp to head into battle. At 10:00 A.M., the men were put under arms. At 11:00 A.M., they formed up into order of battle. Reuber and his comrades gathered their gear and marched toward the rebel fortifications on Guana Heights. It was time for Johannes Reuber to show his fidelity to his king.

Approaching the heights, notwithstanding the British advice, the Rall, Lossberg, and Knyphausen Regiments marched in the usual Hessian formation with closed ranks, deviating from standard practice only by putting detachments of Jägers ahead as advance skirmishers.[21]

Once they came upon their first group of rebels, the effectiveness of using Jäger skirmish lines, followed closely by the grenadiers carrying bayonets, became apparent. The Jägers maneuvered forward using a sophisticated communication system of hand and arm signals, hunting horns, and whistles. They unleashed deadly fire from behind trees, crawled on their bellies across fields, and flushed out rebel positions. When the grenadiers brought up a cannon and charged with bayonets, the rebels fled.[22]

Wiederhold was angered by the scene unfolding before him:

> We attacked them, hit them hard, and took many prisoners. . . . With eight men and two subordinate officers, I captured 19 of them who had hunkered down in almost impenetrable bushes. They fell down on their knees before me and called for quarter. But before I gave it to them, they had to beg the king for mercy and pardon with their heads bare and their hands folded. They did so with tears in their eyes.

The prisoners explained to Wiederhold that they had been told that if the Hessians captured them, they would "immediately scalp them, mutilate all their limbs, and whatever other such atrocities there are."[23]

Reuber and his comrades climbed up the steep Guana Heights, some moving through the woods and others on Flatbush and Bedford Roads, with the Jäger skirmish lines advancing ahead of them. The troops moved up the heights in good order, flags flying, bands playing, the men pulling cannons through the woods. The day was warm but not as hot and humid as it had been the previous week when the oppressive heat had made their uniforms stick to their sweaty skin.[24]

Scouts reported that the woods in front were full of rebels. Reuber was ordered to proceed up the dirt road that led through the woods and passed over the crest of the heights. He had been training for two years for this moment. Fifty rebels with flags burst from the woods. Colonel Rall gave the order to fire. The Hessians closed ranks, the drummers banged out a loud steady march, Reuber and all the men around him fired, and as smoke from the discharges hung in the air, the rebels promptly surrendered. The Americans threw down their weapons and shouted for "pardon!" Many turned their guns upside down and put their hats under their arms. Some got on their knees and begged for mercy.[25]

Reuber watched as a fight soon broke out, but not with the rebels, most of whom were crawling on their hands and knees, groveling for mercy. Colonel Rall and General Mirbach were screaming at each other over whose troops would have the honor of carrying the captured American flag. As the men watched in wonder, the rebels, dirty, barefoot, and in short linen jackets, lay on the ground while the flag, red with the word "Liberty" in the center, was yanked back and forth between the angry officers.

Finally, Rall snatched it away and yelled, "Nothing doing, General! My grenadiers captured the flag and they shall keep it. No one will take it from them." Mirbach stormed away swearing he would report Rall to the prince.[26]

In Piel's regiment, the Lossberg, fifty men volunteered to rush ahead into the rebel-held woods. They charged with their bayonets fixed. They inflicted many casualties, mostly bayonet wounds. A few moments later they emerged with sixty-four prisoners.[27]

By the end of the day, Rall added another American regimental color to his collection. Reuber looked proudly at the American colors flying in the hands of Hessian flag bearers. The sight of the colors flapping in the breeze added to his contempt of the Americans' fighting abilities. An officer wondered if such a misfit enemy would bring the regiment the honor it deserved. To most eighteenth-century armies, losing a regimental flag in battle was seen as a dishonorable calamity. Reuber and his comrades could not have imagined on this victorious day that they would soon feel the same pain and dishonor as the rebel prisoners who were now cowering before them.[28]

Reuber looked at the rebels. They had no uniforms and were dressed for farming or manual labor, in shirts and breeches. Most of the officers were no better dressed than the men. One admitted he was a schoolmaster by trade. A schoolmaster! The Hessians laughed. And who was their general, the town baker? One Hessian in the group spoke English, and the men prodded him to ask the rebels how "contrary to the laws of God and man, have [they] set themselves against their king?" The rebels' response made them pause. The schoolmaster/officer told them he had taken an oath with his students that "so long as there flowed a drop of blood in their veins they would fight against the King." And the students had sworn to this and had brought their schoolmates to fight. With a sweep of the hand, the schoolmaster/officer pointed to his class: the young lads who now sat shivering on the ground in a fearful surrender.[29]

The Hessians had swept through this poorly trained group with ease, but listening to the translation of the rebels' beliefs, some in the regiment began to realize that the Americans were obsessed with the concept of liberty and were determined to overthrow the king. If there was someone to train them, someone to lead them properly in battle, they could become more of a problem than the day's relatively bloodless surrender had suggested.[30]

Word came that Howe's flanking movement along the unguarded Jamaica Pass had succeeded. Caught between the Hessian attack on their front and Howe's attack on their flank, the rebel lines collapsed. The rebels were in full retreat across the entire front.

"Our first advance was an attack on the rebels who defended themselves far worse than one would have expected of such enthusiasts for Freedom," a Hessian chaplain reported. "The slaughter was terrible, but more on the part of the English, into whose lines our men drove the rebels like sheep."[31]

Many rebels had hardly fired a shot, and some threw away their weapons, but not all of them folded so easily. Two of the best regiments in the rebel army, Smallwood's Marylanders and Haslet's Delaware Continentals, made a desperate stand in front of Gowanus Creek, an eighty-yard-wide muddy stream that the retreating Americans could wade and swim across to reach the safety of the fortifications in Brooklyn Heights. Although the British and Hessians attacking them were six times their number, the two rebel regiments fixed bayonets and charged, a tactic the king's troops were accustomed to administering, not receiving. The courageous men from Maryland and Delaware eventually had to fall back, but not until they had slowed the British advance long enough for other units to escape across the creek.[32]

A Connecticut militiaman, Joseph Plumb Martin, remembered seeing his fellow rebels forced into the creek: "When they came out of the water . . . looking like water rats, it was a truly pitiful sight. Many of them were killed in the pond and many more drowned."[33]

Of the approximately 270 men who had made the stand, fewer than a dozen survived.

The rebel survivors of the battle abandoned Guana Heights and fled to Brooklyn Heights. The Americans had had more than 1,300 killed or captured, and many more, particularly the poorly trained militia, had run away or hid in the woods. No reliable estimate of American wounded was recorded. The British had about 350 casualties. The Hessians lost thirty-one men.[34]

For Reuber and Piel it was a blessed day. They were safe and none of their friends had been killed.

Once inside the fortifications of Brooklyn Heights, Washington tried to rally his men, but soldiers were pouring in with gruesome wounds. Farmers with their families huddled inside, terrified, adding to the chaos. Over a thousand cattle had been brought in earlier to keep them from being taken by the British. Nervous from gunfire and scared by the sight of mud-covered soldiers, the cattle mooed loudly and stampeded around the camp. On the plains in front of the fortifications, the British army formed once again for attack. Everyone knew this could be the assault that ended the war. Behind him, Washington could see the East River; in front were more men than he had ever seen in his life. Rank upon rank of enemy soldiers marched toward them—British soldiers in red, blue-coated Hessian infantry, and Jäger light infantry in green jackets with bright crimson lapels—as officers on horseback rode up and down the ranks preparing them for battle. Thousands of gleaming bayonets advanced on the American fortification. And then, unbelievably, they halted and set up camp.

The British knew that a large part of the Continental Army was trapped in Brooklyn Heights and that with the Royal Navy behind them on the East River, the Americans were cut off from Manhattan with no way to retreat and no way to be reinforced. Destruction of the American army seemed inevitable, and most British and Hessian officers wanted to storm the American lines, but General Howe had different ideas. He had not forgotten last year's "victory" at Bunker Hill.

Howe had learned his lesson then and knew that attacking uphill against the entrenched rebels in their fortified positions, even if successful, would mean enormous casualties for the king's troops. Instead, he moved his army closer to the rebel fortifications and settled in for a siege. It would take a little more time, but he believed this approach doomed Washington's army.

"The entire army broke camp and moved nearer to the enemy," Piel wrote in his diary on August 28, 1776. "We established our camp on a height from which we could see over the entire fortified [rebel] camp."[35]

Then Providence interceded: the wind shifted, rising from the northeast, blowing the British ships out of the East River into the harbor. The rain grew into a great storm, a nor'easter that raged for the next three days, slowing Howe's engineers and making life a muddy misery for the soldiers.[36]

"From two o'clock in the afternoon until seven o'clock in the evening," Lieutenant von Bardeleben wrote, "it rained without letup and very heavily. Our tents were so wet that they were barely able to keep the water out."[37]

Washington saw his chance.

The next day, August 29, Piel stayed in camp while a Lossberg Regiment patrol led by Lieutenant Georg Zoll ventured into the two hundred yards separating the armies and detected preparations for a rebel evacuation. Zoll's report was quickly passed up the chain of command to Howe.[38]

Howe dismissed the report, as it seemed preposterous to believe that the rebel army on Brooklyn Heights could abandon their fortifications unseen and march to the East River docks where somehow there would be dozens of boats and sailors waiting to carry the army across the mile-wide East River. And all this would need to be done without being detected by the British Army or the Royal Navy.

Yet that was exactly what Washington was determined to do.

The American leader convened a council of war with his generals on August 29. The council resolved unanimously to move the army across the river into Manhattan.

Washington began a campaign of disinformation to fool his own men and the enemy. He spread the lie that fresh troops were coming from New Jersey to relieve the tired soldiers on Brooklyn Heights. Washington ordered all available vessels near Manhattan to be commandeered for the supposed "reinforcement" of the troops in Brooklyn Heights.[39]

The rebels had two regiments from Essex County, Massachusetts: mariners from Marblehead in Colonel John Glover's 14th Massachusetts and fishermen from Salem, Lynn, and Danvers in Colonel John Hutchinson's 27th Massachusetts. At ten in the evening, they quietly slipped out of the lines and rendezvoused at the Brooklyn Ferry. At midnight, in a pouring rain, officers began marching soldiers out of the entrenchments. The men were sworn to march in silence. As they did so toward the Brooklyn dockside, Washington had a skeleton force slip into the entrenchments to feed the campfires and cry out like sentries.[40]

At the landing, the Massachusetts sailors and fishermen loaded the men onto shallow draft vessels. The retreat continued as fast as Glover's and Hutchinson's men could row. The summer night was brief. Time was running out, and it appeared Glover's men couldn't complete the task before daybreak.

At 4:00 A.M., the first light began to illuminate the horizon. British engineers, only a few hundred yards from the American lines, finally became suspicious and ordered their men to arm and make a sortie. Rebels were still on the wharves awaiting boats. Glover's men were losing their race against time. The men still on the dockside would soon be casting shadows in the morning light.

Then, incredibly, Providence stepped in once again. For in the eyes of the Americans it was certainly a heavenly force that was sending a thick fog over Brooklyn so Glover's men could continue rowing undetected as the sun rose and the British remained blind to their activity.

"A thick fog arose," recalled a Delaware soldier. "It was the pillar of a cloud to our enemies and favorable to us."[41]

When the fog finally lifted, a detachment of Hessian soldiers broke through the unmanned rebel fortifications. They rushed to the dockside to find the last of the rowboats pulling away. Under a hail of gunfire, they forced one to turn about, but the others faded away into the shoreline of Manhattan. From Washington's ten-thousand-man army, they could report to General Howe the capture of just three rebel soldiers.[42]

Washington's amphibious evacuation of his army was a tactical masterstroke. Glover and Hutchinson executed the plan flawlessly. Yet the Hessians were unfazed and unimpressed.

"At daybreak this morning," Piel wrote, "we became aware that the enemy had left his fortified camp and the whole island."

The Mirbach quartermaster recorded in the regimental journal: "During the night the enemy evacuated all their works and returned to New York."

"In the morning, no enemies were to be seen," Bardeleben wrote nonchalantly.

Reuber did not even bother to mention it in his diary.[43]

General Heister was frustrated. Despite the Royal Navy's tactically brilliant amphibious assault on Brooklyn, and a near-perfectly executed attack by the Hessians on the rebels at Guana Heights, Washington's army was still intact and safely across the river in Manhattan. Heister had wanted to attack the rebel lines right away but had been overruled by Howe.[44]

On the morning of August 30, the Rall, Lossberg, and Knyphausen Regiments climbed the muddy slopes of the abandoned rebel fortifications and helped themselves to food, ammunition, and huge, fat, roaming cattle. The rebels, Wiederhold wrote to a friend, had left behind "Every kind of food humanly possible; there we had great fun. I had five cows and two pigs brought from there by a couple of men."[45] They marched through the empty fortifications to the Brooklyn Ferry and set up camp along the East River. Reuber felt great comfort watching the massive British warships anchored a few hundred yards away, knowing their devastating firepower protected the army from attackers.

Gazing across the East River, the men could behold the rebel-occupied Manhattan. This sparsely populated island, a tapestry of tree-clad rolling hills interspersed with farmland and untouched meadows, presented a magnificent vista.

"New York island is the prettiest place I have ever seen," exclaimed a normally reserved Jäger, who was awed by the sight of homes perched on the commanding heights flanking the river.[46]

"Too bad that such unsettled people possess such a blessed land. Livestock in abundance! Wheat, corn, and every possible grain of the best sorts, enough! Fruit, chestnuts, some other nuts, cherries, apricots, peaches, whole forests of them, and just like at home, oak trees and other kinds of woods," Wiederhold wrote.[47]

For the next two weeks, they rested by the Brooklyn shoreline. Then on September 15, Reuber watched the spectacular sight of warships with gun ports open and cannons jutting out, lining up in the waters across the East River from Manhattan. A small armada of flat-bottomed landing craft, filled with the king's troops, emerged from Newton Creek along the Brooklyn shorefront and headed for Manhattan, depositing wave after wave of troops onto the sands of Kip's Bay while the warships fired thunderous salvos into the rebel lines. The Americans fled, and within a matter of hours almost all of Manhattan was in British hands.[48]

Washington rallied his men at the northern tip of Manhattan on the rocky summit of Harlem Heights where the next day they made a brave stand in a bush-covered ravine behind a post-and-rail fence. The British fell back, checked for the first time by an American army. Although the fight at Harlem Heights was a small affair, it had consequences out of proportion to the small number of troops involved. The British had 140 casualties, a price too high for such a trifling battle, and as he had experienced at Bunker Hill and Dorchester Heights, Howe saw again what wizards the rebel engineers were and how dangerous an entrenched American force could be to his own.[49]

The two armies settled in along the northern periphery of Manhattan and quietly faced each other over the next few weeks. In the month since the Hessians had arrived, the British had retaken Long Island (which at the time consisted of Brooklyn, Queens, and Long Island proper), Staten Island, and almost all of Manhattan. Most important, they had done it while suffering fewer than five hundred casualties.

FREDERICK II, LANDGRAVE OF HESSE-KASSEL, AND HIS FAMILY

Top, Portrait of Frederick II, Landgrave of Hessen-Kassel, c. 1770, by Johann Heinrich Tischbein. (*Museo Nacional de Bellas Artes de Cuba*). Bottom, Landgrave Frederick II with his family, 1754, by Johann Heinrich Tischbein. (*Hessen Kassel Heritage*)

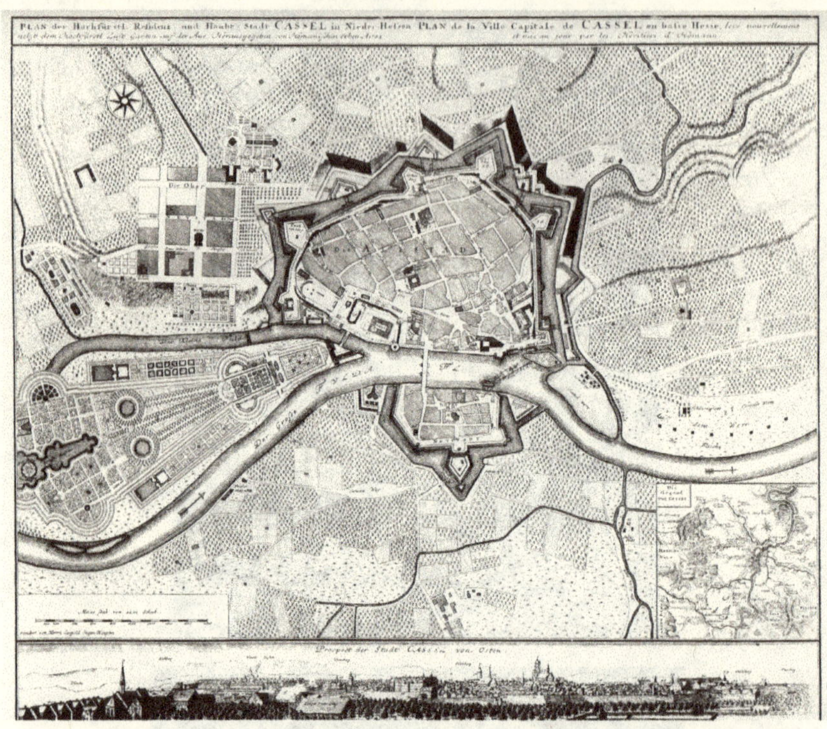

KASSEL AND THE CONSCRIPTION OF GERMAN SOLDIERS

Top, Plan of the city of Kassel, 1742. (*Wikipedia Commons*) Bottom, Albert Bobbett, "Conscription of German Soldiers for Service in America," (1877). (From *Our Country: A Household History for All Readers*, Volume 2, by Benson J. Lossing, Johnson & Miles, New York, 1877)

THE EMBARKATION OF THE HESSIAN REGIMENTS

Top, “Hessians departing for America, 1776.” (*Wikipedia Commons*) Bottom, a uniform study by J. H. Carl, 1784.“Fusilier Regiment von Knyphausen.” (*Anne S.K. Brown Military Collection. Brown University Library*)

KIP'S BAY LANDING AND THE BATTLE OF WHITE PLAINS

Top, "The British landing at Kip's Bay, New York Island, 15 September 1776," by Robert Cleveley, 1777. (*Wikipedia Commons/Royal Museums Greenwich*) Bottom, The Battle of White Plains, October 28, 1776: General McDougal's men occupying Chatterton Hill by George Albert Harker. (*Wikipedia Commons*)

THE BATTLE OF FORT WASHINGTON

Top, British encampment on the Dyckman farmstead on the northern edge of Manhattan before the Battle of Fort Washington by John Ward Dunsmore, 1915. "A view of the attack against Fort Washington and rebel redouts near New York on the 16 of November 1776 by the British and Hessian brigades, drawn on the spot by Thomas Davies, Royal Regiment of Artillery." British troops launched an amphibious landing against the fort from the East River while Hessian troops attacked on land from the Bronx. (*New York Public Library*)

WASHINGTON'S CROSSING AND THE ATTACK ON TRENTON

Left, Emanuel Leutze, *Washington Crossing the Delaware*, 1851. (*Metropolitan Museum of Art*) Top, *Washington crossing the Delaware: on the evening of Dec 25th. 1776, previous to the battle of Trenton*, 1876, Currier & Ives. (*Library of Congress*) Bottom, *The Battle of Trenton* by Charles McBarron. (*U.S. Army Center for Military History*)

THE SURRENDER OF THE HESSIANS

Left, John Trumbull, *The Capture of the Hessians at Trenton, December 26, 1776*, 1786–1828. (Yale University Art Gallery) Top, "Colonel Rahl [Rall] from Trumbull's Battle of Trenton," from the *Pictorial Field-Book of the Revolution*, 1850. (*New York Public Library*) Bottom, *Victory at Trenton*, 1845. The mortally wounded Rall was assisted to his quarters in the background where he soon expired. (*Anne S.K. Brown Military Collection. Brown University Library*)

LEGACY

Top, "The visit of William IX, Elector of Hesse to Amschel Mayer de Rothschild," by Moritz Daniel Oppenheim, c. 1850. (*Wikipedia Commons*) Bottom: A mother and children viewing *George Washington Crossing the Delaware* in 1905. (*Metropolitan Museum of Art*)

CHAPTER 14

The Battles of the Bronx and Westchester

October 12–November 1, 1776

Most of Howe's army spent the next several weeks behind fortified positions across from Washington's army in Harlem at the northern tip of Manhattan. Once again, haunted by the memory of failed, bloody, frontal assaults against the rebel fortifications at Bunker Hill, Howe, as he had done in Brooklyn, chose not to launch a frontal attack against the formidable-looking rebel lines.

Howe was eagerly awaiting the arrival of the fleet carrying six thousand British soldiers and the four thousand men of the 2nd Hessian Division; however, the fleet was delayed. This delay might explain Howe's lack of urgency. The arrival of the fleet was unpredictable, and as the days stretched into weeks without reinforcements, Howe reluctantly concluded he would have to proceed with the forces he had, but the nearly seven weeks he had wasted would come back to haunt him. Had he been more decisive, more of a risk taker, and bolder, he likely would have won the war before winter set in. Time and again, Howe demonstrated a lack of daring and purpose of spirit that George Washington possessed.[1]

Howe's army now occupied New York City and most of the island of Manhattan, but Washington's army, though battered, was alive and functioning. Furthermore, Howe was beginning to feel the difficulty of having his supply base more than three thousand miles away in England. Many of his troops were low on supplies, notably tents, a situation exacerbated by a shortage of wagons and horses. Most of the men were sleeping in barns or in fields.[2]

The only major Hessian forces remaining in Brooklyn were the Mirbach Brigade, consisting of the Lossberg, Knyphausen, and Rall Regiments (which included Jakob Piel, Andreas Wiederhold, and Johannes Reuber respectively).

On September 17, two days after Howe's forces liberated New York City from the rebels, the Mirbach Brigade marched north from Brooklyn and established its encampment along the East River opposite the notoriously turbulent waters of the Hell Gate portion of the river (near present-day Queens). As the night of September 20 gave way to the early hours of the 21st, the brigade's night watch observed flames and smoke billowing from Manhattan across the East River, creating a tragically magnificent glow against the night sky. Fires sweeping through New York City were causing the glow. The origin of the fires remained a mystery, but the flames consumed hundreds of buildings, perhaps up to a thousand.

A Hessian quartermaster, from the relative safety of a ship in the harbor and with a clear view of the lurid scene, was mortified by the sight. "Where a beautiful city once stood, we saw nothing but the ruins of buildings," he wrote in his journal.[3]

The fires and subsequent plundering of New York City had no effect on the Hessians in Queens. They slept in a variety of improvised structures, including brush huts, booths, and wigwams. Some soldiers rolled themselves in blankets and slept under the stars, enjoying the cool autumn weather in New York. As the days passed, the men saw that they would be stationed in Queens for a while and so assembled large regimental tents and erected wooden field huts.

Notably absent from this period was any large-scale looting in the region. Much to their chagrin, the men were under strict orders not to plunder; and for the most part they obeyed, although the British admitted that some of the troops had committed "great irregularities as of late." Howe ordered the provost marshal to "execute on the spot any soldier he finds guilty of Marauding." The soldiers were frustrated because, much to their surprise, many of the locals were rebel sympathizers, and to the Hessians, the local population's disloyalty to the king made them prime targets for plundering.[4]

"When the army was on Staten Island," wrote a British officer, "we were made to expect that as soon as we should land on this island, many thousands of the inhabitants would show their loyalty and join the [British] Army. But we have seen very little to induce us to believe that the inhabitants of this island are more loyal than others."[5]

The question of civilian loyalties was complicated. One Hessian officer noted:

> Many subjects are returning to their lawful government, and on Long Island the villages of Gravesend, New Utrecht, Flatbush, Brooklyn, and the Ferry are filled with returned fugitives. Most of them, however, find their houses empty, their belongings destroyed, and windows broken; nor will they ever recover their cattle. These loyalists must distinguish themselves from the rebels by wearing red ribbons on their hats.[6]

General Mirbach became ill, and Colonel Rall assumed command of the brigade. He appointed Jakob Piel as his brigade major. With the well-respected thirty-six-year veteran Rall now in charge, the brigade's name changed from the Mirbach Brigade to the Rall Brigade.[7]

Howe allowed several weeks for his army to rest and restore themselves, though this did waste precious warm, dry campaigning weather. Finally, on October 12, he put into motion a plan for an amphibious landing to outflank Washington. The logical place to land was on one of the inlets along the Bronx coastline. Howe chose Throgs Neck, about twelve miles from the English base in Manhattan. By landing his expedition on the Bronx mainland, Howe was positioning his troops northeast of Washington's army, just a few miles from both the King's Highway—the road connecting New York to Boston and the King's Bridge, the major link spanning the Harlem River between northern Manhattan—and the mainland. By controlling the King's Highway, Howe could jeopardize Washington's supply line from New England, and by controlling the King's Bridge, Howe could cut off Washington's only escape route from Manhattan, stranding his army on the island. Landing his troops on the Bronx coastline was a cautious, indirect move, but Howe hoped it would force Washington to withdraw from the northern end of Manhattan without a fight.[8]

While the Hessian commander, General Heister, would lead the Hessian corps and the light infantry from several English regiments, Howe made sure the British Army controlled the operation by placing the expedition under the command of two experienced English officers, Generals Henry Clinton and Charles Cornwallis.

On October 11, forty-five days after landing on the beaches of Brooklyn, the invasion fleet began to assemble on the East River; an armada of small vessels and large, powerful warships lined up along the shore.

"At 3 o'clock," wrote a British officer, "all the Gunboats, flat boats, Batteaux [shallow-draft, flat bottom-boats], Launches . . . came up from the harbour, and drew up on the shore. . . . They amounted to about 150. Armed vessels and transports . . . came up with the flood tide."[9]

The Rall, Lossberg, and Knyphausen Regiments had spent the past few weeks exploring the gentle terrain of Long Island, savoring the pleasant aromas arising from a countryside rich with "a multitude of meadows, tilled fields, fruit trees of every kind and fine houses." They meandered down roads shaded by apple and peach trees. Standing downwind in Jamaica, Queens, they inhaled the sweet, hay-like scent of the region's sole tobacco fields.[10]

Most of the inhabitants had fled, and the Hessian army occupied nearly empty, spacious villages with quaint, Anglicized Dutch names like Bushwick (Boswijck), Brooklyn (Breuckelen), Flatbush (V'Lacke Bos), and Gravesend (s'Gravenzande). Some of the villages consisted of a single tree-lined street. As on Staten Island, the inhabitants appeared prosperous, with farmers owning large landholdings. Herds of cattle grazed on lush fields, and the men noted the pervasive scent of grass. Wherever they strolled, they saw barns crammed full of farmers' wealth, and wagons carrying barrels of grains and hemp down to the riverside docks. After seeing such an abundance of produce and farmland, the Hessians found it difficult to understand the colonists' motivation for rebelling against their king.[11]

"The whole island is like a painted landscape," wrote a Jäger. "You can hardly go an English mile . . . without finding houses. The inhabitants are lively, and usually rascals at heart. The air here is . . . very pleasant."[12]

The six-week respite of the Rall Brigade had come to an end. At five in the evening, the officers informed the men they would be boarding boats for an invasion of the Bronx. The soldiers struck their tents an hour later and marched to Hell Gate, a treacherous stretch of the East River that earned its grim name from the violent waters churning through narrow passages between menacing rocks. At ten in the evening, they boarded an array of transport ships, sloops, and schooners. At four in the morning, "they began to move with the tide, passed up the East River and through the Hell Gate with great rapidity," a British officer recorded.[13]

"Here one sees the remains of many wrecked ships," a terrified Hessian officer wrote of Hell Gate. "The passage is so narrow that one can throw an object from the ship to the land on either side."[14]

Several of the English captains later declared that this was a "most hazardous enterprise to go through a channel with such a fleet [150 vessels] and before it was daylight." Their concerns seemed justified when an unexpected fog descended, obscuring the buoys and markers that had been fixed to guide their passage. It was too late to postpone the movement; the ships were already being carried by the tide and the wind into Hell Gate"[15]

From his transport, Reuber gazed down at the eddies and swirling water. To him, Hell Gate was a spiraling, revolving nightmare. The rushing water reminded him of a swollen river surging over a dam spillway. He feared the whirlpool would take hold of his ship and "draw it in and spin it around until it grounds" against the rocks.[16]

Jakob Piel, Andreas Wiederhold, and most of the brigade were unfazed by the notorious rapids. Piel casually wrote in his diary that the Rall Brigade "crossed over the [Long Island] Sound," and Wiederhold simply noted "we crossed in boats."[17]

As the fleet neared the Bronx coastline, the nonchalant attitude of the troops stood in marked contrast to their earlier anxieties. These men from landlocked Hessen-Kassel had transformed into veterans of water transport and amphibious landings. In just six months, they had sailed from Bremelehe on the North Sea to Portsmouth on the English Channel, from Portsmouth to Staten Island, from Staten Island to Brooklyn, and now from Queens to the Bronx.

Only weeks before, during the invasion of Brooklyn, they had stood nervously aboard transport ships, praying and singing religious hymns. Now they showed little fear and scant interest as Throgs Neck came into view—a surprisingly small peninsula, merely a narrow spit of land jutting from the mainland of the Bronx.

"We were shipped over an arm of the sea," a soldier from the Knyphausen Regiment wrote dispassionately. But he excitedly added, "I received a letter from home today."[18]

One gunboat did not make it across. It drifted into a violent eddy that grabbed it and hurled the doomed vessel onto adjacent rocks. Four artillerymen drowned and their cannons were lost. A boat with a detachment of grenadiers got caught in a whirlpool that sent it spinning round and round but after several turns threw it safely onto the shore.[19]

The remainder of the invasion fleet crossed without incident.

"To see ships of war of 44 guns, frigates, transports full of troops, horses and wagons, and flat boats with troops and artillery, attempting and accomplishing so difficult an undertaking, with such trifling loss, [which] to any other nation the obstacles would have seemed insurmountable" a British lieutenant proudly wrote in his diary.[20]

The first phase of Howe's plan worked. Fearful that his supply line to New England would be cut and worried that loss of the King's Bridge would leave his army stranded on Manhattan, Washington began moving men north to counter Howe's maneuver.[21]

As it had done a few weeks earlier in Brooklyn, the Royal Navy executed a flawless landing. Fearsome British warships floated on the waters of the East River, standing guard as sailors rowed transport barges packed with four thousand soldiers onto the Throgs Neck shoreline. The Royal Navy was once again masterful in planning and executing a large amphibious operation. Fog descended, hiding the invasion fleet as it sailed quietly, the only sound coming from oars rhythmically hitting the water. The soldiers disembarked, waded through the shallow surf, and emerged undetected on a small rocky beach. They experienced no casualties and no resistance from the Americans.[22]

But someone had miscalculated.

The British had misjudged the landing site at Throgs Neck. General Howe had ordered the navy to deposit the army on what he thought was a peninsula jutting out from the Bronx but was itself a tiny island (Washington described it as "a kind of Island") separated from the mainland by salt marshes and a creek with only a single, narrow wooden causeway and bridge connecting it to the Bronx.[23]

The British army now found itself bottled up on a spit of land surrounded by water. This was a potentially dangerous situation, but the Hessian soldiers were unconcerned, likely due to their ignorance of tides and waterways. Alerted by local farmers, a small force of Americans arrived on the shore. The Hessians watched helplessly as a mere twenty-five men of the 1st Pennsylvania Regiment, under the command of a twenty-two-year-old physician, Colonel Edward Hand, calmly pulled up the planks of wood from the bridge and then hunkered down at the base of the now uncrossable causeway. To make matters worse, Hand's regiment had riflemen who carried long-range, highly accurate weapons. The Pennsylvania riflemen could settle in safely out of musket range and pick off the enemy one by one. Two dozen rebels had effectively stopped four thousand of the king's troops. The Hessians watched optimistically as the water dropped at low tide, revealing a creek that they believed at first glance gave them access to the mainland. However, the creek had a deep channel lined with unpassable, gooey mud banks, so they were still stuck.[24]

The Americans were soon reinforced with 1,200 men and positioned a cannon to cover the narrow bridge and blast anyone foolish enough to try to tiptoe across the remains of the bridge. Howe was stymied and called a halt to the operation while he considered his options. The English army made camp, most of the men sleeping on the ground under the stars as the navy had not yet brought up their tents. A British drawing of the battle would refer to the impassable causeway as "Bridge Broke down by Americans," but it was the bravery and ingenuity of a few American soldiers, not a broken bridge, that stopped the British invasion force.[25]

The Americans cannonaded the British through the night, but their fire was inaccurate, and only six English soldiers were killed. Though the Hessians were calm and confident throughout the ordeal, they were quite useless stuck on the tiny island. Howe again wasted precious time, leaving the men on Throgs Neck for five days. If nothing else, it was a pleasant spot where men with tents were able to pitch them on level ground. They also enjoyed good drinking water from three freshwater springs. Most important, the campsite was safe since the obstacles that prevented them from marching off the island also prevented the rebels from attacking.

Winter was approaching, which meant the end of the autumn campaign season was only a few weeks away. Washington's army and his supply lines were vulnerable. Finally, on October 17, Howe reboarded his four thousand troops onto his eighty-ship fleet and the next day landed the men a few miles to the east—on a small peninsula jutting from the mainland known by the locals as Pell's Point or Rodman's Point (present-day Pelham Bay in the Bronx).[26]

The landing at Pell's Point was an amazing feat; in a matter of days, the navy landed four thousand men at Throgs Neck, reboarded them from there, and landed them at a new site. Boarding the ships and landing on enemy territory no longer fazed the Hessians. They were greeted at Pell's Point with attacks and ambushes by General John Glover's Brigade of 750 Marblehead sailors, the same men who had bravely evacuated Washington's army to Manhattan after the disastrous Battle of Brooklyn. Glover deftly maneuvered his small force, hiding behind stone walls, coordinating rotations of troops, and ambushing overly confident British regulars. But none of the skillful displays of arms by the rebels impressed or alarmed the Hessians. This was only the second battle for Reuber and Piel, yet neither bothered to mention the fight in their diaries.[27]

Andreas Wiederhold had marched inland from the landing area behind a battalion of English light infantry, but the light infantry had foolishly not sent out skirmishers to reconnoiter, and they were ambushed by rebels who lay hidden behind a stone wall. The rebels waited until the enemy was within a few yards before jumping up to let loose a heavy discharge into the British ranks. Neither the ambushes nor rebel cannon fire slowed down Wiederhold, and he killed his first rebel with a rifle shot.

"I skirmished with the enemy, for which I sent one of them into the next world with my rifle," he dispassionately noted in his diary.[28]

Glover finally, voluntarily, withdrew from the field, satisfied that his actions had delayed the British for a day. His brigade had fired more than twenty-five volleys, or about four thousand musket balls, at close range of thirty to fifty yards into compact enemy columns along a narrow roadway; moreover, his men had rested their muskets on stone fences, allowing his troops, who were considered excellent shots, to ensure that their aim was true. According to one of the American commanders, Glover's men were "Calm as though expecting a shot at a flock of pigeons or ducks." Howe claimed his losses were slight, but this was undoubtedly an attempt at saving face, as Hessian and British deserters told the Americans that Howe lost eight hundred to one thousand men. After the battle, the Hessians used St. Paul's Church, in the Eastchester section of the Bronx, as a hospital, and its records indicate that about a hundred more Hessians died there and were buried in a large sandpit in the church's cemetery.[29]

Tactically, Howe had succeeded. He had forced Washington to leave Manhattan, and the British army was now within striking distance of the road linking Boston to New York, threatening to cut off Washington from his source of supplies in New England. He had left Washington only one viable option: to march farther north, away from Manhattan and toward New England, to the safety of the Hudson Highlands, where harsh terrain would perhaps shelter the rebel army. First, though, Washington had to stop at the village of White Plains on the east side of the Bronx River where newly arrived supplies from Connecticut, including badly needed pork and flour, were being stored and guarded by only three hundred of the rawest colonial militiamen. With Howe's forces also gathering east of the river, this was a risky move.[30]

Inexplicably, Howe failed to pursue the Americans and instead remained at Pell's Point for two days, finally marching inland to New Rochelle, where he again dithered, eventually marching farther inland on October 28. Glover's actions and Howe's procrastinations gave Washington precious time to safely evacuate north from Manhattan and march the twenty-five miles to White Plains. The village was small but vital, with several key roads passing through it from all directions, and like Gettysburg almost a century later, the town drew the opposing armies like a magnet to its tranquil plains.[31]

If the British had not been delayed a whole day by Glover's men, and if Howe had not vacillated, he could have cut off Washington's retreat and forced a fight in the open. The American high command was flabbergasted that Howe made no attempt to hinder their long caravan of 150 slow-moving wagons bearing baggage, artillery, and military stores, strung out along fifteen miles of the roads between Harlem Heights in Manhattan and White Plains. Washington realized that the American army was in great peril. If the British got to White Plains before the Americans did, then Washington's army could be starved, and possibly broken.[32]

Meanwhile, in New York City, civilians and soldiers working along the East River in Brooklyn and Manhattan heard strange music drifting up from the waterway. The four thousand Hessians of the 2nd Division, who had been delayed in sailing from Europe, having embarked on June 9, several weeks after the 1st Division had sailed, had landed in New York. Despite having practically no time to recover from their four-month transatlantic journey, they were in "high spirits," and they undoubtedly unnerved rebel sympathizers watching from the shore as, with the polished buttons of their uniforms glistening in the sun, they sailed up the East River on flatboats with drums beating, trumpets sounding, and banners embroidered with the tongue-wagging Hessian lion waving in the breeze. They landed a few miles from New Rochelle and immediately joined Howe's army in White Plains. They were under the command of Lieutenant General Wilhelm Freiherr von Knyphausen and were looking for a fight.[33]

The locals would later recall that daybreak in White Plains on October 28 arrived with the promise of an uncommonly beautiful Indian summer day. As the soldiers awaited their orders, many scavenged the ground, feasting on the fallen ripe fruit of chestnut trees, the plump morsels bursting through their prickly shells, their sweet scent mingling with the crisp autumn air. Young drummers, their youth belying their skills, beat a call to arms, shattering the morning stillness, as sunrise revealed a pristine landscape.

Washington had positioned his army on three hills that formed a line over three miles long, with Hatfield Hill on the left, Purdy Hill in the center, and, dominating the battlefield, Chatterton Hill on the right. The geography of his defensive line was strong, but there was an obvious potential flaw that made Washington's choice questionable. The Bronx River flowed between Chatterton Hill and Purdy Hill; if attacked, forces on Chatterton Hill would be difficult to support, as only one small bridge spanned the river. Although Chatterton was the highest hill in the area, the American troops stationed there were for all practical purposes isolated from the rest of Washington's troops on Purdy and Hatfield Hills. Washington compounded Chatterton Hill's vulnerability with a second questionable decision. He placed only a few thousand troops, under the command of Major General Alexander McDougall, to defend Chatterton Hill and put the bulk of the army—about ten thousand men—under the command of Israel Putnam and William Heath on the other side of the river to defend the smaller hills, Purdy and Hatfield.[34]

Chatterton Hill was undermanned and isolated, but the prominence had geographic characteristics that were likely to make an assault a bloody affair for the attackers: It was tall and lined on its eastern face with steep slopes and had the natural water barrier of the Bronx River at its base.

Arising early, Howe marched his army to White Plains in two columns with the green-coated Jäger skirmishers marching ahead, scouring the woods for rebels and protecting the army from ambushes. Following behind them, local Tories acted as guides, leveling fences and removing obstacles from the army's path, preparing the way for safe passage across the countryside.[35]

As they neared White Plains, the road became narrow and of poor quality, which forced the army to march in single file.[36]

The men finally came off the road and saw before them Washington's army entrenched in the hills. Leaving the road behind them, they fanned out across a broad field at the base of the rebel-occupied hills. Howe positioned his fourteen thousand men in a straight line facing the rebels head on. Howe's right flank was predominantly British troops under General

Clinton and his left flank predominantly Hessian troops under General Heister.

The Rall Regiment had the honor of heading the army's column on the left, marching behind a protective screen of Hessian dragoons on horseback and Jägers who fell back when they made contact with Washington's army. Rall's men were about a half mile from the Bronx River and Chatterton Hill when the probing Jägers ran into the two-thousand-man force of Brigadier General Joseph Spencer's New England soldiers. Spencer, a veteran of the Seven Years' War, was considered one of Washington's best officers, but many of his soldiers were untested in battle. Musket shots rang out, shattering the quiet morning, sending birds flying off in a panic, and alerting the Hessian vanguard that they had walked into an ambush. The Jägers and dragoons fell back onto Rall's Brigade. The Americans were behind stone walls, trees, and wooden fences. Rall immediately understood that the small rebel force was not trying to defeat them but was instead tasked with harassing and slowing the Hessian advance.[37]

Rall took the initiative and, without waiting for orders from his superiors, rallied his men to charge at the rebels. At first the Americans stood their ground, using the technique that the Hessians had seen Glover use at Pell's Point, pausing behind stone walls to return fire. The king's troops were infuriated. To them there was something ungentlemanly in the rebels' technique of popping up from behind the stone walls and log fences that crisscrossed the American countryside.[38]

Then the mounted Hessian dragoons joined in the attack. They charged at Spencer's brigade. The horsemen terrified the American militiamen as they rode into the rebel lines, scattering soldiers and chasing down those who fell behind. The cavalrymen slashed at the frightened rebels with long swords and fired on them with pistols and muskets. The rebels on Chatterton Hill tried to aid the New Englanders with covering fire, but Spencer's men were panic stricken by the dragoons, and the American lines broke. However, unable to vault the high stone walls, the dragoons lost momentum, and the Americans were able to fall back and cross the Bronx River in an orderly manner, even keeping their gunpowder pouches dry as they slogged through the water. They soon joined their comrades on Chatterton Hill.[39]

Rall's regiment marched to the river, but the Hessians hesitated at the water's edge. The river was running high due to recent rains, and even at the ford the water was up to their chests. Rall urged them across, and the regiment crossed the river and marched to the base of Chatterton Hill opposite the American right flank. The prominence was a 180-foot steep upthrust of bedrock, the result of a prehistoric continental collision, in a way symbolic of the clash between the New and Old Worlds that was about to unfold on its steep slopes. Rall's men began a charge up the hill, but the Americans had set up an ambush behind a stone wall. They waited until the Hessians were within a few yards and poured a volley into them. Rall saw the futility in launching an unsupported attack and withdrew his men to the base of the hill where they wrung out their wet uniforms while awaiting further orders.[40]

A few hundred yards to Rall's right, the Knyphausen Regiment with Andreas Wiederhold arrived at the edge of the Bronx River. Wiederhold could see that the rebels atop Chatterton Hill were in a formidable position. The task of attacking the rebels' position was made even more daunting by the forty-foot-wide Bronx River flowing along the hill's base.

The day was hot, sunny, and dry with temperatures more like summer than the approaching winter. Banners and pennants hung limp during this breezeless day. The strains of martial music played by twenty regimental bands floated across the countryside and mixed with the loud singing of Hessian regiments. There was a splendid grandeur to the sight of the two armies spread across the hills and fields: the soldiers aligned in disciplined columns, the polished arms *and* superb equipment of the Royalists reflecting the midday sun. The Americans, plainly clothed and insufficiently armed, were a stark contrast to the British Army that was clothed in an array of colors: the bright red of the British uniforms, the forest green of the Hessian Jägers, and the blue of the Hessian infantrymen. All around them lay the lush green of the surrounding White Plains countryside, but the Hessian officers knew that the grandeur of the scene before them was an illusion; officers like Wiederhold were experienced enough to know that their regiments faced a difficult task. They understood that to attack Chatterton Hill would mean marching onto the muddy banks of the Bronx River, crossing this "rather deep" river, and then climbing up the side of the hill through thick woods, all while under fire from the rebels massed atop the hill.[41]

About seven hundred yards from Chatterton Hill, Howe's men hauled artillery pieces up Wolf Pit Hill, a small elevation named for the animal traps dug there in the valley's wilder days. Wolf Pit's elevation was only slightly less than Chatterton's, making that hill an excellent platform for bombarding the Americans on Chatterton. With the battle about to begin, the British realized that their gun crews were missing. Without an experienced, well-drilled team, the guns were useless. Improvising, Howe borrowed gun crews from the Royal Navy. Accustomed to naval warfare, the sailors weren't experienced in the finer points of hillside elevation and ballistics needed to effectively target the Americans. Many of their balls overshot Chatterton Hill, while others fell near their Hessian comrades.[42]

Luckily, General Heister had brought fifteen of his own guns and Hessian gun crews along, including howitzers, short-barreled cannons that fired hollow iron balls filled with gunpowder. If aimed properly, the iron balls exploded above the heads of the target, terrifying and maiming enemy soldiers. For an hour the Hessian guns bombarded the American positions, inflicting serious damage. The shells burst into jagged chunks of metal in the air above the rebels, bringing the militia to the brink of panic.[43]

From his position at the base of the hill, Johannes Reuber could see the armies readying for battle. He heard the first crash of artillery, a thunderous roar that drowned out the music of the regimental bands, and soon cannons from both sides were firing.[44]

The rebel entrenchments on the hill formed a strong defensive position, but the hill's geology in some ways worked against the defenders. The hill's rocky apex made it impossible to dig trenches. Rebel spades struck only impenetrable rock. Improvising as the British Army drew near, the rebels scampered through the dirt of farmer Michael Chatterton's recently harvested cornfields, scavenging empty stalks to hastily construct something that looked like breastworks but were actually piles of earth laid upon heaps of corn stalks that to the British and Hessian troops in the valley looked formidable.

Chatterton Hill was moderately steep—difficult to climb, but climbable; however, it was heavily wooded. Even worse for the king's troops, the top was cultivated and divided by stone walls. Here Washington had placed artillery under the command of twenty-one-year-old Alexander Hamilton. Although his battery contained only two guns, Hamilton shrewdly positioned them on a rocky ledge near the top of the hill, making it deadly to troops trying to ascend the hill.[45]

McDougall's troops on Chatterton Hill were some of the best soldiers in the Continental Army mixed with inexperienced militia. On the far right was Spencer's Brigade, soaking wet and sweaty from being chased by Rall through the Bronx River and up Chatterton. In the center were Colonel William Smallwood's Maryland Regiment and Colonel John Haslet's Delaware Regiment, the two regiments whose bravery had saved the army at the Battle of Brooklyn. The rugged Marylanders were supported by

Colonel Morris Graham's less experienced New York Militia. Haslet's Delaware Regiment was supported by Major John Brooks's less-experienced Massachusetts Militia. On the left were Colonel Rudolphus Ritzema's 3rd New York and Alexander McDougall's 1st New York. Lieutenant Colonel Samuel Webb's Connecticut Militia and Colonel Charles Webb's 19th Continental were on the extreme left.[46]

The order was given to attack, and the Hessian line charged the hill, but first the entire attacking force had to cross the Bronx River.[47]

The men of the Lossberg Regiment, with Jakob Piel, raced forward, running through the grass to the wet soil of the riverbank. Soldiers waded into the river, but it was deeper than anticipated, and the men hesitated. At that moment, British soldiers under Major General Alexander Leslie's command who were a few hundred yards to the right of the Lossberg Regiment began to charge uphill. Stuck at the river's edge, the Lossberg Regiment were now humiliated by the Redcoats taunting them, telling them to get out of their way. The British crossed the river and charged up the thickly wooded hill with bayonets fixed. At first they had momentum, but the Americans on top of the hill rained lethal volleys down on the British. Hamilton's artillery sent men running for cover. The British attack paused and finally halted with many casualties sustained.[48]

With Leslie's Brigade no longer a threat, the rebels turned their fire onto the Lossberg Regiment. Still standing at the river's edge but now under fire from the rebels atop Chatterton Hill, Piel and his comrades had no choice. They could stay where they were and be picked off by rebel fire or they could cross the river and charge up the hill.

The regiment surged into the river, carefully keeping their cartridge pouches above the water line as the Americans fired down at them. The regiment emerged from the water into a new terror: a tall field of grass that a gunpowder spark or musket ball had set on fire. Now the men held their cartridge pouches on their heads lest the flames ignite their own ammunition.[49]

For the first time since arriving in the New World, the soldiers of the Lossberg Regiment witnessed a substantial number of their comrades falling in battle. The situation grew increasingly dire, with dozens already dead or wounded. By nightfall, nearly a tenth of the regiment, approximately fifty men, would be casualties.[50]

Just a few months earlier, the king's representative, William Faucitt, had stood at the docks of Bremerlehe on the North Sea, looking down on the Lossberg Regiment. There were stories circulating about this regiment from

Rinteln. They were Hessian, but some saw them not as proper Hessian soldiers since Rinteln was a walled city in what had been the Earldom of Schaumberg, which only became part of Hessen-Kassel when the line of the Schaumberg family died out. The regiment contained many deserters from foreign countries and suffered the largest number of desertions during the march to the North Sea. There had also been doubts about the Rall Regiment. It was an open secret that Landgrave Frederick had taken the best soldiers from the Rall Regiment for his own guards. Now the outcome of the battle depended on the actions of these two maligned regiments.

Lieutenant Colonel Scheffer, who had taken command of the Lossberg Regiment when Colonel Heinrich von Heeringen died of dysentery that September, was leading the regiment for the first time in a major battle. Years later, the British commander Cornwallis would speak of how highly the Lossberg Regiment distinguished themselves at this moment. Jakob Piel and his comrades pushed up the heavily wooded hill, stomping through burning grass as smoke rose around them. Men burned their feet when their shoes caught fire. Unsure if a rebel ambush lay behind the next tree, they nevertheless pushed on, even though they had no Jäger woodsmen to scout ahead of them.

At first the hill seemed unmanned, but the calm was deceptive. The Americans were still there, but they had withdrawn up the hill to the apex of the prominence from where they now surprised the Hessians with heavy fire. The men of the Lossberg Regiment did not waver. They continued their uphill charge and crashed into the rebel lines. Soldiers like Piel could see that the rebels were not doing what the king's army had come to expect of the Americans. They were not running away from the sight of fearsome, brass-hatted, bayonet-wielding Hessians. The Americans were holding firm behind their fake cornstalk breastworks with loaded muskets, and the Hessian attack was in danger of collapsing.[51]

Fate once again brought the Rall, Knyphausen, and Lossberg Regiments together at a decisive moment.[52]

The Knyphausen Regiment, situated to the left of the Lossberg Regiment, was stuck at the base of the hill, the men having not yet crossed the Bronx River. The soldiers warily stepped into the water but quickly drew back as with each step the river grew deeper till it reached up to their waists. Andreas Wiederhold knew they were wasting precious time. The Lossberg Regiment, to their right, was in trouble. Wiederhold took matters into his own hands. He and Lieutenant Johann Briede strode confidently into the river, encouraging the regiment to follow them. Inspired by their officers, the men overcame their hesitancy and followed. But the far side of the riverbank posed a dangerous challenge. It was muddy, slippery, and steep. Their passage was partially obstructed by beaver dams and tree trunks that had been accumulating for many years. The Hessians, landlubbers terrified of water, struggled through the obstacles, climbed up the riverbank, and stumbled out of the river. The rebels then fired from the woods, but the soldiers of the Knyphausen Regiment, even as they scampered up the steep muddy riverbank, did not panic and were soon charging uphill.[53]

In the confusion, they somehow crossed behind the Lossberg Regiment, advanced with artillery from both armies firing overhead, and ended up with the Lossberg Regiment on their left. This unplanned positioning proved to be advantageous as the battle progressed. The Prince Carl and Dittfurth Hessian Regiments, who had both initially balked at wading into the Bronx River, were finally coaxed to cross, and with the English 2nd Brigade, they joined the uphill attack.

The Americans' right flank on Chatterton Hill was about a half-mile to the left of the attack being led by the Lossberg Regiment. It was here that Rall's attack had sputtered out earlier, but now the thirty-six-year veteran had time to take a look around and saw that the troops on the American right flank were vulnerable; they were isolated, with no troops protecting their rear. He realized that if he moved quickly, he could roll up the rebel army's right flank. Rall's decision proved the decisive moment of the battle.

Rall saw that the British and Hessians in the center of the attack, including the Knyphausen and Lossberg Regiments, were charging up the steepest part of Chatterton Hill. When Rall received orders to attack, rather than charging straight uphill, he led his men west (to the left) making a long loop at the base of the hill, which brought him to the gentler western slope, on the Americans' flank. Without hesitating, Rall ordered his infantrymen and his horsemen to attack.

Although he was only a private with less than a year of military experience, Johannes Reuber was savvy enough to understand what Rall was doing.

"Rall realized the circumstances," Reuber would later write. "Rall commanded the regiment to turn left and down the mountain . . . and up the mountain again . . . and we were in back of the Americans after a while."[54]

Rall was moving quickly against the exposed American flank. He sent the dragoons ahead, galloping speedily, hooves kicking up dirt. With kettle drums beating and trumpets blaring, they unnerved the rebel militia. Panic stricken by a sight so novel and unexpected, many members of the militia fled as the British cavalry furiously chased them over the hill.[55]

Rall then ordered his men up the western edge, hitting the rebels in the flank and rear. As Rall had anticipated, the western end of Chatterton Hill was not as steep as its center, making the charge uphill easier and less dangerous. Rall's men ran through burning hillside wheatfields set alight by errant musket sparks. The remaining Americans on top of the hill fired down on the Hessians. Reuber and his comrades pushed upward through choking smoke and musket balls. Keeping order, not allowing the chaos of the wheatfield fires, smoke, and bullets to disrupt their orderly advance, they crested the hill and formed up to fight on level ground. The Americans no longer had the advantage of firing down on their attackers. They were now trapped between Rall on the west and the main attack led by the Knyphausen and Lossberg Regiments on the east. The rebels fought in the style they were most comfortable with, crouching and shooting from behind farmer Chatterton's stone walls, but their position was untenable, and they began retreating along the hilltop, abandoning the right flank of the hill and stumbling toward the center.[56]

As had happened in the Battle of Brooklyn, the king's forces were slowed down by the hard-nosed Maryland and Delaware Regiments. These valiant soldiers once again stood firm, allowing the other Americans on the hill to make an orderly retreat. As the Hessians crested Chatterton Hill, they mistook the blue-coated Delaware men for blue-coated Hessian infantrymen, prompting hasty orders to cease fire. As the tenor of the war constantly swung between merciless and gentlemanly, the Delaware men held their fire, announced their correct identity, and then the shooting resumed. New York and Connecticut soldiers, including militiamen with little battlefield experience, participated in holding the line and keeping the retreat orderly. Webb's 19th Continentals were the last to leave Chatterton Hill, marching in good order onto the bridge, crossing the Bronx River, and joining Washington's men on Purdy and Hatfield Hills.[57]

Safely atop Chatterton Hill, Reuber waited for orders to pursue the retreating rebels, but no such orders came. He watched the sunset until it became so dark he could not see his hand in front of his face. Finally orders came, but they were not what he'd been expecting. Each man was ordered to start a fire and make noise so the enemy would think reinforcements were arriving. It did not make sense. They had driven the rebels off Chatterton Hill. Why did they need to intimidate them with an illusory group of reinforcements? Why not get some sleep and attack them again in the morning? Reuber was awakened throughout the night by horses whinnying; dragoons were riding back and forth for no good reason except to aid the ruse. Cannons creaked, adding to the subterfuge, as they were rolled in useless circles on the hilltop. A constant rattling of chains and hollering of make-believe orders added to the cacophony. The wounded of both sides lay on the hill, some crying and whimpering, awaiting transport back to New York. Baggage and tents would not reach the battlefield until the next day, so the men slept —or at least tried to sleep—with their muskets, on the ground, under the stars.[58]

The morning of October 29 brought no new orders from General Howe. The two armies were of equal strength, approximately thirteen thousand to fourteen thousand men each, and Howe saw that Washington's position on Purdy Hill and Hatfield Hill was strong, though not impregnable. While casualty figures from the campaigns of 1776 were notoriously unreliable, from this battle, British and Hessian casualties were likely 200 to 350 killed and wounded; incomplete American reports suggest that their casualties totaled about 100. The Lossberg Regiment sustained the most damage with about 50 casualties.[59]

Howe was inclined to wait two days until reinforcements arrived from New York. His de facto second in command was Henry Clinton, whose personality was an odd mixture of socially awkward and militarily aggressive. He reconnoitered the field and reported back that defeating the rebel army would require a coordinated attack with diversionary assaults and a rapid repositioning of cannon, but the day passed uneventfully as Howe was still debating his options as the sun set.

The next day, October 30, passed, again with no action on Howe's part. That night a heavy rain fell, what the locals called a "fall soaker," and the storm continued throughout the 31st, leaving the soldiers miserable, guarding trenches ankle deep in water, and sleeping on wet, muddy fields.[60]

The rain cleared on the morning of November 1. Washington understood that his position had vulnerabilities, particularly the flat fields that lay between Purdy and Hatfield Hills. Howe, his army strengthened by reinforcements from New York, and after days of contemplating sophisticated strategies, finally decided on a tactically simple attack against the vulnerable center of Washington's defenses. As the Hessians advanced across the field and up the slopes of the encampment, the Americans were strangely quiet, and the Hessians received no fire. Reaching the encampments, they found them empty. During the night, under the cover of the storm, Washington had quietly moved his army a few miles north, pivoted ninety degrees, and set up a new, more-secure defensive line along five hills that ran east to west.

The Americans had once again displayed their remarkable ability to calmly retreat and reorganize under duress, frustrating their enemy's efforts and ultimately snatching victory away from them.[61]

Just as he had done a few days before at Chatterton Hill, Howe probed the American left flank, but he sent his main attack against the American right flank. Once again, Howe turned to the Rall Regiment. Along with Leslie's Brigade and the distinguished Scottish regiment the 42nd Highlanders, Rall was ordered to launch an uphill assault, this time on Miller Hill. The hill was a 360-foot elevation at the western end of the American defenses; this represented the right flank of Washington's army.

The following morning, November 1, the Rall Brigade left their camp on Chatterton Hill, crossed the Bronx River on the Dobbs Ferry Road Bridge, and turned north, marching parallel to the Bronx River. Just as they had done at Chatterton, they looped around and attacked the western slope of the hill. This meant they were bunched together with Miller Hill in front of them and the river behind them.[62]

Reuber saw that once again, the Rall Regiment was being ordered to perform an uphill attack. As they picked their way through the marshes along the Bronx River, they looked up and saw the Americans standing behind newly built ramparts. To the Hessians, the Americans seemed like magicians when it came to engineering. They had thrown up breastworks in a matter of hours. Neighboring trees had been felled, their branches sharpened, and the trunks laid out horizontally with the sharpened branches pointing out toward the king's troops.

Trying to form an attack in the tight space between the river and the base of the hill, the Hessians could see a strange-looking defensive line. The Americans had added strength to their line in a most imaginative manner. There were large stalks in a nearby cornfield. The Americans had begun pulling these up and were taking up large lumps of earth held together by the tree roots in the process. The stalks were then placed one on top of another with the tops of the stalks pointing inward and the roots with their lumps of earth facing out. This pile of wet topsoil made a strange defensive line that would not stop the Hessians but would leave them exposed to gunfire as they pushed through the piles of soggy earth.[63]

But what the king's troops did not know was that John Glover had once again outfoxed them. He had positioned six cannons on Miller Hill that he kept judiciously out of sight while waiting for the Hessians, British, and Scots to form lines at the base of the hill.[64]

Once the enemy was in position, he unmasked his cannons, pulling them to the top of the hill. From their vantage point at the base of the hill, the Hessians saw the cannons pointed down at them. Glover opened fire on the exposed troops. Still at the base of the hill, Reuber saw that the American artillerymen were firing over the heads of their own troops. The cannonballs were crashing all around him; on impact some just threw up dirt, while others killed comrades. One cannonball decapitated a Hessian artilleryman, an event that likely inspired the region's most enduring Halloween story, Washington Irving's "The Legend of Sleepy Hollow." Atop Miller Hill, an American officer noted that Glover's cannonade "made them run and scamper in the greatest confusion I ever saw."[65]

The British attack never really got started. Glover's cannons wreaked havoc on the exposed troops. Reuber had never seen so many casualties. With more than 150 men already dead or wounded, Leslie called a retreat. Reuber heard Rall order the men to turn to the right and fall back. Still stuck between the river and the hill, they had to withdraw while under fire from rebels. They soon crossed the Bronx River and found refuge on Travis Hill, which was small and unoccupied. They hid there until sunset and then slunk back to camp.[66]

The Battle of White Plains was over. The fight had been far bloodier than either side expected, and there was no clear winner. Tactically, Howe had won the day, driving Washington from the field, but Howe had failed in his strategic objective of destroying the rebel army. With Washington's march encumbered by the ox-drawn wagon train moving at a rate of about two miles an hour, the American army traveled north, tattered but intact, to the safety of the Hudson Highlands.[67]

The Rall Brigade had shown bravery and tenacity at Chatterton Hill and Miller Hill. So Howe presented the brigade with a special commendation. Notably, the Lossberg Regiment, its reputation previously tainted for supposedly harboring too many deserters, was praised by General Cornwallis. Colonel Rall and the soldiers of his brigade were proving to be reliable, proficient fighters.[68]

CHAPTER 15

Fort Washington: The Hessians' High-Water Mark

November 16, 1776

HOWE COULD DISCERN that Washington was assuming a defensive posture and was not an immediate threat. Washington had withdrawn his army north to New Castle, where the terrain was rugged and unfamiliar to the British, a region that was easy to defend and a good place to regroup. But the campaign was exacting a toll on Washington. He had lost control of Staten Island, Long Island (including Brooklyn and Queens), lower Westchester, and the entire island of Manhattan except the garrison at Fort Washington. The Americans had hoped that in conjunction with Fort Lee on the New Jersey coast, Fort Washington would effectively block the Hudson River from the British fleet.

Washington's lack of experience in large-scale strategic decisions now began to show. Howe had several options to choose from, the most obvious being to attack Fort Washington, the last rebel-held territory in Manhattan. As he had done in New York, Washington foolishly tried to stymie all of Howe's options, dividing his forces in front of the numerically superior British.

He sent seven thousand men to the northeast to guard the roads leading to New England, three thousand men to the north to guard the fortifications in the Hudson Valley, five thousand inexperienced militia to Fort Lee to protect New Jersey, and three thousand men to Fort Washington in Manhattan. Then he personally took two thousand men west across the Hudson River to help in the defense of New Jersey.[1]

On the morning of November 4, after only a two-day rest in White Plains, Howe, who until now had moved cautiously, suddenly ordered his army to retire from the field. He marched his men seven miles due west from White Plains to Dobbs Ferry, where warships on the Hudson River could resupply the army. The reason for his urgency might have been that a rebel officer, William Demont, betrayed the Americans. On the night of November 2, Demont snuck out of Fort Washington and delivered to Howe plans of the fort's layout and a description of its garrison.[2]

The Knyphausen Regiment was ordered to guard the baggage and artillery train that followed the army to Dobbs Ferry. Wiederhold was uneasy, as the regiment was ordered to march in front of the slow-moving cannon and wagons, leaving those wagons in the rear unprotected. As night fell, other officers realized the precariousness of the situation as the regiment made its way along rutted roads through dense, almost-pitch-black woods. Wiederhold was relieved to receive orders telling him to halt and remain in place until all the vehicles had passed.

"We received those orders and remained standing until no more cannons or wagons passed," he recalled. "We asked the drivers if they were the last ones. No, they said, there are another seventeen wagons to the rear, which cannot proceed because some of them have broken down."

Two hundred rebel militia, ironically under the command of a prominent German-American tailor and tavern keeper from Reading, Colonel Harvey Haller, were following the wagon train, waiting to pounce. The Hessian officers on the scene realized the danger and quietly gathered alongside the road. Wiederhold emphatically stated he felt it "reasonable and proper" that they march back to the last of the broken wagons to give such aid as needed. The other officers agreed, and the Knyphausen Regiment marched through the pine-scented woods unsure if they were heading into an ambush. They waited in the darkness, listening for rebels, but all they heard were saws cutting, hammers banging, and wagon taskmasters whispering orders in German. Rebels could be heard in the underbrush creeping closer, but none of the militia had the courage to attack the regiment of Hessians.[3]

It was a moment of little significance in a bloody campaign, but it once again showed the British officers the mettle of the Hessians.

Dining comfortably in a Loyalist mansion in the village of Dobbs Ferry, on a bluff a few miles north of Manhattan, Howe and Clinton sat down to devise a plan to capture Fort Washington, the last piece of rebel-held territory in Manhattan. Below them, the sound of water-driven mills churned on the river. Capturing the fort would give the British complete control of Manhattan and New York City. Overcoming Howe's fear of direct assaults on fortified entrenchments, the generals plotted a three-pronged assault to capture their prize. By November 10, Howe had thirteen thousand men converging on Fort Washington and was once again forcing Washington to dance to his tune.[4]

Located on the highest point of Manhattan, Fort Washington appeared to one nineteenth-century historian as "precisely such a spot as in an ancient Greek city would have been chosen for its Acropolis." The fort overlooked the Hudson River and the important King's Bridge, which linked Manhattan Island to the mainland. Directly across the river, Fort Lee sat atop the New Jersey Palisades. Together, Washington had naively believed, the two forts would be an impenetrable barrier to the Royal Navy.[5]

Washington had linked the two forts with a *cheval-de-frise*, an underwater barricade with chains, partially sunk ships, and sunken wooden barriers that stretched across the river to keep the Hudson closed to the British fleet, but this plan had already failed. A month earlier, three British warships, the *Roebuck*, *Phoenix*, and *Tarter* had sailed up the Hudson, smashed through the underwater obstruction, and passed upriver undeterred by the batteries at Fort Washington and Fort Lee.[6]

Washington's inclination was to abandon Fort Washington. Since it and Fort Lee had failed to close off the Hudson to British warships, Fort Washington was now of little use. But Major General Nathanael Greene, a reliable and talented officer, pleaded to hold onto the fort. He argued that it was strong enough to withstand an attack and that the garrison could be ferried over the Hudson to Fort Lee if the situation deteriorated.[7]

Against his better judgment, Washington gave in to Greene. He left Colonel Robert Magaw with three thousand men to defend the fort, including reinforcements later sent over from Fort Lee.[8]

The results of this decision would be disastrous.

After resupplying in Dobbs Ferry, Howe continued his rapid pace, marching south to the King's Bridge. On November 10, the Rall Brigade made camp near this vital link between Manhattan and the mainland.[9] The brigade was assigned to General Knyphausen's corps of the 2nd Division. The next day, a contingent from the Lossberg Regiment entered Manhattan by crossing the King's Bridge, which was now in British hands. They marched to within three miles of Fort Washington and were one of several detachments that built fascines, bundles of sticks bound together and placed at their camp's perimeter to hinder any attempt by the rebels to covertly enter the camp.

A British general, Sir Martin Hunter, summed up the feeling of most of the soldiers on the eve of the attack on Fort Washington: "Fort Washington, a remarkably strong work both by nature and art. It was the only post the enemy had now left on York [Manhattan] Island; of course, it was absolutely necessary for us to be in possession of it."[10]

This was the first time any of Rall's men were in Manhattan. The sparsely populated island was a magnificent sight in 1776. They could not see New York City, which was about twelve miles to the south, but they could see the 280-foot precipice on which Fort Washington stood, and for a rare moment, some of the men began to have doubts.[11]

"Here was a hard nut to bite," was Wiederhold's reaction on seeing the pentagonal fort, with its huge earthwork walls sitting atop a steep hill of multilayered, coarse-grained, metamorphic rocks, rising in forest-clad precipices; the structure dominated the landscape and was protected by mile-long outer defensive works. The cliffs leading up to the fort were steep, rugged, and marred by large stones. It was an attacker's nightmare.[12]

Howe, surprisingly, was undisturbed by the geography and spoke glowingly of the still mostly pristine countryside of northern Manhattan. He was bewitched by the flow of the East River wandering through the valley below.

"This spot of Rocks, Woods & Fields is the finest & most romantic Landskip [landscape] that the Imagination could conceive," he gushed uncharacteristically. He told his aide that he preferred the region of Fort Washington to any spot he had seen in Italy.[13]

Putting aside his romantic image of the region, Howe mounted heavy guns in front of the Rall Brigade from where the artillery could fire on Fort Washington's outer works, but the attack was delayed until the 16th due to rain and Howe's desire to reconnoiter and gather intelligence on the fort. Howe, with thirteen thousand men, planned to envelop the fort. General Knyphausen's 2nd Division along with the Rall Brigade would attack southward from the King's Bridge region. Lord Hugh Percy would lead troops northward from New York City, attacking the fort from the south. Lord Cornwallis with General Edward Matthews would cross the Harlem River on transport ships and attack from the east. Lieutenant Colonel Thomas Sterling with the 42nd Highlanders would make a feint by landing on the shore of the Harlem River several miles southeast of the fort.[14]

Finally, after several rain delays, the men were awakened in the darkness on the morning of November 16. By five thirty, an hour before sunrise, the Rall Regiment with Johannes Reuber, the Lossberg Regiment with Jakob Piel, and the Knyphausen Regiment with Andreas Wiederhold joined the two columns marching to King's Bridge, which spanned Spuyten Duyvil Creek. The creek separated the Bronx mainland from Manhattan, connecting the Hudson River on Manhattan's western shore to the East River on Manhattan's eastern shore. Some men walked across the bridge into Manhattan; others entered boats for the quick ferriage across the creek. Once established on Manhattan, they marched into the woods and fields just outside Fort Washington.

The column on the right was commanded by Colonel Rall and contained the Lossberg, Rall, and Koehler Regiments. The column on the left was commanded by Major General Martin Schmidt and contained the Wutginau, Knyphausen, Huyn, and Buenau Regiments. While these men were scurrying into position, the Waldeck Regiment was deposited on the shore by the indefatigable British Navy flatboat men who had ferried the regiment up the Hudson River the night before. The regiment joined the right-side column.[15]

Sixty-year-old Lieutenant General Wilhelm von Knyphausen commanded the attack. As mentioned earlier, he was a grim, determined, often-silent nobleman with the ramrod-straight posture of a lifelong soldier. He was known for his peculiar habit of buttering his bread with his thumb. Jägers in their green uniforms and one hundred hand-picked soldiers, including Andreas Wiederhold, led the advance, spreading out in the darkness, probing, looking out for ambushes and unexpected obstacles. Wiederhold was surprised and impressed when General Knyphausen joined the frontline troops. As the sun rose, he could be seen clearing obstacles, tearing down fences with his hands, and motivating the troops to push on. But Wiederhold soon became anxious as rebel cannon and musket fire began to land near the general.[16]

Wiederhold led part of the advance guard up the hill toward the rebel fort. Artillery fire from Howe's army and from Royal Navy ships on the Hudson and East Rivers sent cannonballs screaming overhead, the shells coming from so many directions that the rebels would be unsure where the main attack was coming from. Wiederhold scrambled across the heavily wooded hillside, keeping his balance as he scurried over rocks and thick tree roots. His men followed without hesitation. If there was ever a time to question why they were fighting thousands of miles from home in someone else's war this was the moment. But there were no significant desertions, no shirking of duty or hesitancy to advance. If there were doubts in the soldiers' minds, they were overcome by years of training and decades of tradition that had instilled in them a sense of discipline and devotion to their principality.[17]

Abruptly, much to the consternation of the Hessian officers, Howe ordered a halt. The least important aspect of his battle plan, the feint by Colonel Sterling with the 42nd Highlanders, was behind schedule. The normally reliable Royal Navy had blundered by neglecting a minor detail: No one remembered that the Harlem River was a tidal river, and at the hour of the planned landing, the tide was low and the flatboats could not get to the shore. Furious, Knyphausen had to call back all the soldiers who had advanced up the hill. They would have to wait in line at the bottom of the hill for hours.[18]

Wiederhold was fuming. The element of surprise was lost and the momentum of the attack squandered. He was convinced that the delay would cause additional casualties. Finally, at 11:00 A.M., the signal was given to renew the attack, as the Wutginau, Huyn, and Buenau Regiments joined in with the Knyphausen Regiment.[19]

"Now we began the real attack," Wiederhold later wrote.

He led his men in the advance force back through the woods and up the hillside toward the fort. The rebels were firing down on the attackers. The Americans hid behind rocks and fallen trees. The hillside was "rutted up by entrenchments." Rebel artillery and muskets fired from behind large boulders pushed together to form redoubts. Wiederhold felt a sharp pain in his face and saw blood dripping down his front. The rebels had riflemen who could hit a target over two hundred yards away. They often targeted officers. Wiederhold's fingers probed some more, and he pulled his hand back with relief. It was only a flesh wound caused by a branch shot off a tree. The captain and lieutenant who outranked him were not as lucky. Both were shot dead by marksmen, and Wiederhold was now in charge of the advance force.[20]

Looking up, Wiederhold could see a nearly insurmountable precipice topped by formidable rebel earthworks. A quartermaster surveying the scene noted that Fort Washington was on such a steep summit that it was more like a cliff that was on all sides surrounded by thick forests and marshes. "Nature has contributed far more than skill to its fortification," he noted.[21]

At the foot of the heights was a massive abatis covering three acres and made of felled trees tied together with their ends sharpened to a lethal tip that pointed downhill. Looking beyond this defensive line was another barrier of felled trees, and another one above that. Adding to the danger of Wiederhold's position was a muddy swamp at the base of the heights.[22]

Under the constant fire of rebel muskets, Wiederhold was resigned to the dangers but not discouraged as he led his men to clear the obstacles. The remainder of the Knyphausen Regiment joined in. Rebel artillery fired shells into rocks and trees, showering the Hessians with splinters and fragments of stone. The men realized that some of the shells were coming from British ships on the Hudson River that were overshooting the rebel fortification.[23]

Ignoring the musket and cannon balls landing all around them, the Hessians removed the obstacles by hand, breaking through the abatis. The same men who a few weeks before had hesitated to cross the Bronx River at the base of Chatterton Hill now waded freely through the swampy morass. They pushed through bulrushes as tall as a man, the plants' little spikelets scratching at any exposed skin. Reaching dry land, they quickly formed up and charged uphill toward the rebels.[24]

Firing down at the Hessians were some of the best soldiers in the Continental Army, Colonel Moses Rawlings's Maryland and Virginia riflemen, veterans of frontier fighting and of the recent battles in Brooklyn and New York. They were tough, cocky marksmen with their technologically advanced Pennsylvania rifles. They fought from outside the fort, firing from behind rocks and trees then darting to other concealed spots to reload and fire again.[25]

Wiederhold could see the riflemen who were directing this deadly fire into the Hessian ranks. The first assault failed as well as the second. Undaunted, the Hessians pushed on, and Wiederhold led his men toward the top of the hill.

Johannes Reuber was with Rall's regiment to the right of the Knyphausen Regiment. His regiment surged forward up a steep, wood-covered, broken hill that rose from the Spuyten Duyvil Creek behind them and was known by the locals as Cock Hill. The Lossberg, Waldeck, and Koehler Regiments joined in the attack led by Colonel Rall. To Reuber, it seemed as if all "[hell] broke loose" when cannonballs and grapeshot fired from land and sea exploded on and near the fort. Ignoring the cannonading, he plunged forward with his comrades. The men of the Rall Regiment scrambled up the hillside, kicking loose rocks and stones, some of which tumbled down. Reuber watched helplessly as a nearby soldier plummeted to his death and another tumbled down, shot dead.[26]

The climb was steep, and Reuber had to grab onto dense evergreen shrubs. The hill was pockmarked by abandoned rebel entrenchments. Reuber could not stand fully erect, but he clawed his way up the hill. As he neared the top, trees and big rocks came tumbling down, pushed over the side by rebels. He wavered, and soon the whole attacking force started to waver, when suddenly Colonel Rall shrewdly ordered the drums to beat out and the trumpets to blow a Hessian marching tune.[27]

"Suddenly all that were still alive shouted, 'Hurrah,'" Reuber later recalled. Rall's farm boys charged to the top as, to their left, Wiederhold and the Knyphausen Regiment also crested the ridge. There transpired the extraordinary sight of rebels and Hessians running toward the fort, friend and foe mixed together, no one firing as each side tried to reach the fort's entrance before the other. Reuber and Wiederhold ran across the plain and took shelter in a ditch at the base of a mound next to the fort's earthen walls. Other soldiers from the Rall Regiment halted under the cover of large rocks that formed a natural rampart known locally as the Death Gap.[28]

From the safety of the ditch, Reuber heard the sound of officers frantically barking orders, the sounds of German and English intermingled in the mayhem, but the combatants were too close together and moving too quickly to stop, reload, and fire a musket.

The Americans were fleeing, most running into the fort, others dropping their weapons and surrendering. Two hours earlier, Percy's attack from the south had broken into the southern end of the rebel lines and Stirling's attack, which originally was to be nothing more than a feint from the East River, had broken through the rebels' eastern lines.

"The Light Infantry embarked in flat-bottomed boats at King's Bridge, and proceeded up the East River under a very heavy cannonade," General Martin Hunter wrote of the crossing of the East River, which was supposed to be a feint but turned into a ferocious firefight. "The Light Infantry landed under so very heavy a fire of cannon and musketry that the sailors quitted their oars and lay down in the bottom of the boats. In this situation we must have remained exposed to the enemy's fire had not the soldiers taken the oars and pulled us on shore."[29]

Rall had faced a spirited fight against his attack from the north, but with the Hessians now on the plateau outside the fort's walls, the Americans' resistance was crumbling.[30]

It was now evident that the Americans had miscalculated. Fort Washington appeared formidable with its large earthen walls on top of a steep hill, but defending its outer works required more men than Washington had assigned to the location. The rebel lines had been undermanned, and the soldiers, despite putting up a brave defense, finally succumbed under the relentless pressure from the king's troops. The inside of the fort was too small for the retreating American army. By 2:00 A.M., 2,800 Americans were crowded into a fort built for fewer than half that number, with British and Hessian troops pressing in from all sides and British artillery trained on the fort. A protracted bombardment would have meant the slaughter of everyone inside.[31]

General Knyphausen, usually a reserved, taciturn veteran, was moved by the courage and sacrifice of Rall's men who had been shot, hit with boulders, tumbled down hills, but never broke. Meeting with his staff behind a large stone barn on a hill north of the fort, Knyphausen directed Rall, whose men, Knyphausen announced, had earned the distinction to send forward a demand for surrender. Calling a company commander to him, Rall said, "Hohenstein, you speak English and French, take a drummer with you, tie a white cloth on a gun-barrel, go to the fort and call for a surrender."[32]

Captain George Hohenstein, with rebel gunshots still kicking up the dirt around him, frantically waved his white cloth as a young drummer accompanied him toward the American lines, the drummer anxiously beating his drumhead until their mission was finally understood and they were allowed to enter the earthworks. He allowed himself to be blindfolded and was escorted into the fort, where he promised the Americans that their men would receive better terms surrendering to Knyphausen than to the British.[33]

"The Hessians," Hohenstein promised, "make impossibilities possible." He gave his word that all rebel officers would retain their private property if the Americans would lay down their arms and free all prisoners, but the Hessian commanders would not allow the rebels to march out with the honors of war; there would be no flag waving and no regimental musicians playing. The Americans agreed. At 4:00 A.M., they hoisted a white flag of surrender over the fort and began the humiliation of walking the gauntlet between the Rall and Lossberg Regiments, the defeated Americans lined up on an open meadow owned by a local tobacco merchant, Blazius Moore.[34]

According to their diaries, Wiederhold watched the rebels lay their weapons at his feet while Reuber and Piel stood in their respective regimental line as the dejected prisoners filed past them without incident. But other witnesses reported a less peaceful scene. As the men filed out, some Hessians stepped forward to violently rob the prisoners of their clothing and belongings until some British officers took the matter in hand and diverted the defenseless prisoners in another direction.[35]

"Despite the strictest orders," wrote Chaplain Philipp Waldeck, "the prisoners received a number of blows. Especially comical, I watched the treatment handed out by a Hessian grenadier. . . . The grenadier grabbed [a rebel] on the ears with both hands. . . . Another grenadier tied him up with a scarf. Two others hit him on the sides of his head. A third gave him a kick in the rump, so that he flew through three ranks."[36]

General Knyphausen looked on with disdain when the Hessian infantrymen robbed the prisoners, but he remained silent and did not intervene. Some of his men were provoked by a skirmish from the week before in which the Americans killed thirteen Hessian soldiers and proceeded to strip them of their uniforms, leaving the corpses naked.[37]

Captain Alexander Graydon of the 3rd Pennsylvania Battalion found the surrender process terrifying. He wrote that after surrendering, a British officer rode up screaming, "What! Taking prisoners! Kill them! Kill every man of them!" After Graydon talked his way out of this precarious situation, a Hessian threatened him. "He was as much of a brute as anyone I have ever seen," wrote Graydon. "[H]alf unsheathing his sword . . . he grinned out in broken English, 'Why you rebel, you damn rebel!" Other officers threatened to hang Graydon.[38]

The resistance and marksmanship of the American riflemen, with their deadly, long-range guns, had angered many Hessians. They found the American way of fighting to be ungentlemanly and dishonorable: hiding behind trees, stone walls, and boulders, shooting at the Hessians and then running away as soon as they had fired. This had been the bloodiest battle of the war for the Hessians, with 330 men killed or wounded. Many of the dead soldiers were buried where they fell or in a large trench near the fort. A butchery of prisoners might have ensued if some nearby British officers had not interceded. Some Hessians were brandishing their bayonets when the British stepped in.[39]

Praise for Knyphausen's troops, particularly the Rall Regiment, poured in. Ambrose Serle, private secretary to General Howe, declared: "The Honor of the Day is imputed to Genl Knyphausen. The Hessians behaved with incomparable Steadiness and Spirit." Sir George Osborn, an inspector of foreign troops who reported on the condition of the Hessians to Parliament, felt that the Hessians rendered a service to the king that day that no other army could match. One British officer said their fight on the hillside was comparable to Hannibal crossing the Alps. In Knyphausen's honor, the fort was renamed for him. With no mention of any bullying, robbing, or beating of any American prisoners, Wiederhold wrote, "This day brought us Hessians glory which could be shared by every good man of honor."[40]

Unbeknownst to Wiederhold and his comrades, the day would be remembered as the high-water mark of the Rall Brigade in America. Although none of them could see it through the glow of victories and praises, a darker fate was on the horizon.

PART IV

New Jersey

CHAPTER 16

The Palisades: Scaling the Unscalable

As the victorious Hessians settled into the region near the newly renamed Fort Knyphausen, the former Fort Washington, a sense of unease hung over the British high command. The approach of winter, and with it the close of the campaigning season, loomed mere weeks away. The dropping temperatures gave cause for concern among the British. The waterways encircling New York City were prone to icing over, posing a threat of immobilizing the royal fleet. The charred ruins of half of New York City offered scant shelter for the troops, and both armies had depleted the region's food supply.

But as General Howe stood in Manhattan, his gaze fixed east across the Hudson River to New Jersey, he saw opportunity. Fort Lee stood vulnerable, and the unspoiled farmlands and towns of New Jersey beckoned, promising sustenance and shelter for his army through the winter months ahead.

Promptly, and with uncharacteristic decisiveness, Howe formulated a strategy to seize Fort Lee and occupy the northern regions of New Jersey. Echoing his previous assault on Fort Washington, he issued immediate orders for an attack. A formidable force of five thousand men, under the command of General Charles Lord Cornwallis, and supported by the Royal Navy, would cross the Hudson and assault Fort Lee. With Fort Lee destroyed and northern New Jersey secured as a source for food and shelter during the winter, Howe aimed to dispatch forces to seize Newport, Rhode Island's ice-free deep-water port where the fleet would be free of the perils of the soon-to-be-frozen waterways of New York.[1]

The Rall Brigade received high praise for the fighting spirit displayed throughout the campaign, particularly the assault on Fort Washington. In a letter to Lord Germain, secretary of state for the colonies, General Howe praised the Hessian troops under the command of Lieutenant Generals Heister and Knyphausen, who he noted had "exhibited every good disposition to promote his Majesty's interests, and justly merit my acknowledgment of their services."[2]

Yet for reasons that are unclear, the Rall Brigade was excluded from the attack on Fort Lee. It may be that Howe's staff felt they needed a respite. The soldiers seized the opportunity for a bit of levity.

They raced to the shoreline and plunged into the Hudson River's frigid waters. Moments later, wet, naked soldiers stood shivering on the riverbanks, having underestimated the water's biting chill. Others whiled away the time hunting in the nearby woods. "I shot a large hare . . . and some squirrels," one soldier confided in his diary, his disappointment palpable as he noted that the partridges proved "too quick" to be caught.[3]

On the night of November 19, while the Rall Regiment slept, sailors from the Royal Navy ferried General Cornwallis's five thousand-strong invasion force across the Hudson River in a fleet of landing barges and bateaux. As they journeyed, standing in the transports dressed in full uniform, they were drenched by a relentless downpour. A thick, dense fog enveloped the convoy, the vessels silently gliding through the mist until they reached the base of the towering New Jersey Palisades.

Atop a five-hundred-foot, nearly vertical cliff that rose from the water's edge stood Fort Lee.

With the wonderful contempt of a sailor for a soldier, Captain Andrew Snape Hamond, stationed aboard the HMS *Roebuck* on the Hudson River, wrote, "When his Lordship [Cornwallis] came to see the place, the path [up the side of the cliff] seemed so narrow & difficult of access, that he could not be persuaded it was the right spot, and went alongshore 2 or 3 Miles further to look for a better [landing area]."[4]

Cornwallis's skepticism was understandable. One American writer recounted the Palisades as rocky heights springing up "like everlasting walls, reaching from the waves into the heavens." Another writer described the region as "Sheer rock cliffs, often three hundred or more feet in height, they make a western wall for the majestic Hudson [River]."[5]

Finally, Cornwallis, resigned to his fate, permitted the men to disembark at the original landing site.

As they ascended, the troops grasped at trees and rocks, climbing single file up a fracture in the cliffs that formed a steep, slippery trail a mere four feet wide. Those leading the climb inadvertently kicked loose stones and dirt, which cascaded down onto the men behind them, but the troops persevered. Artillerymen and sailors hoisted thousands of pounds of cannons and ammunition up a narrow, rocky road to reach the summit of the precipice.[6]

Those troops who remained in Manhattan, including the Rall Regiment, gazed across the river in awe at the site where Cornwallis's troops had disembarked.

"The opposite shore, where these troops landed, were surrounded with cliffs of a frightful height," one Hessian officer reported. "[S]everal hundred, courageous men [rebels] posted on these heights could have held off our entire corps, and could have killed the greatest part."[7]

When word reached Fort Lee that the British had landed only a few miles away, panic gripped the American garrison. Within minutes, most of the men abandoned their posts and began a hasty march south, away from the looming threat of Cornwallis's army. In their frenzied retreat, they left behind valuable equipment, many carrying only blankets and rifles. Incredibly, some stopped to eat a hasty breakfast, while others plundered the liquor supply, became inebriated, and were captured by the British.[8]

Washington hastened to the fort without delay. He managed to rally most of the men but now faced a critical decision. He could venture west to the Watchung Mountains, where the hilly terrain would offer a strategic advantage against a British pursuit. From there he could summon the portions of his army he had scattered across northern New Jersey and New York. However, seeking refuge in the mountains would effectively relinquish New Jersey to the British. The alternative was to press on south to Philadelphia, traversing the populous central region of the state.[9]

Washington's plan posed a formidable challenge: to elude the British, his army would be compelled to cross four rivers—the Hackensack at the village of Hackensack, the Passaic at Acquackanonk Landing, the Raritan at Brunswick, and last, the Delaware at Trenton. He knew that each crossing, with the British in pursuit, would be fraught with peril.[10]

With no time for planning, he relied on years of experience and a finely honed instinct at this critical juncture: He resolved to march his army the hundred miles to Philadelphia, with the hope of gathering regiments and militia along the journey.

The sick and wounded would be dispatched across the Watchung Mountains to Morristown, where they could recuperate in relative safety. His decision made, he promptly commenced the march, leading the men away from the vulnerable fort, west toward New Bridge over the Hackensack River.[11]

As Washington's army hastily retreated southwest, Cornwallis's troops ascended the hill to Fort Lee. On reaching the summit, the king's troops were taken aback by the sight that greeted them. The fort was far less formidable than they had been led to believe. Its earthen walls stood a mere six feet high, offering little in the way of protection. The rifle pits, too, were unimpressive—shallow holes in the ground, devoid of any cover. The American author and soldier Thomas Paine dismissed Fort Lee as nothing more than a "field fort," its sole purpose to temporarily delay an advancing enemy.

Officers broke open the fort's storehouses and found them filled with corn. The panicky rebels had abandoned supplies sufficient to equip an army: One thousand barrels of flour, 12 precious cannons and 7 mortars, 8,000 cannon shot, 4,000 cannon shells, 2,800 muskets, and a staggering 400,000 cartridges. Bereft of their cannons and ammunition, the rebel army appeared to most of the British as no more than an incensed mob.[12]

As Cornwallis assembled his troops on the Palisades and marched them toward Fort Lee, a revealing incident occurred, exemplifying the strategic challenges faced by the British. A company of Hessian Jägers, led by sixteen-year veteran Captain Johann Ewald, was gathering intelligence. While conversing with local farmers, Ewald spotted "a great glitter of bayonets and a cloud of dust." Recognizing that this was the garrison fleeing Fort Lee, he ordered his Jägers to press forward and engage the American stragglers. Ewald dispatched a request for reinforcements to Cornwallis. Much to Ewald's dismay, instead of reinforcements, Cornwallis surprisingly sent orders for Ewald's immediate withdrawal.

"Let them go, my dear Ewald, and stay here," Cornwallis directed. "We do not want to lose any man. One Jäger is worth more than ten rebels."

This was a revelation for Ewald. "Now I perceived what was afoot. We wanted to spare the King's subjects and hoped to terminate the war amicably."[13]

The experience of American artilleryman Joseph White confirmed Ewald's suspicion. Though officers warned White he must "fight his way through, or be prisoners," British soldiers allowed his group to pass unharmed when fleeing Fort Lee.[14]

These incidents highlight the quandary General Howe faced: His excursion into New Jersey had been *too* successful, with the Americans abandoning Fort Lee without putting up a fight. Cornwallis now faced no significant rebel forces to stop him from liberating most of New Jersey. Howe had not anticipated such a massive collapse of the American army, and he lacked a plan for pursuing the retreating rebel forces. His rapid, overwhelming success was drawing him farther into New Jersey than he had intended. The enemy he had beaten in Brooklyn had over ten thousand men. The rebel forces in New Jersey under Washington's direct command now amounted to no more than four thousand soldiers. Howe was more concerned about securing the ice-free port in Rhode Island for the British fleet than he was about destroying the remnants of the rebel army. With winter approaching, he doubted there would be sufficient time to both destroy Washington's army and sail for Rhode Island. He ordered the fleet to sail to Rhode Island "with the first fair wind."[15]

As twilight descended on the evening of November 20, the Rall Brigade remained peacefully encamped in Manhattan by Fort Knyphausen (formerly Fort Washington). They were undoubtedly tired by three months of campaigning, a fact reflected in the absence of entries in any of the surviving diaries for that day. The soldiers likely spent the evening huddled around the warmth of their campfires, seeking respite from the cold and the rain while reflecting on the remarkable events of the past few months.

While the Rall Brigade rested, across the river in New Jersey the mud-splattered American army fleeing south from Fort Lee endured what one soldier described as "a very wetting rain." In the darkness, the American soldiers crossed the Hackensack River, making their way into the village over the wooden structure known locally as the New Bridge. The twelve-year-old bridge was constructed of timber posts driven into the riverbed and covered by planks. Under the weight of several thousand bedraggled rebels, the aging bridge likely creaked and swayed, adding to the soldiers' discomfort and sense of urgency as they sought to put distance between themselves and their British pursuers.[16]

"The night was dark, cold, and rainy," recalled a Hackensack resident. "They [the rebels] marched two abreast, looked ragged, some without a shoe to their feet, and most of them wrapped in their blankets."[17]

Soldiers shivered in the cold rain, but their tents were back at Fort Lee. They were forced to spend the night on the village green, huddled beneath their blankets for whatever meager warmth they could find. Many of these men had joined the army in July and August, and their summer clothing, reduced to rags by the hardships of campaigning, offered little comfort in the face of the bitter weather.[18]

Washington's army found itself in a dire situation. The majority of its supplies had been abandoned during the retreat, and the ranks were thinning as men deserted or prepared to leave when their one-year tour of duty ended in just a few weeks. To make matters worse, the British Army in New Jersey, bolstered by reinforcements, would soon outnumber Washington's forces by nearly five to one.

Cornwallis, his troops approaching Hackensack, maintained a cautious distance, menaced the retreating American army, but refrained from engaging it in battle. Nestled on the fertile plains of New Jersey, the village of Hackensack lay on flat, open country. Stretched alongside the river and its neighboring surrounding salt marshes, the settlement boasted large prosperous farms where plump Dutch horses grazed in fields fragrant with the sweet aroma of clover. Bountiful apple orchards dotted the landscape, and a large, sturdy grist mill, its wheel creaking rhythmically, slowly ground the village's grain. It was a region of fertile soil heavily laden with crops and tidewater streams described as "the very garden spot of America." Cognizant of the region's Loyalist sympathies and aware of how easily his soldiers could succumb to the temptations of such a bountiful region, Cornwallis issued strict orders forbidding his troops from plundering the local farms or homes. However, his directives were largely ignored, and so began a pattern of looting and abuse that would soon, much to the general's chagrin, spread throughout nearly all of New Jersey.[19]

The plundering was so rampant General Howe wrote back to England asking for more guards (military police) to restrain the men. "I beg . . . to request an additional number of officers to the Guards," Howe wrote to Lord Germain, "although the men behave with great spirit, yet the temptations of plunder are so great that it is not in the power of a few officers to keep the men under restraint."[20]

After just one night in Hackensack, a Hessian officer wrote in his diary: "During the night all the plantations in the vicinity were plundered. . . . Whatever the soldiers found in the houses was declared booty."[21]

According to British witnesses, the pilfering was not limited to the king's troops. Runaway slaves, Irish servants, and even an Indigenous man named Peacock joined in the rampant looting. The local population quickly learned that the marauding soldiers' allegiances were not to king or colony but to opportunity, as they indiscriminately targeted Loyalist and rebel sympathizers. Loyalists who had welcomed the king's troops as liberators were shocked to be plundered. Families, in desperation, knelt together in the fields burying their money and jewels. The village's women were sent away on horseback with bags of flour and butter to sustain them in their uncertain fate.[22]

Although the Hessians did not yet perceive it, the predatory actions of some of their comrades was reinforcing the already dubious reputation of the Hessians from liberators into invaders in the eyes of many Loyalists. Despite their largely disciplined conduct, the stain of indiscriminate plundering tarnished the reputation of the entire contingent, sowing seeds of distrust and resentment that would bear bitter fruit in the months to come.[23]

That night, November 20, the British encamped on the eastern bank of the Hackensack River, their presence a stark contrast to the beleaguered rebels huddled on the other side. The flames of hundreds of campfires reflected off the water's surface, illuminating the gloomy night as the men huddled for warmth around the burning timbers. Even though the New Bridge spanning the Hackensack River was intact, and the river was only one hundred to two hundred feet wide and easily fordable, the British made no threatening moves until the next day.

When Cornwallis finally launched his assault on the morning of November 21, his troops were surprised by the fierce resistance of the Americans. Washington's tenacious rear guard, positioned in houses on both sides of New Bridge, unleashed a barrage of fire on the advancing British troops. For several hours, the Americans held their ground. They were not behaving like a defeated army. A Hessian officer later recalled that the rebels "defended themselves very well."

Unfortunately for the king's troops, the British high command failed to grasp the enemy's resolve, continuing to underestimate the determination and fighting spirit of the Americans. This hubris would eventually lead to a series of British and Hessian miscalculations, resulting in disasters that would significantly impact the course of the war.

CHAPTER 17

New Jersey: Conquered but Still Defiant

By the time Cornwallis's advance guard finally managed to cross the Hackensack River on November 22, Washington's army had abandoned the village and was several miles away. The Americans, undeterred by the inclement weather, were steadily retreating southwest toward their next obstacle: the Passaic River and the hamlet of Acquackanonk Landing (the modern-day city of Passaic).

The region's topography presented the British with an exceptional opportunity to destroy Washington's forces. The rebel army was east of the Hackensack River. To the west of Washington was the Passaic River. To the south, the two rivers converged, forming treacherous salt marshes that led into Newark Bay. Cornwallis's troops loomed menacingly to the north. In essence, Washington's army was trapped on a peninsula, and their fate hinged on their ability to traverse the Passaic River.

Washington, a former surveyor, was undoubtedly aware of the precariousness of their situation. Until his forces successfully crossed the Passaic, they remained ensnared on the peninsula, and the likelihood of their army being cornered and annihilated by the British was alarmingly high.[1]

That same day, Howe crossed over to Fort Lee from Manhattan and joined Cornwallis at Fort Lee. The abandoned fort lay in disarray, bearing witness to the rebels' frenzied retreat. The Union Jack flew overhead. British soldiers lazily dipped their canteens in a fresh-water well that the Americans had been kind enough to dig. Howe surveyed the scene, noting the evidence of the rebels' panic. As they walked through the fort, they passed rows of empty stone huts, each equipped with fireplaces and wooden doors. Cornwallis inspected the structures while his officers quipped about how the rebels had thoughtfully provided them with winter quarters. There was even a slaughterhouse. The pathways between the tents were marked by pieces of tree bark affixed to posts, bearing the names of New York's more prominent streets chalked on them, such as "Broadway" and "Pearl Street."[2]

Howe, moved by his troops' accomplishment, penned a letter to Lord Germain describing how the rebels had "escaped in the utmost confusion, leaving all their artillery and a large quantity of stores and provisions, their tents standing, and kettle upon the fire." With a touch of smugness and humor, he added, "His Lordship [Cornwallis] encamped that night near the fort, making use of the enemy's tents." Despite the opportunities that lay before Howe in New Jersey, his mind was elsewhere. Rather than staying the night, he chose to return to New York City for a 10:00 P.M. dinner engagement.[3]

Cornwallis and many of his officers, witnessing the disarray of the abandoned fort and the haste of the rebels' retreat, now believed that Washington's army was so demoralized it would disintegrate if pursued further.

"This is now the time to push these rascals," Lieutenant Frederick Mackenzie of Howe's staff wrote in his diary, "and if we do, and not give them time to recover themselves, we may depend upon it they will never make head again."[4]

Samuel Webb of Washington's staff lamented: "I can only say that no lads ever shew greater activity in retreating than we have since we left You. Our Soldiers are the best fellows in the World at this Business."[5]

General Clinton proposed that the troops assigned to the Rhode Island expedition be reassigned to a landing in New Jersey to intercept the rebels fleeing from Cornwallis:

> "The rebel army being greatly diminished by losses in battle and desertion, I proposed that my detachment, being at that very time embarked and ready for any move, should be thrown on the shore in the Jerseys either at Elizabethtown or Amboy for the purpose of cooperating with Lord Cornwallis. . . . Failing [to convince General Howe] . . . I finally proposed to Lord Howe to take me with him up the Delaware and place me at Philadelphia."[6]

Clinton did not know that Howe had long ago decided, writing Lord Germain in August, that any movement into New Jersey beyond Fort Lee would be solely to capture winter quarters and settle down until spring and not to destroy Washington's army or capture Philadelphia. And nothing that had happened since then seemed to change his intentions.[7]

Standing amid the wreckage of what had once been Fort Lee, Howe gazed out over the towering cliffs of the Palisades to the British-controlled Hudson River and across to the shoreline of Manhattan, now firmly in British hands. Despite the magnificent view, Howe's perspective remained limited. Rather than being energized by the opportunity to destroy Washington's battered army, he remained focused on securing winter quarters, obtaining forage, and capturing an ice-free port in Rhode Island. Howe preferred to wait until the passing of the upcoming winter season before setting out to attack Philadelphia and deliver a decisive blow to Washington's forces. In contrast, Howe's officers were urging him to attack Washington's army while it was vulnerable. Torn between their advice and his own inclinations, Howe began to implement a series of compromises that would ultimately alter the course of the war with consequences that would reverberate across the Atlantic Ocean, angering and humiliating Landgrave Frederick in Hessen-Kassel.[8]

The king's forces were successfully driving Washington out of New Jersey with minimal casualties on their side. However, at this critical juncture, Howe's indecisiveness muddled the situation. He agreed to allow Cornwallis to advance on Washington's army but with certain restrictions. Cornwallis could proceed only as far as the village of Brunswick, a march of thirty miles south, and he was required to await reinforcements from New York before doing so. Howe encouraged Cornwallis to shadow Washington, following him cautiously from a distance but not engage him in battle. Unlike some of his more optimistic officers, Howe was content with chasing Washington out of New Jersey and waiting for the winter to pass before launching a full-scale attack.[9]

Howe was trying to use the victory at Fort Lee as the springboard for fulfilling all his goals: secure winter shelter and forage for his troops, capture Rhode Island, and destroy Washington's army.

Washington persisted in his retreat. On November 21, having successfully delayed Cornwallis's vanguard from entering Hackensack, he withdrew his forces from the village. He marched the main body of his army southwest across the Passaic River to the village of Acquackanonk Landing. Having successfully crossed the Passaic, his army was no longer trapped on a peninsula with Cornwallis.[10]

Cornwallis could do nothing as Washington slipped farther away, since Howe's orders compelled him to remain in Hackensack until reinforcements arrived.

As dawn broke on the next day, November 22, Washington's forces abandoned their position in Acquackanonk Landing. The weather took a turn for the worse, and a cold, persistent rain began to fall, transforming the once-solid farm roads into a quagmire. Fearing that Cornwallis was closing in, Washington ordered the destruction of the bridge spanning the Passaic River. Drenched by the heavy downpour, Washington's rear guard set to work with axe and saw, hurling timbers into the river and sawing away the upright piles. They set fire to the remaining structure to ensure its complete destruction.[11]

As the rear guard worked to delay Cornwallis, Washington's advance guard reached the next town on its route, Newark. The men staggered in soaked to the skin, muddy, and exhausted. The following day, November 23, the bulk of his army entered Newark.

On November 25, two days after Washington's army entered Newark, Cornwallis finally received the reinforcements he had been waiting for. The majority of his men, however, were still two rivers behind Washington, stationed at Fort Lee and in the Hackensack area. On the 26th, Cornwallis led his reinforced corps out of Hackensack and captured Acquackanonk Landing. Surprisingly, despite the Continental Army being a mere nine miles away in Newark, Cornwallis declared a day of rest for most of his men. The British, wrote Thomas Paine, "seemed extremely desirous that we should leave town without their being put to the trouble of fighting for it." It wasn't until November 28, two days later, that Cornwallis decided to march on Newark. The British anticipated that Washington would defend the town, but when Cornwallis's advance guard arrived at one in the afternoon, they found it deserted.[12]

While Cornwallis advanced unopposed into Newark, the Rall Brigade, which had languished in inactivity near Fort Knyphausen for nine days, finally received orders to redeploy closer to the Hudson River in anticipation of joining Cornwallis's invasion of New Jersey. After three more days of inaction, the brigade was ferried across the Hudson River to Fort Lee where, according to Reuber, the men bivouacked "under the open sky, without tents."[13]

The next morning, the Rall Brigade marched into Hackensack. Washington had abandoned it more than a week prior, leaving it relatively unscathed. The village consisted of about 160 homes primarily owned by descendants of Dutch and French settlers who had arrived in the region in the seventeenth century. These early settlers had initially forged friendships and settled among the tepees and wigwams of a Native American village situated along the banks of the Hackensack River. However, the devastating impact of European diseases, particularly smallpox, combined with the relentless influx of settlers ultimately displaced the native population.[14]

Wiederhold was impressed with Hackensack, finding the townsfolk to be well-educated "Hollanders." The village green presented a charming tableau of Jersey Dutch prosperity bordered by a sandstone Dutch church with a large, brass, rooster-shaped weather vane atop its steeple. Adjacent to the church stood a modest stone courthouse and a local inn, while across the green, a grand mansion constructed from dressed stone with walls three-feet thick added to the village's air of permanence and stability. At the far end of the green, a "very handsome" pole fence completed the picturesque scene. The people spoke Dutch, wore traditional Dutch attire, bestowed Dutch names on their children, and taught them the traditional Dutch skills of barreling cider and farm work, all with the diligent perseverance characteristic of the Old World.[15]

But by the afternoon, Hackensack had lost its air of innocence, as the village green was teeming with resting Hessian troops. They anticipated being greeted as liberators by the local Tories, but the region had been recently plundered by troops from Cornwallis's initial invasion force. To the

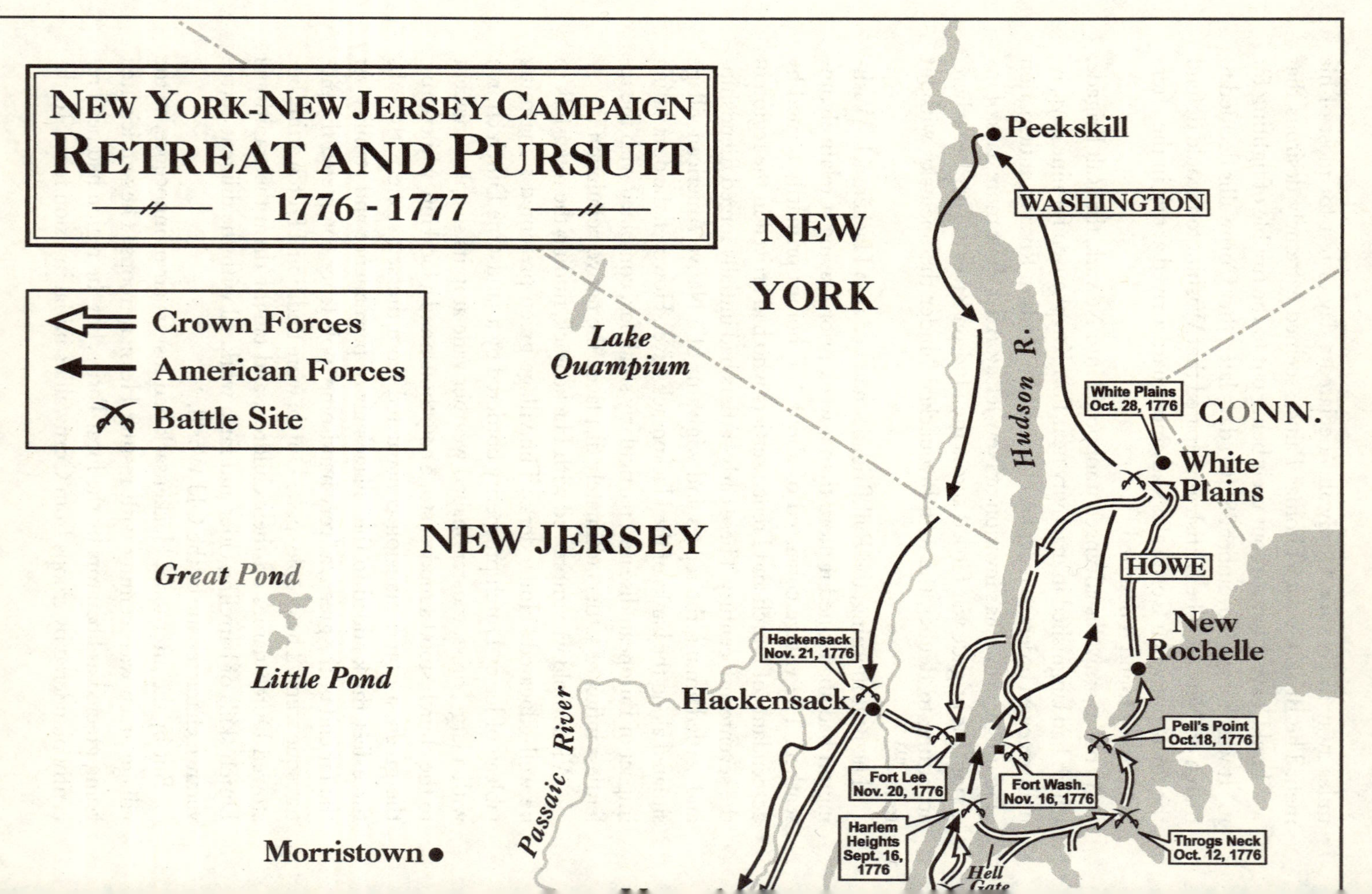
NEW YORK-NEW JERSEY CAMPAIGN
RETREAT AND PURSUIT
1776 - 1777
Crown Forces
American Forces
Battle Site
NEW YORK
NEW JERSEY
CONN.
Peekskill
WASHINGTON
Hudson R.
White Plains
White Plains Oct. 28, 1776
HOWE
New Rochelle
Lake Quampium
Great Pond
Little Pond
Hackensack
Hackensack Nov. 21, 1776
Passaic River
Fort Lee Nov. 20, 1776
Fort Wash. Nov. 16, 1776
Pell's Point Oct.18, 1776
Harlem Heights Sept. 16, 1776
Throgs Neck Oct. 12, 1776
Hell Gate
Morristown

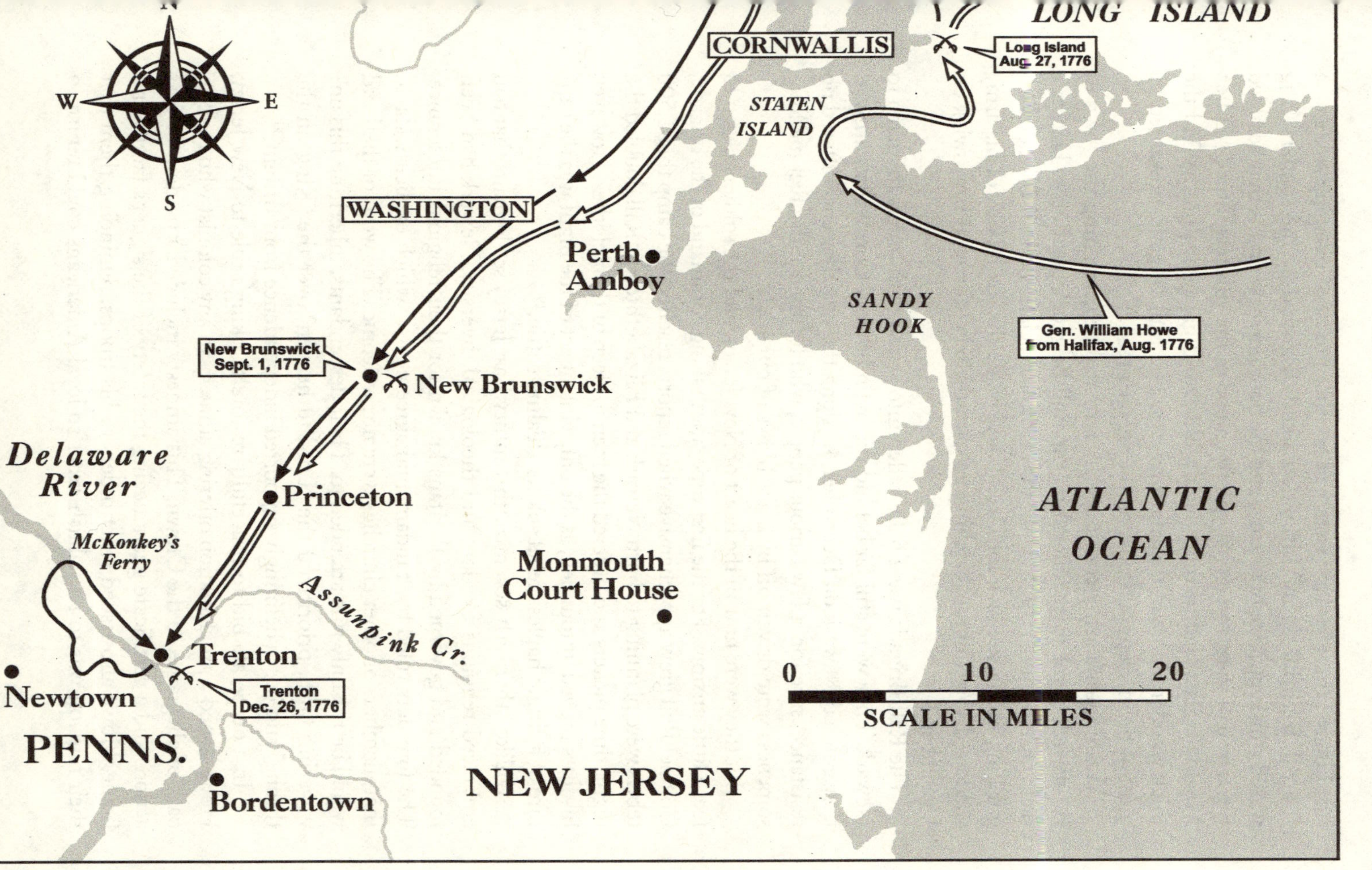
LONG ISLAND
CORNWALLIS
Long Island Aug. 27, 1776
STATEN ISLAND
WASHINGTON
Perth Amboy
SANDY HOOK
Gen. William Howe from Halifax, Aug. 1776
New Brunswick Sept. 1, 1776
New Brunswick
Delaware River
Princeton
ATLANTIC OCEAN
McKonkey's Ferry
Monmouth Court House
Assunpink Cr.
Trenton
Trenton Dec. 26, 1776
Newtown
0
10
20
SCALE IN MILES
PENNS.
NEW JERSEY
Bordentown
N
W
E
S

inhabitants, the Hessians were just another group of pillaging soldiers, a "horrid, frightful sight." Intimidated and disgusted by the soldiers' long waxed whiskers, large brass caps, and the booming bass drums that heralded the arrival of these foreign troops, the mood of the villagers turned somber. Most villagers, clad in their quaint, old-world garments, hid behind the thick wooden doors of their farmhouses. The Rall Brigade, unwanted by most of them, slept outdoors on the village green.[16]

Washington's army continued its retreat south, reaching the town of Brunswick, some forty miles from the Rall Brigade's position in Hackensack, on November 29. Inexplicably, Cornwallis left the Rall Brigade languishing in Hackensack for several days while the main body of his army shadowed Washington, catching up with the rebel forces at Brunswick on December 1.[17]

The Rall Brigade was finally called into action with orders to march to Newark. They were still far behind the main body of Cornwallis's army as they entered Newark on December 4. Along the way they encountered no resistance, save for "a few curious people, who for their indiscreet meddlesomeness were driven off by a few blows of our sticks."[18]

But they were now in the heart of New Jersey, and the soldiers began to feel a little anxious. For the first time since taking command of the brigade, Colonel Rall grew apprehensive when reports reached the camp that 1,500 rebels were planning to burn Newark and Elizabethtown. Rall doubled the night-time pickets and ordered the men to sleep in their clothes. However, his fears proved unfounded, as the only violent act of the night was the capture of a single hapless rebel soldier stealing cattle.[19]

Unlike other early seventeenth-century East Jersey settlements that had embraced religious freedom and theological diversity, Newark had been founded and governed by Puritans known for their religious intolerance. The founders ruled by "fundamental agreements," which explicitly stated that members of other churches were not welcome. The word of the Lord would be the only rule attended to. Their descendants, inheriting this unwavering faith, prioritized the "Lord in heaven" over the "King on the throne" and overwhelmingly supported independence from Britain.[20]

In a desperate bid to peacefully restore the king's rule to New Jersey, Howe issued a proclamation offering amnesty to any colonist who took an oath of allegiance to the Crown. This amnesty included a pardon for past actions and a certificate guaranteeing the safety of the signer's family and home. Howe also issued strict orders to his troops, reminding them that their mission was to reestablish order so loyal Americans could return to their rightful king. Howe was beginning to understand that support for the Crown was feeble in the colonies. The Revolution was taking on the characteristics of a civil war, and the tendency of the soldiers of both armies to pillage added to the cruelty.[21]

The British General Staff in New York tried to maintain discipline within the ranks of the king's troops, issuing orders cautioning soldiers to maintain proper decorum when entering towns. This included dressing neatly, avoiding boisterous behavior, and refraining from smoking tobacco in public. Additionally, any soldier who succumbed to carnal temptations and contracted a venereal disease would be responsible for the cost of his own treatment. Above all, the Hessians were to prioritize harmonious relations with the English troops or face severe repercussions.[22]

If Cornwallis hoped to win the hearts and minds of the American citizenry, the demeanor of the Hessians did little to advance his cause. Their militaristic appearance and somber temperament starkly contrasted with the villagers' deep-seated aversion to the military and a standing army. The sight of Hessian troops marching into town with menacingly sharp bayonets projecting from their muskets, and their officers brandishing long, ceremonial pikes and gleaming short swords struck terror into the hearts of Newark's residents. This sparked a panicked exodus, with families hastily piling their possessions onto wagons and clogging the roads in a desperate bid for escape.[23]

Although the Hessians were apprehensive about the local population, often unsure which civilians they could trust, the soldiers were captivated by the countryside. Newark's 140 dwellings were surrounded by magnificent, fertile land. The region's waterways teemed with seafood. Almost none of the Hessians had ever seen anything like the unique meadows of New Jersey, known locally as salt hay meadows. They were filled with tall-standing hay that was extraordinarily rich in nutrients and salt, providing for easy grazing of cattle.

The autumn air carried the crisp scent of forests filled with oak, chestnut, hickory, and elm trees, along with the sweet aroma of sap oozing from maple trees.[24]

A Hessian lieutenant waxed poetically about the region: "I prefer this province to any other I have seen in America so far. It is not very mountainous. . . . It is well cultivated, and I find excellent fruits everywhere and very many cattle." But his colorful descriptions foreshadowed grim events, as both armies' admiration for the New Jersey countryside would soon degenerate into greed and violent behavior.

Colonel Carl von Donop, a seasoned veteran, immediately saw the region's potential: "The local area seems to be very fertile and is well cultivated." Ominously, he added, "I hope that this expedition [into New Jersey] will contribute greatly to our better subsistence in the upcoming winter quarters." The New Jersey farms, rich with produce, were far more accessible to the British Army than the supply ships sailing the Atlantic from England, and the colonists could sense the predatory hunger in the eyes of the king's troops.[25]

Dwindling supplies compelled General Howe to order his army in New Jersey to forage for food and fuel. While the British commander instructed his men to pay for requisitioned goods, these foraging expeditions often devolved into outright plunder. Loyalists and Patriots fell victim to the soldiers' depredations, eroding local support for the Crown as the once-peaceful countryside was now filled with the sounds of panic and chaos. Families were waking on winter mornings to the sound of horses' hooves crunching on the snow-covered fields as British and Hessian soldiers seized hay, oats, and livestock. A local pastor reported that the foraging parties were often brutal in their treatment of civilians: "Great have been the ravages committed by the British troops in this part of the country. Their footsteps are marked with ruin and desolation of every kind. The murders, ravishments, robbery and insults they were guilty of are dreadful."[26]

Documenting sexual abuse by soldiers was difficult due to the mores of the eighteenth century, but the evidence was overwhelming that rape was occurring on a large scale. In Newark it was reported: "Three women of the town were basely ravished by them [British troops] and one of them was a woman of near seventy years of age. . . . Yea, not only the common soldiers, but officers went about the town by night, in gangs, and forcibly entered into houses, enquiring for women."[27]

The looting of a judge's house in Newark demonstrated how the pillaging was often of a cruel and demeaning nature highlighted by senseless violence: "Justice John Ogden . . . had his house robbed of everything they could carry away. They ripped open his beds, scattered the feathers in the air, . . . broke his desk to pieces and destroyed a great number of important papers."[28]

For the next three days, instead of joining Cornwallis in his southward pursuit of Washington, the Rall Brigade was surprised by orders to march southeast to the waterside village of Elizabethtown, situated on the harbor opposite Staten Island. General Howe then informed Colonel Rall that the brigade would be wintering in New Jersey. Consequently, the men's tents and baggage were loaded onto boats bound for New York, leaving the soldiers to find shelter in confiscated homes or sleep exposed to the biting cold of a New Jersey winter.[29]

As the boats laden with their gear sailed away to Staten Island, the brigade concluded they would be wintering in Elizabethtown. The military campaign of 1776 was drawing to a close. At last, after nearly a year away from their families, a perilous four-thousand-mile transatlantic journey, and multiple hard-fought battles, the Rall Brigade believed they had earned a respite. They looked forward to recuperating, and they took pride in their role in suppressing what they viewed as an unjust rebellion—an achievement that would surely earn them a lifetime of honor back home.

They were soon proven wrong.

CHAPTER 18

Destroy or Appease?

After abandoning Newark on November 28, Washington's beleaguered army trudged south through a relentless deluge. For twenty-five grueling miles, the sodden troops slogged on, some men barefoot, others with threadbare boots squelching in the mud. Washington was conducting a relentless, organized retreat despite severe shortages of tents and proper clothing, and the loss of thousands of men whose one-year enlistments had expired. His immediate objectives were clear: preserve his army and prevent the British from crossing the Delaware River into Pennsylvania, where they could threaten Philadelphia. The situation was dire, with many men, including officers, demoralized after the loss of so many soldiers and so much equipment.

On November 29, they staggered into Brunswick on the banks of the Raritan River, their ranks thinned to a mere 3,400 men. Philadelphia lay fifty miles distant. All that stood between the capital of the rebellion and

Cornwallis's forces was Washington's diminished but determined army, and the icy waters of the Delaware River.[1]

Cornwallis pursued Washington to Brunswick, marching on muddy roads through heavy rains and cold winds. On December 1, his advance guard reached the eastern bank of the Raritan River, where Washington's forces stood ready on the opposite shore. Sensing an opportunity, Cornwallis dispatched his light infantry to seize the sole bridge spanning the Raritan. Washington, recognizing the imminent threat, turned to twenty-one-year-old Captain Alexander Hamilton, commander of the Independent Company of New York State Artillery. Hamilton swiftly brought his five guns to bear, unlimbering them with practiced efficiency, and began a thunderous artillery duel with the British across the river. Washington's men succeeded in partially destroying the bridge. American riflemen concealed in abandoned houses along the shore added their fire to the fray. The combined effect of Hamilton's barrage and the marksmanship of the American riflemen thwarted Cornwallis's advance. As dusk settled over the battlefield, Washington feigned a defense of Brunswick and ordered his troops to evacuate and resume their march south. Hamilton's guns continued their bombardment, pinning down the British while the Americans withdrew under the cover of darkness. Cornwallis held most of his troops on the north bank of the Raritan River until the next day, when his engineers repaired the bridge and his army marched into Brunswick.[2]

"Having the bridge repaired," wrote a British officer, "we took possession of the town, in which the rebels left several of their sick, and dead."[3]

Howe, wary of a rumored rebel attack from the north, commanded Cornwallis to hold his position and refrain from pursuing the retreating Americans. Meanwhile, Washington continued his strategic withdrawal, leading his weary troops thirteen miles farther south to the village of Kingston, near Princeton, where they camped in the open.[4]

With the Delaware River a mere twenty-five miles distant, Washington and Howe found themselves at a crossroads, each facing a pivotal decision that could dramatically alter the course of the war. For Washington, a misstep could spell the demise of the fledgling struggle for independence. Conversely, an error in judgment by Howe could mire the British in a protracted conflict, tarnishing his military reputation and leaving open a slim, yet tangible, chance for an American triumph.

Howe, a seasoned commander with three decades of military experience and leader of the largest army on the continent, would make some of the war's most critical missteps in the weeks to come—while Washington was about to make one of the war's most prescient decisions.

The British found themselves, ironically, hindered by their own rapid success. Cornwallis had fulfilled Howe's initial objectives in a mere twelve days: Fort Lee fell to British forces, securing British control of the Hudson River, and eastern New Jersey was firmly in their grasp, ensuring ample shelter and provisions for the impending winter. However, the complete destruction of Washington's army, while a tantalizing prospect, had not been part of Howe's original directives.

Cautious and methodical, Howe had instructed Cornwallis "not to advance beyond Brunswick." Howe's staff reported that on December 3 and 4, Cornwallis was "standing quietly at Brunswick . . . [with] orders not to advance," while, in an astonishing display of inaction, Howe remained in New York, perusing correspondence. Finally, on December 5, recognizing the need to assess the situation at Brunswick firsthand, Howe surprised his staff by boarding a sloop to Elizabethtown. For some unexplained reason, instead of moving rapidly to Brunswick, Howe passed the day inspecting abandoned rebel fortifications. That night, Howe stayed in the small town of Amboy as a guest of General Grant in the house of the former royal governor, William Franklin, Benjamin Franklin's illegitimate son. The three-story house was less than two years old and the finest in town. It was not until the following day, December 6, that Howe finally departed for New Brunswick, arriving at four in the afternoon. Having left his army stranded in New Brunswick awaiting his arrival, Howe had squandered four invaluable days that could have been used to press his advantage against the retreating American forces.[5]

Finally on the front lines at New Brunswick, Howe needed to decide whether to pursue Washington's army or go into winter quarters.

Cornwallis informed Howe that his army would face difficulties in pursuing Washington. Cornwallis believed his men and his horses were fatigued. Since the fall of Fort Washington on November 16, his army had captured six towns, and most of his men had been on the march for at least twelve days, some as many as sixteen days. In the march to New Brunswick, some men did not have time to bake their flour into bread. A chaplain in a Waldeck Regiment reported that the men had lived on bread and schnapps for the last six days. Some men were marching with worn-out boots, others barefoot. The approaching winter presented a precarious situation. Cornwallis needed shelter for his troops, a task made more challenging by the destruction of nearly half the buildings in British-occupied New York during the great fire of September. Neither the farms in New York nor the Royal Navy, whose ships, like Cornwallis's men, were worn out, could fully resupply his army. Reclaiming New Jersey would ease the burden of providing shelter and provisions. Furthermore, Cornwallis remained concerned about rumors of General Lee attacking from the north. He knew that Lee had a considerable body of troops and an excellent reputation among the British officers.[6]

"I remember Colonel Griffin, an adjutant general of the rebel army, met me on the march," Cornwallis later said, "and I was unwilling he should see . . . [my] troops, as they were so few."[7]

But most of his senior officers believed that Washington's army, which was only about twelve miles away in Princeton, was weak and could be caught and destroyed.

Clinton wrote that "the rebellion was on the brink of being wholly crushed."[8]

"Washington's army was so reduced," believed one British officer, "that the bets were ten to one that we should not have another campaign."[9]

"We all think our cause is nearly ruined," confessed a rebel officer to a Loyalist gentleman. "[O]ur army is just disbanding . . . and the King's troops are severely pushing us."[10]

Howe was pleased to learn that large numbers of Loyalists were entering the British camp to sign the oath of allegiance. Local residents assured Howe that the rebel army was in a wretched condition with less than eight thousand men and many deserting daily. They assured Howe that if the campaign were continued, the enemy army would disperse and break up.[11]

"Several distinguished persons arrived from Pennsylvania," wrote a Hessian officer, "who implored [Howe] to press General Washington as closely as possible so that we might overtake him in the vicinity of the Delaware [River] by which his retreat would be cut off. There we could surely destroy his disheartened army. Indeed, one of them, Mr. Joseph Galloway, was so enraged over the delay of the English that he said out loud, "I see, they don't want to finish the war!"[12]

Galloway, an ardent Loyalist, was furious that Washington was cheeky enough to remain for "a week so near the superior force of the British Army, with a large river in his rear to cross. . . . But here on this, as on every other occasion, he relied on the indolent progress of the British Army."[13]

Howe was finally convinced.

He countermanded his directives. The army was ordered to advance deeper into New Jersey. Howe would command a column marching from New Brunswick to Princeton. Cornwallis would lead a second column that would march west of Howe's column, protecting its right flank in case of the still-feared surprise attack by Lee's rebel army.[14]

Howe was too late.

As the British would soon discover, while they had wasted precious time, Washington had been utilizing the reprise with deadly efficiency, swiftly constructing a plan to save his army and laying the groundwork for a potential, unexpected rebel counterstroke.

That afternoon, in Elizabethtown, the Rall Brigade was relaxing, preparing for winter quarters. Most of their baggage had been dispatched to Staten Island for storage until the spring campaign.[15]

"This is a large and beautiful place, which is divided by a medium sized river [the Elizabeth]," Wiederhold wrote of Elizabethtown. From the center of town, one could see the low-lying meadows and swampy ground that flanked the red limestone banks of the river. During high tide, the flat land along the riverside was submerged as the waters rose.[16]

Winter was almost upon the brigade. The soldiers could smell the briny scent of the nearby marshes and ocean, and they could feel the chill of winter creeping into the crisp morning air.

The town itself was well-cultivated, a stark contrast to the humble villages of Hessen-Kassel. The townsfolk tended to numerous gardens and orchards, prompting one visitor to effuse, "It might truly be said that Elizabethtown was situated in a garden."[17]

A regimental chaplain from Waldeck, elated at the prospect of comfortable winter quarters for his men, marveled at the "splendid, well-situated houses" of Elizabethtown. They were, he wrote, "always pleasing and bear witness to the good taste of the inhabitants." He was particularly impressed by the intricate woodwork, a testament to the skilled artisans and craftsmen prevalent in America. Even the home of a local coppersmith, he noted with surprise, was "furnished and wallpapered in a manner not to be expected from a man of his class."[18]

The battle-hardened veterans of the Rall Brigade likely could not resist smiling at Elizabethtown's unique method for raising poultry. The town's geese were outfitted with three footlong sticks fastened crosswise around their necks, an ungainly contraption designed to prevent them from squeezing through fences.

"They look extremely awkward," said one observer, "and it is very diverting to see them in this attire."[19]

Despite being stationed in hostile territory, the men couldn't have asked for better accommodations and were in good spirits. However, their contentment was short-lived. Orders arrived unexpectedly from General Howe. To the men's dismay, they were instructed to prepare for an immediate march. To add to their frustration, the brigade was being split up. The Lossberg Regiment, including Jakob Piel, was instructed to remain in Elizabethtown with orders to catch up with the rest of the brigade when reinforcements arrived from New York. The Knyphausen and Rall Regiments, with Andreas Wiederhold and Johannes Reuber respectively, were commanded to march to New Brunswick, where they would rejoin the main body of the British Army.[20]

The Knyphausen and Rall Regiments promptly set out for New Brunswick. Some troops sailed up the Raritan River, others went by foot. After traversing approximately twelve miles of flat countryside, they crested a hill. Below them, nestled in a valley, the Raritan River snaked through, its banks made of red limestone, and on the far side was New Brunswick.

The town itself, with its prosperous-looking homes—some made entirely of wood, others of brick—spread out from the riverbank. In the distance, large farms peppered the landscape with spacious orchards full of peaches and apple trees, and enormous barns large enough to hold a threshing room, lofts of hay, and cattle under one roof. Massive clay ovens were set outside at a prudent distance from the farmhouses.

Cherry trees, barren from the cold of winter, lined Albany Street, the town's main thoroughfare. Many homes boasted small balconies in front, where, as one traveler observed, "the people sat in the evening, in order to enjoy the fresh air, and to have the pleasure of viewing those who passed by." The most unique structures of New Brunswick, which undoubtedly the Hessians had never seen before, were homes with a peculiar construction: houses with brick facades facing the street, while the remaining three sides were constructed of simple wooden planks. But on this day, as the British and Hessian troops entered the town, the streets were eerily deserted, the balcony benches empty save for a few stalwart Loyalists. In the midst of this unsettling quiet, plump guinea hens roamed freely through the mostly deserted town. Their large, rotund bodies, topped with comically small heads and covered in black feathers speckled with countless white dots, provided a stark contrast to the tense atmosphere.[21]

The following day, the troops marched twelve miles to the village of Kingston, located just north of Princeton. As they settled in for the night, whispers of rebel attacks and potential ambushes spread through the camp, unsettling the weary soldiers. Their respite was short-lived; after only an hour's rest, the Knyphausen and Rall Regiments received orders to embark on a forced march toward Maidenhead, a small settlement south of Princeton on the road to Trenton. Tensions escalated when reports arrived of "armed country people" assailing and setting ablaze several of the army's supply wagons. This news undoubtedly heightened Colonel Rall's apprehensions.[22]

"During this dark and quiet night an alarm was sounded and we had to proceed all night until we arrived [near] Princeton," wrote Reuber.

"Just as I was about to go to bed at 10:00," wrote Wiederhold, "we had to fall out in the greatest haste. During the night we marched eighteen miles to Maidenhead, where we lay a day and a night in bivouac [outdoors with no tents]."[23]

Exhausted from their march, Reuber and his comrades collapsed in a field and quickly fell asleep. Awakened by the rising sun, Reuber felt an unfamiliar chill and realized that a blanket of snow had covered him during the night. As he looked around, he saw snow-covered shapes beginning to stir and rise from the ground, and he realized they were his fellow soldiers, their forms unrecognizable under the white blanket. The scene had a ghostly appearance, made more unsettling when the men discovered they had been sleeping among graves in a cemetery.

Major Rall rode up to the cemetery's front gate on horseback. Surveying the eerie scene before him, he issued orders: General Howe wanted the brigade back on the road resuming its march to Trenton within two hours. Those with provisions should prepare their meals now.[24]

CHAPTER 19

Stolen Boats

At four on the morning of December 7, under General Howe's command, the main body of the British Army finally departed the region around New Brunswick for Princeton, having frittered away six crucial days. Washington, recognizing the opportunity, had seized on this welcome break to set in motion plans to salvage his battered army.[1]

Six days earlier, on December 1, with the British poised to enter New Brunswick, Washington had already set his sights on the one geographical feature that could prove pivotal to his army's fate: the Delaware River. If he could successfully cross the Delaware into Pennsylvania, the river, combined with the region's harsh winter weather, the local militia, and the remnants of his own army, could collectively serve as a formidable barrier to the British advance. Yet for Washington, defense alone was not enough. The American commander yearned for an opportunity to strike back.

"As nothing but necessity obliged me to retire before the Enemy and leave so much of the Jerseys unprotected," he wrote to Congress, "I conceive it to be my duty, and it corresponds with my Inclination, to make head against them, so soon as there shall be the least probability of doing it with propriety."[2]

Against seemingly insurmountable odds, Washington contemplated a strategy that no one in the British or Hessian high command had seriously entertained: a daring counterstrike against Cornwallis's army. With greater foresight than his enemy, Washington made one of the most prescient decisions of the war. He entrusted a courier with a secret order for Colonel Richard Humpton, commander of the 11th Pennsylvania Regiment. Humpton, one of Washington's most reliable officers, was instructed to gather all the boats on the Delaware River and secure them on the west bank near Trenton. "You are to proceed . . . to Collect all the . . . boats you can and have them Secured . . . in the most expeditious manner."[3]

Washington's strategy served multiple purposes. It ensured that a flotilla would be at his disposal to ferry his army across the river to the relative safety of Pennsylvania while simultaneously he denied the British any means of river passage when they reached the shore. Furthermore, should the opportunity arise, these same boats could transport his forces back to New Jersey, enabling a swift and unexpected counterattack.

Washington's obsession with obtaining all the boats on the river quickly spread to his subordinates. Militiamen from Pennsylvania, Continental soldiers, and local Patriots joined in the frenzied hunt to gather up every kind of watercraft and secure them under guard on the Pennsylvania side of the Delaware. They scoured the river for vessels, even traversing its tributaries. From small rowboats to large ferries, they cleared the New Jersey shore of anything that would float. Washington ordered his quartermasters and his staff to join in the endeavor, issuing multiple orders throughout the week to ensure that the British would find no boats within forty miles north or south of Trenton.[4]

The New Jersey militia went to work with a vengeance. Captains Daniel Bray, Jacob Gearhart, and Thomas Jones and their men of the 2nd Regiment of the Hunterdon County militia cast about for "boats of every kind." Soon they were untying dockside ropes and dragging beached vessels across the frozen mud of the riverbanks. They worked during rainstorms that hit the region and were often forced to stand in the river's cold water as they commandeered and pirated ships belonging to Patriots and Loyalists alike. Their relentless searching yielded so many vessels that they needed to hide the fruits of their labor in unmapped inlets, up narrow creeks, and behind wooded islands on the Pennsylvania side of the river. With a deliberate thoroughness they collected practically every boat along forty miles of the river. They executed their mission so rigorously that when the Tory Joseph Galloway went looking for vessels on the Jersey shore, he found only a solitary scow and six dilapidated boats.[5]

On December 2, with Cornwallis still in New Brunswick, Washington defied conventional military wisdom and divided his forces despite the looming threat of the much larger British army less than twenty miles distant. He marched about half the army to Trenton to help transport the army's supplies to the Pennsylvania side of the Delaware River. He left the other half, about 1,400 strong, in Princeton to "watch the Motions of the Enemy and give notice of their Approach."[6]

Washington's army, weary but resolute, descended on Trenton around midday on December 2. The boats his men had commandeered were now brought over to the Trenton side to facilitate the transportation of the army's supplies across the river. For five grueling days and nights, while the British remained encamped in New Brunswick, the Americans toiled ceaselessly.

The riverbank was transformed into a scene of frenetic activity. Under a bleak winter sky, men strained and grunted, hauling equipment, artillery, and horses onto the waiting boats. As darkness fell, the work continued unabated. The shoreline came alive with the warm glow of enormous bonfires. Their flames cast a flickering light over the scene, illuminating the faces of the soldiers as they wrestled with their burdens. The air was filled with a cacophony of sounds: the splash of oars, the creaking of vessels, and the voices of hundreds of men hollering in their difficulties of getting horses and artillery onto the boats.

Charles Wilson Peale, the renowned artist, watched from the Pennsylvania shore, his heart heavy with a mixture of awe and dread. He described the spectacle as "a grand, but dreadful appearance." The relentless labor, the harsh conditions, the sheer desperation of the scene—it all coalesced into a vision that seemed "rather the appearance of Hell than any earthly scene."[7]

Despite the cold, the rain, and the exhaustion, the Americans persevered. Boats continually passed and repassed. The river, once a barrier, now served as their lifeline, carrying the tools and supplies they needed to continue the fight.

By the evening of December 6, a sense of relief settled over the American camp. The herculean effort to transport their supplies, wounded, artillery, and horses across the Delaware was finally completed. There was no word of any movement by Cornwallis in New Brunswick so Washington decided to march the men with him at the Delaware River to Princeton, where the two segments of his army would unite.

On the morning of December 7, reports reached Washington that altered the strategic landscape. The British forces under Cornwallis were finally on the move, departing New Brunswick and marching toward Princeton. Faced with this new intelligence, Washington countermanded his previous orders, recognizing that the planned march to Princeton was no longer viable. Instead, he initiated a full retreat across the Delaware River into Pennsylvania. This decision prioritized the preservation of his army. By withdrawing to the relative safety of the Pennsylvania shore, Washington would deny the British an opportunity to engage his forces on unfavorable terms. Moreover, it would buy him time to regroup, resupply, and consider his next move.[8]

As intelligence had forewarned Washington, the British forces under Howe departed New Brunswick on December 7. Howe had finally recognized the strategic advantage of pursuing Washington's retreating army and extending British control to the Delaware River. Based on Howe's correspondence and his actions, it is fair to say that in his mind he saw a map of New Jersey unfurled, with a sweeping expanse of red denoting British-controlled territory stretching from Fort Lee on the Hudson River to Trenton and Burlington on the Delaware. But what he visualized was an illusion. A more accurate representation of the situation would have depicted isolated red dots—signifying major cities under British control—surrounded by blue—representing vast stretches of rebel-held countryside, British strongholds isolated in a sea of rebel activity.

Signs of danger were all around, but Howe failed to appreciate how fragile and vulnerable Britain's control of New Jersey truly was. This vulnerability was starkly illustrated by the very nature of the march he was now undertaking. The old stagecoach road from New Brunswick through Princeton to Trenton, rather than being a secure route through pacified territory, required substantial protection for the commanding general. Howe's vanguard consisted of 150 British cavalry, complete with horse-drawn cannons, supported by four battalions of English infantry to protect the general against surprise attacks.

"The rebels were always barely ahead of us," wrote one of his aides, but "since General Howe was with the vanguard we advanced very slowly, and the rebels had time to withdraw step by step without being engaged." While ensuring Howe's safety, this cautious approach allowed the Continental forces to withdraw unchallenged, preserving their strength for future engagements.[9]

Heavy rains muddied the roads, further impeding the already sluggish progress of the British. One hundred fifty Patriots, unfazed even by Howe's cannon-carrying vanguard, suddenly burst from dense woods lining the road. In a swift and violent ambush, they struck down several British scouts before vanishing back into the forest.[10]

The British were starting to feel the pressure of being in hostile territory. There was no real "rear" to the British Army since the rebels were all around. Accustomed to more conventional warfare, British officers were forced to confront an uncomfortable truth: Mere rumors of rebel activity, or small bands of determined Patriots, could significantly delay and disrupt the movements of much-larger, better-equipped British forces.

The general and his troops labored all day to cover the fourteen miles to Princeton. As evening fell, they finally entered the nearly deserted town, its streets empty and buildings abandoned. British and Hessian soldiers embarked on a spree of plunder and destruction. The venerable library at the College of New Jersey (now Princeton University), a repository of knowledge and culture, fell victim to this rampage. Valuable books were callously stolen or, in a particularly poignant act of vandalism, tossed into campfires, their pages providing a fleeting warmth against the winter chill. This scene—priceless tomes crackling in the flames while soldiers huddled around them for warmth—served as a stark metaphor for the broader destruction wrought by the war.

Besides using books for fuel, in a quest for warmth the soldiers stripped wood from houses, tore down wooden fences, cut down fruit trees, and pilfered firewood from Patriots and Loyalists alike. British officers commandeered almost all the town's residences, completing the transformation of Princeton from a peaceful college town to an occupied military outpost.[11]

This scene of destruction in Princeton illustrated a harsh reality of the war: The line between military necessity and wanton destruction was often blurred, and the civilian population, regardless of their political leanings, often bore the brunt of an army's needs and frustrations. General Howe was acutely aware that his soldiers' reckless behavior undermined his efforts at pacification. Washington faced the same challenge. In all three armies—American, British, and Hessian—edicts against plundering were issued and reissued, offenders arrested, and in the most egregious cases, such as rape, the death penalty was imposed.

While plundering was a widespread problem, there were differences in its nature and scale. American soldiers' looting tended to be more disorganized and smaller in scale, compared to the more systematic pillaging by Hessian and British troops. However, this distinction offered little comfort to the victims. Some of Washington's men were guilty of grave offenses, including violent assaults, sexual offenses, and arson, even targeting fellow Patriots at times.[12]

Although Reuber, Wiederhold, and Piel were conspicuously silent on the matter of plundering in their writings, this omission is deeply misleading. The Hessian armies were, in fact, notorious for their extensive pillaging. Their plundering operations were often of a far grander scale than those carried out by the Americans. A wealth of eyewitness accounts and historical records verify that while the American and British armies certainly engaged in plundering throughout New York and New Jersey, the Hessians' activities were distinguished by their greater scale, efficiency, and brazenness.

Both Hessian and American soldiers had been promised prize money as a reward for their conquests. However, a crucial difference lay in how each force defined "booty." Only captured military equipment and firearms were considered legitimate prizes for Washington's troops. The Hessians, on the other hand, operated under a much broader definition of legitimate contraband that included personal property seized from civilians.

When the Hessians left a town, they were almost always followed by a convoy of wagons overflowing with plundered goods. In a two-week period in New Jersey along the Delaware River, the Hessians filled several hundred wagons, carriages, and carioles. A British officer observing their rapacity remarked, "Indeed, they spare nobody, but glean all away like an Army of Locusts."[13]

According to many eyewitnesses, the Hessian women traveling with the army were the most merciless plunderers of all. "A scene of promiscuous pillage was in full operation," wrote an eyewitness in Piscataway, New Jersey. "Here a soldier was seen issuing from a house armed with a frying pan and gridiron and hastening to deposit them with the stove over which his helpmate kept watch. The women who had followed the army assisted their husbands in bringing the furniture from the house or stood sentinels to guard the pile of kitchen utensils and other articles already secured and claimed by right of war."[14]

The artist Charles Peale wrote of a New Jersey farmer that the Hessians "have taken every shirt he had, except the one on his back. . . . They have taken hogs, sheep, horses and cows, everywhere; even children have been stripped of their clothes—in which business the Hessian women are the most active—in short the abuse of the inhabitants is beyond description."[15]

Howe understood that the pillaging and acts of violence perpetrated by the king's troops, were fueling the growing resistance among the people of New Jersey to fight back. The previous day's ambush exemplified the increasing opposition his army faced. Bands of armed men in civilian clothing roamed the countryside assaulting British couriers, attacking foraging parties, and firing on sentries. Howe's aide noted that in a two-day period, the rebels had captured an escort with eight baggage wagons, made prisoners of several letter couriers, ambushed a number of patrols, and stole seven hundred oxen and nearly one thousand sheep and hogs from the British commissary. Many of these rebel attackers had signed General Howe's oath of allegiance to the Crown, but it was likely that most did so out of pragmatism rather than genuine allegiance, seeking to safeguard their families and property.[16]

A British captain astutely observed that the signers "swallow their Oaths of Allegiance to the King and Congress alternately, with as much ease as your lordship does poached eggs."[17]

The once tranquil country lanes of New Jersey were now actively traversed by irregular fighters, militia, and detachments of the Continental Army who harassed, shot at, and killed the king's soldiers. "It is now very unsafe for us to travel in jersey," wrote an aide to General Howe. "The rascal peasants meet our men alone or in small, unarmed groups. They have their rifles hidden in the bushes, or ditches, and the like. When they believe they are sure of success and they see one or several men belonging to our army, they shoot them in the head, then quickly hide their rifles and pretend they know nothing."[18]

The killing of British soldiers by armed civilians dealt a significant psychological blow to the British, but the disruption of communication posed an even more significant long-term threat. Simple communication between the various segments of Howe's army was becoming increasingly dangerous. Soldiers learned to avoid traveling alone on the roads, instead moving in large convoys and only a few days each week.

Howe and Cornwallis's successes in New Jersey unleashed a storm of lawlessness and resentment that threatened the stability of the British occupation.

PART V

Trenton

CHAPTER 20

Small Town at the Crossroads of History

ON DECEMBER 8, 1776, the British Army, having spent the previous day in Princeton, embarked on an eleven-mile march to Trenton. The temperature had risen into the 40s, and the weather was calm, making for a pleasant march. Encountering no resistance, they arrived at their destination at 2:00 P.M. Trenton, with its one hundred or so homes, was situated on a flat, sandy plain next to the Delaware River. The town was laid out perpendicular to the river, with its northern end slightly elevated and its southern reaches extending to the riverbank. Trenton's proximity to the Delaware made it a crucial point in the ongoing chase of Washington's elusive army.

As the British neared, the town's inhabitants rushed forward, pleading with Howe to hurry. They claimed the last remnants of Washington's forces were just then embarking on boats to cross the river. Howe, ever cautious, suspected a trap. He feared that Washington might have artillery on the Pennsylvania side. He held back the main force, venturing toward the riverbank with only a small contingent of Jägers and light infantry, Cornwallis at his side. The Jägers, eager to seize the moment, broke into a trot, hoping to catch Washington's rear guard before they slipped away. But they were too late. The last boats were already pulling away, leaving the Jägers stranded on the shore.[1]

As Howe had feared, the American artillery, stationed across the river, began bombarding his men. "A terrific fire" erupted from all their batteries. The light infantry and Jägers were forced into a hasty retreat, losing thirteen men in the blink of an eye. Despite the intense barrage, General Howe remained. He stood with unwavering calm for over an hour as cannonballs crashed around him. "Wherever we turned, the cannonballs hit the ground," one soldier later wrote, marveling at how they had not all been killed. Then, just as Howe prepared to move back into town, a cannonball struck the soft ground near him, spraying dirt across his body and face. Howe simply wiped it off and continued his withdrawal.

After finally turning his back on the enemy and returning his gaze to the landward side of Trenton, Howe ordered his men to find quarters for the night.[2]

The brief but intense bombardment served no significant military purpose. Yet it spoke volumes about the contrasting motivations of the two armies. Howe and Cornwallis exemplified a traditional European notion of bravery and honor in their steadfastness under fire. The Americans, in turn, demonstrated their resilience and defiance. They were not a defeated army but one willing to fight back, even in the face of overwhelming odds.

On December 9, 1776, the first full day of British occupation of Trenton, as the Hessian and British troops were settling into position in and around the town, Howe ordered a thorough search of the Delaware River for boats. Although a crossing of the Delaware by the British was unlikely, Howe wanted to be prepared should the opportunity arise. The mission was deemed so critical that over six thousand soldiers were roused in the middle of the night to scour the riverbanks. Cornwallis led a contingent twenty-one miles north and west to Coryell's Ferry on the Delaware, while a second detachment was sent to reconnoiter the great bend in the river near Trenton. Colonel Donop marched seventeen miles south to explore the river near Bordentown. The three search parties toiled through the night and most of the following day but found that Washington's men had brought every vessel on the Delaware River to the Pennsylvania shore, fastened down and placed under the watch of Continental soldiers.[3]

The week spent by Patriots, such as Richard Humpton, confiscating every vessel on the Delaware effectively halted Howe's pursuit of the Americans at the river's eastern bank. The British forces' frustration was evident in Howe's aide's words: "It is a great pity that we cannot get across the Delaware River. If we could, nothing would stand in the way of our getting to Philadelphia before the year is out."[4]

Howe spent the week in Trenton unable to pursue Washington across the Delaware. He rode up and down the river scouting the ground, ignoring musket and cannon fire from the Americans on the Pennsylvania shore. The weather was turning cold, with temperatures dipping into the 20s, and snow was imminent. He decided it was time to end the 1776 campaign. Following European armies' standard practice, Howe prepared to move the troops into winter quarters. He informed Lord Germain that the weather had become "too severe to keep the field."[5]

Confident that the war was nearing its end, Howe believed he could conclude the "unpleasant business" in the spring. His beliefs were based on the Continental Army's poor battlefield performances, the rebels' current ragged condition, his knowledge of the looming expiration of many of Washington's soldiers' enlistment, and his contempt for the colonists as citizens and soldiers.

The rebel general Charles Lee was captured on December 13 in northern New Jersey, further bolstering Howe's confidence. Howe and many British officers held Lee in high regard, considering him the rebels' most capable general.

Despite some inner doubts, Howe outwardly expressed assurance that with the onset of winter, he could now safely disperse his forces across New Jersey to protect the state's Loyalists and maintain law and order. Over breakfast with his officers, Howe outlined his winter strategy: Defend as much of New Jersey as possible by establishing cantonments in sixteen towns spanning about sixty miles from Burlington in the south to Paulus's Hook (modern-day Jersey City) in the north. As a show of force, a forward line of cantonments would be established in three towns on the Delaware River, each manned by a full brigade of Hessians; the most southern would be Burlington, then six miles to the north, Bordentown, and seven miles to the north of Bordentown, Trenton. Howe believed these brigades, placed about six miles apart, would be close enough to support each other and sufficiently far apart to have their own fields for foraging.[6]

In assigning officers to the cantonments, Howe placed General James Grant in overall command, stationing him at New Brunswick. Grant, who hailed from one of Scotland's most influential aristocratic families, was clan chief and owner of a great Scottish estate. Despite his high social standing and the royal family's favor, Grant proved to be a disastrous military leader throughout the war.

His physical appearance matched his temperament: squat and bulldog-faced, with a personality that inspired contempt among his own men. One major bluntly assessed him as "without abilities, or the least knowledge of his profession." The choice of Grant was particularly ill suited for this command, which required a leader capable of adapting to American warfare tactics. Instead, Grant's deep-seated contempt for the Americans blinded him to the strengths of their resourceful and determined army.[7]

Colonel Carl Emil Ulrich von Donop, a thirty-six-year-old aristocrat, was chosen to command the troops at Bordentown and Burlington, with oversight of all three Delaware River cantonments, including Rall's force at Trenton. His noble background shaped every aspect of his command. Like General Grant, he hailed from a noble family and was well connected, having served as a personal assistant to the landgrave. He joined the American expedition with dreams of conquering not just the colonies but Peru and Mexico.

Von Donop's rigid adherence to social rank influenced his leadership. He treated officers of lower standing (the landgrave's social classes seven through twelve) curtly while showing deference to his superiors (social classes one through six), often addressing them in French. His letters revealed a courtier's sensibility—one observer noted their "fulsome flattery" and "flowery phrases." Describing the British landing in Manhattan, he wrote with theatrical flair, "Picture to yourself, illustrious prince, the most splendid stage-setting of the opera and the descent of King Jupiter himself, and you will have an idea of our military spectacle."[8]

Howe's decision to pair this aristocratic officer with Rall, a gruff commander of humble origins, proved another critical miscalculation in the chain of command.

Twelve miles inland from these forward positions on the river, Howe planned to establish a strong garrison at Princeton. He was convinced that the Princeton garrison and the garrisons on the Delaware River could support each other in case of an attack, even though the closest one, Trenton, was twelve miles away. North of Princeton, fourteen cantonments would stretch across the state from New Brunswick to Hackensack. The three cantonments on the Delaware River would be manned primarily by Hessians, while the cantonments stretching across New Jersey would be manned by mostly British soldiers.

Despite his outward assurance, Howe privately harbored doubts about his strategy. General Clinton had warned him that a chain of posts across New Jersey would be vulnerable to rebel attacks. The Americans, Clinton cautioned, were "trained to stratagem and enterprise . . . they knew every trick of that country of chicane," a reference to the region's winding, unpredictable roads.[9]

In correspondence with Lord Germain, Howe admitted that the chain was "rather too extensive." Nevertheless, he justified his decision to extend the outposts over such a large area as necessary "to afford protection to the inhabitants." He believed that the Hessian troops stationed at the hazardous forward posts along the Delaware River were of such high quality that they "will be in perfect security.[10]

Johannes Reuber, Jakob Piel, Andreas Wiederhold, and their comrades in the Rall Brigade at Trenton were about to learn the hard truth about that supposed "perfect security," as they found themselves isolated and vulnerable on the banks of the Delaware.

Upon first glimpsing Trenton, an officer in the Lossberg Regiment, likely voicing the sentiments of his Hessian compatriots, remarked with disdain, "This town consists of about 100 houses, which many are mean and little, and it is easy to conceive how ill it must accommodate three regiments."[11]

Contrary to the Hessian officer's disparaging assessment, Trenton in 1776 was far from "mean and little." The town was the result of a vision shared by a group of settlers who harnessed the power of nature to create a community that, while modest in size, loomed large in stature and influence.

European settlement of the Trenton region began in 1678 when Mahlon Stacy, a Quaker from Yorkshire seeking refuge from religious persecution in England, purchased two proprietary shares of a new settlement in the wilderness along the Delaware River. Leaving behind the comforts of his Yorkshire estate, Stacy embarked on a perilous four-month journey across the Atlantic Ocean, braving winter seas alongside his family, servants, and a group of fellow Quakers aboard the sailing ship *Shield.* Their destination: the falls of the Delaware, where they would lay the foundations for what would one day become the city of Trenton.[12]

As the *Shield* approached the North American coastline near the entrance to Delaware Bay, a fierce gale propelled it farther upriver than any European vessel had previously ventured. As night fell, the winds drove the ship toward the shore, entangling its rigging in the branches of overhanging trees. While the crew struggled to free the sails, one seaman gazing at the surrounding landscape remarked with a hint of prophecy that this place would make an excellent site for a city. Four years later, William Penn founded the city of Philadelphia here.[13]

Pressing on, the *Shield* continued its journey upriver until one morning the passengers awoke to an extraordinary sight: Overnight, the Delaware River had transformed into a vast, gleaming expanse of ice. Undeterred, they disembarked, cautiously making their way across the frozen river to begin their new lives in this uncharted wilderness. Their fledgling settlement, situated at the edge of the river's frozen falls, was humbly named Friends at the Falls of the Delaware, or, as it was quaintly rendered in the records of the time, "Ye ffalles of ye De La Warr."[14]

The region was rich in meadows and woods, with creeks and rivers to power mills. Mahlon Stacy chose his land with great care, claiming a fertile tract that straddled both banks of a creek flowing into the Delaware River. The indigenous Lenape people had long known this waterway as Assunpink, meaning stony watery place. Recognizing the creek's potential, Stacy harnessed its flowing waters to power a gristmill, laying the foundation for future prosperity.[15]

These original settlers found their lives freed from government interference, their growth dependent upon their abilities, their imagination, and the "will of the lord." They cut timber to build homes and developed their properties as they saw fit.

The region's land was fertile and lush, a fact Stacy eagerly shared in letters home to England: "We have peaches by cart loads. The Indians bring us seven or eight fat bucks of a day. Without rod or net we catch abundance of herrings after the Indian manner in pinfolds [intricate handmade fish traps]. Geese, ducks, pheasants are plenty. Swans abound. Oysters are excellent, six inches long."[16]

The settlers traded goods with the Lenape for land, forging a fragile relationship that allowed their community to grow in this wild and bountiful land.

"The first comers," wrote Mary Murfin, the daughter of an original settler, "made an agreement with the Indians for their land, being after this manner: From the river to such and such creeks, and was to be paid in goods ... say, so many matchcoats, guns, hatchets, hoes, kettles ... all in number as agreed upon by both Indians and English."[17]

She later wrote coldheartedly: "It may be observed how God's providence made room for us in a wonderful manner in taking away the Indians. There came a distemper among them so mortal that they could not bury all the dead. . . . It was said that the old Indian king spoke prophetically before his death, and said, 'the English should increase and the Indians decrease.'"[18]

Economic activity was unregulated except for royal province-wide regulations governing fair weights. Even a century later, most government-controlled licenses in the region involved only ferries and taverns. The men of the settlement only had to give the royal government some service in the building of highways and assure the government that any beer the families sold was "strong and wholesome ... [containing] four bushels of malt to a hogshead."[19]

By 1714, the area, still not yet officially a town, had four families. Stacy was separated from his neighbors by woods with only a footpath to travel. The land was still so pristine that the Royal Book of Surveys for the region listed Mahlon Stacy's land simply as starting at the "black walnut tree by the Delaware River."[20]

In 1714, Stacy's son sold a significant portion of the family's land holdings to William Trent, an enterprising Philadelphia merchant. Trent's acquisition proved transformative. Leveraging his business acumen and strategic partnerships, including a notable alliance with William Penn, Trent rapidly ascended to prominence as a highly successful wholesale and retail merchant and shipowner. In one year, he exported a staggering 30 million pounds of tobacco.[21]

The settlement steadily grew, evolving from a cluster of homesteads to a village of about five hundred inhabitants by 1719. Recognizing its growing importance, the governor of West Jersey directed that the county courts should convene there. The town, in recognition of Trent's influence and contributions, gradually became known as Trent's-town, then Trent-town, and finally, Trenton.[22]

The town's principal source of income and influence was its strategic location. It sat about thirty miles north of Philadelphia along "the Falls" of the Delaware, where the river rushed so rapidly over protruding rocks that one could hear the water crashing. The turbulent water was the sound of prosperity, as the rocks jutting above the water line formed a natural barrier to larger vessels. These rocks made Trenton the head of navigation—the farthest point upriver from the Delaware's mouth that sloops, the single-masted sailboats that were the workhorses of colonial trade, could reliably reach. All shipping commerce that reached Trenton had to be unloaded and either reloaded onto ships on the other side of the falls or put on wagons. Only small, flat-bottomed, shallow draft boats could traverse the falls. They carried the produce from farmers on both sides of the river and unloaded their goods in Trenton for the wagon ride to Philadelphia. Sloops and ferries were continuously passing and repassing on the river, carrying travelers and their horses. This shallow, rocky stretch of the Delaware River bestowed on Trenton the economic benefits of loading and unloading fees, multiple ferries, busy taverns, and riverside jobs such as oarsmen and baggage carriers.[23]

Adding to its importance, Trenton also sat astride the main postal and transportation route between the bustling cities of New York and Philadelphia. Stagecoaches, carrying passengers and mail, traversed this vital artery, with the majority relying on the ferries at Trenton to cross the Delaware River. This confluence of water and land routes positioned Trenton as a key hub in the colonies' emerging transportation and communication network.[24]

By the time of the American Revolution, Trenton had been the county seat for almost sixty years and thus was a center for legal business. Lawyers entered town in wagons, sulkies (small single carriages), and public stagecoaches. The hotels and taverns were thronged with lawyers, jurors, and witnesses eating and sleeping in close proximity to each other.[25]

Trenton in 1776 was a pleasant, unplanned jumble of breweries and druggists, merchants' warehouses, churches and taverns, elegant mansions, and one hundred modest frame dwellings. Only a third of the residents were involved with agriculture. The town had a surprisingly large amount of industry. Mahlon Stacy's original hewn-log-sided mill along the Assunpink had been replaced by William Trent with a three-story stone building that ground and sifted wheat twenty-four hours a day. Two ironworks were built, Samuel Henry's on the Assunpink and Benjamin Yard's plating mill at the mouth of a small stream, Petty's Run. Trenton was a jumble of activity with silversmiths, gunsmiths, blacksmiths, shoemakers, bakers, coopers, chair makers, corset makers, a tannery, and a large dry-goods store. The town had fifteen lawyers, one sheriff, a county court building, four places of worship, and a jail.[26]

Carriages and horsemen passed and repassed through Trenton on their journeys to New York and Philadelphia, stagecoaches and mails came and went regularly, ships loaded and unloaded, merchants and officials, judges, lawyers, farmers, and peddlers found lodgment here.

Trenton was a lively, vibrant town—and then the Hessians arrived.

CHAPTER 21

Danger, Distrust, and Fatigue

When the men of the Rall Brigade arrived in Trenton, what they saw was a dreary, mostly deserted town. Almost all the inhabitants had left at the approach of the king's forces. The Hessians saw ahead of them at least four months of being crammed into small houses with six or seven of their unbathed comrades in one room. A town with no fun, no recreation. A miserable place to recuperate after having fought five battles in three months. The more-experienced soldiers realized that occupying the town was dangerous, a defender's nightmare. Roads converged on the town from every direction, offering an advancing enemy multiple avenues of approach. The proximity to the Delaware River allowed the Americans to cross in small detachments, strike, and quickly retreat unmolested back across the water. A surrounding countryside of dense forests gave cover to small groups of Americans who harassed and sometimes ambushed the king's troops.

None of the Hessian had anything good to say about the village. While they would be standing in the freezing cold on picket duty or walking day and night in the snow on patrols, their comrades in New York would be enjoying parties and celebrations throughout the winter.[1]

Trenton was laid out in the north-south direction, perpendicular to where the Delaware River met the Assunpink Creek. Some one hundred of the houses were in the main part of the town (north of the river), and the remainder were on the other side of the town (south of the Assunpink Creek). Most of the larger houses were on the two main streets in the center of town, King Street and Queen Street, which ran nearly parallel in a north-south direction from the river and united at a junction north of the village.[2]

King and Queen Streets formed a distinctive, funnel-like shape through Trenton. At their southern end near the river, the two streets were set wide apart. As they ascended north, the distance between them narrowed until they converged at a junction atop a small hill, the highest point in town. Many of the Hessian officers were well versed in military history, and this topographical feature, with its narrowing terrain leading to an elevated position, would not have been lost on them. It bore an uncanny resemblance to the battlefield of Agincourt, where in 1415, French knights had made a fateful charge uphill across a narrowing field, only to be crowded together and massacred by the English forces positioned on the high ground. If the Americans were to seize control of the hill where King and Queen Streets met, the Hessians could find themselves in a predicament reminiscent of the French at Agincourt.[3]

However, this tactical vulnerability seemed a distant concern to the Hessian command, notably Colonel Rall and General Grant. They dismissed the possibility of a successful American attack on Trenton, believing Washington's ragtag army incapable of launching such a complicated mission, which would require transporting thousands of soldiers with horses and artillery across the ice choked Delaware River. Even if, by some miracle, the Americans managed to cross the river, the Hessians were confident that such a force could not approach undetected.

By December 14, all three regiments of the Rall Brigade had fully assembled in Trenton. A light snow fell, the delicate flakes vanishing into the dirt the moment they touched the ground. The narrow streets, now crowded with soldiers, carried the pungent aroma of semifrozen horse manure mingled with the earthy scent of mud and unbathed men. Colonel Rall's blue-coated regiments were joined by a colorful array of reinforcements: a blue-coated artillery detachment with their distinctive long, tapered boots distinguishing them from the infantry; fifty additional Jägers under the command of Lieutenant Fredrich Wilhelm von Grothausen, clad in their traditional green coats with crimson lapels and carrying their grooved-barrel rifles, widely regarded as the most lethal weapon of the era. Tasked with scouting and carrying messengers were twenty of the Queen's Light Dragoons (light cavalry) resplendent in their bright red uniforms and brass helmets adorned with red horsehair, creating a striking contrast against the winter landscape. Altogether, the brigade now numbered about 1,400 men.[4]

Standing in the street, Andreas Wiederhold looked beyond the brigade's bright uniforms and martial pageantry to see its true form. He noted the brigade's deteriorating condition: Uniforms bore ragged holes and hastily stitched patches. Elbows and knees were threadbare, the fabric nearly transparent from constant use. Once-bright blue coats were now faded from sun and rain and stained with mud and worse. "Our poor worn out soldiers," he bemoaned, "denuded of small clothes and uniforms." A Lossberg officer's correspondence confirmed these observations, noting, "Our people begin to grow ragged," and warning that the situation would only worsen since "our baggage is left at New York."

The approaching winter magnified these deficiencies. The men's thin uniforms offered scant protection against the cold, and officers voiced concerns to Rall about the lack of adequate winter undergarments. While the brigade possessed warm overcoats, these were reserved for soldiers on picket duty, leaving most of the troops exposed to the elements. The condition of the brigade's footwear was most alarming. The shoes of many of the men had worn-out soles, exposing bare feet to the frozen ground. So many shoes were falling apart that officers now submitted urgent requests to the quartermaster for replacements, a clear sign of the brigade's decline.[5]

The toll of illness was severe, with fevers sweeping through all the Hessian brigades, hitting older officers particularly hard. The Lossberg Regiment lost Colonel Heeringen to dysentery. Compounding these troubles, the British Army's equipment proved poorly suited to the New World's climate and terrain. The army's tents were poorly constructed and "leaked like sieves in the American downpour." For much of the campaign, the men had been forced to sleep without tents, bivouacked under the open sky.

Many of the troops believed the fluctuating temperatures—warm autumn days that quickly turned frigid at night—were contributing to the high incidence of dysentery.[6]

The casualties from months of fighting had further thinned the ranks. Record keeping was inconsistent, but the scale of losses was clear. The Hessian army's baptism of fire in America came at the Battle of Brooklyn, where the Rall Brigade suffered only two killed and twenty-five wounded, a deceptively mild introduction. The battles that followed were far bloodier, with hundreds of Hessians killed or wounded. At Fort Washington, the Lossberg Regiment sustained forty-three wounded in just a few hours, and even smaller skirmishes like the Battles of Pelham and Miller's Hill resulted in hundreds more casualties combined.[7]

Two senior officers shared Wiederhold's concerns. Major Friedrich von Dechow, commander of the Knyphausen Regiment, met with Lieutenant Colonel Francis Scheffer of the Lossberg Regiment. Both seasoned officers—Dechow had fought under Frederick the Great and was twice wounded at Fort Washington, while Scheffer had served for thirty-five years and had been awarded the order Pour la vertu militaire (Award for Military Virtue) for his brave conduct at the Battles of Fort Washington and White Plains—they shared a growing alarm about the shape of the brigade. Bypassing both Rall and Grant, they warned General von Heister directly that illness, exhaustion, and winter's hardships had dangerously reduced their effective fighting strength.[8]

The temperature in Trenton was just above freezing. Bivouacking under the stars was no longer a viable option, but finding suitable quarters for this influx of soldiers was a challenge. The optimal location, the naturally elevated junction of King and Queen Streets at the north of town, offered the best defensive position against a surprise attack and the greatest distance from the sporadic shelling by rebel artillery across the river. But that area was sparsely populated, offering limited lodging.[9]

Reluctantly, Rall billeted most of his men on and about King and Queen Streets in the southern part of town, close to the Delaware River and within reach of Washington's cannons. The Hessians commandeered private houses, assigning about twenty-five soldiers to each. The few remaining citizens of Trenton, many surreptitious Patriots, could only watch helplessly as the town's five houses of worship, its schoolhouse, the post office, even the courthouse with its jail, were repurposed into makeshift barracks. Three of the town's most prominent inns, the City Tavern, the Bull's Head Tavern, and the True American Inn, which usually offered shelter and warm food to travelers, were requisitioned and filled with Hessian soldiers, their hearths now used to warm shivering troops rather than weary travelers.[10]

Loyalist refugees fleeing the rebel army found themselves sharing an old stone barracks from the French and Indian War with the brigade's Jägers. Even worse, the wives and children of the brigade's Hessian soldiers arrived in town. The women were notorious for their cruel plundering, considered more brutal than their husbands'. They were quartered in the barracks with the fleeing Loyalists. The stone walls of the barracks offered poor insulation against the weather, and the occupants were cold and miserable.[11]

Commerce in Trenton came to a standstill. Though some townspeople continued doing business with the occupying forces, most fled. Those who remained found themselves living "shoulder to shoulder" with the Hessian army. Some locals sought protection by taking General Howe's oath of allegiance to the king. A Hessian officer noted this trend with suspicion: "A great many came to headquarters in Trenton, were accepted, and dismissed with the protection. Unfortunately, it was not discovered until too late that many, on the other hand, had come only to look around and spy." While many, perhaps the majority, took the oath hoping the occupying troops would protect and not plunder their families, their hopes for fair treatment often proved futile.[12]

One resident of the town, remembering her childhood, recalled the brass-helmeted Hessians strutting about and the atmosphere of fear permeating the town. "We lived in momentary dread of their appearance," she wrote. "And our worst fears were soon fulfilled." One night, a group of huge, aggressive Hessian soldiers, accompanied by their wives, burst into her home "jabbering away in harsh, guttural tones." They declared their intention to take up quarters in the house. The children watched in horror as their mother was grabbed by one of the Hessian women who ripped a silver shoe buckle from their mother's shoe, striking her in the face with its heel when she resisted.

The mother pleaded with the Hessians that her husband was an officer in the British Army (he actually was in Washington's army), and the Hessians toned down their intimidating attitude. That night, the terrified family crowded together in one bedroom, listening helplessly as the Hessians ransacked their home. Closets, pickle jars, and canisters of preserves were opened and emptied, with the invaders helping themselves "like a swarm of locusts."[13]

The atmosphere in occupied New Jersey was one of mutual suspicion. While civilians feared the king's troops, the soldiers themselves harbored deep mistrust of the local population. General Howe threatened summary execution for partisan fighters, declaring, "Small straggling parties not dressed like soldiers and without officers . . . who presume to molest or fire upon our soldiers . . . will be immediately hanged without trial as assassins." However, just as Howe's oaths of allegiance failed to shield loyal subjects from the depredations of his own forces, his harsh decrees proved equally ineffective in curbing the raids and ambushes carried out by bands of irregular rebel troops. This cycle of fear and retaliation only served to deepen the divide between occupiers and occupied.[14]

Colonel Rall, following orders to establish a formal headquarters in Trenton "to mark his honor and authority," selected the spacious home of Stacy Potts, a prominent Trenton citizen. Potts, a grandson of Thomas Potts, traced his lineage to one of Trenton's original settlers who had braved an Atlantic crossing on the *Shield* with Mahlon Stacy in 1678. His first name, Stacy, reflected the intermarriage of the neighboring Stacy and Potts families in the early days of the settlement.

Stacy Potts' wealth was evident in his commodious two-story wooden frame house, boasting multiple rooms and several fireplaces. To the Hessians, the home was like the grand manor of a nobleman. Behind the residence lay an elegant garden bordered by Petty's Run, a stream that flowed into the Delaware River. The garden's well-tended flowers served a dual purpose: beautifying the property and masking the pungent odors from Potts' nearby tannery along the stream. The sweet fragrance of goldenrods, black-eyed Susans, and purple coneflowers competed with the unpleasant scents of the tanning process, including cow urine, decomposing animal flesh, and stagnant water vats. Downstream, Potts operated a steelworks near the Delaware's mouth. One of his business associates was John Fitch, who would later gain fame as the inventor of the steamboat.

Rall likely chose the Potts residence for the comfort it offered, including eight bedrooms, numerous fireplaces, and a stable sufficient to contain eight horses, with room for hay to keep them. The fact that he would be sharing quarters with several unmarried young ladies of the Potts family might have influenced his decision. Potts was a Quaker who had signed no allegiances to either side; but despite his political aloofness, he was respected and trusted by Loyalists and Patriots alike.[15]

The decision to station most of the soldiers along King and Queen Streets was born out of necessity, offering little in terms of defense. To rectify this, Rall billeted troops in homes and buildings on the outskirts of town. This approach served two purposes: It offered quarters for the men and created a defensive ring around Trenton of pickets and guardhouses to provide early alerts in case of attack.

Moving clockwise from the Princeton Road on the periphery of the town's northern border, a chain of picket stations, guard houses, and buildings to quarter the men included:

Princeton Road (Fox Chase Tavern): Seventy men, led by four officers, stood watch here, forming the northernmost outpost.

Assunpink Bridge (True American Inn/Johnathan Richmond's Inn): Positioned southeast of town across the Assunpink Creek, near the flour mill, this post was occupied by eighteen men and one officer to guard the bridge connecting Trenton's Queen Street with the road to Bordentown.

Ferry Road (Royal Oak Inn): Just south of the Assunpink Creek Bridge, on the road to Bordentown, twenty-five men and six officers were stationed at the road to the Trenton Ferry. They guarded the Trenton Ferry and the road to Bordentown. Situated near the riverbank, these men had strict orders to stay out of sight during daylight to avoid drawing fire from American artillery across the river. They were relieved under the cover of darkness to minimize exposure to enemy batteries.[16]

River Road (two-story Stone Barracks): Built during the French and Indian War on the southern border of town on River Road, this sturdy structure housed approximately 150 infantrymen, fifty Jägers, and Tory refugees who had come to town seeking British protection.

River Road (the Hermitage): About half a mile from the two-story Stone Barracks lay the large country estate of General Philemon Dickinson of the Continental Congress and the Continental Army. The estate was now repurposed as a post controlled by Jägers. Their mission was to watch the river closely, and patrols were often sent upstream to guard against American crossings. Pickets were dispersed across the grounds, taking positions in the servants' quarters, barn, greenhouse, vegetable garden, and two separate huts, one behind the barn and another up the road. Each morning, three or four British dragoons scouted the river as far as Yardley's Ferry, about four miles upstream.

Pennington Road (Alexander Calhoun's house and merchandise store): This site, at Alexander Calhoun's house and merchandise store, about a quarter mile outside the northern edge of town on Pennington Road, was held by a company of Lossberg infantry under Captain Ernst von Altenbockum, a seasoned, twenty-two-year veteran.

Pennington Road (Howell cooper shop and residence): A little farther down the road from von Altenbockum, on a remote stretch of Pennington Road, fifteen men and one officer were posted at the home of coopers (barrel makers) Richard and Arthur Howell. The residence served as both a picket and an alarm house where soldiers would gather when an alarm was sounded.

Crosswicks Creek Drawbridge: Four miles south of Trenton, on the road to Bordentown, stood a drawbridge surrounded by thick, mostly unsettled woods. Though it was two miles nearer to von Donop's position in Bordentown, von Donop used his seniority to shift responsibility for this isolated outpost to Rall. In the event of a rebel attack, the one hundred men and four officers at the bridge were under orders to retreat to Bordentown.[17]

To bolster Trenton's defenses, Rall established a network of patrols to circle the town. The main circuit commenced at the Fox Chase Tavern outpost northeast of town on the Princeton Road. From there, the patrol marched to the west on Pennington Road passing the picket stations at the Howells' cooper shop and at Alexander Calhoun's house. Turning south, they traversed the network of picket and guard stations that ringed the town until they reached River Road. Along the Delaware River, south of town, the Hermitage and Stone Barracks outposts guarded River Road. A chain of sentries completed the defensive ring by looping north back to the Fox Chase Tavern. Additional patrols protected the vital riverside regions on the south end of town near the Assunpink Bridge and the Trenton Ferry. Small squads of infantry and cavalry patrolled about five miles north of town to protect the Yardley and Howell Ferries. On occasion, but not every day, they might patrol an additional five miles to the McKonkey and Johnson's Ferries. The erratic and inconsistent decisions about patrolling as far as McKonkey's Ferry would soon have profound consequences for the Hessians stationed in Trenton.[18]

With pickets, guard stations, and patrols keeping watch, the final defensive measures needed to secure the town were the placement of the brigade's artillery, establishment of alarm posts, and construction of redoubts.

The brigade's officers recommended two locations for the cannons: the intersection of King and Queen Streets provided an elevated position from which the cannons could protect most of the Trenton houses quartering troops, and at the Assunpink Bridge, where artillery pieces could safeguard the bridge, the nearby Trenton Ferry, and the road to Bordentown.

WASHINGTON'S
CROSSING TO TRENTON
DECEMBER 25-26, 1776
American Forces
Hessian Forces
Hessian Guard Post
Hessian Sentry
A Fox Chase Tavern Ensign Gräbe
B Howell's Cooper Shop Lt. Wiederhold
C Calhoun's Merchandise Store Capt. von Altenbockum
Bear Tavern
Pennington
Johnson's Ferry
McConkey's Ferry
Jacob's Creek
SCOTCH ROAD
BEAR TAVERN ROAD
NEW JERSEY
Beatty's Ferry
Birmingham
Howell's Ferry
Greene's Division
PENNINGTON ROAD
Delaware River
Yardley's Ferry
Sullivan's Division
RIVER ROAD
PRINCETON
The Hermitage
Upper Trenton Ferry
Trenton
Stone Bridge
PENNSYLVANIA
Ewing's Force (failed to cross)
BORDENTOWN
South Trenton Ferry
0
2
SCALE IN MILES
N
S
E
W
1. Dec. 25, 1776, 4:00 PM: Preparations begin for Washington's crossing. This includes 2,400 troops, 18 cannons, 50–75 horses, and commanders Sullivan, Greene, Glover, and Knox.
2. Dec. 25–26, 11:00 PM – 4:00 AM: Main force completes river crossing, but later than expected.
3. Dec. 26, 6:00 AM: Washington splits his troops for a two-pronged march toward Trenton.
4. Dec. 26, 8:00 AM: Washington's forces reach Trenton and open fire — Battle of Trenton begins.
5. Dec. 26, 9:30 AM: Battle ends: ~900 Hessians captured, ~100 killed.

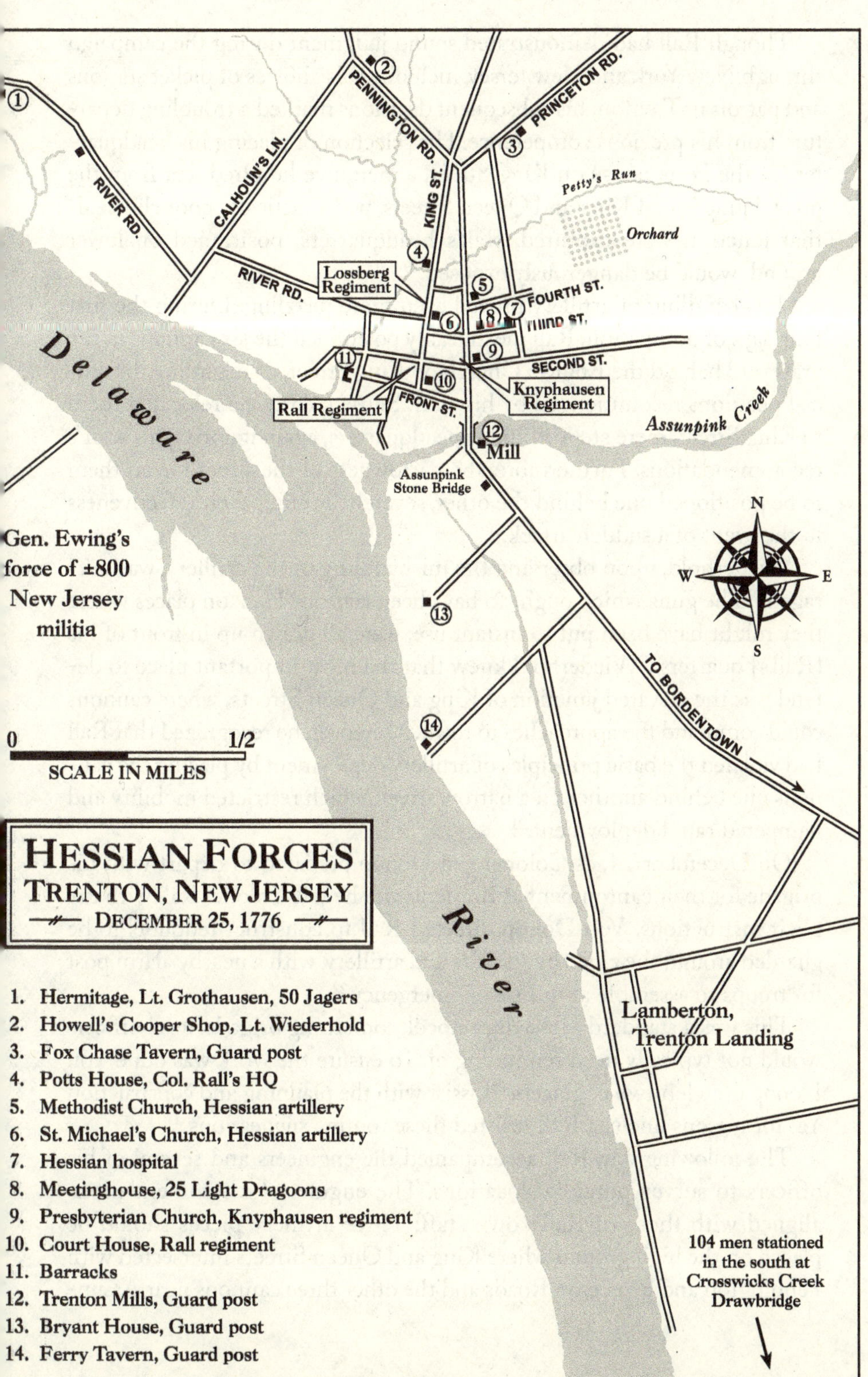

PENNINGTON RD.
PRINCETON RD.
RIVER RD.
CALHOUN'S LN.
KING ST.
Petty's Run
Orchard
RIVER RD.
Lossberg Regiment
FOURTH ST.
THIRD ST.
SECOND ST.
Delaware
Rall Regiment
FRONT ST.
Knyphausen Regiment
Assunpink Creek
Mill
Assunpink Stone Bridge
N
W
E
S
Gen. Ewing's force of ±800 New Jersey militia
TO BORDENTOWN
0
1/2
SCALE IN MILES
HESSIAN FORCES
TRENTON, NEW JERSEY
DECEMBER 25, 1776
River
Lamberton, Trenton Landing
1. Hermitage, Lt. Grothausen, 50 Jagers
2. Howell's Cooper Shop, Lt. Wiederhold
3. Fox Chase Tavern, Guard post
4. Potts House, Col. Rall's HQ
5. Methodist Church, Hessian artillery
6. St. Michael's Church, Hessian artillery
7. Hessian hospital
8. Meetinghouse, 25 Light Dragoons
9. Presbyterian Church, Knyphausen regiment
10. Court House, Rall regiment
11. Barracks
12. Trenton Mills, Guard post
13. Bryant House, Guard post
14. Ferry Tavern, Guard post
104 men stationed in the south at Crosswicks Creek Drawbridge

Though Rall had demonstrated sound judgment during the campaign through New York and New Jersey, including his choices of picket stations and patrols in Trenton, his subsequent decisions marked a troubling departure from his previous competence. His selection of placing his headquarters in the Potts house on King Street, a mere five hundred feet from the pivotal junction of King and Queen Streets, was a tactically poor choice. If that junction were captured, Rall's headquarters, positioned on lower ground, would be dangerously exposed.[19]

His handling of artillery proved even more puzzling. During the first four days of occupation, Rall inexplicably positioned the six cannons in the graveyard behind the English Church on King Street, disregarding the crucial positions recommended by his staff. Subsequently, he relocated them to King Street, mere steps from his headquarters, again ignoring his staff's recommendations. Furthermore, the narrowness of the street forced them to be positioned one behind the other, severely limiting their effectiveness in the event of a sudden attack.[20]

Wiederhold, upon observing the mishandling of the artillery, was outraged. "The guns which ought to have been stationed . . . on places where they might have been put to instant use, were all drawn up in front of his [Rall's] quarters." Wiederhold knew that the most important place to defend was the elevated junction of King and Queen Streets, where cannons could command the approaches to town. Moreover, he recognized that Rall had violated the basic principles of artillery deployment by placing the cannons one behind another on a narrow street, which restricted mobility and hampered rapid deployment.[21]

On December 14, as Colonel von Donop prepared to depart with his brigade for their cantonment at Bordentown, he left Colonel Rall with explicit instructions. Von Donop directed Rall to construct redoubts to be guarded around the clock by soldiers and artillery, with a nearby alarm post for troops to assemble at in case of emergency.[22]

This was a standard Hessian protocol, something brigade-level officers would not typically need reminding of. To ensure the work was done, von Donop even left two engineers to assist with the planning and construction Yet for reasons unclear, Rall resisted these routine suggestions.[23]

The following day, Rall accompanied the engineers and several of his officers to survey potential locations. The engineers' recommendations aligned with those of Rall's own staff: Three artillery pieces should be placed on the high ground where King and Queen Streets intersected with Pennington and Princeton Roads and the other three cannons near Assunpink Bridge. Despite approving these plans, Rall failed to issue orders to commence construction.

A few days later, von Donop, concerned by the lack of progress, again sent Rall a message urging him to fortify the positions. Surprisingly, instead of heeding his superior's directive, Rall dismissed the matter, telling the messenger, Captain Reinhard Martin of the Hessian engineers, that he did not think redoubts necessary since the rebels were a miserable lot incapable of mounting an effective attack. Captain Martin later complained that he felt Rall was mocking him.[24]

A delegation of officers—Wiederhold; Piel; artillerist Lieutenant Friedrich Fischer, Lieutenant Georg Zoll, adjutant of the Lossberg Regiment; and Major von Dechow—personally appealed to Rall, urging him to begin construction of the redoubts. Rall was again dismissive of the need to build fortifications, declaring that the way to beat the rebels was with bayonets, not trenches. Furthermore, he refused to assign emergency assembly points for the troops, a standard military precaution in case of a surprise attack.

Major Dechow persisted. "Colonel, it does not cost anything" to build redoubts. "If it does not help, it also does no harm!" He suggested that Wiederhold oversee the construction. But again, despite the reasonableness of the offer, Rall remained obstinate. According to Wiederhold, Rall laughed at the suggestion and walked away.[25]

Perhaps to protect himself from accusations of insubordination, Rall wrote to Colonel von Donop, explaining that redoubts would be of little use in Trenton, as the enemy could approach from any direction. It was not an unreasonable argument, but as Dechow had stated, there was nothing to lose in building the fortifications, as a small group of soldiers could construct them in a day. Ultimately, Rall's intransigence prevailed. No redoubts were built, and only two alarm posts, located on King Street near his headquarters and at the picket station in the Howell residence on Pennington Road, were designated.[26]

With cannons poorly positioned, no redoubts constructed, and only two alarm posts established, Trenton's defense rested solely on the stamina of pickets and patrols. This required a substantial commitment of manpower, with roughly four hundred to five hundred men—about a third of the brigade—deployed each day. As they paced on the town's frost-covered ground, the soldiers tried to ignore the coldness seeping into their wet, dilapidated shoes. The grueling schedule, the cold, windy weather, and long hours on their feet took a toll on the soldiers.[27]

During the initial days of the occupation, soldiers coming off duty at 4:00 P.M. stacked their arms in front of their commander's quarters and were instructed to sleep "under arms"—fully dressed and ready for action. After long shifts of patrolling in the frosty cold, the men were forced to sleep in full uniform, leather straps cutting into tired shoulders, the weight of ammunition pouches pressing against their sides. Some companies endured this punishing routine for three consecutive nights before receiving a night's rest.

The demanding schedule exhausted the men. Each day soldiers, their faces drawn and pale, their bodies shaking with fever, staggered into the brigade hospital in the Presbyterian Parsonage on Third and Queen Streets. Finally, after about a week, the system was modified so each regiment was only on duty for twenty-four hours every third day, with the nighttime guards and sentinels relieved at 9:00 A.M., predawn detachments at 2:00 P.M., and pickets at 4:00 P.M.. The schedule also included a daily parade at 11:00 A.M..

The brigade's artillery horses fared no better. They remained harnessed day and night, steam rising from their flanks in the cold air, waiting for an emergency that might require rapid deployment.

In addition, patrols were needed to guard the river from rebel crossings. As dawn broke, while darkness still engulfed the little town, a "heavy patrol" departed the Fox Chase Tavern on Princeton Road. The soldiers' footsteps echoed down empty streets past the English Church, where two artillery pieces hitched up and joined the patrol. A witness described it as an early morning "commotion" through the sleeping town with the cannons' creaking wheels, hoofbeats of the horses' ample gait, and the soldiers' boots in step on the cold, hard dirt of Queen Street. The patrol proceeded to Assunpink Bridge and Trenton Ferry, ensuring that the Delaware River downstream from town was safe. Each morning, three or four British dragoons riding at a slow pace trudged northward from the Hermitage, examining the Delaware upstream from the town. Throughout the day, patrols of Jägers examined the river upstream.

Lieutenant Wiederhold was infuriated by the seemingly endless patrols and guard duties interspersed with nights of trying to sleep fully clothed: "The duties were exceptional, guard duty, special detachments, picket duty without end . . . [which] served no purpose, . . . Senseless employment throughout the day."

But what particularly incensed Wiederhold was Rall using the troops, notably the brigade's musicians, to have a daily musical parade marching around the English Church. The sounds of oboes, trumpets, flutes, and drums filled the air while exhausted troops looked on. Wiederhold fumed that they looked like a "Catholic procession." Rall would follow the parade during the changeover of the guards, clearly enthralled by the melodies but never taking time to meet with the staff officers coming off duty to discuss the status of the garrison.

As the sun set and the temperature dipped below freezing on the evening of December 14, marking the end of the Rall Brigade's first full day of occupying Trenton, the soldiers settled into their makeshift sleeping quarters. What was about to follow were eleven days of relentless, dreary discomfort, monotony, fear, and mounting anxiety—eleven of the most trying days in the lives of the soldiers.

The twelfth day would bring something far worse.

CHAPTER 22

The Tide Begins to Turn

The Donop and Rall Brigades stood as the vanguard of the most powerful army on the continent, the front line of a vast empire whose power stretched from London to the Delaware River. Undefeated since their arrival in the New World, the Hessians had amassed victory after victory, striking fear into their enemies. Yet despite their fearsome reputation, subtly, but undeniably, the situation had shifted. The occupiers now found themselves on the defensive.

The raids began almost immediately after their arrival in Trenton. American militia and ununiformed partisans roamed the countryside. They avoided direct confrontation with occupied towns, instead targeting vulnerable foraging parties and messengers traveling between outposts. As each day brought new attacks, Rall began to lose men, and morale among his troops began to waver, leaving his troops exhausted and uneasy.

Over two thousand men, poorly bathed and in worn clothing, were crammed into a few hundred dwellings in Trenton and Bordentown. Posted just across the Delaware from Washington's most experienced Continental troops, the Rall Brigade in Trenton were the most exposed. They slept fully clothed, wary of a surprise attack. Most of their time was spent on patrol, trudging through the chill of winter, on the lookout for ambushes. There were no glorious battles to be fought, only the constant harassment by rebel forces. Any patrols that ventured beyond the defensive perimeter would be attacked by local militia. Having control of all watercraft on the river, small detachments of Continentals would cross the river daily and attack the Hessian pickets. A Lossberg Regiment officer lamented, "We are obliged to be constantly on our guard and very severe duty. . . . Notwithstanding we have marched across this extremely fine province of New Jersey. . . . Yet it is by no means freed from the enemy, and we are insecure both in flank and rear."[1]

In the half-light of dawn on December 16, three boats slipped from the Pennsylvania shore into the Delaware's icy waters. They carried thirty rebels toward the New Jersey bank, their approach masked by American artillery fire that shattered the morning quiet. Landing near Trenton Ferry, the raiders stormed a house serving as a Hessian picket station. Its seven defenders fled without resistance. Though Rall dispatched reinforcements, the raiders had already withdrawn across the river. "I cannot understand the object of the enemy in making this crossing," Rall wrote to von Donop, promising to strengthen the post with thirty additional men.

Rall's superior officer, thirty-eight-year-old Colonel Carl von Donop, reporting to General Grant, dismissed the raid with aristocratic disdain. "After this the rascals went off taking away as their only prize a pig." Neither he nor his fellow commanders grasped the psychological impact of these seemingly minor incursions. The raid, the second on this station, forced Rall to tie down thirty soldiers—3 percent of his brigade—at Trenton Ferry.[2]

The Americans maintained their pressure. On December 17, rebels ambushed British dragoons patrolling near Pennington. "Opened on them with a terrific fire," read one report, and when the dragoons withdrew, the attackers "fired rapidly on them, killed a horse, and wounded a dragoon." Rall dispatched yet another patrol to locate the wounded man.[3]

That same morning brought fresh alarms. "This morning at daybreak another party of rebels made a landing at the same place as they did the day before," Rall reported. Once again, he sent reinforcements, and once again, the raiders withdrew. Four miles north, seventy-five rebels crossed forcing Rall to divert twelve Jägers and two dragoons "to ascertain the facts." These raiders departed with willing local collaborators, "a family . . . with three cows and some furniture."[4]

The pattern of rebel harassment continued. On December 19, rebels wounded a dragoon near Maidenhead, a small village just south of Princeton. Responding to the earlier attacks on Trenton Ferry, Rall established a heavy morning patrol, complete with artillery, which marched from Fox Chase Tavern to Trenton Ferry. Johannes Reuber described the patrol: "Early in the morning Commander Rall selected a strong force from his brigade, also a cannon, and we must march in two divisions, along the Delaware to see about the Americans making an effort to cross the Delaware for an aggression." The patrol did see Americans on the other side of the Delaware but no signs of aggressive activity, so the patrol with Reuber returned to town.[5]

The same day brought fresh troubles later. Just two miles from Trenton on the Princeton Road, three soldiers of the Lossberg Regiment vanished while foraging. The incident so unsettled Rall that he appealed to General Leslie in Princeton to "post some troops at Maidenhead in order to keep open the communication with Princeton." His growing anxiety showed in his admission to Leslie of "constant alarms and troubles" in Trenton.[6]

The American pressure continued mounting. On December 20, in a freezing rain that left the men wet and shivering, Lieutenant von Grothausen led a patrol of twenty Jägers and four dragoons from the Hermitage picket on River Road. Four miles upriver, they encountered 150 rebels. The Americans withdrew after a brief exchange of fire, leaving behind only a wounded horse. The next day's toll was heavier—a dragoon shot dead on patrol.[7]

Narrow country roads with surrounding thickets made the dragoons easy targets for rebel ambushes. One officer lamented that the vaunted, usually proud dragoons "were so frightened when they were to patrol that hardly any of them were willing to venture it without infantry, for they never went out patrolling without being fired upon or having one wounded or even shot dead."[8]

Until this point, the river crossings by the Americans had been done during the day; on the evening of December 20, they attacked at night. They rowed silently in the dark with blackened faces, snuck ashore at the ferry landing, and set houses on fire. Rall sent reinforcements, including Johannes Reuber, and the rebels fled back across the river. The pressure on the soldiers was mounting as demonstrated in Reuber's strange and ominous description of the attack in his diary: "Nights, negroes and others wanted to beat us up."[9]

General Howe's threat to hang armed civilians "not dressed like soldiers ... who presume to molest or fire upon [British] soldiers" proved ineffective against the growing American resistance. The British and Hessian commanders, trained in European warfare, found themselves confronting an enemy who refused to follow conventional rules of winter campaigning. As Howe declared the British offensive complete, the Americans seized the initiative.

The rebels struck in a haphazard and indiscriminate manner, but their tactics were effective. Irregular forces from New Jersey increasingly coordinated with local militia and Continental Army detachments, striking suddenly before vanishing into inaccessible terrain. Howe's cantonment system—posts separated by open country, connected by lonely roads that passed through woods and thickets—made them particularly vulnerable to such tactics.[10]

The impudence of these raids became clear during Howe's return to New York. Despite an escort of twenty dragoons surrounding him, forming a security zone a quarter-hour's march in all directions, the commander in chief nearly became another casualty. His dragoons discovered five armed men concealed in a ditch. The Americans fired and fled, but mounted pursuers captured them. Two of the rebels suffered wounds, and only the intervention of Howe's aide prevented their death at the hands of enraged dragoons.[11]

Even the commander in chief of the British Army was not safe on New Jersey roads.

Rall dispatched two dragoons to Princeton through freezing rain with urgent correspondence. Within an hour, they were ambushed. One dragoon fell dead, and the other's horse collapsed beneath him. Snatching the letters, the survivor mounted his dead comrade's horse and galloped back to Trenton. Alarmed by the attack, Rall immediately assembled a contingent of one hundred men and a piece of artillery to ensure the letters reached Princeton. Included in the correspondence was a request to General Leslie to station troops at Maidenhead.[12]

In his letters, Rall pleaded with his superiors that the combination of a strong outpost at Maidenhead and more frequent patrols on the road would keep open communications between Princeton and Trenton. Rall claimed that between 40 and 150 rebels were operating in the area, making it, as he described, "so unsafe on this side of the river." Just weeks earlier, Rall had confidently stormed Chatterton Hill and the heavily fortified Fort Washington. Now his insecurity was palpable, as evidenced by his decision to deploy one hundred men to deliver mail.

General Grant, receiving Rall's forwarded request for reinforcements, was unimpressed. Annoyed at Rall for sending a hundred men, which Grant saw as a foolish overreaction, he expressed his displeasure to Colonel von Donop about Rall's hundred man "spectacular gesture," declaring that Rall "is making much more of the rebels than they deserve."[13]

For Wiederhold, this incident became a nightmare, as he was sent with the one-hundred-man contingent to help with the artillery. He was a seasoned veteran used to fighting in all sorts of weather, but this night "the weather was exceptionally bad," he uncharacteristically complained. "We delivered our letter, slept on god's earth during the night, and returned home early next morning without seeing or hearing anything." He was embarrassed when the British soldiers in Trenton laughed at the sight of one hundred Hessians delivering a bunch of letters. "The Englanders made great fun of us, and it was truly laughable, because a non-commissioned officer and fifteen men were adequate to execute this."[14]

For the troops, the situation was deteriorating and morally disheartening. The Lossberg regimental journal recorded, "The road between Trenton and Princeton was now so unsafe, that no one would travel along it without a sufficient escort."[15]

When Colonel von Donop requested troops from Rall to better fortify his cantonment in Bordentown, Rall replied:

> It is impossible, my brother, to spare a battalion of my brigade as I am liable to be attacked at any moment. I have the enemy before me, behind me and at my right flank. The road from here to Princeton is very unsafe so that I have to send your letter by an escort of fifty men. . . . I beg therefore to be relieved of this request and not be placed in certain danger. I have not made any redoubts or any kind of fortifications because I have the enemy in all directions. It is then, my brother, absolutely impossible.[16]

Perhaps no letter or diary entry provides a better insight into the dispirited morale of the king's troops in New Jersey as they tried to cope with the hit-and-run tactics of the Americans than this letter of condolence sent by Colonel William Harcourt to Admiral Francis Geary, the father of a slain dragoon:

> It is with infinite reluctance I find myself under the very disagreeable necessity of communicating to you an event which must, I am persuaded, give you the utmost concern. Cornet [Francis Geary] having been ordered to advance with a party some miles into the country to procure intelligence of the enemy's situation, was upon his return from that duty fired upon by a party of the rebels, who had concealed themselves on each side of the road by which he proposed to have passed. Unfortunately, a ball took place, which in one moment deprived you of a son, and the regiment of an officer, whose loss cannot be sufficiently lamented.[17]

Now a strange incident occurred. General Leslie, appreciating Rall's predicament, deployed dragoons to Trenton and Maidenhead. Reuber watched the arrival of "Three English regiments from Princeton to Trenton for reinforcement and when they came to town and major Rall settled them, they were ordered to turn around and march back to Princeton." Why Rall would decline reinforcements at this precarious moment remains a mystery. Rall wrote to Leslie, "As there were no more attacks on this post, I have sent the battalion back"—a statement that makes no sense as there were attacks the very day these troops arrived.[18]

Washington and Rall developed starkly different approaches to protecting their forces along the Delaware. Rall relied heavily on intensive foot and mounted patrols circling Trenton, backed by picket stations. His British dragoons and Hessian Jägers ventured along the river. Despite direct orders from Colonel von Donop and urgings from his engineers, he refused to construct redoubts. His artillery deployment was minimal—typically a single gun accompanying riverside patrols making the artillery a mere extension of his patrols rather than a formidable defense. Lieutenant Wiederhold noted with frustration that Rall's entire strategy centered on defending the town itself, ignoring the surrounding approaches.[19]

Washington recognized the strategic importance of the Delaware River. He ordered the construction of redoubts at vital points along the river, ensuring constant surveillance of enemy movement. A Hessian officer remembered that Washington's men "occupied the opposite bank for 30 English miles or more, entrenched and constructed strong batteries at some places. Six or eight [Hessian soldiers] could not move together outside the town [Trenton] without being fired upon from these guns."[20]

Washington's men lived near the riverbank "crouched in the bushes," as one of them wrote, or behind little wooden-and-dirt ramparts. Some built wooden shanties from boards, but many slept in the woods without tents or blankets. Almost every soldier had the same type of experience along the Delaware. Private Thomas McCarty wrote, "The night past it snowed and it rained part of the night, was somewhat colder than usual." He was nursing a painful finger that had lost its nail, and the following night things worsened. His wooden hut burned down, leaving him with only the clothes on his back.[21]

Washington had scouting parties constantly out trying to discover Howe's plans. Guards stood watch at all twelve ferry crossings. Above all, Washington prioritized having the ability to raise an early alarm and gather intelligence. Colonel Joseph Reed, his aide, captured the essence of this strategy in a letter to Washington: "We must depend upon intelligence of their Motions—to which no Expense must be spared." Washington's network of observation posts served to warn of enemy movement and to gather intelligence about British dispositions.[22]

For months, the Hessian troops had relentlessly pursued the Continental Army across New Jersey, inflicting a series of crushing defeats. Lieutenant Piel of the Lossberg Regiment recalled their confidence: "The rebels had never successfully opposed us." Yet the Americans, though driven from every battlefield, refused to break. By mid-December, they had begun turning the tables on their pursuers. Small bands struck at isolated patrols and foraging parties, taking prisoners and occasionally killing the king's troops.

As winter settled over New Jersey, both armies appeared to adopt defensive positions. Yet beneath this surface calm, preparations continued on both sides. This apparent quiet would not last long.

CHAPTER 23

Fate Intervenes

On December 22, Washington gathered his officers for a council of war. The army's growing strength, he told them, finally permitted thoughts of offensive action. The discussion turned quickly to the possibility of striking an isolated enemy outpost in New Jersey. The officers reached swift agreement: The time to strike was now. Delay would be equal to defeat.

Their plan was simple, but bold: They would cross the Delaware at McKonkey's Ferry, march nine miles during the night, and attack Rall's isolated garrison at Trenton before dawn on December 26. Colonel Henry Knox, the chief of artillery, wrote his wife, "A hardy design was formed of attacking the town by storm." The next day, secret orders went out to senior commanders. After five months of retreat, the Continental Army would take the offensive. To General Gates, Washington confided simply, "We may yet affect an important stroke."[1]

Despite efforts at secrecy, Washington's plans began leaking to the British.

In Trenton, rumors of an impending American attack on Trenton began to circulate. Private Johannes Reuber captured the Hessian response: "The inhabitants of the city circulated a rumor that the rebels wanted to surprise us. We did not have any idea of such a thing and thought that the rebels were unable to do so." Colonel Rall shared this skepticism. The idea that Washington's beleaguered army could cross the river undetected to strike a garrison of over one thousand Hessians seemed implausible.[2]

General Grant, despite mounting evidence of an attack by the Americans, remained contemptuous. He assured Rall that the rebel army "does not exceed 8000 men who have neither shoes nor stockings, are in fact naked, dying of cold, without blankets and very ill supplied with Provisions." To von Donop, he wrote dismissively, "I can hardly believe that Washington would venture at this season of the year to pass the Delaware at Vessels Ferry [McKonkey's Ferry] as the repassing it may on account of the ice become difficult."[3]

On Christmas Eve, two Continental Army deserters brought a warning to Trenton. Under questioning by Lieutenant Piel and Colonel Rall, they revealed that Pennsylvania militia had drawn four days' rations and were preparing to march.[4]

More warnings followed. Dr. William Bryant, a Loyalist physician from near Trenton Ferry, sought out Rall with news from an informant who had crossed the river: The rebels had drawn several days' rations and planned to strike Trenton. Rall dismissed this intelligence with contempt: "This is all idle! It is old women's talk!"[5]

General Leslie sent word from Princeton that he had information that an attack was imminent. On Christmas Day, a Bucks County resident named Wahl approached Rall: "Colonel, take care, they're going to attack you." Rall's response was brief: "Let them come."[6]

And come they did.

With many enlistments expiring at the end of the month, Washington's already battered army was about to shrink below one thousand men. With no victories behind him, the cause seemed lost. But Washington had the backing of his generals and over two thousand devoted soldiers willing to try one last gamble. Determined and focused, he wrote, "It is in vain to ruminate upon or even reflect upon the authors or causes of our present fortunes." In other words, Washington was not looking back. He planned to change the direction of the war before the month ended, but for his course of action to succeed, his troops would need to demonstrate precise timing and the strict adherence to orders—talents they had yet to prove.[7]

At four o'clock on Christmas afternoon, as Rall settled into his game of checkers at the Potts house, drums began beating along the American side of the Delaware. The Continental Army formed for its usual evening parade, but something was different. Every man was ordered to carry a musket, even the musicians. New flints and sixty rounds of ammunition were distributed to each man along with three days' rations of salted meat and hard bread. Breaking with custom, officers withheld their destination from the troops. Washington had ordered "a profound silence to be enjoined, and no man to quit his ranks on pain of death."[8]

Washington's plan called for his 2,400 troops to reach their assembly point, behind the Pennsylvania hills forming a valley along the river near McKonkey's Ferry, by sunset at 4:41 P.M. "As soon as it begins to grow dark," his orders specified, they would quietly march to the ferry landing and begin crossing the Delaware River under cover of night.

If all went well, the army would complete its passage, reassemble on the New Jersey shore, and divide into two wings by midnight, leaving five hours to march ten miles to Trenton for a predawn attack. The left wing led by Nathanael Greene would strike the northern end of Trenton. The right wing led by John Sullivan would strike the southern end of town. Two small supporting forces, 800 men under the command of Brigadier General James Ewing and 1,200 led by Colonel John Cadwalader, would land south of Trenton.[9]

The schedule began unraveling almost immediately. A massive ice jam on the river prevented both Cadwalader's and Ewing's crossings. And despite meticulous planning, most of Washington's main force did not reach their assembly points until after 6:00 P.M., almost two hours behind schedule.[10]

Washington's three-pronged attack was on the verge of collapse. Only his men at McKonkey's Ferry remained—and they were two hours behind schedule.

As the troops assembled at McKonkey's Ferry, the sky was clear with scattered clouds, but some of the men sensed a slight change overhead.

While Washington's attack force assembled just ten miles away at McKonkey's Ferry, Rall was reading correspondences and preparing a ride through Trenton to inspect his outposts. Rall's mood vacillated between bold confidence and growing unease as reports of rebel activity increased. His confidence in open battle remained absolute. General Grant likely added to Rall's moments of overconfidence when he minimized the dangers with boastful letters that claimed he could, "Keep the peace in New Jersey with a corporal's guard."[11]

This bravado surfaced repeatedly in Rall's dealings with his officers. When Major von Dechow urged moving the brigade's vulnerable baggage from the town center, Rall dismissed his concerns: "The rebels will not come, but if they do and can take me, they can have all the stores and the baggage to my very last wagon." Asked about constructing fortifications, his response was equally dramatic: "Let them come! . . . We want no trenches! We will go at them with the bayonet."[12]

Yet in private correspondence, Rall painted a darker picture. He spoke of how his regiment was "extremely fatigued" from miserable weather and endless harassment. He worried that he had only two officers fit for duty, and he knew that the Lossberg Regiment fared even worse. The pressure never eased. Each night he kept one regiment awake, dressed and ready for a fight. Three times in the last four days—December 22, 23, and 25—the entire brigade turned out for alarms.[13]

"We have not slept one night in peace since we came to this place," wrote an officer of the Lossberg Regiment. "The troops have been laying on their arms every night and they can endure it no longer." Captain von Altenbockum reported his men at the Pennington Road picket had been "under arms three consecutive nights, and then off duty for one night."[14]

Many of the soldiers thought Christmas Day would bring a respite, but it did not. Contrary to later legend, there was no revelry or heavy drinking in the Hessian camp. That morning, General Grant warned that elements of Washington's army might strike. The Americans, he wrote, had learned of weakness in the Hessian positions at Trenton and Princeton. Grant emphasized that his source was "undoubtedly true" and urged Rall "to be upon your guard against an unexpected attack at Trenton." The letter's urgency was evident in its timing, having been written at "past 11:00 at night."[15]

That afternoon, Rall rode out to personally inspect his pickets. Though he found nothing to alarm him, his actions belied his earlier dismissals of attack warnings: he quietly doubled the picket strength around Trenton to one hundred men, a tacit acknowledgment of the warnings he had publicly dismissed.

At 4:00 P.M., American drums along the Delaware's eastern shore began to beat ominously. Rall paid them no mind.[16]

As daylight waned and darkness descended on December 25, two very different scenes were unfolding. Washington's regiments were approaching their assembly point, a valley near McKonkey's Ferry whose hills sheltered them from the enemy across the river. Nine miles downriver in Trenton, Colonel Rall, after a day of ominous warnings but no action, sat down by the warmth of a roaring stone fireplace to play checkers with his host Stacy Potts. Rall enjoyed refreshments served by the Pottses' daughters, just as the American troops were beginning to maneuver horses and artillery onto ice-slicked boats.

It had been a sunny day with the temperature in the twenties and a light wind out of the north. In the early afternoon, the barometer fell, the wind shifted to the northeast, and clouds rolled in. The farmers and hunters of both armies could read the signs of a change in the weather. They did not need a falling barometer to tell them trouble was on the horizon. By late afternoon they could feel the wind growing stronger, and they could see clouds racing across the sky. A nor'easter was sweeping up from the south. One of the Continental privates recalled "that no sooner had the sun set than it began to drizzle." By the time he reached the assembly point at McKonkey's Ferry, the drizzle had become a driving rain.[17]

Now, as so often happens in war, fate stepped in.

At about 7:30 P.M., gunshots cracked through the freezing air along Trenton's northwest edge near Pennington Road—the very road on which Washington planned to advance in a few hours. The shots came from a small band of Virginia raiders operating without Washington's knowledge or consent. Washington's main army remained at McKonkey's Ferry, where the ice-choked Delaware slowed its crossing. Though unconnected to Washington's carefully planned operation, these unauthorized shots would reshape the coming battle.

At first only a single shot rang out, followed by a few scattering shots, then silence. Rall rose from his game of checkers to investigate. The source was quickly discovered. Forty or fifty rebels had burst from the woods near the Howell cooper shop on Pennington Road north of town, overwhelming the sixteen-man picket led by twenty-six-year-old Corporal William Hartung. In moments, six Hessians lay wounded, bleeding in the freezing darkness. Seeing that the Americans outnumbered them, the ten uninjured men, carrying their injured comrades, fell back to Captain von Altenbockum's post at Alexander Calhoun's merchandise store.[18]

Von Altenbockum gave Hartung eight of his own men to go back and search the woods around the Howell cooper shop. His men scoured the region just beyond the picket stations. Finding nothing, von Altenbockum sent thirty men from the Rall Regiment to look for the enemy farther up the road.[19]

In town, all the regiments raced into the street fully armed. The Rall Regiment formed up outside the English Church. Rall concluded that this was likely the attack he had been warned about all week, and he marched his regiment up King Street to the high ground at the junction of Pennington and Princeton Roads.

The patrol that von Altenbockum had sent out returned after traveling about two miles up the road without encountering any rebels.

Rall sent Wiederhold with ten men to reinforce the picket post at Howell's cooper shop, increasing its strength to twenty men. Von Altenbockum brought his men back to their warm, dry quarters at Alexander Calhoun's merchandise store. Their guns were stacked, but the soldiers were under strict orders to remain fully clothed in their damp uniforms. Being extra cautious, von Altenbockum split the troops between Calhoun's house, the Howell cooper shop, and two nearby houses. Von Altenbockum met Colonel Rall and his regiment at the head of King Street. Rall listened to von Altenbockum's story of the attack.[20]

Still concerned that this might be the attack he was warned about, Rall ordered two companies to advance, supported by dragoons and a single cannon. In the numbing cold of Christmas night, Lieutenant Colonel Balthasar Brethauer, the inspector of guards, accompanied the force as they checked each outpost in turn. Finding no sign of rebels in the dark woods, Rall returned his men to their positions.[21]

The size of this attack convinced Rall that this was the long-predicted rebel assault. The casualty count—six Hessians wounded by a force of fifty rebels—exceeded any raid that week. Major von Dechow pressed for immediate action, urging Rall to dispatch strong patrols of infantry, artillery, and dragoons to ensure that the rebels were not crossing at the ferry landings. Rall waved off the suggestion, cursed, and dismissed the rebels as "country clowns."[22]

Von Dechow, frustrated by his commander's indifference, took matters into his own hands. He posted armed sentinels before every house occupied by his regiment and ordered the sentinels to make sure that the men remained inside, ready for alarm.[23]

Lieutenant Wiederhold was furious, declaring a few days later, "A more vigilant commander would have issued orders to reconnoiter all the roads up to the river and the ferries. . . . This would have revealed [Washington's] whole plan and turned the scale." Like von Dechow, Wiederhold acted on his own initiative, posting seven pickets in the field and on the roads. As further insurance he sent out "one patrol after another to prevent being surprised."[24]

With the weather worsening, Rall was confident the Americans would not try another raid that night. He accepted an invitation to a late supper at the house of Postmaster Abraham Hunt. A wealthy merchant known for maintaining cordial relations with both sides, Hunt had cultivated a reputation for hospitality that transcended political divisions. His parlor was renowned for its evening gatherings: clay pipes sending smoke to the rafters, card games stretching into the night, and fine liquors flowing freely.

While his men maintained their posts in the darkness, Rall passed Christmas evening in Hunt's well-heated parlor. Though no direct evidence exists of Rall drinking excessively, he most certainly would have imbibed liberally of the liquor in this festive atmosphere, and the comfortable setting stood in marked contrast to the vigilance required of his command. Yet Rall felt secure. Every approach to Trenton was watched by his sentries, their breath visible in the cold darkness as they stood at their posts, muskets at the ready.

At McKonkey's Ferry, the ice-choked Delaware River proved more formidable than anticipated. Sleet and hail pelted the men as they crossed. Sixteen-year-old fifer John Greenwood found inspiration even in misery: "The noise of the soldiers coming over and clearing away the ice, the rattling of the cannon wheels on the frozen ground, and the cheerfulness of my fellow comrades encouraged me beyond expression."[25]

The army would be at its most vulnerable when crossing the river. For this hazardous task, Washington chose twenty-five Durham boats seized from their owner, the Durham Iron Works. Washington knew that these vessels, unique to the Delaware region, were the workhorses of river commerce. Stretching more than fifty feet in length, Durham boats looked like huge canoes, but the appearance was deceptive. They were actually flat bottomed. Washington was counting on their reputation for carrying enormous loads of cargo—up to seventeen tons—on an incredibly shallow draft of merely twenty inches, making them very stable, even in rough conditions. The other essential vessels on this stormy evening were the local ferry boats. Like the Durham boats, they were flat-bottomed craft designed for shallow water.[26]

For the crossing, Washington again turned to John Glover and his Marblehead seamen and fishermen—the same men who had saved the army after the disastrous Battle of Brooklyn. Their seafaring experience would prove crucial this night as they needed to navigate swift currents, swirling eddies, and treacherous chunks of ice on the Delaware River. Joining them were seasoned watermen from the Philadelphia waterfront and local ferrymen familiar with the river's nighttime passage.[27]

The troops moved silently through the valley toward McKonkey's Ferry House. Cresting the hill that had hidden them from enemy view, they encountered a confused and chaotic scene at the ferry landing. Many soldiers wore tattered, faded, and dirt-stained clothing and broken shoes. The moonless night and driving rain limited visibility, but the soldiers—few of whom could swim—saw clearly enough the dark river filled with ice floes rushing past in the swift current. Many took off their backpacks, sat on the ice-laden grass, and waited somberly as more units arrived, adding to the confusion.

Glover's men began loading the Durham boats. "Boats were in readiness," Major James Wilkinson later wrote, "but the force of the current, the sharpness of the frost, the darkness of the night, the ice which . . . [formed] during the operation, and a high wind, rendered the passage of the river extremely difficult."[28]

The soldiers stood rigid, grasping the sides of the boats as Glover's men thrust the soldier-laden vessels into the current, leaning hard against their poles. They used poles, oars, and even musket butts to deflect ice from the boats' sides. Thomas Rodney, a signer of the Declaration of Independence, recalled it as "a severe night as I ever saw." The wind was blowing very hard "and the night was very dark and cold."[29]

Washington placed Colonel Henry Knox in charge of loading. Nearly three hundred pounds and taller than Washington himself, Knox had followed an unlikely path to command. In his Boston youth, he rose from street-gang fighter to become one of the neighborhood's most feared brawlers. Yet he was also a voracious reader who taught himself military tactics and eventually opened his own bookstore.

Drenched in rain and pelted with hail, Knox stood his ground, bellowing commands. He steadied frightened horses at the ferry landing while his artillery men maneuvered eighteen cannons, some weighing 1,750 pounds, across the ice-covered riverbank. Working in teams, they lifted each piece carefully onto the waiting ferries. "The floating ice in the river," Knox wrote his wife, "made the labor almost incredible. However, perseverance accomplished what at first seemed impossible."[30]

The success of the crossing owed much to Knox's direction and the skill of Glover's seamen as they fought the ice-choked river through total darkness. General Nathanael Greene captured the conditions succinctly: "We crossed the Delaware on the 25th of December at night, 8 miles above the town, in one of the severest hails and rainstorms I ever saw."[31]

Incredibly, almost miraculously, not a single soldier, cannon, or horse was lost in the crossing.

At about 3:30 A.M., the last of the cannon were being wheeled off the ferry boats onto the New Jersey shoreline. General Adam Stephen's Virginia Brigade had crossed first, forming a protective arc of sentries around the landing area. The operation stood three hours behind schedule, Washington's men were drenched, and hail pelted them mercilessly. "Worst day of sleet rain that could be," one private recalled.[32] Washington knew the army could not reach Trenton before sunrise. As his men struggled with the storm, he debated abandoning the mission. He concluded that retreat now posed greater danger than advance. His choice of the mission's password reflected his resolve: "Victory or Death." Two forty-man advance parties moved out immediately to establish roadblocks around Trenton, followed by Stephen's Virginia Brigade with orders to kill or capture Hessian sentries.[33]

The weather was emerging as a critical factor. The storm was descending on both armies with such force that survivors of the battle would recall its intensity in their memoirs and letters decades later.

"Rain, hail, sleet and a dense fog. . . . A more cold, gloomy, cheerless and disheartening night and morning can scarce be imagined. It seemed as though the very elements had conspired against us," remembered a continental soldier years later.[34]

The march from the ferry house to Trenton began between 3:30 and 4:00 A.M., almost four hours behind schedule. Portions of the road proved too treacherous, forcing the soldiers to walk single file along the road's snow-covered shoulders. The column of soldiers, artillery, and wagons stretched more than a mile. Local residents, aware of the unfolding events, guided the army through the darkness, riding ahead disguised as farmers and ax-carrying woodcutters.[35]

The troops pressed through dark woods. Knox's artillerymen maneuvered their heavy cannons across swollen creeks and overflowing tributaries. Rain and sleet lashed at the men as they trudged forward, heads bowed against the wind. "It rained, hailed, snowed, and froze," fifer Greenwood remembered, "and at the same time blew a perfect hurricane." At least two soldiers, overcome by cold and exhaustion, collapsed along the side of the road and froze to death.[36]

At the hamlet of Birmingham, only halfway to Trenton, the storm intensified. Sleet stung faces and slowed progress until they were "not advancing faster than a child 10 years old could walk." Washington, seeing dawn approach at nearly six o'clock, urged his men forward, stressing unity and obedience to officers.[37]

At Birmingham the road split, and as planned, the main force divided. The left wing, led by Nathanael Greene, consisted of General Adam Stephen's troops forming the advance party, followed by the Virginian and Pennsylvania brigades of Generals Hugh Mercer, Matthias Alexis Roche de Fermoy, and Lord Stirling. Greene would lead the division inland toward the northern sector, targeting the Howell house and Calhoun house picket stations and the elevated junction of King and Queen Streets. This would put him on a collision course with Andreas Wiederhold.

John Sullivan, who had fought Hessians at Long Island with pistols in both hands, would lead the right wing down River Road, past the Hermitage and Stone Barracks, to strike Trenton's southern quarter. Sullivan's division consisted of Colonel John Stark and his 1st New Hampshire Regiment forming the advance party, followed by the other New England brigades of Colonel John Glover, General Arthur St. Clair, and Colonel Paul Sargent.

Each column had an artillery detachment.

Knox's artillery would give Washington unprecedented firepower—almost eight guns per thousand infantry men with a total of eighteen guns against the Hessians' six. One artillery expert described this ratio as "an almost unheard of proportion" in that era. This gave the Americans a tremendous advantage, particularly if the weather remained bad, as artillery pieces were more reliable than muskets in foul weather.[38]

Washington ordered the officers to set their watches to match his own. With snow and hail beating down on them, they pulled out their large pocket watches and matched them with the general's timepiece—one of the first recorded instances of synchronized timepieces in a military campaign.[39]

Ahead of the army, about three miles from Trenton, advance parties had been busy putting up roadblocks, cutting off Trenton's communications with the northern and western countryside. There was a surprising flow of civilian traffic on these country roads in the early hours of a severe storm. Washington's advance guards detained a number of unsuspecting civilians—doctors and midwives on their rounds, farmers heading to market, and young men out courting who suddenly found themselves facing a bayonet instead of a pretty maiden.[40]

CHAPTER 24

The Battle of Trenton

December 26, 1776

THE HESSIAN GARRISON followed its morning routine, unaware of the approaching enemy. Along the river, small Hessian outposts guarded the Assunpink Bridge, the Trenton Ferry, the Stone Barracks, and the Hermitage—all of which had remained quiet during the evening. Between these formal positions, solitary sentries stood watch in the snow-covered fields, their isolated posts forming a web of surveillance around the town. Within Trenton itself, one regiment remained on alert while the others slept fully armed. A mounted patrol circled the perimeter, methodically checking each outpost.

At 4:00 A.M., two brass guns were hitched to the artillery horses on King Street for the daily patrol over Assunpink Bridge to the Trenton Ferry. When the gunners reported for orders, they found Colonel Rall still asleep in the warmth of his quarters. Lieutenant Piel directed them to Major von Dechow, the duty officer of the day, who canceled the patrol due to the severe weather—a decision that would prove fatal.

The decision to cancel the patrol troubled Wiederhold. Just a few hours earlier, von Dechow had expressed anxiety about a possible rebel attack. Now, as the storm worsened and the sky darkened, the major was choosing a warm bed over security thoroughness. Had the patrol crossed Assunpink Bridge as usual, they might have discovered Ewing's force, revealing Washington's plan. Instead, von Dechow stayed in quarters while Rall slept until half past seven.[1]

The Hessians' failures in security continued to mount. The Jägers at the Hermitage typically conducted dawn patrols at 5:00 A.M., sending two dozen infantry and several light horsemen to scout the River Road. But this morning, deterred by the storm, they dispatched only three men, who ventured barely a mile before turning back to report the road clear. A proper patrol would likely have encountered Sullivan's advancing division. Like Major von Dechow's cancellation of the patrol to Assunpink Bridge, this abbreviated reconnaissance squandered another opportunity to detect Washington's approach.[2]

Around 7:30 A.M., just after sunrise and a few miles from Trenton, the main columns of Washington's army reached the advance parties. Suddenly, through the storm emerged fifty Continental soldiers, moving north away from Trenton, in the wrong direction, toward Greene's division. Washington was stunned to recognize men from General Adam Stephen's Virginia Brigade, led by Captain George Wallis. Without notifying Washington, Stephen had authorized a raid into Trenton the previous day, seeking revenge for a fallen comrade. While Washington's army had been assembling for the crossing, Wallis and his men had struck a Hessian outpost, claiming to have killed or wounded fifteen sentries.[3]

Washington, angrier than his officers had ever seen, confronted Wallis: "You, sir, may have ruined my plans by putting them on guard!" Then, mastering his fury, he invited Wallis's men to join the attack.

The situation appeared dire: dawn breaking, surprise potentially lost, troops drenched and exhausted from the relentless storm. Yet Washington judged retreat more dangerous than advance. The march would continue.

The Americans were less than two miles from Trenton. Though sunrise had come at 7:20, the storm that had plagued their march now shielded them from detection. "A really terrible storm with snow and strong hail mixed together," one officer reported. Another remembered "a constant fall of snow . . . [and] rain," noting that the sky was "dark and stormy so that we could not see very far ahead."[4]

At 7:45, scouts reported to Washington that they had located the Howell cooper shop, a few hundred yards ahead. Washington's intelligence about Hessian positions, gathered from scouts and local patriots, was proving to be accurate. While his men remained concealed in the thick woods, Washington deployed his left wing in three columns: General Mercer's Marylanders and Connecticut men on the right; Stephen's Virginians and Stirling's Virginians, Pennsylvania Rifles, and Delaware men in the center; and Fermoy's Pennsylvanians on the left. Virginia infantry under Captain William Washington and Lieutenant James Monroe formed the vanguard.

On Washington's command, the three columns advanced through the heavy snow and sleet. Washington led from the center, his men surging forward, as one historian described, "half running, half sliding." As they emerged from the darkened woods, Washington set a "long trot." In the distance, they saw a door open at the cooper shop and a single Hessian emerged.[5]

Inside the cooper shop, Lieutenant Wiederhold had maintained vigilant security through the night. He had posted seven additional nighttime sentries. His sentries made a chain stretching from the cooper shop south to the Jägers at the Hermitage on the River Road and north to the outpost on Princeton Road. He dispatched "one patrol after the other to prevent being surprised." At sunrise, his night sentries reported "everything quiet." Earlier, his morning patrol had returned without incident. "At daybreak," he recalled, "I sent out my last and actually strongest patrol. It returned as it became full daylight, reported everything quiet and that there was nothing to be seen or heard." But the relentless storm and days of constant alerts had taken their toll. His men, as Wiederhold subsequently acknowledged, were fatigued and less alert. He allowed seventeen of his men who had finished their picket duty to shelter in the shop's warmth.

"The night passed quietly," he wrote in his diary. "I drank a little coffee and after that I decided to take a brief walk."[6]

Wiederhold knew that his homeland would never compare to the vastly powerful British Empire—an empire that stretched from India to the Alleghenies, protected by hundreds of ships of the Royal Navy that dominated "the seven seas." At 8:00 A.M., when he pushed open the door of the Howell family cooper shop, stepping outside for one final check, he was unaware that he was stepping onto the most vulnerable point of the entire British Empire. Nor could he imagine that in just a few moments, the next phase of his life would begin, and it would be humiliating, dangerous, and eventually, amorous.

Through swirling snow, he caught movement in the distance.

His first thought was of the inspector's morning patrol, but as he stood in the doorway, more shapes emerged, snow-covered figures materializing from the storm like ghostly apparitions. Their numbers multiplied rapidly as they advanced through the fields and along Pennington Road, more appearing from the dark forests.

This was no raid.

Wiederhold, who had dismissed the patriots as "evil and disobedient rebels . . . who are disloyal to God and the King," now faced the full weight of their assault. A figure in the distance—perhaps David Lanning of the Hunterdon County militia—raised his musket and fired at Wiederhold. Two more shots followed. Wiederhold shouted to his men, "Der Feind! Heraus!" (The enemy! Turn out!). The sleepy, uniformed pickets seized their dry muskets and rushed out to form a line. The seven pickets Wiederhold had earlier posted in the fields and on the road came running, alerted only now by the gunfire after failing to detect Washington's approach.[7]

"They fired three salvos at me and the seventeen men that I had under arms," Wiederhold later wrote. "After the third round I gave the order to fire." Both sides missed in this first exchange, but the Americans kept coming. The Hessians "engaged them until nearly surrounded by several battalions." As more Americans poured onto the field, threatening to overlap his flanks, Wiederhold ordered a retreat toward Captain von Altenbockum's outpost. He could now see the full scope of the attack: Mercer's brigade advancing southwest of Pennington Road toward the center of town, Stephen and Stirling holding the middle of the line and pressing toward the northern end of Trenton, and Fermoy's troops moving east toward Princeton Road.[8]

At the Calhoun house, von Altenbockum heard the firing and immediately roused his men to form a line outside of the house. Wiederhold, seeing his own position threatened with encirclement, fell back to join Altenbockum's Lossberg men. "*Herr Kapitän, ich werde mich auf Ihrem rechten Flügel formieren!*" (Captain, I will form on your right wing!)

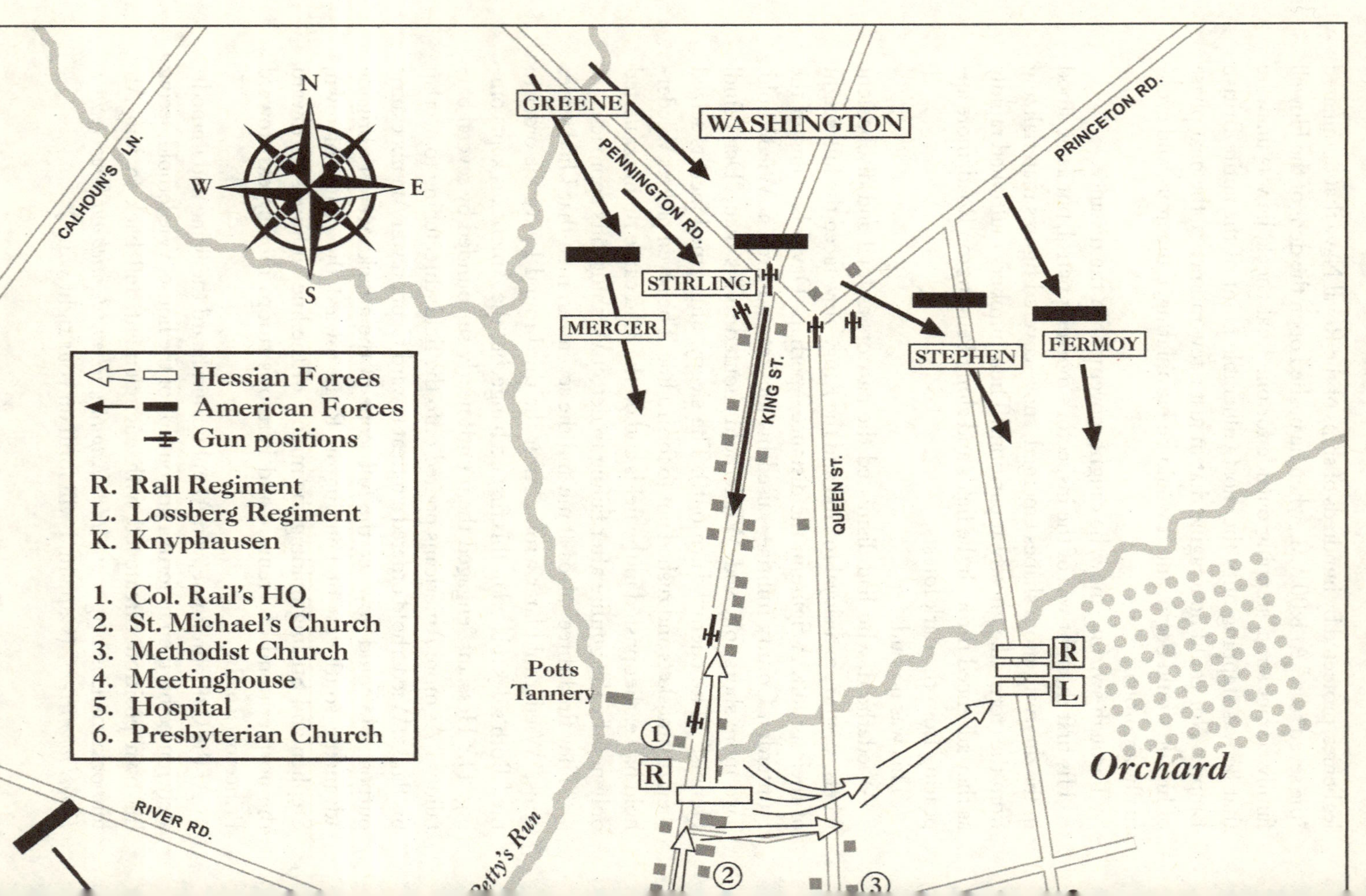
GREENE
WASHINGTON
PRINCETON RD.
PENNINGTON RD.
CALHOUN'S LN.
N
W
E
S
STIRLING
MERCER
STEPHEN
FERMOY
KING ST.
QUEEN ST.
Hessian Forces
American Forces
Gun positions
R. Rall Regiment
L. Lossberg Regiment
K. Knyphausen
1. Col. Rail's HQ
2. St. Michael's Church
3. Methodist Church
4. Meetinghouse
5. Hospital
6. Presbyterian Church
Potts
Tannery
1
R
R
L
Orchard
RIVER RD.
2
3

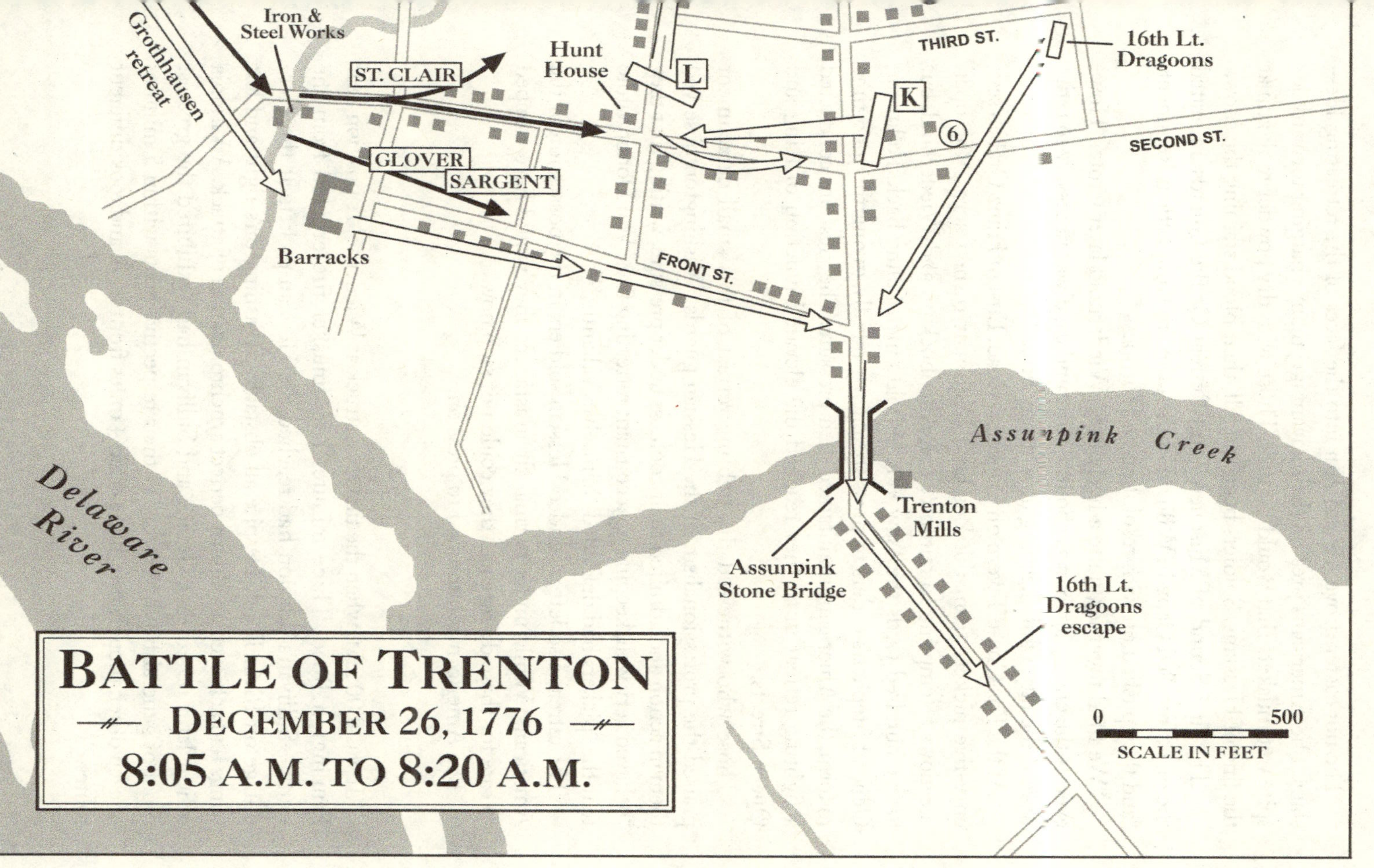

Grothhausen retreat
Iron & Steel Works
ST. CLAIR
Hunt House
L
K
6
THIRD ST.
16th Lt. Dragoons
SECOND ST.
GLOVER
SARGENT
Barracks
FRONT ST.
Assunpink Creek
Trenton Mills
Assunpink Stone Bridge
16th Lt. Dragoons escape
Delaware River
0
500
SCALE IN FEET
BATTLE OF TRENTON
DECEMBER 26, 1776
8:05 A.M. TO 8:20 A.M.

The nor'easter drove ice and rain into the faces of the retreating Hessians. The Americans pressed their advantage, many charging forward despite wet muskets that would not fire. Those with dry powder took aim at the line of Hessians. Soldiers began to fall, their blood staining the snow.

"The first Sound of Musquetry and Retreat Of the Guards animated the men," recalled Captain William Hull of the 7th Connecticut Regiment, "and they pushed on with resolution and firmness."[9]

"We fired together, quite a lively fire," Wiederhold later wrote. "However, as the enemy again was about to surround us, it was necessary to retire toward the city, while keeping up a steady fire."[10]

At the Fox Chase Tavern on Princeton Road, Ensign Franz Gräbe's seventy-five pickets from the Lossberg Regiment rushed across the open meadows attempting to reinforce von Altenbockum and Wiederhold, but at five hundred yards they saw Wiederhold's men falling back. Following General Stephen's orders to press the enemy rapidly, giving them no time to form, the Americans maintained their pressure. The Hessians conducted a fighting retreat until they reached the elevated junction of King and Queen Streets.

Those who witnessed the fighting retreat of this small detachment praised the professionalism of the Hessian guards. Washington observed them in action and admired their coolness under pressure, writing that they "behaved very well, keeping up a constant retreating fire." Von Donop wrote that the "pickets had defended themselves valiantly."[11]

The retreat also left wounded Hessian soldiers in the possession of the Americans. While under normal circumstances they would have stopped to care for these dying men, they could not stop now.

The American column had to press on.

It was 8:00 A.M. when the first shot struck at Wiederhold's position near Pennington Road. Three minutes later, musket fire erupted from the south—Sullivan's division had reached the Hessian pickets at the Hermitage on River Road. Despite all obstacles, Washington's right and left wings had achieved an almost perfect synchronization of attack. A Virginia officer later noted that Greene and Sullivan had "exhibited the greatest proof of generalship by getting to their respective posts within 5 minutes of each other, though they had parted 4 miles from town and took different routes."[12]

Sullivan's advance along River Road was spearheaded by Captain John Flahaven's New Jersey Continentals, with the brigades of Stark, Sargent, and St. Clair following. They encountered the first Hessian picket post three-quarters of a mile from Trenton, just short of the Hermitage.

There, Lieutenant Friedrich von Gröthausen commanded fifty Jägers, his men dispersed across the estate's two hundred acres, positioned in servants' quarters, barns, the greenhouse, and outlying huts.

A lone picket in his wooden hut by River Road saw the American column emerging from the storm. He fired once and fled. When Gröthausen heard this shot and the gunfire erupting from Pennington Road, he gathered his Jägers and moved north to support Wiederhold, still believing he faced another raid. His Jägers had covered barely a thousand feet when they saw columns of troops materializing through the snow—not raiders but battalions of Continental soldiers spreading across the fields.[13]

The Jägers faced John Stark's New Hampshire men. Stark was already legendary for his tenacity—in his youth, captured by the Abenaki and forced to run a gauntlet of warriors armed with sticks, Stark had seized the first warrior's stick and proceeded to beat him. The impressed Abenaki had adopted Stark into their tribe.

Now, finding his men's powder wet in the storm, he ordered a bayonet charge against the Jägers, whose accurate rifles lacked bayonets. Unable to meet cold steel with cold steel, most of Gröthausen's men abandoned their equipment and fell back to the Stone Barracks. There, despite reinforcements, the defense quickly collapsed. "The enemy made a momentary show of resistance by a wild and undirected fire from the windows of their quarters," Major James Wilkinson recalled, "which they abandoned as we advanced."[14]

Sullivan's artillery opened with canister shot, sending hundreds of iron projectiles into the Jäger line. The bombardment served a dual purpose: scattering the enemy while signaling Washington that Sullivan's division had engaged. The weather was "extraordinarily bad"—dark and snowy. Gröthausen, without artillery to respond, now faced fire from two directions as General Dickinson's batteries opened from across the river. Shells crashed into the riverside ice while others plowed into the frozen ground, sending troops scrambling for cover. In an ironic turn, Dickinson found himself firing on the Hermitage, his own elegant country estate.[15]

Caught between Stark's bayonet charge and artillery fire, the Jägers saw American forces advancing through town to their right while Dickinson's guns pounded from the Delaware to their left. The only escape lay straight ahead across the Queen Street Bridge spanning Assunpink Creek. Most of Gröthausen's Jägers took this route while others, more desperate, attempted to ford the freezing stream. Gröthausen's actions would not be the last panicky or cowardly act this day.[16]

Jakob Piel, having already failed twice that morning to wake Colonel Rall, bypassed headquarters. Instead, he ordered the thirty-man watch guard to investigate the firing on King Street, gathering other soldiers emerging onto the street to join them. When Piel returned to headquarters, he found Rall at the window in his nightclothes. "What is the matter?" Rall asked. "Do you not hear the firing?" Piel replied. "I will be there immediately!" Within moments, Rall was dressed and mounted.[17]

The sound of battle had roused the town's garrison. The three Hessian regiments, their men having slept in uniforms with cartridge boxes strapped on, assembled quickly in the streets. The Rall Regiment formed on King Street near their colonel's headquarters, collecting their regimental flags. Rall told the Lossberg Regiment to assemble down the block in the graveyard by the English Church. Two blocks west, the Knyphausen Regiment gathered by the Quaker Meeting House on Queen Street.[18]

Washington's men were advancing with unexpected speed, charging relentlessly through the storm. "We barely had time to take up our weapons before we lost many people in the city," Jakob Piel later wrote.[19]

To the south, Sullivan's force split into two columns—St. Clair's troops pressing up King and Queen Streets while Stark and Glover's men raced for the Assunpink Bridge. "Indeed," noted one American officer, "I never could conceive that one spirit should so universally animate both officers and men to rush forward into action."[20]

Near the junction of King and Queen Streets, Wiederhold and von Altenbockum maintained their organized retreat, but the race was turning against them. "No one came to see what was happening, nor to reinforce and assist us," Wiederhold recorded. With Washington's men threatening to envelop their position and no reinforcements in sight, they abandoned the crucial high ground. "I positioned myself in the city at the first houses and fired at the enemy, who were forming for battle on the city's heights," Wiederhold wrote. The two commanders then separated—von Altenbockum's men retiring down Queen Street while Wiederhold's force threaded through gardens between houses, seeking cover from American fire now commanding the junction.[21]

~

From the captured heights where King and Queen Streets merged, Washington surveyed the battle below. Infantry formed around him, leaving space for the guns to be dragged into position. Though the storm obscured Washington's view of River Road, the growing sound of artillery and musket fire confirmed Sullivan was advancing into the southern end of town toward Assunpink Bridge, threatening to sever the Hessians' southern escape route along Bordentown Road. To the west, Mercer's Brigade crossed the snow-covered fields, breaking into houses along King Street. His men stormed the homes, establishing firing positions at windows where American riflemen could keep their powder dry while picking off Hessian soldiers, particularly their officers. Others from Mercer's Brigade advanced quietly through gardens, greenhouses, walkways, and back alleys to penetrate deeper into Trenton.

Below, the Hessian regiments were forming in the streets, but to Washington's experienced eye something was wrong. He sensed that Rall's men were hesitant and unsure of their next move. Now was the time for his overpowering artillery power to be brought in.[22]

Through the storm, American artillery men had kept their guns' touch holes and muzzles dry, their vigilance now proving crucial. Captain Thomas Forrest's men unlimbered the Pennsylvania battery's two 6-pounders and two howitzers. Captain Alexander Hamilton's two New York guns and Captain Baumann's three 3-pounders joined them as Stirling's and Stephen's troops formed their lines.[23]

Bauman, reading the terrain through the wind-driven snow, shrewdly positioned his guns on a ridge overlooking the town, securing both a clear field of fire and flank protection for Mercer's advancing forces. Hamilton's guns, now commanding the north end of King Street, faced directly at the Hessian pieces being wheeled into position below.

Lieutenant Piel saw the danger materializing above them and ordered the Hessian artillery men into action. Twenty-three-year-old Lieutenant Johannes Engelhardt, barely a year in service, led his men to retrieve the artillery horses from Queen and 4th Street near the Methodist Church. They hitched the teams to their two 6-pounders and waited for orders.[24]

Rall screamed, "My god, Lieutenant Engelhardt . . . the pickets are already back, take the cannon forward!" Engelhardt's crew advanced up King Street, unlimbered their guns, and positioned their horses behind. Nine American guns now faced their two.[25]

The Hessians fired first, their synchronized shots thundering through the town. The American response was murderous—eight of Engelhardt's

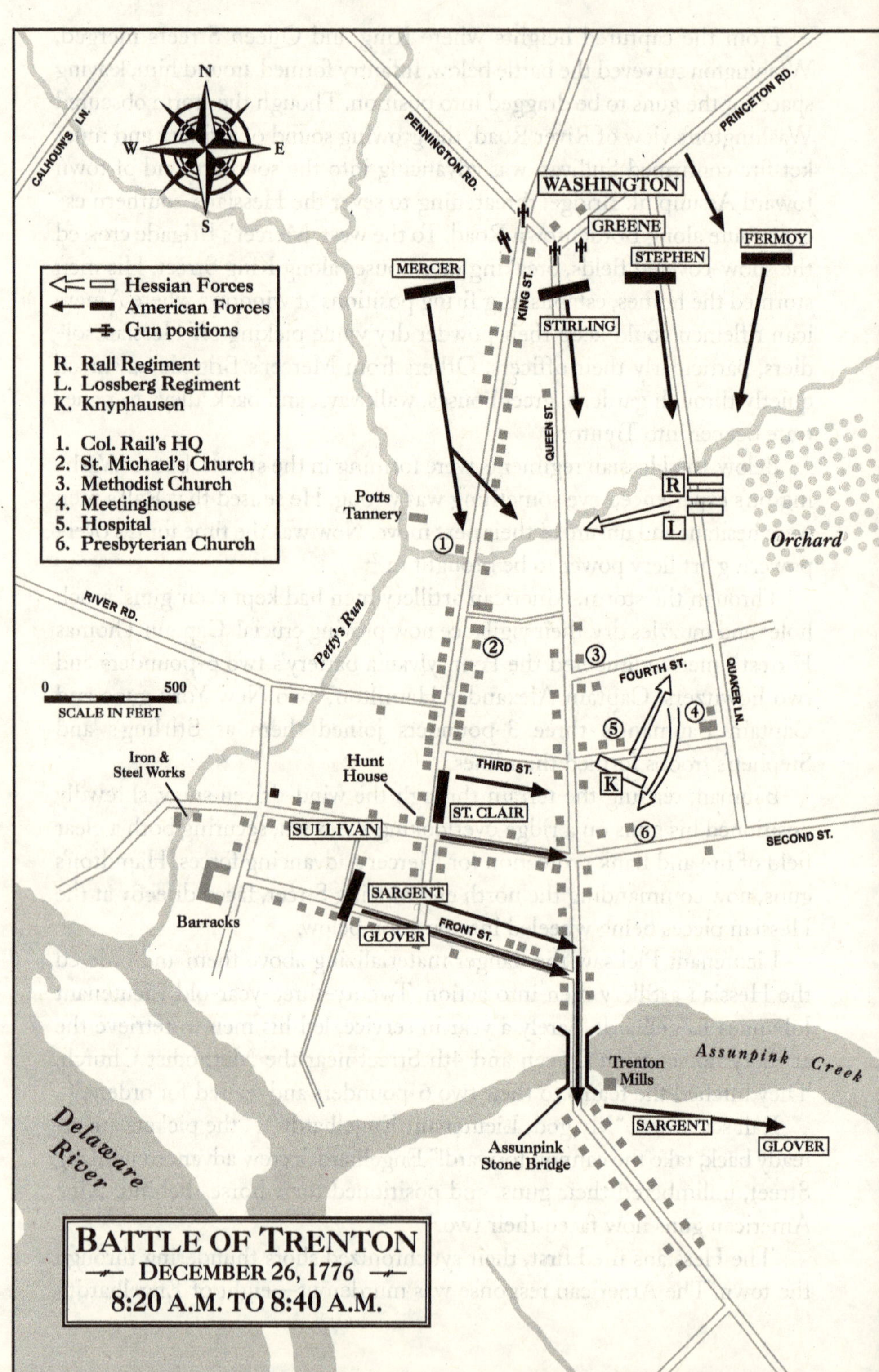
N
W
E
S
CALHOUN'S LN.
PENNINGTON RD.
PRINCETON RD.
WASHINGTON
GREENE
FERMOY
STEPHEN
MERCER
KING ST.
STIRLING
QUEEN ST.
Hessian Forces
American Forces
Gun positions
R. Rall Regiment
L. Lossberg Regiment
K. Knyphausen
1. Col. Rall's HQ
2. St. Michael's Church
3. Methodist Church
4. Meetinghouse
5. Hospital
6. Presbyterian Church
R
L
Potts Tannery
Orchard
RIVER RD.
Petty's Run
FOURTH ST.
QUAKER LN.
0
500
SCALE IN FEET
Iron & Steel Works
Hunt House
THIRD ST.
K
ST. CLAIR
SULLIVAN
SECOND ST.
SARGENT
Barracks
FRONT ST.
GLOVER
Assunpink Creek
Trenton Mills
SARGENT
GLOVER
Assunpink Stone Bridge
Delaware River
BATTLE OF TRENTON
DECEMBER 26, 1776
8:20 A.M. TO 8:40 A.M.

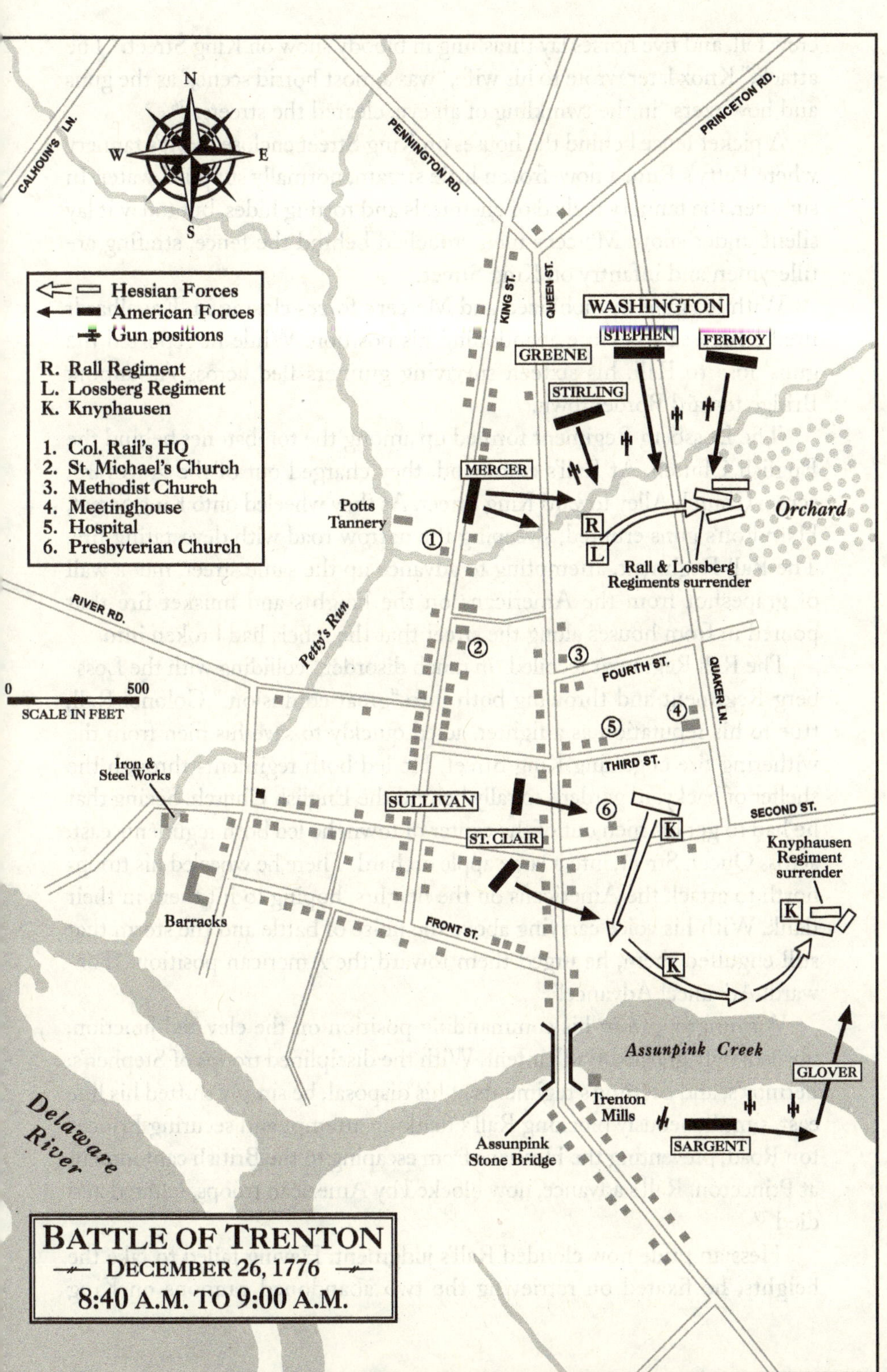

N
S
E
W
CALHOUN'S LN.
PENNINGTON RD.
PRINCETON RD.
KING ST.
QUEEN ST.
Hessian Forces
American Forces
Gun positions
R. Rall Regiment
L. Lossberg Regiment
K. Knyphausen
1. Col. Rall's HQ
2. St. Michael's Church
3. Methodist Church
4. Meetinghouse
5. Hospital
6. Presbyterian Church
WASHINGTON
STEPHEN
FERMOY
GREENE
STIRLING
MERCER
Potts Tannery
Orchard
Rall & Lossberg Regiments surrender
RIVER RD.
Petty's Run
FOURTH ST.
QUAKER LN.
THIRD ST.
0
500
SCALE IN FEET
Iron & Steel Works
SULLIVAN
ST. CLAIR
SECOND ST.
Knyphausen Regiment surrender
Barracks
FRONT ST.
Assunpink Creek
GLOVER
Trenton Mills
SARGENT
Assunpink Stone Bridge
Delaware River
BATTLE OF TRENTON
DECEMBER 26, 1776
8:40 A.M. TO 9:00 A.M.

crew fell, and five horses lay thrashing in bloody snow on King Street. "The attack," Knox later wrote to his wife, "was a most horrid scene," as the guns and howitzers "in the twinkling of an eye, cleared the streets."[26]

A picket fence behind the houses on King Street enclosed Pott's tannery where Petty's Run, a now-frozen little stream, normally supplied water. In summer, the tannery reeked of chemicals and rotting hides, but today it lay silent under snow. Mercer's men crouched behind the fence, strafing artillerymen and infantry on King Street.

With his guns immobilized and Mercer's forces closing in, Engelhardt fired a final salvo before abandoning his position. While he reported the guns' loss to Rall, his sixteen surviving gunners fled across Assunpink Bridge toward Bordentown.[27]

The Lossberg Regiment formed up among the tombstones behind the English Church. At Rall's command, they charged out of the graveyard, across Church Alley toward King Street. As they wheeled onto King Street, Hamilton's guns erupted, sweeping the narrow road with devastating fire. The Rall Regiment, attempting to advance up the same street, met a wall of grapeshot from the Americans on the heights and musket fire that poured in from houses along the street that the rebels had broken into.

The Rall Regiment recoiled "in much disorder," colliding with the Lossberg Regiment and throwing both into "great confusion." Colonel Rall, true to his reputation as a fighter, acted quickly to save his men from the withering fire engulfing King Street. He led both regiments through the shelter of backyard gardens to rally behind the English Church. Seeing that he had to get his men out of the center of town, he led both regiments east, across Queen Street, into a large apple orchard. There he wheeled his troops north to attack the Americans on the heights, hoping to hit them in their flank. With his voice carrying above the noise of battle and the storm that still engulfed them, he urged them toward the American position, "Forward! Advance! Advance!"[28]

Washington, from his commanding position on the elevated junction, immediately grasped Rall's intent. With the disciplined troops of Stephen's, Fermoy's, and Sterling's regiments at his disposal, he simply shifted his line east, simultaneously blocking Rall's flanking attempt and securing Princeton Road, preventing the Hessians from escaping to the British cantonment at Princeton. Rall's advance, now blocked by American troops, faltered and died.[29]

Hessian pride now clouded Rall's judgment. Having failed to take the heights, he fixated on retrieving the two abandoned cannons on King

Street—a matter of honor that paled against the urgent need to withdraw his men to defensible ground.

"The grenadiers stormed to recapture the cannons!" wrote Reuber. Like many others in his regiment, Reuber revered his colonel. As one historian noted, "They would have followed him to Hell, and that was where he led them."[30]

Through gunsmoke and sleet, Rall led his men out of the apple orchard and back into town with colors flying and drums beating. They marched directly into a firestorm of musket balls and cannon shots: Mercer's sharpshooters struck from any shelter that kept their muskets dry, Stirling's infantry advanced steadily down from the heights, and Washington's artillery continued its relentless bombardment.

With courageous tenacity, the Rall Regiment recaptured their guns. "Although we went against enemy cannon, we retook our cannon," Reuber wrote triumphantly. But victory proved fleeting. As Rall's regiments, their ranks broken and intermixed, struggled in the storm, "As violent a Storm ensued of Hail & Snow as I ever felt," recalled one officer. Most Hessian muskets failed to fire in the wet conditions. Then came the crack of musket fire from the south: Sullivan's division had reached King Street, threatening to envelop Rall's position.[31]

The Americans, having captured and then lost the Hessian cannons, were determined to either destroy or recapture the guns. "Suddenly the rebels advanced unbelievably severe against us . . . and captured our cannons in front of the regiment," Reuber wrote. The rebels' fearlessness shocked the Hessians.

Colonel Knox spotted the guns and roared to Sergeant White's New England gunners, "My Brave Lads, go up and take those two field pieces sword in hand." Captain William Washington and Lieutenant James Monroe, the future president, led Virginia infantry in a fierce charge. "Captain Washington rushed forward, attacked and put the troops around the cannon to flight," Monroe later wrote. At the other gun, White charged the lone remaining gunner, sword raised, yelling, "Run you dog!" The gunner fled.[32]

"Now we lost the greater part of our artillery and the rebels were about to use them," Reuber wrote. "The rebels, in three lines, marched around us and brought seven cannon into the main street."[33]

Through a driving rain and cannon smoke, the center of Trenton dissolved into chaos. The Rall and Lossberg Regiments intermingled in confusion as rebels pressed in, their musket fire crackling from houses, from cellars, and from behind fences. With the regiments' ranks uneven and fragmented, they could not mount a proper bayonet charge.

In the southern part of town, the Sullivan division's main objective was to secure the Assunpink Bridge by seizing Front Street and Queen Street, the two roads leading to the stone arches of the old, narrow bridge. Control of the bridge would cut off the Hessians' only escape route. Minutes earlier, the rebels had captured the Hermitage. At the Stone Barracks—a potential strongpoint—Lieutenant von Gröthausen's Jägers fled after just one exchange of fire. As the fleeing Jägers ran toward Assunpink Bridge, a lone Hessian guard called to his comrades through the storm, "You gentlemen, will you not stay here with me?"

"It won't be long till they have your [dead] body," a Jäger private shouted back as he ran away.[34]

Not a single diary or report mentions the Queen's Light Dragoons—though surely, they cut a magnificent figure in their bright red uniforms and brass helmets as they skedaddled across Assunpink Bridge at the first sound of battle. These men, whose motto proudly proclaimed "Aut cursu, aut cominus armis" (Either in the charge or in hand-to-hand combat), fled alongside the unarmed: drummers, hautbois players, army surgeons, and camp women.[35]

Just a block away, the Knyphausen Regiment stood at Queen Street and 2nd Street with colors unfurled, waiting fifteen crucial minutes for orders. Above the roar of battle, they could hear the fighting intensify in the northern quarter but remained idle without command. While awaiting the orders, Major von Dechow galloped through the storm to the bridge, ordering the guards to hold at all costs. Rall's orders finally came through: One company would guard the bridge, four would advance up King Street.[36]

The Knyphausen attack faltered almost immediately. As they reached the intersection of King Street and Second Street, Sullivan's men unleashed a murderous fire on the advancing Hessians. Some of Knyphausen's men fell back from Second Street and tried to run northward up King Street, but through the drifting smoke, they could see American forces on King Street bearing down on them from the north.[37]

In the forefront of the fight was the indefatigable John Stark and his New Hampshire boys. "The dauntless Stark, who dealt death wherever he found resistance, and broke down all opposition before him," Wilkinson wrote in his memoirs. Stark sent a seventeen-man party under the command of the massively rotund Captain Ebenezer Frye to harass the Knyphausen Regiment's flank. The squad, much to everyone's amazement, captured sixty very embarrassed Hessians.[38]

Wiederhold, having broken away from the fighting around Rall's regiment, made his way down Queen Street and joined the Knyphausen Regiment on 2nd Street. He was furious that Rall kept ordering attacks into the center of town. Wiederhold saw that the best option would be to gain control of the bridge. "What nonsense this was!" he wrote. The Hessians had already been forced out of the city once. He wondered why Rall would "try to retake . . . a city which was of no value and which had been left 10 or 15 minutes previously, which was now filled with . . . the enemy in houses, and behind the walls and fences."[39]

The Knyphausen Regiment fell back along 2nd Street, near the entrance to the bridge, where their formation was disrupted by a tide of fleeing panicky soldiers, stragglers from all three Hessian regiments, terrified Loyalists who feared being taken by rebels, Engelhardt's artillerymen, and camp followers.[40]

General Sullivan, seeing the situation as Wiederhold did, ordered St. Clair to continue driving the Knyphausen Regiment from King Street to Queen Street while Glover and Sargent's men seized the bridge, captured those attempting to flee, and secured the vital heights beyond the creek.[41]

The Knyphausen Regiment finally broke. Major von Dechow and his horse were both shot; he mounted his adjutant's horse despite his wound. Leading his men out of the town into an apple orchard, he sought escape via a path to Samuel Henry's ironworks. He hoped to find a path leading away from Assunpink Creek and the town but, unfamiliar with the terrain, instead mistakenly led them toward the creek—and the Americans who awaited them.[42]

The Rall and Lossberg Regiments withdrew from town, their ranks intermingled and soldiers scattered. At the edge of the open fields off 4th Street, Rall wheeled his disorganized men to face Trenton. Though he and his officers struggled to restore order, many officers who had maintained discipline lay dead in the streets behind them.

"Forward March!" Rall commanded. "And attack them with the bayonet." He knew a disciplined bayonet charge was the Hessians' deadliest weapon. But musket shots from houses and artillery blasts from Washington's cannons shattered their advance, throwing troops already disoriented by the surprise rebel attack and the storm into deeper confusion. Through smoke and sheets of freezing rain, soldiers could barely distinguish friend from foe. The regimental band struck up, trying to rally the men. Colonel Knox witnessed "The hurry, fright, and confusion of the enemy."[43]

American sharpshooters targeted Hessian officers. The toll of dead and wounded commanders mounted steadily. At Queen Street below Church Alley, as gunfire from the houses intensified, Colonel Rall was shot. He claimed it was a slight wound, but his officers saw him weakening. Still mounted, he continued urging his men forward.[44]

A group of Hessian infantry made a stand in narrow Church Alley, hoping to prevent a rout. Jakob Piel suggested to Rall they should retreat across Assunpink Bridge. Rall sent him to reconnoiter the bridge. At Queen and 2nd Streets, trying to peer through rain and hail, Piel nearly walked into Sullivan's men, mistaking them for Knyphausen's regiment. He was within thirty paces of being taken prisoner when he realized his mistake. After surveying the area, he reported to Colonel Rall that it was too late, the Assunpink Bridge was held by the Americans.[45]

Rall, bleeding but still mounted and shouting orders, called out, "All who are my grenadiers, forward!" His men hesitated as Sullivan's artillery opened fire from 2nd and Queen Streets, catching them from behind. As Rall ordered retreat to the apple orchard beyond 3rd and 4th Streets, he slipped from his horse, two wounds in his side. He lay on the ground in his own blood; then, leaning on two soldiers, he was walked to the Methodist Church at Queen and 4th Streets.[46]

The retreat Rall had ordered east into the fields was in chaos. The regiments were so confused and mixed together that it was impossible to reestablish order. The regiments' surviving officers huddled in the rain to plan a breakout through the orchard. They led the men through rows of apple trees to a place where they could begin their escape. They were startled to find Stephen's and Fermoy's Continentals waiting in two perfect lines, cannons at the ready. Instantly the guns opened fire and drove the bewildered Hessians back among the apple trees. These were not the inexperienced rebels who had run away like rabbits at the Battle of Brooklyn. To make sure that the Hessians got the message, the Americans brought forward their six-gun battery from the elevated junction and placed the cannons in front of them.[47]

American officers shouted terms through English-speaking Hessians and through their own German-speaking officers from Pennsylvania's German Battalion: Throw down your weapons and surrender or we will shoot you down. The Americans advanced to within sixty feet. The English-speaking Hessian officers called out to the American officers who were now mounted in front of them that they understood they would have to surrender. Lieutenant Colonel George Baylor, Washington's aide, rode out to meet Lieutenant Colonel Scheffer and Major Von Hanstein. The Hessian flag bearers, reluctantly, slowly, lowered their standards; officers placed their hats on raised swords in surrender. Some soldiers smashed their muskets against the frozen ground in anger, others hurled them into the orchard. Angry infantrymen cut the straps on their cartridge pouches. The officers of the Rall and Lossberg Regiments quietly surrendered their swords to General Stirling.[48]

The Knyphausen Regiment was now alone. Major von Dechow, his pain unbearable, dismounted in the freezing rain. The regiment retreated across soggy ground along the Assunpink Creek, where von Dechow, growing weak, passed command to Captain Bernard von Biesenrodt. It would be the last time they would see the major; he would die of his wounds the following night. Biesenrodt attempted one desperate rush at the narrow bridge but found it strongly guarded by Sargent and Glover's New Englanders, their artillery commanding the approach from heights beyond the creek.[49]

Searching for a ford, Biesenrodt led his men along the waterway until they found themselves trapped: wooded heights before them, a tributary of the Assunpink behind, their boots sinking into swampy ground. The situation was desperate and quickly turned lethal when American artillery opened fire from across the creek. "Two enemy battalions, with four cannons, marched up close in front of us and seized the right flank which was our only escape, the only possible place of rescue," Wiederhold wrote in his diary. The wounded von Dechow had seen enough and ordered surrender through Captain Ludwig Lowenstein. When his officers ignored him, von Dechow, determined to find a ford across the Assunpink Creek, even though almost none of the Hessian soldiers knew how to swim, had a corporal tie a white handkerchief to a spontoon and he hobbled to surrender at a nearby blacksmith's house.[50]

Some men, convinced that their commander's surrender had exposed their position, followed Lowenstein through the underbrush. Glover's Brigade called mockingly from the far bank that they'd found "the best place for fording." The ice-cold water was neck deep with treacherous mud below. Three soldiers drowned in the attempt, tragically swept away by the current, while others struggled back to shore.[51]

Biesenrodt, a veteran of twenty-one years' service, still refused to yield despite American cannon trained on his position. When Major Wilkinson approached under a flag of truce, Biesenrodt threatened to shoot him. Only after General St. Clair sent over an ultimatum—"If you do not surrender immediately, I will blow you to pieces"—did Biesenrodt negotiate through Lieutenant Wiederhold. The captain secured only the retention of officers' swords and baggage before leading his men up to surrender.[52]

As the Hessians laid down their muskets, American troops tossed their hats skyward. The Battle of Trenton was over, but the repercussions were just about to begin.

PART VI

Aftermath

CHAPTER 25

Victory and Defeat

WASHINGTON HAD WON his first battle as commander in chief. The Hessian occupation of Trenton was over. The victorious Americans had captured more than 950 Hessian soldiers along with their camp followers. The Hessians were exhausted and demoralized and did not know what the future held for them.

As for the victors, Washington had little time to celebrate as he faced his next challenge. British forces remained strong just six miles north in Maidenhead. Five miles beyond was the British garrison at Princeton, as well as other British outposts throughout New Jersey. He also did not know the disposition of von Donop's Hessians south of Trenton. Since Cadwalader's men had been unable to cross, Washington had no troops to guard the road to Bordentown. Washington believed he might be exposed from both the north and south. His immediate concern was evacuating his army and Hessian prisoners along with the army's horses, artillery, and supplies, back across the Delaware. The need to cross the river gained urgency from an unexpected quarter, as recorded by Joseph Reed, Washington's adjutant: "There was a great Quantities of Spirituous Liquors at Trenton which the Soldiers drank too freely. . . . And they would not be able to put up a . . . Defense in Case of Attack."[1]

Mortally wounded, Rall was carried to his headquarters at the house of Stacey Potts. Before evacuating, Washington and Greene visited the dying colonel, who pleaded for kindness toward his men. Washington granted his request without hesitation. Through the night, Rall suffered in constant pain before dying on the evening of December 27. Though buried in the Presbyterian Church, his grave has been lost to time.

It had been an adventurous day. Few of the men in either army realized the adventure was not over.

The army trudged back to Johnson's Ferry through continuing sleet and rain. The crossing proved as treacherous as before. One boat, carrying Hessian officers, swamped and drifted nearly two miles downstream, forcing its occupants to "wade about 200 feet through the angry waters" to reach the shore.[2]

The Continental Army had endured over twenty-four hours of constant action—marching thirty miles as they were continuously snowed and rained on without rest. Captain Hull captured the army's exhaustion: returning to quarters, he sat down to a bowl of hasty pudding, fell asleep midmeal, and was found the next morning on the floor, spoon still in hand.[3]

The Hessian officers were confined to the ferry house at McKonkey's, but the enlisted men were immediately marched to Newtown to be confined in the town's Presbyterian Church and the Bucks County Jail. None of the prisoners received much food that night, if any.[4]

After being captured and placed on a boat, Wiederhold faced the Delaware's ice-choked waters. "We had to resign ourselves to the possibility of death," he wrote. Though he had shown no fear on the battlefield, the river terrified him. Wind and current drove his boat two miles downstream, unable to reach shore. Rather than spend the night trapped on the drifting boat, he jumped into chest-deep water, breaking through ice to reach land. His diary entry that night showed that even in his desperate struggle with the river, thoughts of that day's battlefield dishonor haunted him: "Instead of a promotion and a good nest egg, we return home to an unhappy Prince with wasted bodies."[5]

Adding to his discomfort, he had to spend the night wet and cold in a little room at the ferry house with twenty-six fellow officers, all of whom "could hardly stand, without food or drink." Incredibly, two days after what was likely the worst day of his life, Wiederhold and his fellow officers received extraordinary invitations: dinner at General Stirling's and George Washington's respective houses.

Wiederhold beamed when Stirling, his recent battlefield opponent, praised his handling of the pickets' fighting retreat. In his diary, he wrote proudly of Washington's keen interest in his tactical analysis of the battlefield and the general's commendation of his "alertness and defense" at the guard house. His pride swelled further when Washington singled him out to discuss the battle and afterward wrote his name on the general's blackboard.

The atmosphere was much different when on December 31 the Hessian prisoners were loaded onto farm wagons and paraded through Philadelphia. All the Hessian diary entries from that day mention that the streets were filled, and Washington made sure they were paraded down every thoroughfare. At first the people of Philadelphia approached them with food and drink, but then old women came up screaming at them, and the mood of the crowd changed. "Our entrance seems splendid," Wiederhold wrote, but soon "we had to put up with a great deal from the rabble."[6]

Unlike Wiederhold's harrowing crossing, Jakob Piel passed safely across the Delaware at Johnson's Ferry. He stayed in the same crowded room at the ferry house as Wiederhold, and he received the same invitation to dine with General Stirling, who promised, "Your General von Heister treated me like a brother when I was a prisoner, and so, gentleman, you should be treated by me in the same manner."

An awkward dinner moment provided deep insight into the Hessian mindset. When a local pastor attempted to "convince us of the correct view of the Americans in this war," Piel responded firmly, "We had not been sent to America to determine which of the parties was in the right, but to fight for the King."[7]

Meeting Washington left a lasting impression on Piel. He later wrote that he was surprised, "In the face of this man nothing of the great man showed for which he would be noted. His eyes have no fire, but a slight smile in his expression when he spoke inspired love and respect."

During the parade, he faced real danger: "The people were so angry and so threatening . . . [they] nearly overpowered the guards." The entire American escort struggled to protect the Hessians from the mob.[8]

The common soldiers faced starker conditions. Reuber's crossing of the Delaware was uneventful, but unlike the officers who slept in taverns and homes, he was "confined in a rotten prison." His meals consisted of bread "shaking down out of a basket from above into the bare prison courtyard and onto the snow." The Philadelphia parade proved especially dangerous for the infantrymen: "The people were so angry and so threatening towards us and nearly overpowered the guards . . . we Hessians had to march into the barracks at once and the entire American escort had to control the angry people."[9]

Congress believed exposure to American liberties and opportunities might convince their Hessian prisoners to forsake their prince and homeland. Rather than imprisonment, American officials offered them paid work, telling Reuber and his comrades, "Those who wish to work on the land for the farmers, shall be allowed to do so."

In the fertile farmland of Lancaster, Pennsylvania, and Winchester, Virginia, Reuber and his captured comrades found an unexpected peace. The Americans, confident their Hessian prisoners would choose to stay, allowed them to roam up to ten miles from their assigned homes.

When a prisoner exchange was arranged in August 1778, Reuber chose his homeland over America. Traveling to New York City, he rejoined the re-formed Rall Grenadier Regiment, spending the war's final four years fighting through the Carolina and Georgia campaigns.

In September 1783, he boarded a ship at New York, retracing his seven-year-old journey back to Bremerlehe. Back in Hessen-Kassel, his regiment's final march led to Kassel's Holland Gate, where their new commander, Marquis Luigi D'Angelelli, received the regiment and led them through familiar streets. Reuber watched with pride as D'Angelelli received "the five flags which had been lost at Trenton on 25 December 1776 but had been retaken in the hard fought battle near Charleston at Stono Ferry." Landgrave Frederick himself reviewed their final parade.

Though the regiment disbanded, the military bureaucracy had one last claim on Reuber. His official discharge was delayed until he trained a group of recruits. He was allowed to return home and await instructions on training the recruits. He lived peacefully and waited for orders that never came. His discharge papers finally arrived in 1807—twenty-three years late.

In his diary's final entry, as the last Hessians returned from America in spring 1784, Reuber wrote: "After all were back in their former garrisons, with God's help, this American campaign is finished. What will happen now we can only wait and see."

While Reuber adapted to American farm life, his fellow officers Piel and Wiederhold experienced their captivity differently, though both were granted the privilege of countryside residence rather than prison confinement.

Piel found no comfort in America. "The farther we travel," he wrote, "the less pleasing it is to us. We see always more woods and fewer houses, and these should sooner be called huts than houses." He dismissed Dumfries, Virginia, as "a wretched town," Millerstown, Pennsylvania, as mere "wooden houses and poor German inhabitants," and Charleston, Maryland, as "a terrible place." He avoided the locals, writing, "Most of them are such blind Patriots and such eager adherence to their false political system, that for us no happiness is to be found in their company."[10]

His days in America after the Battle of Trenton were uneventful. When exchanged in April 1778, he served in Quebec until war's end.

Wiederhold's captivity proved more colorful. In Fredericksburg, Virginia, he moved easily in high society, noting the inhabitants were "the most polite and friendly in America, regardless of social position or political inclination." The highlight of his "incarceration" was entertaining sixteen ladies—including Washington's sister and nieces—with claret, muscatel, chocolate, and music. Hessian prisoners played flute and violin while Wiederhold accompanied on guitar. Wiederhold strongly hints at an affair in his diary, but to guard this "Special situation," he felt it was prudent "not to write more." The cryptic reference makes one wonder if this explains the extra child on his genealogy chart. Unfortunately, and perhaps due to jealousies his relationships caused, in May 1778 he was sent to Philadelphia.[11]

In September 1779, while sailing for Quebec after a prisoner exchange, his vessel was severely damaged in a storm and drifted aimlessly. Finally, a ship approached that Wiederhold presumed was British, as he wrote in his diary. "But oh! How are our hopes betrayed! For when they came near and hoisted their flags of thirteen stripes, our joy was turned into sorrow." Recaptured by the Americans, he would not return to New York City until a prisoner swap in 1780."[12]

Between his adventures, Wiederhold's prescient observations captured America's environmental transformation. He noted how unrestricted hunting had killed off wild turkeys from settled areas, though they remained "plentiful" in Native American territories. Looking at the seemingly endless forests, he warned, "The Americans are very wasteful with their wood. If they continue in this way . . . wood will become rare and expensive."[13]

By 1781, despair had crept into his correspondence. He feared the war would be lost and all sacrifices made by him and his comrades rendered meaningless. "Will no power in Europe intervene and support the English?" he wrote home from New York. "Thus, despite all the unspeakable costs and exertions incurred, the whole cause is lost."[14]

His letters to Hessen-Kassel consistently show his dislike of New York City. The only exception being his attendance of a demonstration of an "electricity making" machine which was being used by at least one participant to help cure erectile dysfunction.[15]

Despite his hardships, Wiederhold remained committed to the Hessian system of raising revenues through military service: "From a political point of view, it is not to our advantage if England is reduced too far, since that is the only source from which the Guineas and the advancements for the Hessian revenues and troops flow."[16]

He was ashamed of his army's defeat. "Our period has come to an end, We will soon return home with very slow steps—although not with victories and honors, but with sorrow. It's true! I'm going home now, but I wish to do so with greater satisfaction, and in order to satisfy my suffering as a soldier a little more, I would rather that the satanic rebels and especially the cheesemongers [cheese sellers, an insulting reference to the Americans] were first chastised and humbled."[17]

His contempt for America ran so deep that he declared he would rather have a "mediocre farm in Hesse than the largest plantation here." The only ones who should be grateful for America, he believed, "are those who were sentenced to hang in Europe and to avoid such a fate had sought refuge here."[18]

Wiederhold was an emotional, complex man. He killed in battle without hesitation. He unflinchingly criticized his superiors. He was a romantic. He seemed to have a talent for finding calamities—captured at Trenton, shipwrecked in the Atlantic—and an equal talent for finding romance: a landlady in Bremerlehe, a second landlady in Bremerlehe, a beautiful woman left behind in Hessen-Kassel, and George Washington's nieces.

But most of all, he hated the Americans. He hated their concept of liberty. He hated their new nation. He hated almost everything about the Americans and their United States of America.

Even George Washington's beautiful nieces could not soften his heart.

CHAPTER 26

Repercussions

WHILE HIS TROOPS assaulted Fort Washington in November 1776, losing 58 dead and over 250 wounded, Frederick embarked on a long-anticipated Italian journey. With good weather and little snow, his stagecoaches and eleven-person entourage crossed the Alps. By December 20, they reached Venice, where Frederick began a royal shopping spree for antiquities.[1]

On Christmas Eve, as Washington prepared to strike the Hessian garrison at Trenton, Frederick attended midnight mass at St. Mark's Church. The following evenings, while his army faced humiliation on the banks of the Delaware River, he enjoyed comedies and operas at St. Benedetto's Theatre. Showing that he could connect with the common man, he insisted on traveling incognito and, as one companion noted, "even chose to sit with the commoners at public events, refusing the elegant boxes assigned to him."

"To our knowledge," an Italian newspaper observed, "almost no foreign prince who visits the city of Rome has kept it secret as the landgrave of Hessen-Kassel." By January 15, 1777, after an arduous crossing of the snow-covered Apennines, his entourage entered the Vatican. Four days later, Frederick was granted an audience with the pope. A Protestant member of the party recorded how "the non-Catholics made deep bows to His Holiness without being obliged to kiss his slippers."

The trip ended abruptly when Frederick announced "urgent business" in Kassel. He arrived home March 28, his trunks filled with antiquities and artwork—and news of Trenton awaiting him.

Frederick's fury over the Trenton disaster demanded satisfaction. His letters revealed both shame and threats of retribution. He wanted an explanation for the humiliation and punishment for those responsible. He ordered an exhaustive investigation, a process that would stretch across five years.

Suspecting a cover-up among his officers, he wrote bitterly, "My sensitive feelings are not quieted and the painful shock not lessened by keeping from me the details of this affair."

From General Knyphausen, he demanded "all the information necessary to give light on this unlucky business and enable me to judge of the proper sentence." Unwilling to wait for the troops' return from America, he ordered an immediate court-martial, which met periodically in Philadelphia from April 1778 until its conclusion in New York City on December 13, 1781.[2]

Even two years after the battle, Frederick's contempt for the rebels remained undiminished. He insisted that at Trenton, "Determination and courage would undoubtedly have enabled them [Rall's Brigade] to break their way through a motley militia which had lost its [courage] because of our previous victories."[3]

The Hessian War Commission's verdict reached Kassel on April 15, 1782. They recommended pardons for all living officers while placing full blame on two men who could not defend themselves: the deceased Colonel Rall and deceased Major von Dechow.

"Colonel Rall and Major von Dechow in many respects acted culpably and laid the foundation for the bad fate of the brigade," the commission declared, recommending pardons for all surviving officers. All the members of the court-martial agreed "the disaster at Trenton was due to the neglect of Rall."[4]

Perhaps the only surprise of the extensive five-year investigation was that the commission absolved the three groups who fled across Assunpink Bridge. The commission, through a twisted, Talmudic-like logic, justified each group's retreat: the Jägers, with their long-range rifles that lacked bayonets, were not equipped for close-quarter street fighting; the pickets had defended themselves honorably before withdrawing under heavy fire; and the artillerymen, having lost their guns, had nothing left to fight with.[5]

Frederick had asked for an "Adjust and impartial."[6]

What he got was a kangaroo court—a court that conveniently laid all the blame on two dead officers.

The news of Washington's victory spread quickly through the colonies, producing a marked change in public sentiment. A British land agent in Virginia observed a remarkable metamorphosis: "The minds of the people are much altered. A few days ago [they] had given up the cause for lost. Their late successes have turned the scale and now they are all liberty mad again." Most telling was his observation of the tangible effect on military recruitment—from complete stagnation to "men coming in by companies."[7]

Soldiers, civilians, and patriotic leaders all spoke about the new spirit of hope, the belief that the rebellion could succeed. Having survived the perilous Christmas Day crossing and the subsequent battle at Trenton, fifer John Greenwood wrote, "The success of this maneuver gave new life to our almost expiring hopes." Contemporary letters and diaries largely glossed over the military details of the engagement, focusing instead on its profound impact on morale and the renewed confidence in the revolutionary cause.[8]

British observers recognized the significance of this shift. Ambrose Serle, Admiral Howe's secretary, wrote with concern that the rebel victory at Trenton would "revive the drooping spirits of the rebels and increase their force." His fears proved prescient, as evidenced by a Pennsylvania soldier's observation that "our militia are flocking in from all quarters."[9]

Yet this renewed spirit faced immediate challenges. Washington's army remained severely depleted, with a third of his force incapacitated. The bitter winter weather persisted, and the Delaware River, which often froze at this time of year, could become a highway for British forces to strike Philadelphia. Nevertheless, this new confidence manifested in bold decision-making: Washington convened a council of war that chose to capitalize on their momentum with another offensive across the Delaware.

The British command's response revealed the extent of the setback. General Howe delayed nearly a month before informing Lord Germain, "Trenton has thrown us further back than it was first apprehended, from the great encouragement it has given to the rebels." Significantly, Howe's previous confidence in his Hessian auxiliaries had diminished, as evidenced by his observation, "I do not now see a prospect of terminating the war, but by a general action, and I am aware of the difficulties in our way to obtain it, as the enemy moves with so much more celerity than we possibly can."[10]

The battle had shattered more than just the myth of Hessian invincibility—it had fundamentally altered the psychological landscape of the American Revolution. What emerges from the historical record is not merely a tactical victory but a moment of profound transformation in how both sides viewed the potential trajectory of the war.

On October 31, 1785, Frederick was enjoying a typical day in his residence. After his daily parade with the Swiss Guard and Privy Council paperwork, he was having lunch with the landgravine's ladies when he suddenly became still and hunched forward in his chair. Death came with such quiet swiftness that his dining companions continued their conversations, not yet realizing their prince had passed away.[11]

His son William, only recently reconciled after twenty years of estrangement, would inherit a complex legacy. The American war's profits had funded Frederick's dreams: patronage of arts, government reforms, and social improvements. At his funeral, a college professor proclaimed, "He made his residence, the residence of the muses, doing everything that he could to promote the Enlightenment."[12]

When William rushed to Kassel to open the treasury's well-guarded vault, he discovered the full measure of his father's financial success. Despite Hessen-Kassel's modest size, the soldier trade had made Frederick one of Europe's wealthiest rulers. British subsidies during the American Revolution brought 19 million thalers to Hessen-Kassel (nearly $4 billion in 2025), leaving Frederick a profit of 10 million thalers (about $2 billion).[13]

Even the soldiers prospered from the war in America, though at terrible cost. By the war's third year, they had sent home 600,000 thalers ($120 million) but paid for this wealth with 5,000 dead comrades and 1,300 wounded. Frederick tried to ease their burden by remitting 2.17 million thalers ($434 million) in taxes to soldiers' families. In a final irony, he sent 324 thalers ($65,000) to his Enlightenment mentor Voltaire, listed simply as "gratitude."[14]

William was likely stunned by the scale of his inheritance in his father's art gallery. Rembrandts, Rubenses, and Van Dykes adorned the walls—over nine hundred precious paintings forming one of Europe's finest collections, particularly strong in seventeenth-century Dutch and Flemish works.[15]

British gold had transformed the Kassel of William's youth. The dreary, shabby city had become one of Germany's notable capitals, yet beneath its improved facade, the principality struggled. Frederick's final four years saw him issue 250 ordinances, trying to accelerate economic growth while maintaining social justice. He left William a government with a unique, but often not very effective, mixture of socialism and capitalism.[16]

Frederick's reforms were evident throughout Hessen-Kassel: courts modernized, schools rebuilt, farming methods upgraded. Stone by stone, Kassel changed—its antiquated walls pulled down as modern avenues took shape.[17]

William viewed the welfare state that Frederick had built with distaste. Where Frederick had built a system for relief of the poor, easing peasants' burdens and reducing their taxes, the new landgrave marked the start of his reign by slashing government expenditures.

Most of Frederick's reforms were withering even before William took control. Frederick's bureaucracy, meant to serve the people, instead suffocated them with rigid, uncompromising, arbitrary rules. Officials proposed absurd measures—like monitoring the fidelity of soldiers' wives whose husbands were fighting in America—and even tried banning hot chocolate as morally corrupting. Nature, too, worked against reform. Hills made roads nearly impossible to maintain, and droughts in 1784 and 1785 destroyed crops. Neighboring states enforced harsh trade barriers, strangling Hessian commerce. Through it all, the largely illiterate peasantry resisted change.[18]

One deputy captured Frederick's failures bluntly: Despite "best intentions.... Some of his programs have not only failed to have the desired effect but... have considerably worsened the problem." The Jewish expulsion policy demonstrated this perfectly. By driving Jewish families from rural areas, Frederick had inadvertently stripped nobles of laborers, Jewish farmers of livelihoods, and Christian peasants of financial services the church prohibited. In 1785, acknowledging these cascading failures, he reversed the policy.[19]

In June 1765, William's life took an unexpected turn when he bought a few antique coins from a young coin dealer. Despite his youth, the twenty-year-old dealer displayed wisdom, cleverness, meticulous attention to detail, and exceeding trustworthiness. William departed their initial meeting satisfied with his bargain purchase, unaware that the astute dealer had willingly accepted a loss to cultivate a relationship with the wealthy landgrave.[20]

This seemingly trifling transaction of a few antique coins profoundly altered William's life and shaped the future of European banking. The young coin dealer was Mayer Amschel Rothschild, and his dealings with

William marked the genesis of his banking empire. With great care and foresight, Rothschild built on that first transaction, gradually expanding from coins to metals and eventually to international loans. He deftly demonstrated to William the extraordinary profits that could be reaped from lending to royal borrowers. Perhaps even more valuable was Rothschild's extensive network, which possessed the capability to safeguard the landgrave's wealth from the grasp of political adversaries.

In recognition of Rothschild's invaluable services, William bestowed on him the title of court factor, designating him as his personal financial manager and a member of the court. He granted him a Judengasse permit, allowing him to walk the streets on Sundays and Christian holidays when other Jews were barred. Likely influenced by Rothschild, William further demonstrated his esteem by abolishing laws requiring Jewish merchants to identify their market stalls as non-Christian.

William built his inheritance into vast wealth but lacked his father's drive to improve his subjects' lives. Where Frederick had sought reform, his son pursued profit.

Frederick's reign had brought more changes than most European monarchs attempted, yet few of his initiatives truly challenged existing institutions. Frederick's blend of socialism and capitalism produced more failures than successes, his enlightened absolutism ultimately achieving only modest gains.

Some reforms succeeded: Agricultural techniques were modernized, textiles grew from a local craft to an international export, and unemployment held at 4 percent—far below Berlin's 15 percent and Munich's 11 percent. Yet without the soldier trade's profits, the principality would have faced bankruptcy. Despite Frederick's efforts, Hessen-Kassel remained what geography had ordained: an agrarian society wresting life from stubborn soil.

The new century brought changes Frederick could not have foreseen. The soldier trade that had funded his dreams soon yielded to citizen armies. Nationalism and liberalism threatened the very existence of small principalities. William spent his reign maneuvering through European politics, particularly during the Napoleonic Wars. Napoleon bluntly declared his intent to "remove the house of Hessen-Kassel from rulership and to strike it out of the list of powers."

In the end, neither French ambition nor William's financial acumen would decide Hessen-Kassel's fate. In 1866, the principality's ancient fear came true: Prussia absorbed Hessen-Kassel, ending its independence.

Epilogue

The Painting, Dusseldorf, 1849

The American painter Worthington Whittredge had grown bored of the gaiety of Paris. He paid the rent on his studio, had his passport stamped, and bought a railroad ticket to the Art Academy in Dusseldorf. Standing in front of a Dusseldorf tavern, he paused to reflect on the image that gazed back at him from the establishment's window. The ridge of his eyebrows protruded, and his bald, wide skull narrowed at his chin, giving him the appearance of a tall monkey. His lips curved into a smile.

The natural charm he might have found wanting, he compensated for with the talent and dexterity of his hands. This day had been the object of his dreams: to study at the prestigious Dusseldorf Art Academy, to hone his craft under the tutelage of Europe's esteemed masters. With a deep, steadying breath, Whittredge ascended the creaking wooden staircase that led to the studio above the tavern.

Reflecting on his journey, he chuckled at the memory of his first public painting. He had begun as a house painter in Ohio, with local farmers cheering as he completed the word "PORKHOUSE" across the side of a barn and applauding his painting of a brown boot in the window of a shoe store.

Those days in Ohio were behind him. Now he stood at the threshold of the Düsseldorf Art Academy, an institution that reigned over the art world, a place where mediocrity found no refuge and only exceptional skill flourished.[1]

He knew what he was getting himself into—or at least he thought he knew.

At the top of the stairs, Whittredge pushed open the door that led to Emanuel Leutze's studio, a sanctuary where the meister's creative spirit held sway. In a moment, as theatrical as the setting itself, a cannon's roar shattered the stillness, and fragments of shrapnel embedded themselves in the wall adjacent to Whittredge. As the smoke dissipated, it revealed Leutze, a figure of grandeur, standing beneath an American flag, the cord of a miniature cannon in his grasp.[2]

Leutze spoke rapidly, brushing back his thick, flowing red hair with nervous strokes. His face was childlike, effeminate, but Whittredge discerned a spark of frenzied brilliance—almost madness—in Leutze's gaze. Towering and brimming with energy, Leutze greeted his compatriot with a zeal reserved for kindred spirits. Across the room, a "Prussian" battery of miniature cannons was manned by another artist, Andreas Achenbach. Leutze explained he was painting George Washington's crossing of the Delaware River, and the artillery added to the mood of the studio.[3]

Whittredge had journeyed across the sea to learn from a master, but Leutze's focus was on how Americans made the best models when painting soldiers. He expressed that Germans were physically too small to convey the ruggedness of American farmers risking their lives with Washington. Leutze had allowed one European in the painting, a large Norwegian posing as Washington's oarsman, since Leutze figured Scandinavians were familiar with navigating boats in cold weather.[4]

After circling Whittredge and evaluating him, Leutze exclaimed, "Perfect!"

He believed the tall, solidly built Whittredge would make a fine George Washington. Leutze then brought out a meticulously crafted replica of the general's uniform, which a tailor had copied from the original at the Patent Office in Washington, DC. Leutze smiled and drew a draft of beer from a cask behind the twenty-four-foot canvas. Whittredge tried to ask a question about technique, but Leutze ignored him and instead thrust the historic attire into his arms along with the freshly drawn beer. Sipping the brew, Whittredge arrayed himself in the uniform. Leutze screamed for him to freeze; he sought to capture the garment's authenticity, insisting that not a fold be disturbed by needless adjustment.

For two hours, Whittredge stood frozen in Washington's uniform, his luggage from Paris unopened on the floor. His muscles ached and he nearly collapsed from fatigue. When finished, Leutze poured a glass of champagne and insisted Whittredge drink. Exhausted, he complied.[5]

Just then, a friend of Whittredge's from America hobbled up the stairs into the studio. Sickly and walking hunched, the invalid had come to meet the esteemed Leutze. Instead, Leutze bandaged the man and draped him in a blanket. Whittredge watched as his handicapped friend became a wounded soldier huddling against the icy winds on the Delaware River.

Whittredge tried to grasp Leutze's technique as the German completed painting the wounded soldier. Leutze set down his brush and handed a mug of beer to his invalid model. They laughed and drank, then Leutze seized Whittredge, thrusting an oar into his hands and adorning him in a soldier's uniform. Whittredge was now a steersman for Washington's boat.[6]

In the ensuing days, Whittredge helped with various tasks around the studio. His temporary home was a cot placed near the grand but still-headless portrayal of General Washington. Under this looming figure, he rested and dined, while Leutze appeared to forego sleep altogether. Other artists drifted in to labor over their own pieces in the corners of the large studio. Fellow artists shouted encouragement, Leutze barking retorts, the German folk songs from the tavern below mixing with their chatter. In rare quiet moments, Whittredge sat on the paint-splattered floor sipping his beer, marveling at the chaos of creativity swirling around him.[7]

Prussian officials peered through the doorway, their eyes surveying the juxtaposition of "Prussian" and "American" artillery batteries and the strewn copies of Karl Marx's *Neue Rheinische Zeitung* (New Rhenish Newspaper). Scribbling onto their notepads, they exchanged brief, curt nods with Leutze before departing. Whittredge realized the Prussian government still feared the pencil and paintbrush of men like Leutze. The failed democratic uprisings of 1848 had sent shockwaves across Europe, leaving the Prussian authorities wary of influential figures like Emanuel Leutze. The artist's childhood emigration from Germany and his subsequent return to establish progressive artistic circles such as *Der Malkasten* (the Paintbox) only deepened official suspicion. On the surface, *Der Malkasten* appeared harmless, perhaps even frivolous, with its insignia of a double-headed eagle clutching both a latch key and a foaming cup of beer. The Prussian authorities, however, saw little humor in such flippancy. The government, which demanded unwavering loyalty and heroic portrayals of the fatherland, regarded Leutze's allegiance with growing skepticism.[8]

Leutze, with his fiery red hair, restless demeanor, and enthusiasm for Republicanism, harbored no romantic notions about his German upbringing. He had grown up in the impoverished Principality of Württemberg, a region that had once been prosperous until its ambitious prince sided with Napoleon and sent sixteen thousand Württemberg men to their deaths during the disastrous 1812 Russian campaign. Leutze's father's job involved the labor-intensive process of splitting cattle horns, boiling them, and shaping them into combs until, after repeated attempts at dodging the military draft, he relocated his family to Philadelphia. Residing in a house around the corner from Betsy Ross's, the family discovered a world of opportunities, and by age fifteen, Leutze was experimenting with oil paints. Now, at thirty-five, Emanuel Leutze was driven by a desire to remind Americans, who often took their democracy for granted, that the struggle for democratic ideals persisted in Europe.[9]

Leutze brought out a bust of Washington, a precise replica of the mold crafted by the French sculptor Houdon just two years after the war. Using the bust as a reference, Leutze meticulously painted Washington's face, capturing a dignified expression gazing intently yet calmly through the mist toward the unknown perils on the opposite shore.

With the painting nearly complete, Leutze roused his sleeping dog nestled in the corner of the studio. Grabbing the animal by his leash, Leutze romped boisterously through the apartment, the dog barking frantically as his master howled in return.[10]

That night, Leutze mixed the hues for the sky. In the morning, he allowed Whittredge to work with the Dusseldorf artist Andreas Achenbach. Gently, but swiftly, they blended the colors, rushing to form the sky in one session so it would retain its natural color. They drank from the cask of beer, talking and singing as they worked. In a moment of whimsical inspiration, Leutze discharged his miniature cannon, contributing to the creative ambiance of the studio.

Finally, it was done, but Achenbach had a thought: a star. A lone, barely visible star, the last to fade in the morning light. Leutze added it. Leutze joked and laughed with ease, and Whittredge realized how effortlessly painting came to this master artist. Though the German government had succeeded in removing Leutze from the board of the Dusseldorf Artist's Union, labeling him "*ein geburtiger Republikaner*" (a native Republican), gazing upon the star fading over Washington's head, Whittredge knew they had not crushed Leutze's spirit.[11]

* * *

The following year, fire damaged the painting. Leutze received $1,800 from his insurance company for the marred work. The insurers then raffled off the scorched canvas, selling ten thousand chances at sixty cents each. Through this venture, the company not only recovered its payout but also accumulated a surplus. Failing to see the irony, the company donated the profits to the wives and children of the Prussian military.

Leutze proceeded to paint a new copy. The new painting was purchased by the International Art Union, for the extraordinary sum of $6,000 and embarked to New York for a grand display on Broadway. In its debut month on exhibit, more than twenty thousand people paid twenty-five cents each to see *Washington Crossing the Delaware*.[12]

The *New York Evening Mirror* proclaimed that the painting was "the grandest, most majestic painting ever exhibited in America. . . . The scenery, the atmosphere, the ice, the frost particles upon the clothing of the men—the expression of the sturdy oarsmen, and the heroic countenance of Washington, who carries the American Revolution in his heart, are all depicted to life—and in a style to baffle criticism."[13]

Within three months, over fifty thousand visitors had viewed Leutze's work. The *Literary World* said it was "incomparably the best painting yet executed of an American subject." Finally, the painting was sold to a private purchaser for $10,000. On the last night of the exhibit, the gallery stayed open to midnight to accommodate the thousands who came to say goodbye.[14]

Leutze was the toast of the art world. Reviewers spoke of his "masterly excellence" and of the "fearful perils of the Revolutionary army." However, despite the acclaim, Leutze fell short in achieving one of his primary objectives. While the public viewed the painting as a symbol of America's struggle for freedom and a tribute to its heroic past, they failed to recognize it as an allegory of the contemporary Germanic fight for democracy. Leutze expected the exhibition would rally support for the waning German democratic revolution. But when Louis Kossuth, hero of the Hungarian insurrection of 1848, arrived in America, Leutze was unable to raise financial or moral support for his cause. The complexities of the European uprisings were perplexing to Americans, who failed to see the parallels between George Washington's crossing of the Delaware River and the ongoing conflicts behind barricades in the streets of Europe.[15]

The German government permitted Leutze to display the original, fire-damaged painting in Dusseldorf and even honored him with a gold medal. The German rulers could afford to be magnanimous, for by the time

Leutze returned to Germany in 1852, the revolution was effectively defeated. The government-controlled press praised the painting's technical proficiency and American theme, carefully and explicitly noting it to be of "foreign element."[16]

The undamaged copy was eventually donated to the Metropolitan Museum of Art in New York, where copies were made for almost every history textbook used in American schools. The painting has remained on display at the museum for more than 120 years.

The original fire-damaged copy was exhibited across Germany and eventually hung in a Bremen art museum for almost a century. While under the ownership of a German government even more repressive than the autocratic Hessian regime of the eighteenth century, the painting was destroyed by Allied bombers in 1942.[17]

Notes

PREFACE

1. Emanuel Leutze, *Washington Crossing the Delaware*, 1851, oil on canvas, 149 x 255 in. (378.5 x 647.7 cm), permanent exhibit, Metropolitan Museum of Art, New York, accessed March 30, 2025, https://www.metmuseum.org/art/collection/search/11417.

PROLOGUE: BOSTON, APRIL 1775

1. Bob Ruppert, "A Fast Ship from Salem: Carrying News of War," *Journal of the American Revolution*, April 17, 2015, accessed April 17, 2025, Allthingsliberty.com /2015/04/a-fast-ship-from-salem-carrying-news-of-war.
2. Michael Cecere, "The Army of Observation Forms: Spring 1775 in Massachusetts," *Journal of the American Revolution*, May 19, 2025, https://allthingsliberty.com/2025/05/the-army-of-observation-forms-spring-1775-in-massachusetts/; Richard Ketchum, *Decisive Day: The Battle for Bunker Hill* (Doubleday, 1974), 29-33; Allen French, *The Siege of Boston* (Macmillan, 1911), 216-219; Clark Summers, "Ten Rifle Companies: Why Rifles, and Not Muskets?" *Journal of the American Revolution*, October 20, 2023, https://allthingsliberty.com/2023/10/ten-rifle-companies-why-rifles-and-not-muskets/.
3. Eric Robson, *The American Revolution in Its Political and Military Aspects, 1763–1783* (Archon Books, 1965),166.
4. Andrea Hofmeister, "Elementary Education, Schools, and the Demands of Everyday Life: Northwest Germany in 1800," *Central European History* 31, no. 4 (1998): 329-384; Ernst Kipping, *The Hessian View of America, 1776–1783* (Philip Freneau Press, 1971), 5.

CHAPTER ONE: A VILLAGE GOES TO WAR

1. Wolf von Both and Hans Vogel, *Landgraf Friedrich II* (Deutscher Kunstverlag, 1973), 98; Daniel Krebs, *A Generous and Merciful Enemy* (University of Oklahoma Press, 2013), 15.
2. Robert Wright, "Side by Side: British, German and Loyalists," *Johannes Schwab Historical Society* 23 (2020): 3- 25; Krebs, *Generous*, 15.
3. Rodney Atwood, *The Hessians: Mercenaries from Hessen-Kassel in the American Revolution* (Cambridge University Press, 1980), 21. One in every fifteen Hessen-Kassel males served in the military. Krebs, *Generous*, 36.

4. Anna Schnitker, "Writing the Nation," PhD diss. (University of Edinburgh, 2004), 119 n126.
5. Atwood, *Hessians*, 21; Both and Vogel, *Landgraf*, 98; Fritz Redlich, *The German Military Enterpriser and His Workforce* (Franz Steiner Verlag, 1964),187; Krebs, *Generous*, 51.
6. Charles Ingrao, *The Hessian Mercenary State* (Cambridge University Press, 1987), 93-94.
7. Redlich, *German Military Enterpriser*, 187-188.
8. Johannes Reuber, *Diary*, tr. Bruce Burgoyne, in Bruce Burgoyne private collection, 1; Friederike Baer, *Hessians: German Soldiers in the American Revolutionary War* (Oxford University Press, 2022), 40.
9. Krebs, *Generous*, 15. Estimates of the principality's population vary from 275,000 to 350,000.
10. Atwood, *Hessians*, 43, 89, 244; "Colonel Johann Rall," Road to Freedom Biographies, accessed February 4, 2025, https://id3491.securedata.net/imagecog/roadtofreedom/rall.html.
11. Jakob Piel, "Diary of the Hessian Lieutenant Jakob Piel," in *Defeat, Disaster and Dedication*, tr. Bruce Burgoyne (Heritage Books, 1996), 20; Mayo Clinic staff, "Adult Attention-Deficit/Hyperactivity Disorder (ADHD)," Mayo Clinic, accessed April 2, 2025, https://mayoclinic.org/diseases-conditions/adult-adhd/symptoms-causes/syc-20350878.
12. Reuber, *Diary*, Burgoyne translation, 1; Wright, "Side by Side," 17.
13. Atwood, *Hessians*, 37.
14. Unbeknownst to the men, the landgrave had issued the marching orders three weeks prior. Heister Regiment, *Journal of the First Brigade of the von Heister Corps, 1776–77*, microfiche 364, box H, Lidgerwood Collection, Morristown National Historical Park, Morristown, NJ; Reuber, *Diary*, Burgoyne translation, 1.
15. Reuber, *Diary*, Burgoyne translation, 1.
16. Atwood, *Hessians*, 38; Hill, Steven W. Hill, "Hessian Flags in the American War for Independence, 1776–1783." *Military Collector & Historian* (Winter 2003/2004): 226-31; David Norris, "Halberds and Spontoons," *Warfare History Network*, May 2016, accessed April 3, 2025, https://warfarehistorynetwork.com/article/halberds-and-spontoons/. The spears carried by some officers were ceremonial. Spears, also known as pikes, halberds, and spontoons were archaic-looking bladed weapons attached to six-foot-long shafts. Their value as a weapon in Europe had ended with the development of artillery and muskets. They were still used on the battlefield as a signal to straighten formations, set distances between the ranks, and prod men into line.
17. For those interested in Hessian genealogy, Stanford University has an extensive history of the Wiederhold family going back to 1229 CE: Gio Wiederhold, "Wiederhold Ancestors," accessed May 16, 2025, http://i.stanford.edu/pub/gio/personal/ancestors; Atwood, *Hessians*, 49; David Hackett Fischer, *Washington's Crossing* (Oxford University Press, 2004), 58.
18. Reuber, *Diary*, Burgoyne translation, 2.
19. Ingrao, *Mercenary State*, 166; Both and Vogel, *Landgraf*, 156.
20. Both and Vogel, *Landgraf*, 152, 180.
21. Both and Vogel, *Landgraf*, 152.
22. Atwood, *Hessians*, 48-49; Both and Vogel, *Landgraf*, 100.
23. Both and Vogel, *Landgraf*, 99-100; Atwood, *Hessians*, 47; Hill, "Hessian Flags," 226-231.
24. Atwood, *Hessians*, 16; Wright, "Side by Side," 9.
25. Matthew White, "Statistics of Wars, Oppressions and Atrocities of the Eighteenth Century," necrometrics.com, accessed April 2, 2025, https://necrometrics.com/wars18c.htm.
26. Elliot Hoffman, "The German Soldiers in the American Revolution," PhD diss., University of New Hampshire, 1982, 110.

27. Atwood, *Hessians*, 38; Both and Vogel, *Landgraf*, 100; Krebs, *Generous*, 53; Ingrao, *Mercenary State*, 142.
28. Krebs, *Generous*, 53, 61-62, 67-71. Krebs notes that later in the war, foreigners would make up 20 percent of the army after Frederick ordered that only foreigners be recruited as replacements for his troops in North America. Hessen-Kassel's wartime rural-based economy was too fragile to lose more men to recruitment.
29. Both and Vogel, *Landgraf*, 101; Kipping, *Hessian View*, 21.
30. Andrea Hofmeister, "Elementary Education, Schools, and the Demands of Everyday Life: Northwest Germany in 1800," *Central European History* 31, no. 4 (1998): 329-384; Kipping, *Hessian View*, 5; Edward J. Lowell, *The Hessians and the Other German Auxiliaries of Great Britain in the Revolutionary War* (Harper & Brothers, 1884), 21-24.
31. Atwood, *Hessians*, 43. Hessian Army regulations required recruits to be five foot four, but these guidelines were often ignored during times of war. Baer, *Hessians*, 40.
32. Ingrao, *Mercenary State*, 142-143.
33. Horst Dippel, *Germany and the American Revolution* (Steiner, 1977), 9; Baer, *Hessians*, 82.
34. Ingrao, *Mercenary State*, 142.
35. Ingrao, *Mercenary State*, 132; Mark Schwalm, "The Hessian to the British Crown: A Series of Four Lectures," (Messiah College, 1984), 5.
36. Baer, *Hessians*, 7-9.
37. The British recaptured Montreal by the end of the year after Benedict Arnold's failed attempt to capture Quebec.
38. Anthony Mockler, *The Mercenaries* (Macmillan, 1969), 119; Dippel, *Germany*, 121; Ingrao, *Mercenary State*, 138.
39. Wright, "Side by Side," 5.
40. Atwood, *Hessians*, 26; Max von Eelking, *The German Allied Troops in the North American War of Independence, 1776–1783*, trans. J. G. Rosengarten (Joel Munsell's Sons, 1893), 19; Baer, *Hessians*, 16.
41. Ingrao, *Mercenary State*, 141-142.
42. Atwood, *Hessians*, 49-50, 62-63, 77; Lowell, *Auxiliaries*, 58; Benson Lossing, *The Pictorial Field-Book of the Revolution*, vol. 1 (Porter, 1866), 321; Richard Ketchum, *The Winter Soldiers* (Doubleday, 1973), 135.
43. Lossing, *Pictorial*, 1:321; Atwood, *Hessians*, 50, 77; Ketchum, *Winter Soldiers*, 135, 154.
44. The Hessian heavy infantry is sometimes archaically referred to as "Fusilier." A fusil was an outdated, older, lighter version of a musket. Almost all the Hessian units in America carried state-of-the-art muskets.
45. Atwood, *Hessians*, 39; Hoffman, "Soldiers," 93-96; Krebs, *Generous*, 52; Henry Stirke, "A British Officer's Revolutionary War Journal," ed. Sydney Bradford, *Maryland Historical Magazine* 56, no. 2 (June 1961): 156, 165.
46. Heister, *First Brigade*, 4-5; Hoffman, "Soldiers," 93-96; Wright, "Side by Side," 18.
47. Baron Karl Leopold Baurmeister, *Revolution in America: Confidential Letters and Journals 1776 to 1784 of Adjutant General Major Baurmeister of the Hessian Forces*, ed. Bernard Uhlendorf (Rutgers University Press, 1957), 16; Hoffman, "Soldiers," 96-97.
48. Hoffman, "Soldiers," 97; Krebs, *Generous*, 57.
49. Hoffman, "Soldiers," 80; Lossberg Regiment, *Journal of the Regular Corp Under the Command of His Excellency Lieutenant General Lossberg*, microfiche box M, 1, Lidgerwood Collection, Morristown Historical Park, NJ.
50. Heister, *First Brigade*, 4,7; Knyphausen Regiment, *Journal of the Regular Corp Under the Command of His Excellency Lieutenant General Knyphausen*, microfiche box P, 1-3, Lidgerwood Collection, Morristown Historical Park, NJ; Hoffman, "Soldiers," 92.

51. Hoffman, "Soldiers," 95.
52. Atwood, *Hessians*, 52; Fischer, *Washington's Crossing*, 175-176, 383-385; Baer, *Hessians*, 59-61; Georg Pausch, *Journal of Captain Pausch* (Joel Munsell's Sons, 1886), 41; Henry Retzer, "March Route from Hessen to America: Jeramias Kappes," *Johannes Schwan Historical Association* 7, no. 4 (2004): 9.

CHAPTER TWO: FREDERICK: DESPOT OR ENLIGHTENED PRINCE?

1. Atwood, *Hessians*, 13-14, 20; Ingrao, *Mercenary State*, 127.
2. Atwood, *Hessians*, 13, 15, 16, 22-23; Both and Vogel, *Landgraf*, 101
3. Lowell, *Auxiliaries*, 3; Krebs, *Generous*, 25. Krebs describes Hessen-Kassel as part of the "Protestant System" that included "most of the northern states in the Holy Roman Empire, Great Britain, Sweden, Denmark and the Netherlands." The Imperial Knights of the Holy Roman Empire were a unique noble class whose defining characteristic was that they received their lands directly from the emperor and ruled their fiefdoms without any intermediary local princess.
4. Ingrao, *Mercenary State*, 13.
5. Arthur Wyss, 'Friedrich II: Landgrave of Hesse-Kassel," *Allgemeine Deutsche Biographie*, 7 (1878): 524-528.
6. Ingrao, *Mercenary State*, 13-14.
7. Ingrao, *Mercenary State*, 66.
8. Atwood, *Hessians*, 231; Ingrao, *Mercenary State*, 93; Both and Vogel, *Landgraf*, 58.
9. Ingrao, *Mercenary State*, 93-95,107; Both and Vogel, *Landgraf*, 57-58.
10. Ingrao, *Mercenary State*, 15, 21, 53; Both and Vogel, *Landgraf*, 83.
11. Wyss, *Friedrich II*, 524-528; Ingrao, *Mercenary State*, 16; Friedrich Kapp, *The Soldier Trade of German Princes to America*, repr., Project Gutenberg ebook, guttenberg.org, accessed June 18, 2025, https://www.gutenberg.org/cache/epub/47054/pg47054.txt. Kapp states that Frederick found Protestantism "too insufficiently noble." Kapp, *Soldier Trade*, 50.
12. Ingrao, *Mercenary State*, 17.
13. Ingrao, *Mercenary State*, 17.
14. Wyss, *Friedrich II*, 524-528; Ingrao, *Mercenary State*, 17.
15. Both and Vogel, *Landgraf*, 25.
16. Ingrao, *Mercenary State*, 20, 21.
17. Wyss, *Friedrich II*, 524-528; Ingrao, *Mercenary State*, 19.
18. Wyss, *Friedrich II*, 524-528.
19. The derivation of the fort's name from ancient German reflects the fort's reputation: "Magdeburg" from the ancient German word *magado* for mighty and *burga* for fortress.
20. Ingrao, *Mercenary State*, 15; Both and Vogel, *Landgraf*, 18.
21. Both and Vogel, *Landgraf*, 18.
22. Both and Vogel, *Landgraf*, 19; Ingrao, *Mercenary State*, 123; Atwood, *Hessians*, 26.
23. Both and Vogel, *Landgraf*, 26.

CHAPTER THREE: MARCHING TO THEIR DESTINY

1. Ingrao, *Mercenary State*, 166,172; Both and Vogel, *Landgraf*, 154, 156; Atwood, *Hessians*, 2, 33, 252. Kapp feels that Frederick liked playing the "protecter of the Arts," but the spectacular waterworks was really built to obtain good publicity. Kapp, *Soldier Trade*, 51.
2. Bergpark Wilhelmshöhe. UNESCO Application Documents, https://whc.unesco.org/en/list/1413/documents/; Both and Vogel, *Landgraf*, 164; Bergpark Wilhelmshöhe, *UNESCO Application*, UNESCO.org, 5-7, 32-34, accessed April 5, 2025, https://whc.unesco.

org/uploads/nominations/1413.pdf. For more documents and maps of Bergpark Wilhelmshöhe, see UNESCO World Heritage site, https://whc.unesco.org/en/list/1413.

3. Ingrao, *Mercenary State*, 109; Atwood, *Hessians*, 2.
4. Ingrao, *Mercenary State*, 111.
5. Ingrao, *Mercenary State*, 108.
6. Ingrao, *Mercenary State*, 58, 74.
7. Ingrao, *Mercenary State*, 64-65; Both and Vogel, *Landgraf*, 60-61.
8. Ingrao, *Mercenary State*, 167.
9. Ingrao, Mercenary State, 64-65, 167-168; Both and Vogel, *Landgraf*, 60-61, 125, 150, 152, 234; Atwood, *Hessians*, 251.
10. Both and Vogel, *Landgraf*, 125-126, 152.
11. Ingrao, *Mercenary State*, 183, 186.
12. Ingrao, *Mercenary State*, 74, 109.
13. Ingrao, *Mercenary State*, 184-185.
14. Hill, "Flags," 226-231.The Hessian flags were taller than wider, measuring approximately fifty-five by forty-five inches. There were some variations, but the description presented here is fairly typical of a Hessian regimental flag.
15. Dippel, *Germany*, 123.
16. Reuber, *Diary*, Burgoyne translation, 2-3; Retzer, "March Route," 7; Piel, "Diary," 8.
17. Atwood, *Hessians*, 37; Retzer, "March Route," 7.
18. Reuber, *Diary*, Burgoyne translation, 2.
19. Robert Slagle, "The Von Lossberg Regiment" (PhD diss., American University, 1965), 216.
20. The Regiment von Lossberg dated back to 1683 and had its headquarters in Rinteln, a walled city on the Weser River. From the twelfth century to 1640, Rinteln was the principal town of the Earldom of Schaumberg, an independent political entity. In 1640, the ruling line died out, and the Schaumberg territory was eventually divided between three rulers, with Hessen-Kassel receiving the city of Rinteln. Hoffman, "Soldiers," 99.
21. Steven Hill's article on Hessian flags shows the orange Lossberg flag. Hill, "Flags," plate 6. Based on a painting and banner fragments preserved in Rinteln, Robert Slagle believes the Lossberg flag was made of white silk embroidered with a gold crown and an eagle holding an olive branch alongside the motto *Pro Principe et Patria* (For the Prince and the Country). Slagle, "Lossberg," 18.
22. Slagle, "Lossberg," 20.
23. Atwood, *Hessians*, 39; Knyphausen, *Journal*, 2; Reuber, *Diary*, Burgoyne translation, 5, 7.
24. Heister, *First Brigade*, box H, 13. The value of a thaler is based on the calculation that one thaler equals $76 in 2025. This is from the work done by Wolf von Both analyzing Hessian-Kassel's finances as shown in Both and Vogel, *Landgraf*, 91-97. On page 97 is the calculation that one thaler was equal to 30 deutsche marks in 1965. Claude AI and Chat GPT calculations based on silver prices and purchasing power (the number of days that one thaler would pay for a worker's food and lodging) estimate that one thaler equals $200 to $400. (Claude AI Estimate is $200 to $300 and Chat GPT estimate is $200 to $400.) Obviously, deciding on the value of a 250-year-old coin is at best an educated guess. I will use an average of all three estimates, which would be one thaler equals $200 in 2025.
25. Heister, *First Brigade*, 13; Lowell, *Auxiliaries*, 41.

CHAPTER FOUR: SHOPPING FOR SOLDIERS

1. Baer, *Hessians*, 10.
2. Melodie, Andrews, "Myrmidons from Abroad: The Role of the German Mercenary in the Coming of American Independence" (PhD diss., University of Houston, 1986), 37-38.

3. Atwood, *Hessians*, 25; Ingrao, *Mercenary State*, 137.
4. Hoffman, "Soldiers," 82; Baer, *Hessians*, 8-9; Atwood, *Hessians*, 25.
5. Atwood, *Hessians*, 26.
6. Atwood, *Hessians*, 36.
7. Atwood, *Hessians*, 210-213; Ingrao, *Mercenary State*, 144-145; Krebs, *Generous*, 51.
8. Edward Lowell, *The Hessians and the Other German Auxiliaries of Great Britain in the Revolutionary War* (New York: Harper & Brothers, 1884), 42-43; Kenneth Jones, *Johannes Schwalm: The Hessian* (Johannes Schwalm Historical Association, 1976), 11.
9. Lowell, *Auxiliaries*, 42-43.
10. Lowell, *Auxiliaries*, 42-43; Jones, *Schwalm*, 9.
11. Jones, *Schwalm*, 9.
12. Krebs, *Generous*, 43.
13. Baer, *Hessians*, 43; Krebs, *Generous*, 43, 64-65.
14. Baer, *Hessians*, 65; Atwood, *Hessians*, 36.
15. Heister, *North America*, box B, 93; Wiederhold to Gilsa, April 1 , 1776, in Georg Ernst von und zu Gilsa, *The War in America and Enlightenment in Hesse: The Private Letters of Georg Ernst von und of Gilsa (1772–1784)*, ed. Holger Graf (Hessian State Office for Regional History Marburg: Hessian State Office for Historical Regional Studies Marburg, 2010). The letters are viewable on DFG Viewer (https://dfg-viewer.de/en/), a browser web service for displaying digital representations from decentralized library repositories.
16. Hoffman, "Soldiers," 120; Lowell, *Auxiliaries*,14. Ironically, in the light of Germany's future history, the British Army at this time used the same goose step.
17. Atwood, *Hessians*, 40, 43; Faucitt to Suffolk, April 2, 1776, in "Contemporary Observations on the Hesse-Cassel Troops Sent to North America, 1776 to 1781," ed. Albert W. Haarmann, *Journal of the Society for Army Historical Research* 54, no. 219 (Autumn 1976): 131.
18. Baer, *Hessians*, 91-92; Atwood, *Hessians*, 45, 132-133; Krebs, *Generous*, 16, 57.
19. Wright, "Side by Side," 7, 17, 19; Krebs, *Generous*, 57-58; James McIntyre, *Johann Ewald: Jager Commander* (Knox Press, 2020), 21.
20. Hoffman, "Soldiers," 96-97; Atwood, *Hessians*, 68; David Ross, "The Hessian Jägerkorps in New York and Pennsylvania, 1776–1777," *Journal of the American Revolution*, May 14, 2015, accessed May 30, 2025, https://allthingsliberty.com/2015/05/the-hessian-jagerkorps-in-new-york-and-pennsylvania-1776-1777/.
21. Ross, "Jägerkorps"; Atwood, *Hessians*, 132
22. Haarmann, *Observation*, 130.
23. Wright, "Side by Side," 19.
24. Atwood, *Hessians*, 41-42; Slagle, "Lossberg," 12, 17; Krebs, *Generous*, 52.
25. Atwood, *Hessians*, 43; Hofmeister, "Elementary Education," 329-384; Kipping, *Hessian View*, 5; Slagle, *Lossberg*, 11, 13, 17; Krebs, *Generous*, 292n89.
26. Faucitt to Suffolk, March 25, 1776; Kapp, *Soldatenhandel*, 63.
27. Faucitt to Suffolk, April 12, 1776; Atwood, *Hessians*, 43n121.
28. Knyphausen, *Journal*, 1-3.
29. Atwood, *Hessians*, 38-39; Baer, *Hessians*, 46.
30. Atwood, *Hessians*, 38-39; Everett Spees, "The Erbprinz Regiment at Staten Island," *Journal of the Johannes Schwalm Historical Association* 23 (2020): 26-47.
31. Knyphausen, *Journal*, 4; Atwood, *Hessians*, 36; Baer, *Hessians*, 79.
32. Atwood, *Hessians*, 51.
33. Hoffman, "Soldiers," 119; Baer, *Hessians*, 77.
34. Baer, *Hessians*, 78.

35. Reuber, *Diary*, Burgoyne translation, 2; Retzer, "March Route," 7-14; Piel, "Diary," 8.
36. Atwood, *Hessians*, 53.

CHAPTER FIVE: CAN A BROKEN NATION BE FIXED?

1. Ingrao, *Mercenary State*, 21; Wyss, *Friedrich II*, 524-528.
2. Ingrao, *Mercenary State*, 57-58; Both and Vogel, *Landgraf*, 33.
3. Both and Vogel, *Landgraf*, 125.
4. Ingrao, *Mercenary State*, 54-55, 117, 130.
5. Ingrao, *Mercenary State*, 14.
6. Ingrao, *Mercenary State*, 68; Both and Vogel, *Landgraf*, 44.
7. Both and Vogel, *Landgraf*, 43, 63; Ingrao, *Mercenary State*, 45,167.
8. Ingrao, *Mercenary State*, 60-69, Both and Vogel, *Landgraf*, 11.
9. Both and Vogel, *Landgraf*, 41.
10. Both and Vogel, *Landgraf*, 41.
11. Ingrao, *Mercenary State*, 62-63, 91; Both and Vogel, *Landgraf*, 45.
12. Ingrao, *Mercenary State*, 92-95; Both and Vogel, *Landgraf*, 58; Atwood, *Hessians*, 231.
13. Ingrao, *Mercenary State*, 94.
14. Ingrao, *Mercenary State*, 94.
15. Ingrao, *Mercenary State*, 66-67, 102; Both and Vogel, *Landgraf*, 45.
16. Ingrao, *Mercenary State*, 82-83, 92-93; Both and Vogel, *Landgraf*, 38-41.
17. Ingrao, *Mercenary State*, 25-26.
18. Ingrao, *Mercenary State*, 33, 39, 43, 49, 51, 58, 92, 118; Both and Vogel, *Landgraf*, 33,38, 41.
19. Ingrao, *Mercenary State*, 71, 105, 119; Both and Vogel, *Landgraf*, 42.
20. Ingrao, *Mercenary State*, 20, 72.
21. Both and Vogel, *Landgraf*, 41, 43, 44, 46, 47, 48; Ingrao, *Mercenary State*, 49, 67, 147.
22. Both and Vogel, *Landgraf*, 44.
23. Ingrao, *Mercenary State*, 9, 12, 56.
24. Lowell, *Auxiliaries*, 4; Ingrao, *Mercenary State*, 55.
25. Both and Vogel, *Landgraf*, 43; Ingrao, *Mercenary State*, 103, 112, 116.
26. Ingrao, *Mercenary State*, 112-113, 115; Both and Vogel, *Landgraf*, 45, 48, 60, 93.
27. Ingrao, *Mercenary State*, 109, 113-115.
28. Ingrao, *Mercenary State*, 109, 113, 114.
29. Ingrao, *Mercenary State*, 21, 112.
30. Both and Vogel, *Landgraf*, 45-48; Ingrao, *Mercenary State*, 188-192.
31. Both and Vogel, *Landgraf*, 48, 63, 126.

CHAPTER SIX: THE FIRST TIME AT SEA

1. Heister, *North America*, 93.
2. Reuber, *Diary*, Burgoyne translation, 3.
3. Reuber, *Diary*, Burgoyne translation, 4.
4. Krebs, *Generous*, 45-46, 73. Krebs notes many of these marriages were more practical than romantic, as soldiers wanted to ensure housing in barracks and bread rations for their female partners who remained behind.
5. Johannes Reuber and the Rall Regiment sailed for Portsmouth on April 19, arriving in Portsmouth on April 23, and then sailed for America on May 10. Jakob Piel and the Lossberg Regiment sailed for Portsmouth on April 17, but due to unfavorable sailing conditions arrived in Portsmouth on April 26 and sailed for America on May 6. Andre Wiederhold, with a company of the Knyphausen Regiment, sailed for America on May 18 on the *Eagle*.

Atwood, *Hessians*, 52; Baer, *Hessians*, 59-61; Reuber, *Diary*, Burgoyne translation, 5. See table 1 for departure dates.

6. Reuber, *Diary*, Burgoyne translation, 5.

7. Wiederhold to Gilsa, March 5, 1776, Gilsa, *Private Letters*.

8. Wiederhold to Gilsa, April 1, 1776, Gilsa, *Private Letters*.

9. Wiederhold to ST, September 11, 1782, Gilsa, *Private Letters*. There are many hints in his letters that he had an illegitimate daughter. For example, Wiederhold complained: "I haven't received a single letter from Ziegenhain [a small town north of Kassel] for a year. I almost believe that nothing good can come of it and that no one will write to me. . . . I very much request the true situation in Ziegenhain. . . . The girl is not—" and the sentence ended uncompleted, likely an oblique message to his friend about his out-of-wedlock child. Two months later, he was open about the situation: "I see and hear nothing of my child from Ziegenhain, even with the receipts. I hope she isn't so naughty that no one will shout it at me." Wiederhold to Gilsa, December 14, 1782, *Gilsa Private Letters*.

10. Reuber, *Diary*, Burgoyne translation, 5. Most of the women initially left behind would be transported to Portsmouth on later ships.

11. Reuber, *Diary*, Burgoyne translation, 5-6.

12. Reuber, *Diary*, Burgoyne translation, 6. This phenomenon is called St. Elmo's fire, an atmospheric discharge of electricity that appears as light on the extremities of pointed objects such as the masts of ships. In the eighteenth century it was believed to portend good luck since it often occurs near the conclusion of a storm.

13. Heister, *North America*, 86; New York State Historical Association (hereafter NYSHA), "Diary of Voyage from Stade in Hanover to Quebec in America of the Second Division of Ducal Brunswick Mercenaries," *Quarterly Journal of the New York State Historical Association* 8, no. 4 (October 1927): 323-351.

329; Baer, *Hessians*, 82.

14. NYSHA, "Diary," 329-330. The officers involved were from the same fleet as Rall and Wiederhold.

15. NYSHA, "Diary," 329; V. C. Hubbs, *Hessian Journals* (Camden House, 1981), 23.

16. Hubbs, *Hessian Journals*, 22; NYSHA, "Diary," 330.

17. Hubbs, *Hessian Journals*, 23.

18. Reuber, *Diary*, Burgoyne translation, 3-4.

19. NYSHA, "Diary," 332.

20. Zwieback means "twice baked" and refers to sweetened bread and eggs that are baked twice. The sailors' time on deck relaxing is mentioned in most of the soldiers' diaries. Atwood, *Hessians*, 53; Reuber, *Diary*, Burgoyne translation, 8.

21. Phillip Waldeck, *Diary of Philip Waldeck*, personal collection of Bruce Burgoyne, Dover, DE, 10; Margarete Woelfel, trans., "Memoirs of a Hessian Conscript: J. G. Seumes Reluctant Voyage to America," *William and Mary Quarterly* 5, no. 4 (October 1948): 553-570; Reuber, *Diary*, Burgoyne translation, 4.

22. Reuber, *Diary*, Burgoyne translation, 6; Waldeck, *Diary*, 12.

23. Pfister and Seume, *The Voyage of the First Hessian Army* (Heartman, 1915), 9-10.

24. Reuber, *Diary*, Burgoyne translation, 7; Hoffman, "Soldiers," 128.

25. Reuber, *Diary*, Burgoyne translation, 7.

26. Reuber, *Diary*, Burgoyne translation, 7; Karl Rueffer, "Journal of Lieutenant Rueffer of Melsungen," in *The Hesse-Cassel Mirbach Regiment in the American Revolution*, ed. and trans. by Bruce E. Burgoyne (Heritage Books, 2008), 6. Rueffer, "Journal," states that each soldier was issued one-sixth of a bottle of rum daily.

27. Johan Heinrich Bardeleben, *The Diary of Lieutenant von Bardeleben*, trans. Bruce Burgoyne (Heritage Books, 2007), 43.
28. Reuber, *Diary*, Burgoyne translation, 7, 12.
29. Reuber, *Diary*, Burgoyne translation, 8.
30. Lossberg, *Journal Lossberg*,10.
31. Piel, "Diary," 8-9.
32. Reuber, *Diary*, Burgoyne translation, 8.
33. Lossberg, *Journal Lossberg*, 18-19, 23; Reuber, *Diary*, Burgoyne translation, 7-9, 12-15; *Piel*, "Diary," 8-9; Hubbs, "Hessian Journals," 27-28; Retzer, "March Route," 7; Bardeleben, "Diary Bardeleben," 37-39.
34. Lossberg, *Journal Lossberg*, 19; Piel, "Diary,"10.
35. Bardeleben, "Diary Bardeleben," 39

CHAPTER SEVEN: HESSIANS: MERCENARIES OR LEGAL AUXILIARIES?

1. Bergpark Wilhelmshöhe, *UNESCO Application*, UNESCO.org, 5-7, 32-34, accessed May 18, 2025, ttps://whc.unesco.org/uploads/nominations/1413.pdf. For more descriptions and maps of Hercules, see Bergpark Wilhelmshöhe, *Hercules*, Hessen Kassel Heritage, accessed May 18, 2025, https://www.heritage-kassel.de/en/locations/herkules.
2. Estimating the value of eighteenth-century currency in modern currency is a notoriously unreliable task. One of the better currency conversion analyzers is NASA scientist Ian Webster, who uses raw data from the UK Office of National Statistics to calculate inflation. Ian Webster has developed an inflation calculator for the general public: CPI Inflation Calculator, accessed May 18, 2025, https://www.in2013dollars.com/. I have used his calculator to convert British currency in 1776 to current US dollars.
3. Treaty Between His Majesty and the Landgrave of Hessen-Cassel, signed January 15, 1776. See Kapp, *Soldier Trade*, 257, for an English translation from the original French.
4. Baer, *Hessians*, 16; Kapp, *Soldier Trade*, 257.
5. Both and Vogel, *Landgraf*, 100; Ingrao, *Mercenary State*, 138-139; Baer, *Hessians*, 28; Elisa P. Douglass, "German Intellectuals and the American Revolution," *William and Mary Quarterly* 17, no. 2 (April 1960): 200–218; Baer, *Hessians*, 6.
6. Krebs, *Generous*, 29.
7. Krebs, *Generous*, 32-34. For an excellent analysis of changing views on the soldier trade, see H. D. Schmidt, "The Hessian Mercenaries: The Career of a Political Cliché," *History* 43, no. 149 (1958): 207–212. Schmidt follows the controversy from the American Revolution through the Second World War.
8. Frederick the Great to Voltaire, June 18, 1776, in Lowell, *Auxiliaries*, 24-25; Kapp, *Soldatenhandel*, 155.
9. Ingrao, *Mercenary State*, 138-140.
10. Ingrao, *Mercenary State*, 138.

CHAPTER EIGHT: THE ATLANTIC CROSSING

1. Krebs, *Generous*, 73; Heister, *North America*, box B, 85.
2. Reuber, *Diary*, Burgoyne translation, 6; Waldeck, *Diary Waldeck*, 82.
3. Philip Steuernagel, *A Memoir by Philip Steuernagel*, private collection of Bruce Burgoyne, Dover, DE, 11; Woelfel, *Conscript*, 563; Heister, *First Brigade*, box H 26; Bardeleben, "Diary Bardeleben," 33-34.
4. Reuber *Diary*, Burgoyne translation, 8; Rueffer, "Journal," 45.
5. Reuber *Diary*, Burgoyne translation, 8; Waldeck, *Diary*, 87; Baer, *Hessians*, 80; Rueffer, "Journal," 43.

6. Hoffman, "Soldiers," 130; Slagle, "Lossberg," 23.
7. Bardeleben, *Diary Bardeleben,* 44; Rueffer, "Journal," 43.
8. Piel, "Diary," 9. Hubbs reported a similar collision. Hubbs, *Hessian Journals,* 25.
9. C. C. Coester, *The Diary of Chaplain C. C. Coester* (Giebel, Helwig, Krause, 1969), 11; Hubbs, *Hessian Journals,* 19; Bardeleben, *Diary Bardeleben,* 44; Pausch, *Journal,* 33. Chaplain Coester lists the birth occurring on March 23, 1776, at sea aboard the *Jenny.* This date is incorrect, as in March 1776, the regiment was still in Hessen-Kassel. Bardeleben and Coester both record a birth aboard the *Hope* on July 11. Chaplain Coester also records a birth aboard the *Empress* on July 12, 1776.
10. Hubbs, *Hessian Journals,* 19.
11. Bardeleben, *Diary Bardeleben,* 116-117. Coester survived the war, married his cousin, and died in 1790 at thirty-eight.
12. Coester, *Diary,* 11.
13. Coester, *Diary,* 14-15.
14. Reuber, *Diary,* Burgoyne translation, 9-11, 15-16; Piel, "Diary," 8; Waldeck, *Diary Waldeck,* 81; Bardeleben, "Diary Bardeleben,"46; Rueffer, "Journal," 42. The German word for porpoise is "Meerschwein," which translated literally means "sea pig."
15. Lossberg, *Journal Lossberg,* 17.
16. Lossberg, *Journal Lossberg,* 30-31.
17. Piel, "Diary," 10.
18. Bardeleben, *Diary Bardeleben,* 38.
19. Reuber, *Diary,* Burgoyne translation, 11; Hubbs, *Hessian Journals,* 27.
20. NYSHA, "Diary," 326; Piel, "Diary," 8; Reuber, *Diary,* Burgoyne translation, 7; Baer, *Hessians,* 85-86; Bardeleben, "Diary Bardeleben," 226; Rueffer, "Journal," 45-46.
21. Rueffer, "Journal," 45-46.
22 Reuber, *Diary,* Burgoyne translation, 4.
23. Reuber, *Diary,* Burgoyne translation, 11.
24. Bardeleben, *Diary Bardeleben,* 43.
25. Reuber, *Diary,* Burgoyne translation, 11, 14; Hubbs, *Hessian Journals,* 27-8; Heister, *First Brigade,* box H 50; NYSHA, "Diary," 346; Lossberg, *Journal Lossberg,* 19; Bardeleben, *Diary Bardeleben,* 32.
26. Hubbs, *Hessian Journals,* 21, 30; Waldeck, *Diary,* 85; Reuber, *Diary,* Burgoyne translation, 15.
27. Hubbs, *Hessian Journals,* 20, 28.
28. Piel, "Diary," 9-10.
29. Hubbs, *Hessian Journals,* 4. A similar sailor's "baptism" occurred on the *Molly,* Rueffer, "Journal," 46.
30. Reuber, *Diary,* Burgoyne translation, 13.
31. Hoffman, "Soldiers," 415; Johann Ewald, *Diary of the American War: A Hessian Journal* (Yale University Press, 1979), 6.
32. Pfister and Seume, *Voyage,* 24.
33. Heister, *First Brigade,* box H, 52; Bardeleben, *Diary Bardeleben,* 47.
34. Hubbs, *Hessian Journals,* 56; F. Melsheimer, *Journal of The Voyage of the Brunswick Auxiliaries.* Pamphlets of American History (Morning Chronicle Steam Printing, 1891), 44.
35. Lossberg, *Journal Lossberg,* 31; Pausch, *Journal,* 50-52.
36. Hubbs, *Hessian Journals,* 44; Piel, "Diary," 12.
37. Hubbs, *Hessian Journals,* 36, 52, 54; Pfister and Seume, *Voyage,* 26; Woelfel, *Conscript,* 562-563; Bardeleben, *Diary Bardeleben,* 50.
38. Lossberg, *Journal Lossberg,* 33.

39. Hubbs, *Hessian Journals,* 48; Rueffer, "Journal," 45.
40. Heister, *First Brigade,* box H, 51; NYSHA, "Diary," 337.
41. Atwood, *Hessians,* 54.
42. Heister, *First Brigade,* box H, 134; Atwood, *Hessians,* 56; Bardeleben, *Diary Bardeleben,* 50.
43. Rueffer, "Journal," 45-47.
44. Reuber, *Diary,* Burgoyne translation, 15.
45. Reuber, *Diary,* Burgoyne translation, 14.
46. Reuber, *Diary,* Burgoyne translation, 12.
47. Reuber, *Diary,* Burgoyne translation, 17.
48. Reuber, *Diary,* Burgoyne translation, 17, 18; Bardeleben, *Diary Bardeleben,* 50; Piel, "Diary," 12-13.
49. Johann Hinrichs, "Extracts from the Letter Book of Captain Johann Hinrichs of the Hessian Jäeger Corps," *Pennsylvania Magazine of History and Biography* 22, no. 2 (1898): 146-149.
50. Carl Bauer, *Journal of the Hochfuerstlichen Grenadier Battalion Platte from 16 February 1776 to 24 May 1784,* Journal of a Hessian Grenadier Battalion Platte (Koehler), Hessian State Archives at Marburg, in George Fenwick Jones, "Hessian Participation in the Attack on Fort Washington, 1776, and the Occupation of Northern New Jersey, 1777," *Report: A Journal of German-American History* 43 (1996): 81–90.
51. Schwalm, "Hessian *Auxiliaries,*" 25; Reuber, *Diary,* Burgoyne translation, 18; Lossberg, *Journal Lossberg,* 35; Piel, "Diary," 12; Rueffer, "Journal," 49.
52. Reuber, *Diary,* Burgoyne translation, 18.

CHAPTER NINE: THE HESSIANS ARE COMING!

1. William Ukers, *All About Coffee* (Tea and Coffee Trade Journal Co., 1922), ch. 14; Andrews, "Myrmidons," 182-183; Paul Smith, "Josiah Bartlett to John Langdon, May 19 to 21, 1776," *Letters of the Delegates to Congress 1774 to 1789* (Library of Congress, 1976).
2. Andrews, "Myrmidons," 183-4.
3. Andrews, "Myrmidons," 194.
4. Andrews, "Myrmidons," 213-4.
5. Andrews, "Myrmidons," 214-5.
6. Andrews, "Myrmidons," 215.
7. Andrews, "Myrmidons," 216.
8. Andrews, "Myrmidons," 217.
9. Andrews, "Myrmidons," 218.
10. Andrews, "Myrmidons," 203.
11. Pfister and Seume, *Voyage,* 13; Andrews, "Myrmidons," 253.

CHAPTER TEN: LAND OF MILK AND HONEY—AND UNGRATEFUL REBELS

1. The fleet had arrived on August 12, but Howe kept the men on board in the harbor for a few days until the Hessian commander, General Heister, convinced Howe to allow them to disembark.
2. Spees, "Erbprinz," 27, 36; Bardeleben, *Diary Bardeleben,* 54. During their ocean voyage, the Hessians ate mostly salted meats. Some of the ships had cattle on board, which were slaughtered sparingly. Rueffer, "Journal," 44. Heister, *First Brigade,* box H, 69.
3. Spees, "Erbprinz," 31; Bardeleben, *Diary Bardeleben,* 50.
4. Ray Pettingill, trans., *Letters to America, 1776 to 1779* (Houghton Mifflin, 1924), 153.
5. Steuernagel, *Memoir,* 22-23; Heister, *North America,* box B, 180-181; Pettingill, *Letters,* 177; Bardeleben, *Diary Bardeleben,* 52.

6. Bardeleben, *Diary Bardeleben,* 52; Rueffer, "Journal," 50.
7. Spees, "Erbprinz," 26.
8. Rueffer, "Journal," 50.
9. Spees, "Erbprinz," 29.
10. Atwood, *Hessians,* 160; Baer, *Hessians,* 94; Steuernagel, *Memoir,* 23.
11. Lowell, *Auxiliaries,* 59; Heister, *North America,* box B, 179-180.
12. Lowell, *Auxiliaries,* 59; Heister, *North America,* box B, 179-180; Pettingill, *Letters,* 179, 189; Dippel, *Germany,* 4; Steuernagel, *Memoir,* 21, 23.
13. Harry Schenawolf, "A Hessian Soldier's Letter Home Describes Colonial America," contains letter from Johann von Hinrichs to Professor Schlozer, September 18, 1776, Revolutionary War Journal, September 19, 2013, accessed May 20, 2025, https://revolutionarywarjournal.com/hessian-soldiers-letter-home/
14. Dippel, *Germany,* 76-80, 141-145; Atwood, *Hessians,*160-167; Baer, *Hessians,* 94.
15. Wiederhold to Ernst von und zu Gilsa, August 29–31, 1776, in Georg Ernst von und zu Gilsa, German History Intersections, accessed May 20, 2025, https://germanhistory-intersections.org/.
16. Baer, *Hessians,* 89; Spees, "Erbprinz," 31; Harry Schenawolf, "A Hessian Soldier's Letter Home Describes Colonial America," contains letter from Johann von Hinrichs to Professor Schlozer, September 18, 1776, Revolutionary War Journal, September 19, 2013, accessed May 20, 2025, https://revolutionarywarjournal.com/hessian-soldiers-letter-home/.
17. Atwood, *Hessians,* 56; Spees, "Erbprinz," 27; Ambrose Serle, *The American Journal of Ambrose Serle* (Huntington Library, 1940), 71-72, 94; Heister, *North America,* box B, 182.
18. Spees, "Erbprinz," 31.
19. Spees, "Erbprinz," 42n28.
20. Slagle, "Lossberg," 29, Reuber, *Diary,* Burgoyne translation, 1, 19.
21. Spees, "Erbprinz," 29.
22. Spees, "Erbprinz," 33.
23. Spees, "Erbprinz," 36.
24. Spees, "Erbprinz," 36.
25. Baer, *Hessians,* 89-91; Spees, "Erbprinz," 36-37; Serle, *American Journal,* 57-60.
26. Baer, *Hessians,* 103; Spees, "Erbprinz," 32-39; Pettingill, *Letters,* 180.
27. Waldeck, *Diary,* 94.
28. Bardeleben, *Diary Bardeleben,* 53.
29. Lynn Montross, *Rag, Tag and Bobtail: The Story of the Continental Army, 1775–1783* (Harper & Brothers, 1952), 107; Wiederhold, "Diary," 80.

CHAPTER ELEVEN: THE ADVERSARIES

1. Morton Smith, *George Washington: A Profile* (Hill & Wang, 1969), xxv; Edward G. Lengel, *General George Washington: A Military Life* (Random House, 2005), 14.
2. Smith, *George Washington,* xxv-xxvii; Lengel, *George Washington,* 19-30, 36-39, 80.
3. Lengel, *George Washington,* 52, 54-63.
4. Lengel, *George Washington,* 41-44, 64-67; Smith, *George Washington,* xxvi-xxvii.
5. Bruce Bliven, *The Battle for Manhattan* (Henry Holt, 1955), 23-25; Joseph J. Ellis, *His Excellency: George Washington* (Knopf, 2004), 40-72; Paul K. Longmore, *The Invention of George Washington* (University of Virginia Press, 1999), 2-6, 9-11; Thomas Flexner, *Washington in the American Revolution* (Little & Brown, 1967), 40.
6. Longmore, *Invention,* 52-55, 64-70, 82-85, 134-136, 145-146, 157-160.
7. Longmore, *Invention,* 9-11, 52-55, 64-70, 82, 134-136, 138, 145; Richard Ketchum, *Decisive Day*; 87-91; Flexner, *Washington,* 30, 33-35; Herbert Wade and Robert Lively, *The*

Adventures of Two Company Officers in Washington's Army (Princeton University Press, 1958), ch. 2; Charles Knowles Bolton, *The Private Soldier Under Washington* Charles Scribner's Sons, 1902), 25; Lengel, *George Washington*, 106-110.
8. North Callahan, *Henry Knox, General Washington's General* (A. S. Barnes, 1958), 56-59.
9. Flexner, *Washington*, 70-79.
10. I. R. Gruber, *The Howe Brothers and the American Revolution* (University of North Carolina Press, 1972), 57.
11. Fischer, *Washington's Crossing*, 33; Gruber, *Howe Brothers*, 81.
12. Gruber, *Howe Brothers*, 31, 80, 82.
13. Gruber, *Howe Brothers*, 56.
14. Gruber, *Howe Brothers*, 56.
15. Gruber, *Howe Brothers*, 57; Ketchum, *Decisive Day*, 7.
16. New York City geography can be confusing because of the tendency of historians to combine eighteenth-century names with modern names. In the eighteenth century, Manhattan was also referred to as New York Island. Brooklyn was actually the western end of Long Island, so sometimes it is referred to as Brooklyn and other times as Long Island. The Hudson River, which flows along Manhattan's western shore, was also known as the North River. The East River, which flows along Manhattan's eastern shore, was known at its northern end as the Harlem River. The Harlem River connected the Hudson River to the East River.
17. Estimates of the size of Washington's army vary because of fluctuation of its numbers during the summer.
18. Bliven, *Battle*, 330-333; Piers Mackesy, *The War for America* (Harvard University Press, 1964), 33.
19. Bruce Bliven, *Under the Guns: New York: 1775–1776* (Harper & Row, 1972), 332-333.
20. Atwood, *Hessians*, 61.
21. Lowell, *Auxiliaries*, 59; Atwood, *Hessians*, 64; Spees, "Erbprinz," 27.

CHAPTER TWELVE: BROOKLYN: INVASION

1. Spees, "Erbprinz," 38.
2. Spees, "Erbprinz," 39.
3. Spees, "Erbprinz," 39-40; Pausch, *Journal*, 44-45. Hessian quartermasters were undoubtedly angered watching the coin-filled war chest disappear into the lower decks of the British vessel. The British, pleading a shortage of coin, often insisted on exchanging Hessian coins with five pound Sterling banknotes, contemptuously called by the Hessians "those little bits of paper."
4. Spees, "Erbprinz," 38.
5. Spees, "Erbprinz," 40.
6. Waldeck, *Diary*, 416; Coester, *Diary*, 2-3.

CHAPTER THIRTEEN: BROOKLYN: COWARDLY REBELS, CUNNING REBELS

1. Reuber, *Diary*, Burgoyne translation, 19; Eelking, *German Allied Troops*, 28, 30; Fischer, *Washington's Crossing*, 96.
2. Spees, "Erbprinz," 41; Baurmeister, *Revolution*, 35.
3. Spees, "Erbprinz," 41; Heister, *North America*, box B, 177-179.
4. Bardeleben, *Diary Bardeleben*, 54-55.
5. Baer, *Hessians*, 95; Bardeleben, *Diary Bardeleben*, 60; Heister, *North America*, box B, 183.
6. Bardeleben, *Diary Bardeleben*, 54.
7. Fischer, *Washington's Crossing*, 82.

8. Atwood, *Hessians*, 66; Fischer, *Washington's Crossing*, 94-95.
9. Fischer, *Washington's Crossing*, 92-96. Washington did have an excellent cavalry unit in the Connecticut Light Horsemen, but the cavalrymen returned home two months before the battle after a silly dispute with Washington over digging latrines. Fischer, *Washington's Crossing*, 85-86; Montross, *Rag Tag*, 124.
10. Fischer, *Washington's Crossing*, 92-93; Slagle, "Lossberg," 31.
11. Slagle, "Lossberg," 30; Lowell, *Auxiliaries*, 61.
12. Both and Vogel, *Landgraf*, 106-107; *Atwood*, Hessians, 61, 68; Baurmeister, *Revolution*, 36.
13. Hoffman, "Soldiers," 96-97; Atwood, *Hessians*, 68; David Ross, "Jägerkorps," May 14, 2015.
14. Trevelyan noted that they were no longer marching as if crossing the *Friedrichsplatz* in Kassel for the landgrave's birthday. George Otto Trevelyan, *The American Revolution, Vol. 3* (Longmans, Green, 1905), 279.
15. Stephen DeVillo, *The Battle of White Plains* (History Press, 2022), 17; Robert Dunkerly, "How Did They Communicate?" Emerging Revolutionary War Era, February 16, 2016, accessed February 4, 2025, https://emergingrevolutionarywar.org/2016/02/16/how-did-they-communicate/.
16. Fischer, *Washington's Crossing*, 22; Atwood, *Hessians*, 61.
17. Bardeleben, *Diary Bardeleben,* 52; Wiederhold to Gilsa, August 31, 1776, in German History Intersections. For the landgrave's feelings about officers removing their marks of distinction, see Heister, *North America*, box B, 169.
18. Ray Pettengill, *Letters,* 153-154.
19. DeVillo, *Battle*, 17; Bardeleben, *Diary Bardeleben,* 55.
20. Lowell, *Auxiliaries*, 62; Bardeleben, *Diary Bardeleben,* 54.
21. Hoffman, "Soldiers," 96; Atwood, *Hessians*, 82; Ross, "Hessian Jägerkorps."
22. Atwood, *Hessians*, 65; Bardeleben, *Diary Bardeleben,*56; Reuber, *Diary,* Burgoyne translation, 19; Piel, "Diary," 13.
23. Wiederhold to Gilsa, August 31, 1776, in German History Intersections.
24. Eelking, *German Allied Troops*, 31; Reuber, *Diary,* Burgoyne translation, 19. Heister, *First Brigade*, box H, 84, states that General von Heister ordered his troops deployed in small detachments, believing they would prove most effective in Brooklyn's wooded and mountainous terrain. His tactical instincts proved sound. The Heister Regiment's journal reported that "more effective work was done by the small detachments which inspired much fear among the rebels."
25. Lowell, *Auxiliaries*, 67; Atwood, *Hessians*, 68; Slagle, "Lossberg," 39; Bardeleben, *Diary Bardeleben,* 56; Reuber, *Diary,* Burgoyne translation, 19. Reuber's diary dates are incorrect starting in late August; thus I have dated his movements based on other regiments in his brigade.
26. Reuber, *Diary,* Burgoyne translation, 19; Lowell, *Auxiliaries*, 67; Fischer, *Washington's Crossing*, 97-98.
27. Slagle, "Lossberg," 34.
28. Atwood, *Hessians*, 68-70.
29. Bardeleben, *Diary Bardeleben,* 57.
30. Fischer, *Washington's Crossing*, 98, 501n46.
31. Pettengill, *Letters,* 154.
32. Fischer, *Washington's Crossing*, 95; Joseph Plumb Martin, *A Narrative of a Revolutionary Soldier* (Signet Classics, 2001), 24.
33. Martin, *Narrative*, 24.
34. Lowell, *Auxiliaries*, 69; Slagle, "Lossberg," 38.

35. Piel, "Diary," 13; Fischer, *Washington's Crossing*, 99-100.
36. George Athan Billias, *General John Glover and His Marblehead Mariners* (Henry Holt, 1960), 97. Fischer, *Washington's Crossing*, 99; Jonathan Engel, "The Force of Nature: The Impact of Weather on Armies During the American War of Independence, 1775–1781" (master's thesis, Florida State University, 2011), 13.
37. Bardeleben, *Diary Bardeleben,* 58.
38. Eelking, *German Allied Troops,* 37; Slagle, "Lossberg," 37.
39. Fischer, *Washington's Crossing*, 100; Billias, *Glover*, 101.
40. Billias, *Glover*, 99-103
41. Enoch Anderson, *Personal Recollections of Captain Enoch Anderson* (Papers of the Historical Society of Virginia, 1896), 22.
42. Bardeleben, *Diary Bardeleben,* 59.
43. Piel, "Diary," 13; Reuber, *Diary,* Burgoyne translation, 20; Bardeleben, *Diary Bardeleben,* 59; Burgoyne, *Mirbach Regiment*, 10; Johann Zin, "Journal of the Hesse-Cassel von Donop Regiment," in *The Diary of Lieutenant von Bardeleben and Other von Donop Regiment Documents*, trans. Bruce Burgoyne (Heritage Books, 2007), 171.
44. Atwood, *Hessians*, 69.
45. Wiederhold to Gilsa, August 31, 1776, in German History Intersections.
46. Johann von Hinrichs to Professor Schlozer, September 18, 1776, in Pettingill, *Letters*, 181.
47. Wiederhold to Gilsa, August 31, 1776, in German History Intersections.
48. Reuber, *Diary,* Burgoyne translation, 19-20.
49. DeVillo, *White Plains,* 19.

CHAPTER FOURTEEN: THE BATTLES OF THE BRONX AND WESTCHESTER

1. DeVillo, *White Plains,* 19.
2. In 1776, New York City was located in the southern tip of Manhattan. The majority of Manhattan Island was farmland, county homes, and wilderness with few roads. New York City was a small town with buildings, farms, and streets. Locals considered New York City and Manhattan Island separate entities.
3. Bauer, "Journal," 81.
4. Frederick MacKenzie, *The Diary of Frederick MacKenzie* (Harvard University Press, 1930), 39-40, 52; Spees, "Erbprinz," 32-33. Although the Hessians were not indiscriminately plundering, the king's troops were foraging and taking in large quantities of cattle, sheep, and food.
5. Mackenzie, *Diary*, 37, 39.
6. Baurmeister, *Revolution*, 24.
7. Slagle, "Lossberg," 40-41. As per Hessian Army tradition, Rall's name is now used twice. The Rall Regiment retained its name, but the brigade, consisting of the Lossberg, Knyphausen, and Rall Regiments, was now referred to as the Rall Brigade. Also, a few days later, Colonel Heinrich von Heeringen, the commanding officer of the Lossberg Regiment, died of dysentery and was replaced with fifty-four-year-old Lieutenant Colonel Scheffer.
8. Alfred Franko, *Pelham Manor: The Forgotten Battle of the Revolution* (Pelham Manor Bicentennial Committee, 1966), 20; William Hadaway, *The McDonald Papers, Part 1* (Westchester County Historical Society, 1926) 1-2; Billias, *Glover*, 112-113.
9. Mackenzie, *Diary Mackenzie,* 76-77, 85.
10. Johann von Hinrichs to Professor Schlozer, September 18, 1776, in Pettengill, *Letters,* 180.
11. Hinrichs to Professor Schlozer, September 18, 1776, in Pettengill, *Letters,* 177-180.

12. Hinrichs to Professor Schlozer, September 18, 1776, in Pettengill, *Letters,* 179.
13. Mackenzie, *Diary Mackenzie,* 75-76.
14. Bauer, "Journal," 82.
15. Mackenzie, *Diary Mackenzie,* 85.
16. Reuber, *Diary,* Burgoyne translation, 20.
17. Burgoyne, "Diary," 18, 65. Some of the British and Hessian journals and diaries mentioned crossing over from the Jamaica and Flushing section of Queens. From that position there would have been no need to cross the Hell Gate. This may explain Piel's and Wiederhold's nonchalance.
18. Retzer, "March Route," 9.
19. Stirke, "Journal," 160; Mackenzie, *Diary Mackenzie,* 77, 85.
20. Mackenzie, *Diary Mackenzie,* 85.
21. Gruber, *Howe Brothers,* 133.
22. Christopher Ward, *The War of the Revolution* (Macmillan, 1952), 255; Hadaway, *McDonald Papers,* 9-10; David Ludlum, "The Weather of American Independence: The Loss of New York City and New Jersey," *Weatherwise* 28, no. 4 (August 1975): 172-174.
23. Hadaway, *McDonald Papers,* 4, 11. The cause of General Howe's error is unknown. There is one mention in the McDonald papers of a resident possibly tricking the general, but it is more likely that Howe had used outdated or inaccurate maps when making his decision.
24. Franko, *Pelham Manor,* 21; DeVillo, *White Plains,* 23; Hadaway, *McDonald Papers,* 5.
25. Ward, *War,* 255-256; DeVillo, *White Plains,* 24; Billias, *Glover,* 112; Baurmeister, *Revolution,* 58.
26. Baurmeister, *Revolution,* 58; Slagle, "Lossberg," 42; Atwood, *Hessians,* 72; Hadaway, *McDonald Papers,* 14-15; DeVillo, *White Plains,* 25.
27. Hadaway, *McDonald Papers,* 15-16; Billias, *Glover,* 114-118.
28. Burgoyne, "Diary," 65.
29. Franko, *Pelham Manor,* 4; Hadaway, *McDonald Papers,* 18-19; Billias, *Glover,* 116-121. Billias points out on pages 110-111 that the Battle of Pelham Bay has been rightly called "a forgotten battle." The total number of troops was greater than the numbers engaged in such better-known battles such as Trenton, Stony Point, King's Mountain, and Cowpens. Montross said, "One of the oddities of American history is that [the battle] . . . should have been ignored . . . or dismissed as a skirmish." Montross, *Rag Tag,* 148.
30. DeVillo, *White Plains,* 28; Hadaway, *McDonald Papers,* 13-14, 18-19.
31. Atwood, *Hessians,* 73; Hadaway, *McDonald Papers,* 19-20.
32. Franko, *Pelham Manor,* 49-51; Billias, *Glover,* 122-123.
33. Atwood, *Hessians,* 73; Slagle, "Lossberg," 43; Burgoyne, "Diary," 65; Serle, *American Journal,* 127. The 2nd Division troops under the command of Lieutenant General Wilhelm Freiherr von Knyphausen should not be confused with the Knyphausen Regiment, which was part of the Rall Brigade. The 2nd Division consisted of 4,000 Hessians, 670 Waldeckers, a company of Jägers, and 3,400 British recruits. These troops swelled the invasion force to over 37,000.
34. Ludlum, "Weather: New York City," 174; DeVillo, *White Plains,* 47-55; Hadaway, *McDonald Papers,* 40-42; Bauer, "Journal," 83.
35. Hadaway, *McDonald Papers,* 42.
36. Baurmeister, *Revolution,* 63.
37. DeVillo, *White Plains,* 55-56; Slagle, "Lossberg," 45-46.
38. Hadaway, *McDonald Papers,* 43; DeVillo, *White Plains,* 55-56.
39. Atwood, *Hessians,* 74; Reuber, *Diary,* Burgoyne translation, 20; DeVillo, *White Plains,* 56-58; Hadaway, *McDonald Papers,* 43; Lossing, *Pictorial,* vol. 2, 822-824.

40. DeVillo, *White Plains,* 55, 58-59; Hadaway, *McDonald Papers,* 3.
41. Burgoyne, "Diary," 65-66.
42. DeVillo, *White Plains,* 60-61. Wolf Pit Hill was also known as Fisher Hill. See page 60 in DeVillo, where he cites a fascinating obscure book that traces the historical names of places in Westchester County: Richard Lederer, *The Place Names of Westchester County* (Harbor Hill Books, 1978), 158.
43. DeVillo, *White Plains,* 61-62.
44. Reuber, *Diary,* Burgoyne translation, 20.
45. Hadaway, *McDonald Papers,* 63; Lossing, *Pictorial,* 2:822. Some historians question whether Hamilton was actually present at this battle. I have found no reason to doubt his presence. Others claim his men fled when British artillery fired on them.
46. DeVillo, *White Plains,* 60.
47. Slagle, "Lossberg," 48.
48. Slagle, "Lossberg," 47-48; Atwood, *Hessians,* 74.
49. Slagle, "Lossberg," 49, Atwood, *Hessians,* 74-75; Burgoyne, "Diary," 66.
50. Eelking, *German Allied Troops,* 49; Atwood, *Hessians,* 75; Burgoyne, "Diary," 18, 66.
51. DeVillo, *White Plains,* 65.
52. Baurmeister, *Revolution,* 65.
53. Hadaway, *McDonald Papers,* 49.
54. Reuber, *Diary,* Burgoyne translation, 20-21.
55. Hadaway, *McDonald Papers,* 52.
56. DeVillo, *White Plains,* 67.
57. DeVillo, *White Plains,* 67-68.
58. Reuber, *Diary,* Burgoyne translation, 21; Baurmeister, *Revolution,* 65.
59. DeVillo, *White Plains,* 71.
60. DeVillo, *White Plains,* 79.
61. DeVillo, *White Plains,* 80; Hadaway, *McDonald Papers,* 55.
62. DeVillo, *White Plains,* 84.
63. Hadaway, *McDonald Papers,* 58-59.
64. Hadaway, *McDonald Papers,* 83.
65. Hadaway, *McDonald Papers,* 84.
66. DeVillo, *White Plains,* 83-85; Reuber, *Diary,* Burgoyne translation, 5.
67. DeVillo, *White Plains,* 46, 87.
68. Burgoyne, "Diary," 66; Atwood, *Hessians,* 74.

CHAPTER FIFTEEN: FORT WASHINGTON: THE HESSIANS' HIGH-WATER MARK

1. Arthur Lefkowitz, *The Long Retreat* (Rutgers University Press, 1999), 20-24.
2. DeVillo, *White Plains,* 89; Mackenzie, *Diary Mackenzie,* 95-96.
3. Burgoyne, "Diary," 66-68.
4. DeVillo, *White Plains,* 91-93; Baurmeister, *Revolution,* 69.
5. Edward F. Delancey, "The Capture of Mount Washington, November 16th, 1776: The Result of Treason," *Magazine of American History* (February 1877): 7.
6. Franko, *Pelham Manor,* 25; Lefkowitz, *Long Retreat,* 19n1; Serle, *American Journal,* 54. The modern-day George Washington Bridge was built in 1931 along the same position where the *chevaux-de-fris* had been.
7. Lefkowitz, *Long Retreat,* 27; Fischer, *Washington's Crossing,* 111; Ward, *War,* 269.
8. Lefkowitz, *Long Retreat,* 28-29.
9. Lossberg, *Journal Lossberg,* 54; Uhlendorf, *Baurmeister Letters,* 68.
10. Martin Hunter, *The Journal of General Sir Martin Hunter* (Edinburgh Press, 1894), 19.

11. Lossberg, *Journal Lossberg*, 54.
12. Burgoyne, "Diary," 68; Reginald Bolton, *Fort Washington: An Account of the Identification of the Site* (Empire State Society of the Sons of the American Revolution, 1902), 97-98; Ward, *War*, 268-269: Ketchum, *Winter Soldiers*, 124-125.
13. Serle, *American Journal*, 144.
14. Ewald, *Johann Ewald*, 14-15; Baurmeister, *Revolution*, 69-70; Ward, *War*, 27; Burgoyne, "Diary," 68.
15. Bolton, *Fort Washington*, 96; Ketchum, *Winter Soldiers*, 138.
16. Ketchum, *Winter Soldiers*, 134-135; Lossing, *Pictorial*, 2:310; Burgoyne, Defeat, 68.
17. Burgoyne, "Diary," 69; Delancey, "Capture," 76; Bolton, *Fort Washington*, 97-98.
18. Bolton, *Fort Washington*, 97; Ketchum, *Winter Soldiers*, 138, 140; Sagle, *Lossberg*, 57.
19. Burgoyne, "Diary," 69; Ketchum, *Winter Soldiers*, 140.
20. Burgoyne, "Diary," 69; Ketchum, *Winter Soldiers*, 142-144.
21. Bauer, "Journal," 84.
22. Burgoyne, "Diary," 69; Bolton, *Fort Washington*, 43-44.
23. Burgoyne, "Diary," 69.
24. Ketchum, *Winter Soldiers*, 143; Bolton, *Fort Washington*, 101.
25. Bolton, *Fort Washington*, 100; Ketchum, *Winter Soldiers*, 143.
26. Bolton, *Fort Washington*, 30,114; Reuber, *Diary*, Burgoyne translation, 21-22.
27. Ketchum, *Winter Soldiers*, 142; Reuber, *Diary*, Burgoyne translation, 21-22.
28. Burgoyne, "Diary," 68; Reuber, *Diary*, Burgoyne translation, 21-22; Bolton, *Fort Washington*, 115.
29. Hunter, *Journal*, 20.
30. Reuber, *Diary*, Burgoyne translation, 21-22; Ketchum, *Winter Soldiers*, 149.
31. Ketchum, *Winter Soldiers*, 144; Bolton, *Fort Washington*, 47.
32. Bolton, *Fort Washington*, 115.
33. Bolton, *Fort Washington*, 116.
34. Bolton, *Fort Washington*, 117-119; Ketchum, *Winter Soldiers*, 155-156.
35. Bolton, *Fort Washington*, 119.
36. Waldeck, *Diary Waldeck*, 102.
37. Burgoyne, "Diary," 69; Bolton, *Fort Washington*, 119; Ketchum, *Winter Soldiers*, 149, 157; Atwood, *Hessians*, 174; Fischer, *Washington's Crossing*, 113.
38. Alexander Graydon, *Memoirs of His Own Time* (Lindsay and Blakiston, 1846), 205-206. The day before the battle, General Howe, observing proper eighteenth-century European protocols, had formally requested that the American commanders surrender the fort, a request that was quickly rejected. By eighteenth-century laws and customs, the rejection of the surrender request granted the king's troops the legal prerogative to plunder the fort after they captured it. Atwood, *Hessians*, 78; Ketchum, *Winter Soldiers*, 137.
39. Montross, *Rag Tag*, 155, quotes John William Fortesque, *History of the British Army*, vol. 3 (Naval and Military Press, 2021), 193; Ketchum, *Winter Soldiers*, 157; Bolton, *Fort Washington*, 120; Lowell, *Auxiliaries*, 82. There is no proof that the Hessians killed any prisoners. Graydon does write that he was shot at as he tried to surrender, but the Hessians did finally stop shooting when Graydon advanced at them waving his hat in the air. Graydon, *His Own Times*, 204-206.
40. Serle, *American Journal*, 143; *Atwood, Hessians,* 79; Wiederhold, "Diary," 68.

CHAPTER SIXTEEN: THE PALISADES: SCALING THE UNSCALABLE

1. Donald Londahl-Smidt, "British and Hessian Accounts of the Invasion of Bergen County 1776," in *The Revolutionary War in Bergen County: The Times That Tried Men's Souls*, Carol

Karels (History Press, 2007), 17; Gruber, *Howe Brothers*, 135; Howe to Germain, November 30,1776, Northern Illinois University Digital Library, accessed May 19, 2025, https://digital.lib.niu.edu/islandora/object/niu-amarch%3A83831; Rick Spilman, "Update: Looking Back at When New York Harbor Froze," *Old Salt Blog*, January 4, 2018, accessed May 19, 2025, https://www.oldsaltblog.com/2018/01/update-looking-back-new-york-harbor-froze/. Howe may also have been influenced by reports of poverty and inflation in New Jersey that left "the People of that Country [New Jersey] . . . extremely distressed." Serle, *American Journal*, 142-143.

2. Howe to Germain, November, 30, 1776, in Peter Force, *American Archives,* ser. 5, vol. 3 (M. St. Clair Clarke and Peter Force, 1848–1853), 925.

3. Bardeleben, *Diary Bardeleben,* 77-78.

4. William Morgan, ed., *Naval Documents of the American Revolution* (US Department of the Navy, 1976), 266.

5. Adrian Leiby, *The Revolutionary War in the Hackensack Valley* (Rutgers University Press, 1962), 3. The first description of the Palisades is from Washington Irving and the second from New Jersey historian Adrian Leiby.

6. Stirke, "Journal," 164; von Donop to von Heister, November 19, 1776, letter A, in *Lidgerwood Collection.* Morristown National Historical Park, Morristown, New Jersey.

7. Bardeleben, *Diary Bardeleben,*78.

8. Joseph White, "The Good Soldier White," *American Heritage* 7, no. 4 (June 1956): 74-79; Thomas Glyn, *Ensign Glyn's Journal*, ms., 28, Firestone Library Special Collections, Princeton University.

9. Washington had left troops in Peekskill, northern New Jersey, along the Connecticut border and Fort Ticonderoga. Gates to President of Congress, November 27, 1776 in Force, *American Archives,* ser.5 , vol. 3, 874.

10. There were also several tributaries and creeks along the way.

11. William Beatty, "Journal of Captain William Beatty," *Maryland Historical Magazine* 3, no. 2 (1908): 104-106.

12. Thomas Paine, *Collected Writings,* ed. Eric Foner (Citadel Press, 1945), 52; Washington to Hancock, November 21, 1776, in Founders Online, National Archives, accessed May 30, 2025, https://founders.archives.gov/documents/Washington/03-07-02-0136. There are various, slightly conflicting records of the amount of equipment and provisions captured at Fort Lee, but all the accounts agree that the amount was staggering. Friedrich von Münchhausen, *At General Howe's Side* (Philip Freneau Press, 1974); Howe to Germain, November 30,1776, and Howe to Germain, December 20, 1776, Northern Illinois University Digital Library, 926-927, 1316-1317. (Many of the records of British officers and politicians writing about the war can be found in the British Public Record Office, Colonial Office, Class 5 Files, Part 5: The American Revolution, 1772–1784, ed. Randolph Boehm [University Publications of America, 1984]); Washington to Hancock, November 19-21, 1776, in Founders Online, National Archives, accessed May 25, June 24, 2025, https://founders.archives.gov/documents/Washington/03-07-02-0128; Nathanael Greene, *The Papers of Nathanael Greene*, ed. Richard Showman (Chapel Hill: University of North Carolina Press, 1976), 359-363.

13. Ewald, *Johann Ewald,* 18. A few hours later, Ewald's men, moving aggressively on the flank, captured a coach driven by rebels. Again, Ewald was ordered to drop back and remain closer to the rest of Cornwallis's army. This verified Ewald's belief that Cornwallis did not want to destroy Washington's army.

14. White, "Good Soldier," 74-79. Hinrichs wrote in 1778 that Cornwallis had orders to follow but "not molest" Washington's retreating army. Hinrichs, *Extracts*, 149.

15. Gruber, *Howe Brothers*, 135-136; Force, *Archive,* ser.5, vol. 3, 925. Before the Battle of Brooklyn, the estimated number of forces in the American army in the New York area was approximately nineteen thousand. By the end of the New York campaign, that number had dwindled to less than eight thousand. Washington would begin his march south through the Jerseys with about four thousand effectives.

16. Andrew Hunter, *The Revolutionary War Diary of Chaplain Andrew Hunter, New Jersey Brigade, Continental Army,* diary entry for November 21, 1776, Rare Book Library, Princeton University, Princeton, NJ, accessed May 29, 2025, https://revwar75.com/library/bob/HunterDiaries2.htm.

17. Theodore B. Romeyn, *Historical Discourse Delivered on Occasion of the Re-Opening and Dedication of the First Reformed [Dutch] Church, at Hackensack, N.J.: May 2, 1869* (Board of Publication, Reformed Church in America, 1870), 26. Romeyn says the quote came from an anonymous Hackensack resident, but he states that the resident was an eyewitness, implying the witness was credible.

18. Romeyn, *Historical Discourse*, 26; Washington to Hancock, November 19-21, 1776, Founders Online, https://founders.archives.gov/documents/Washington/03-07-02-0128; Frances Westervelt, ed., *History of Bergen County, New Jersey, 1630–1923*, vol. 1 (Lewis Historical Publishing, 1923), 106.

19. Glyn, *Journal*, 28; Ewald, *Johann Ewald,* 18-19; Stephen Kemble, "The Kemble Papers," *Collections of the New-York Historical Society for 1883*, vol. 16 (1884), 96; Leiby, *Revolutionary War*, 7; Londahl-Smidt, "British," 58. Cornwallis believed that the inhabitants of the region were in general loyal to the king and ordered the officers to exert themselves to prevent plundering.

20. Howe to Germain, November 30,1776, Northern Illinois University Digital Library, 926-927.

21. Ewald, *Johann Ewald,* 18.

22. Hunter, *Diary,* November 24, 1776; Leiby, *Revolutionary War*, 73; Edward Dixon, *Scenes in the Practice of a New York Surgeon* (DeWitt and Davenport, 1855), 295.

23. A disgusted von Donop reported to his superiors in New York that the English were "uncommonly engaged" in "infamous plundering . . . in spite of all orders to the contrary," but he could proudly report that Lord Cornwallis had personally assured him that no Hessians were among the marauding plunderers. Londahl-Smidt, "British," 23.

CHAPTER SEVENTEEN: NEW JERSEY: CONQUERED BUT STILL DEFIANT

1. Westervelt, *Bergen County*, 106.

2. Dixon, *Scenes*, 295; T. N. Glover, "The Retreat of '76 Across Bergen County," paper presented at the Society of Hackensack, November 20, 1905.

3. Kemble, "Papers," 101; Force, *Archives*, 925; Münchhausen, *Howe's Side*, 5.

4. Mackenzie, *Diary Mackenzie*,113.

5. Samuel Blachley Webb, *Correspondence and Journals of Samuel Blachley Webb, 1772–1806*, ed. Worthington Chauncey Ford, 3 vols. (Wickersham Press, 1893), 3:172-173.

6. Henry Clinton, *The American Rebellion: Sir Henry Clinton's Narrative* (Yale University Press, 1954), 55.

7. Howe to Germain, November 30, 1776, Northern Illinois University Digital Library, 926-927.

8. Force, *Archives*, 925.

9. Lefkowitz, *Long Retreat*, 80; Clinton, *Clintons Narrative*, 55-57.

10. Wheaton Lane, *From Indian Trail to Iron Horse* (Princeton University Press, 1939), 63; Hunter, *Diary*, November 21, 1776.

11. Washington knew that the destruction of the bridge would be only a minor obstacle to Cornwallis, as the Passaic was fordable at points
12. Cornwallis captured Acquackanonk and was nine miles from Washington is described in Baurmeister, *Revolution*, 73. Newark deserted is described in Archibald Robertson, *Diaries and Sketches in America, 1762–1780* (New York Public Library, 1930), 114; Thomas Paine, *Collected Writings*, ed. Eric Foner (Library of America, 1995), 382; and Serle, *American Journal*, 146. Serle notes that Cornwallis was at Acquackanonk Bridge.
13. Some diaries disagree on marching dates in the weeks following the Battle of Fort Washington. Most of these discrepancies are of no historical importance and have no effect on the accuracy of the information presented by these diaries. I have chosen those dates that seem the most accurate based on a preponderance of evidence and common sense. The correct dates are easily ascertained by correlating the information with other diaries, regimental journals, letters, and orders from the same time period. For those who want more information on this topic or would like to make their own judgments, I suggest using the diaries listed in the bibliography. Rall Brigade moved closer to the Hudson River ferry point is from Rueffer, "Journal," 63. Rall Brigade crossed Hudson to New Jersey is from Piel, "Diary," 19; Wiederhold, "Diary," 70; Retzer, "Journal Knappes," 9; Glyn, *Journal*, 369; and Baurmeister, *Revolution*, 73. Rall Brigade quartered in Fort Lee and Hackensack region is from Reuber, *Diary*, Burgoyne translation, 22, and Wiederhold, "Diary," 70.
14. Wiederhold, "Diary," 70.
15. Leiby, *Revolutionary War*, 3-10; "very handsome" pole fence is from Leiby, *Revolutionary War*, 7; Wiederhold, "Diary," 70.
16. Leiby, *Revolutionary War*, 9; Westervelt, *Bergen County*, 106; Baurmeister, *Revolution*,73; anonymous Hackensack resident in Romeyn, *Historical Discourse*, 27.
17. Wiederhold, "Diary," 70; Baurmeister, *Revolution*, 73-74.
18. Hessian diaries vary on the date for the Rall Brigade entering Newark. Wiederhold, "Diary," 70, says they entered on December 4. Piel, "Diary," 19, says November 30. Knappes lists December 4 as the date of entry in Retzer, "Journal Knappes," 9.
19. Baurmeister, *Revolution*, 74.
20. Frank J. Urquhart, *A History of the City of Newark, New Jersey: Embracing Practically Two and a Half Centuries, 1666–1913* (Lewis Historical Publishing, 1913), 65-68.
21. Force, *Archive*, 928; Serle, *American Journal*, 157.
22. Heister Regiment, *First Brigade*, box H, 157.
23. William S. Stryker, *The Battles of Trenton and Princeton* (Houghton, Mifflin, 1898), 320.
24. Urquhart, *City of Newark*, 95, 103-106, 301.
25. Londahl-Smidt, "British," 23.
26. Force, *Archive*, 928; Urquhart, *City of Newark*, 307.
27. Urquhart, *City of Newark*, 307.
28. Urquhart, *City of Newark*, 307.
29. Wiederhold, "Diary," 71; Piel, "Diary," 19; Retzer, "Journal Knappes," 6; Slagle, "Lossberg," 67.

CHAPTER EIGHTEEN: DESTROY OR APPEASE?

1. Force, *Archives*, 822. The size of the army can be derived from a November 23 note that shows the number of soldiers leaving. Beatty, "Journal," 106.
2. Serle, *American Journal*, 150; MacKenzie, *Diary*, 117; Lefkowitz, *Long Retreat*, 95-97; Ewald, *Johann Ewald*, 24; Robertson, *Diaries and Sketches*, 114-115.
3. Stirke, "*Journal*," 166.

4. Rumors of a ten-thousand-man rebel attack were based on the fact that General Charles Lee, with about four thousand men, had crossed the Hudson into New Jersey from Peekskill, NY, on December 2. Ewald, *Johann Ewald,* 24; Hunter, *Journal*, 22-23; Kemble, *Papers,* 102; Troyer Anderson, *The Command of the Howe Brothers* (Oxford University Press, 1936), 202. For Howe delaying Cornwallis, see William M. Dwyer, *The Day Is Ours* (Viking, 1983), 81; Joseph Galloway, *Letters to a Nobleman, on the Conduct of the War in the Middle Colonies* (London: J. Wilkie, 1780), 48; and Anderson, *Howe Brothers*, 203.
5. Howe to Germain, December 20, 1776, Northern Illinois University Digital Library, 926-927, 1316-1317; Münchhausen, *Howe's Side*, 6; Serle, *American Journal*, 154; Lefkowitz, *Long Retreat*, 115; Proprietary House, "Royal Governor 1774–1776," accessed April 18, 2025, https://www.theproprietaryhouse.org/royal-governor; Lossing, *Pictorial*, 2:10-11.
6. For British worn out, see Ewald, *Johann Ewald,* 24; Franklin B. Wickwire and Mary B. Wickwire, *Cornwallis and the War of Independence* (Faber and Faber, 1971), 92-95; Anderson, *Howe Brothers*, 201-202; Waldeck, *Diary*, 106. For Howe arrives, see Stirke, "Journal," 167. Cornwallis was particularly concerned about the communication link between Brunswick and Amboy. Supplies and troops from New York were carried by the Royal Navy to Amboy on the Staten Island coast and from there up the Raritan River to Brunswick. For rumors of Lee, see Anderson, *Howe Brothers*, 205. For an excellent description of the logistical situation in New Jersey in winter 1776, see William Kidder, *Ten Crucial Days: Washington's Vision of Victory Unfolds* (Post Hill/Knox Press, 2019), 28-29.
7. Anderson, *Howe Brothers*, 203.
8. Wickwire and Wickwire, *Cornwallis*, 56.
9. Hunter, *Journal*, 23.
10. Serle, *American Journal*, 152-153.
11 Ewald, *Johann Ewald,* 24-25.
12. Ewald, *Johann Ewald,* 28. Joseph Galloway was an attorney from Pennsylvania. He represented Pennsylvania at the First Continental Congress but eventually grew disillusioned with the radical direction Congress was taking. He opposed independence and eventually had to flee Pennsylvania. He became a top adviser to General Howe and an intelligence expert, recruiting upward of eighty spies for the British. He eventually became one of the leading critics of General Howe.
13. Galloway, *Letters to a Nobleman*, 48-49.
14. Müenchhausen, *Howe's Side*, 6. He states that the orders were issued "immediately upon our arrival."
15. Baurmeister, *Revolution*, 27.
16. Wiederhold, "Diary," 71; William Dunlap, *A History of the American Theater* (J & J Harper, 1832), 248; Peter Kalm, *Travels into North America* (William Eyres, 1770), 232-235.
17. Kalm, *Travels*, 232-235; Waldeck, *Diary*, 106.
18. Waldeck, *Diary*, 106-107.
19. Kalm, *Travels*, 232-235.
20. Baurmeister, *Revolution*, 27.
21. Wiederhold, "Diary," 71; Retzer, "Journal Knappes," 9; Kalm, *Travels*, 227-231.
22. Journal Regiment Knyphausen, *Journal*, 17.
23. Reuber, *Diary*, Burgoyne translation, 23; Wiederhold, "Diary," 70-71.
24. Reuber, *Diary*, Burgoyne translation, 23.

CHAPTER NINETEEN: STOLEN BOATS

1. Münchhausen, *Howe's Side*, 6.

2. George Washington to Congress, December 5, 1776, in George Washington, *The Writings of George Washington*, collected and ed. Worthington Chauncey Ford (G. P. Putnam's Sons, 1890), vol. 5, 1776–1777.
3. Stryker, *Battles*, 15; George Washington to Richard Humpton, December 1, 1776, in Stryker, *Battles*, 310.
4. William Kidder, *Crossroads of the Revolution: Trenton 1774–1783* (Post Hill/Knox Press, 2019), 100-102.
5. Stryker, *Battles*, 129-130; Force, *Archives*, vol. 5, ser. 3, 1343.
6. George Washington to Congress, December 3, 1776, in Washington, *Writings*.
7. Charles Wilson Peale, "Autobiography, December 8, 1776, entry," unpublished ms., American Philosophical Society, Philadelphia, entry.
8. George Washington to Congress, December 5, 6, and 7, 1776, in Washington, *Writings*
9. Münchhausen, *Howe's Side*, 6.
10. Münchhausen, *Howe's Side*, 6.
11. For a detailed description of the plundering of Princeton, see the seventy-six page booklet Varnum Collins, *A Brief Narrative of Ravages of the British and Hessians at Princeton in 1776–1777* (Princeton Historical Association, 1906.)
12. Collins, *Brief Narrative*, 40-41.
13. Ewald, *Johann Ewald*, 43; Serle, *American Journal*, 120.
14. Dunlap, *American Theater*, 240.
15. Charles Wilson Peale, *The Selected Papers of Charles Wilson Peale*, vol. 1 no. 1 (Yale University Press, 1983), 216.
16. Münchhausen, *Howe's Side*, 8.
17. Marion Balderston, *The Lost War: Letters from British Officers During the American Revolution* (Horizon Press, 1975), 131.
18. Münchhausen, *Howe's Side*, 7.

CHAPER TWENTY: SMALL TOWN AT THE CROSSROADS OF HISTORY

1. Münchhausen, *Howe's Side*, 6-7; Ewald, *Johann Ewald*, 27; Robertson, *Diaries and Sketches*, 115.
2. Münchhausen, *Howe's Side*, 7. The American bombardment was so intense that witnesses to the cannon fire gave conflicting accounts, with estimates of the number of American cannons ranging from eight to thirty-seven.
3. Howe to Germain, November 30,1776, Northern Illinois University Digital Library, 926-927, 1316-1317; Münchhausen, *Howe's Side*, 7-8; Stryker, *Battles*, 28-30.
4. Münchhausen, *Howe's Side*, 8. There were other possibilities for crossing the Delaware. The Loyalist Joseph Galloway claimed to have found forty-eight-thousand feet of wooden boards that could have been used to make small boats to transport the king's troops over to Pennsylvania. There were also at least one hundred wooden houses in the region that could have been stripped of their planks. In Trenton, there were bundles of wire, and several hardware stores and blacksmith shops that could have supplied nails and iron. Small boats and rafts could have been carried overland from the Raritan River. Also, the Delaware often froze over. The great historian William Stryker, in Stryker, *Battles*, has a good description of the situation on page 36.
5. Howe to Germain, December 20, 1776, Northern Illinois University Digital Library, 926-927, 1316-1317. Fischer describes General Howe scouting along the Delaware River, but Fischer gives no citation for the source of this information. Fischer, *Washington's Crossing*, 184-185.

6. Map of British and Hessian garrisons in New Jersey by Captain John Montresor, December 12–13, 1776, as cited in Fischer, *Washington's Crossing*, 186-187.
7. Fischer, *Washington's Crossing*, 183-184. Grant also held his Hessian allies in contempt, and he did not speak German or French, which limited his ability to communicate effectively.
8. Hans Huth, "Letters from a Hessian Mercenary," *Pennsylvania Magazine of History and Biography* (October 1938): 489-492, 494; Howe to von Donop, December 13, 1776, in Stryker, *Battles*, 316-317.
9. Clinton, *Clinton's Narrative*, November 1776.
10. Howe to Germain, December 20, 1776, Northern Illinois University Digital Library, 1316-1317.
11. Anonymous officer of Lossberg Regiment, "Hessian Journal of December 18, 1776, Found at Trenton," *Evening Post* (Philadelphia], July 26, 1777. Reprinted in *New Jersey Archives*, 2nd ser., vol. 1, 432-433. This rare document is also available online through the Hathitrust, accessed 4/19/25, https://babel.hathitrust.org/cgi/pt?id=uc1.31175029470849&seq=438&q1=evening+post.
12. Richard Hoare, *Balby Beginnings: The Launching of Quakerism* (Sessions of York, 2002), 112; Elizabeth Satterthwaite, "Mahlon Stacy, Quaker Founder of Trenton," *Proceedings of the New Jersey Historical Society*, n.s., vol. 9, no. 2 (April 1924): 150-154.
13. Samuel Smith, *The Colonial History of New Jersey* (W. S. Sharp, 1890), 108; WikiTree, "Mahlon Stacey, Sr. (1638–1704)," accessed June 1, 2025, https://www.wikitree.com/wiki/Stacy-192. This site is filled with information about the early Quaker settlers in Trenton, including birth and death records, church records, and DNA records.
14. Edwin Robert Walker, *A History of Trenton 1679 to 1929*, Trenton Historical Society, 1929, accessed June 1, 2025, https://www.trentonhistory.org/His/colonial.html.
15. Walker, *History*, sec. 4, "The Coming of Mahlon Stacy."
16. WikiTree, "Mahlon Stacey, Sr. (1638–1704)."
17. Walker, *History*, sec. 7, "The Account of Mary (Murfin) Smith."
18. Walker, *History*, sec. 7, "The Account of Mary (Murfin) Smith."
19. Charles Boyer, *Old Inns and Taverns in West Jersey* (Camden Historical Society, 1962), 9, 69-70.
20. Francis Lee. *History of Trenton New Jersey*. (State Gazette, 1895.) 16. This page contains a Royal Survey Map of Stacy Mahlon's property from 1712.
21. Walker, *History*, sec. 5, "The Coming of William Trent"; Stephanie Toothman, "Trenton, New Jersey, 1719 to 1779" (PhD diss., University of Pennsylvania, 1977), 109.
22. Toothman, "Trenton," 108-109.
23. Stryker, *Battles*, 90; Walker, *History*, sec. 1, "The Colonial Period", 4. The name "The Falls of the Delaware" led to disappointment with travelers, as the association of the term "Falls" often led to the comparison of the Trenton ripples with the truly grand falls in New York. The descent of the river at the falls was only about eighteen feet in six miles, but it was enough to disrupt navigation.
24. Stryker, *Battles*, 90.
25. Toothman, "Trenton," 225.
26. Toothman, "Trenton," 226, table 6.

CHAPTER TWENTY-ONE: DANGER, DISTRUST, AND FATIGUE

1. Gruber, *Howe Brothers*, 189-190. Gruber lists several correspondents on this page which document General Howe's participation in New York City parties, balls, gambling. and an extramarital affair.

2. Slagle, "Lossberg," 71-73; Kalm, *Travels*, 220; Stryker, *Battles*, 41-42.
3. Battles that involved narrowing terrain include Thermopylae (480 BCE), with the Greek city-state alliance led by the Spartan King Leonidas against the Persians led by Xeres, and the Battle of Stirling Bridge (1297), with William Wallace leading the Scots against the British. Sun Tzu's *Principles in the Art of War* discusses the principle of narrow-terrain fighting.
4. Phineas Pemberton, "The Phineas Pemberton Weather Diary, Philadelphia, 1776–1777," American Philosophical Society, in *American Philosophical Society Transactions*, n.s. 6 (1839), 395, reproduced in *Washington's Crossing*, by David Fischer, appendix K, 399-403; Slagle, "Lossberg," 70-71. The Lossberg Regiment marched from Elizabethtown to New Brunswick on December 9. The next day they marched to Princeton and finally to Trenton on December 14. Stryker, *Battles*, 40, 96-97, 316-317; Howe to von Donop, December 13, 1776, in Stryker, *Battles*, 316; John Mollo, *Uniforms of the American Revolution* (Blandford Press, 1975), 24-32, plate 90.
5. Wiederhold, "Diary," 71; Anonymous officer, "Hessian Journal," 432-433.
6. While variations in temperature can increase the incidence of dysentery, it was more likely eighteenth-century ignorance of proper sanitation, particularly regarding drinking water and sewerage, that led to the outbreak of dysentery. This was a common problem in armies before the age of modern medicine.
7. Bardeleben, *Diary*, 62; Atwood, 75, 81.
8. Stryker, *Battles*, 99.
9. The junction consisted of not only King Street and Queen Street but also Princeton Road, Pennington Road, and a small pathway known as Beakes Lane. For brevity's sake, we will refer to the elevated junction of these four roads as the junction of King and Queen Streets. Also, some writers refer to Princeton Road by its original name, Maidenhead, which was in use in 1776. Other writers use the newer name, Princeton Road. We will use Princeton Road for two reasons: (1) our modern-day readers will likely find it easier to geographically orient themselves via the famous college town and (2) the village of Maidenhead is now known as Lawrenceville. As for our twenty-second-century readers, you're on your own. Stryker, *Battles*, 90-91.
10. Stryker, *Battles*, 94-98; Kidder, *Crossroads*, 124, 125, map, 7-8. Kidder shows that the twenty British dragoons occupied the Friends Meeting House (a Quaker house of worship) on 3rd Street close to Queen Street.
11. Kidder, *Crossroads*, 125.
12. Kidder, *Crossroads*, 125; Baurmeister, *Revolution*, 75.
13. Kidder, *Crossroads*, 125, 126-128.
14. Howe, *Orders*, 429.
15. William S. Stryker, *Trenton 100 Years Ago* (Library of Congress, 1878), 6-7. For a fun, informative source about Stacy Potts that is filled with wonderful footnotes, see the blog from William Covington, *The Frigate South Carolina in the American Revolution: 1778-1783*, accessed June 3, 2025, https://thefrigatesouthcarolina.weebly. com/blog/earlier-connections-between-john-henderson-future-lieutenant-of-marines-on-board-the-frigate-south-carolina-and-mr-stacy-potts-quaker-resident-of-trenton-nj.
16. Stryker, *Battles*, 103-104, 380; Boyer, *Inns*, 175-176. Boyer states that in 1767, Rensselaer Williams moved into the Ligoner Tavern on Queen Street and changed its name to the Royal Oak. In 1773, Williams moved the tavern to the Trenton Ferry, taking the Royal Oak sign board with him. Stryker, in *Battles*, page 380, states that "the Tavern formerly owned by Rennselaer Williams" was the picket post at the Trenton Ferry.
17. Stryker, *Battles*, 90-98, 100-104; Raum, *History*, 107, 327, 329, 330-331; Atwood, *Hessians*, 94. Calhoun's house was at the junction of a country lane, Calhoun's Lane, which

connected Pennington Road on the north side of town with River Road on the south side of town. On page 94, Stryker states that Francis Witt ran The City Tavern, but in *Trenton 100 Years Ago* he states on page 8 that Witt ran The Blazing Star Tavern. It is understandable that there is some confusion, as the owners of taverns in Trenton in the latter half of the eighteenth century changed quite often. The True American Inn is sometimes called Jonathan Richmond's Tavern, a reference to the name of its owner, Jonathan Richmond. For more information on Jonathan Richmond's Tavern, see Stryker, *History of Trenton,* 329, and Stryker, *Battles,* 381. There is a sketch of the tavern in Kidder, *Crossroads,* 124. Piel and Wiederhold both made maps of the Trenton defenses and both are in Stryker, *Battles,* 124-126.
18. Stryker, *Battles,* 379-382. Fischer, *Washington's Crossing,* 396, has an excellent list of the Delaware River ferries.
19. Stryker, *History of Trenton,* 31, 139-140; Stryker, *Battles,* 92.
20. Stryker, *Battles,* 92, 97-98.
21. Wiederhold, "Diary," 72.
22. Alarm posts were designated areas for the troops to form up in case of an emergency. The British built alarm posts in every town they occupied. They also built guard houses for the pickets. Staff officers checked on the guard houses, ensuring that the men were not gambling or "reveling." *Journal of the 1st Brigade of the Von Heister Corp,* box H 160.
23. Stryker, *Battles,* 46-47, 106-107; Kidder, *Crossroads,* 129.
24. Stryker, *Battles,* 106-107.
25. Stryker, *Battles,* 107; Wiederhold, "Diary," 72.
26. Rall to Colonel von Donop, December 21, 1776, in Stryker, *Battles,* 332. Piel does not mention the incident in his diary, nor do any of the other officers who were present. Wiederhold had by this point developed a dislike and disrespect for Rall, so it is unclear how accurate Wiederhold's account is. But it should be noted that in the years following the battle, none of the participants of this dispute—including engineers Captain Georg Pauli and Coronet Carl Levin von Heister, Artillerist Lieutenant Fischer, Colonel Scheffer, Major Dechow, and Reinhard Martin of the Hessian engineers—contradicted Wiederhold's account.
27. The rest of this chapter is based on Stryker, *Battles,* 100-101, 103, 105; Wiederhold, "Diary," 71-72; Reuber, *Diary,* Burgoyne translation, 23.

CHAPTER TWENTY-TWO: THE TIDE BEGINS TO TURN
1. Anonymous officer, "Hessian Journal," 432-433.
2. Stryker, *Battles,* 50-51; Rall to von Donop, December 17, 1776, in Stryker, *Battles,* 323-324; Donop to Grant, December 17, 1776, in Stryker, *Battles,* 50-51. Rall's letters imply that this was the second attack near the Trenton Ferry. Donop's imply that there had been an earlier attack that had driven away dragoons, making for a total of three attacks near the Trenton Ferry.
3. Rall to von Donop, December 17, 1776, in Stryker, *Battles,* 323-324; Donop to Grant, December 17, 1776, in Stryker, *Battles,* 50-51; Anonymous officer, "Hessian Journal," 432-433.
4. Rall to von Donop, December 18, 1776, in Stryker, *Battles,* 326; Anonymous officer, "Hessian Journal," 432-433.
5. Reuber Diary, *Diary,* Burgoyne translation, 23; Anonymous officer, "Hessian Journal," 432-433; Rall to von Donop, December 20, 1776, in Stryker, *Battles,* 329.
6. Rall to von Donop, December 20, 1776, in Stryker, *Battles,* 329.
7. Rall to von Donop, December 20, 1776, in Stryker, *Battles,* 329; Anonymous officer, "Hessian Journal," 432-433.

8. Leonard Lundin, *Cockpit of the Revolution* (Princeton University Press, 1940),188-189.
9. Reuber, *Diary,* Burgoyne translation, 23.
10. Much of the material here is from Lundin's informative and pleasantly readable work *Cockpit of the Revolution*, 179-190.
11. Munchausen, *Howe's Side,* 8.
12. Lossberg Regiment, *Journal*, December 22, 1776; Rall to Colonel von Donop, December 21, 1776, in Stryker, *Battles,* 331-332.
13. Grant to von Donop, December 21, 1776, in Stryker, *Battles,* 329-331; Rall to von Donop, December 21, 1776, in Stryker, *Battles,* 331-332.
14. Wiederhold, "Diary," 72-73.
15. Lossberg Regiment, *Journal Lossberg*, December 22, 1776.
16. Rall to Colonel von Donop, December 21, 1776, in Stryker, *Battles,* 332
17. Lundin, *Cockpit*, 185.
18. Reuber, *Diary,* Burgoyne translation, 23; Rall to General Leslie, December 22, 1776, in Stryker, *Battles,* 70.
19. Wiederhold, "Diary," 71-73.
20. Captain Boking, "Letter from Captain Boking," Von Jungkenn Papers, vol. 1, no. 26, William Clements Library, University of Michigan.
21. Alfred Bill, *The Campaign of Princeton, 1776–1777* (Princeton University Press, 1948), 13, 24; James McMichael, "The Diary of Lieutenant James McMichael of the Pennsylvania Line," *Pennsylvania Magazine of History and Biography* 16 (1892): 139; Thomas McCarty, "The Revolutionary War Journal of Thomas McCarty," *Proceedings of the New Jersey Historical Society* 82 (1964): 29-46.
22. Reed to Washington, December 12, 1776, in Stryker, *Battles,* 322-323.

CHAPTER TWENTY-THREE: FATE INTERVENES

1. Henry Knox to Lucy Knox, December 28, 1776, in Stryker, *Battles,* 371-372; Washington to Gates, December 14, 1776, in Stryker, *Battles,* 190.
2. Reuber, *Diary,* Burgoyne translation, 23.
3. Grant to Rall, December 21, 1776, in Stryker 334-335; Grant to von Donop, December 17, 1776, in Stryker, *Battles*, 51. McKonkey's was also spelled McConkey's. It was sometimes referred to as Eight-Mile Ferry since it is about eight miles upstream from Trenton. Grant referred to it as Vessel's Ferry. We will refer to the ferry as McKonkey's as this was the spelling used by William Stryker.
4. Stryker, *Battles,* 110.
5. Stryker, *Battles,* 110-111. The recorded dates of the many incidents that occurred in the week leading up to Washington's attack vary among the participants. It may be that much of this information was first recorded in a 1778 Hessian court-martial and memories may have faded or had been influenced by subsequent events. In either case, it is undeniable that these events occurred and were of significance. In the next few chapters we will visit these events and the heartaches, successes, bravery, and cowardice that marked this momentous week.
6. Stryker, *Battles,* 110. His name is recorded as both Wahl and Mahl.
7. George Washington to Robert Morris, December 25, 1776, Founders Online, accessed June 2, 2025, https://founders.archives.gov/documents/Washington/03-07-02-0344.
8. John Greenwood, *The Revolutionary Services of John Greenwood*, ed. Isaac Greenwood (De Vinne Press, 1922), 40; George Washington to Robert Morris, December 25, 1776, Founders Online, accessed June 2, 2025, https://founders.archives.gov/documents/Washington/03-07-02-0344; George Washington, General Orders, December 25, 1776, in

Stryker, *Battles,* 113-115; Mercer to Durkee, December 25, 1776, in Stryker, *Battles*, 379; Dwyer, *Day Is Ours*, 227-229.

9. George Washington, General Orders, December 25, 1776, in Stryker, *Battles*, 113-115; Stryker, *Battles,* 129; Mercer to Durkee, December 25, 1776, in Stryker, *Battles*, 359-360, 379; Washington to John Cadwalader, December 25, 1776, Founders Online, accessed June 2, 2025, https:// https://founders.archives.gov/documents/Washington/03-07-02-0342. Hessians referred to Johnson's Ferry as John's Ferry.

10. John Cadwalader to George Washington, December 26, 1776, Founders Online, accessed June 2, 2025, https://founders.archives.gov/documents/Washington/03-07-02-0347; George Washington, General Orders, December 25, 1776, in Stryker, *Battles,* 113-115; New Jersey State Geologist Kemble Widmer discussion of ice on the Delaware River is in Fischer, *Washington's Crossing,* appendixes J and K and page 212; Stryker, *Battles*, 130; Washington to Hancock, December 27, 1776, Founders Online, accessed June 2, 2025, https://founders.archives.gov/documents/Washington/03-07-02-0355; Dwyer, *Day Is Ours*, 239.

11. Grant to Rall, December 21, 1776, in Stryker, *Battles,* 108.

12. Stryker, *Battles*, 107-108.

13. Baurmeister, *Revolution*, 78; Fischer, *Washington's Crossing*, 205.

14. Stryker, *Battles*, 100.

15. Grant to Rall, December 12, 1776, in Stryker, *Battles,* 115-116. In an unusual move, Grant added the time of the letter's creation as "past 11:00 at night." This may have been Grant's way of signaling to Rall how important the letter was.

16. Reuber, *Diary,* Burgoyne translation, 24; Stryker, *Battles,* 117.

17. Greenwood, *Revolutionary Services*, 38; Pemberton, "Weather Diary," December 25, 1776, appendix K in Fischer, *Washington's Crossing,* 399-403; David Ludlum, "The Weather of American Independence: Trenton and Princeton," *Weatherwise* 29, no. 2 (April 1976): 74-83.

18. Stryker, *Battles,* 118-120.

19. Lossberg Regiment, *Journal Lossberg*, December 25, 1776; Stryker, *Battles*, 118.

20. Stryker, *Battles,* 119-120; Wiederhold, "Diary," 73-74. Based on Wiederhold's diary, the post originally had sixteen men, but since six had just been shot, Wiederhold's eleven-man reinforcement brought the number of guards up to twenty-one. The Lossberg Regiment Journal states that the picket was strengthened with sixteen men. See entry for December 26, 1776.

21. Reuber, *Diary,* Burgoyne translation, 24; Lossberg Regiment, *Journal Lossberg*, December 25, 1776; Stryker, *Battles,* 118. The Lossberg Regimental Journal mentions the dragoons; Stryker omits them.

22. Johann Bardeleben, "Report of the Court Martial for the Trial of Hessian Officers Captured at Trenton," *Pennsylvania Magazine of History and Biography* 7, no. 3 (1883): 45-49, accessed June 4, 2025, https://www.jstor.org/stable/20084591.

23. Stryker, *Battles,* 20.

24. Wiederhold, "Diary," 73-74.

25. Greenwood, *Revolutionary Services,* 39. A musician during the war, Greenwood later became a dentist and is most famous for building George Washington's false teeth.

26. M. V. Brewington, "Washington's Boats at the Delaware Crossing," *American Neptune* 2 (1942): 167-170; Lane, *Indian Trail,* 69; Terry McNealy, "The Durham Family and the Durham Boats," *Journal of the Bucks County Historical Society* 7, no. 1 (1990): 14-15; Anonymous, "Ferries," Vertical File of the David Library, Washington Crossing, PA; Stryker, *Battles*, 129-130; Ward, *Revolution*, 293-294. The number of Durham boats used by Washington

has been a matter of debate. James Snell, in *History of Hunterdon and Somerset* (Philadelphia: Everts & Peck, 1881), 50. Snell states there were sixteen. Stryker has an affidavit from the War Department stating that Captain Bray gathered twenty-five boats, but it does not distinguish as to which type of boat they were.

27. C. C. Haven, *Thirty Days in New Jersey Ninety Years Ago: An essay revealing new facts in connection with Washington and his army* (Trenton, State Gazette, 1867), 4-7.

28. Wilkinson, *Memoir of My Own Time* (Abraham Small, 1816) 128.

29. Thomas Rodney to Caesar Rodney, December 30, 1776, in George Ryden, *Letters to and from Caeser Rodney* (Da Capo Press, 1970); Ward, *Revolution*, 294.

30. Washington, General Orders, December 25, 1776, in Stryker, *Battles,* 113-115; Callahan, *Henry Knox*, 18-20; Henry Knox to Lucy Knox, December 28, 1776, in Stryker, *Battles,* 371 372.

31. Greene to Governor Cooke, January 10, 1777, Papers of Nathaniel Greene.

32. McCarty, "Journal," 41. The storm hit with full fury at about 11:00 P.M. Changing from a mixture of snow and ice pellets, then ice pellets alone, and finally a mixture of ice pellets and rain, it was a classic "nor'easter." Ludlum, "Weather: Trenton," 75; L. H. Butterfield, ed., *Letters of Benjamin Rush* (Princeton University Press, 1951), 124.

33. McCarty, "Journal," 41; Washington, General Orders, December 25, 1776, in Stryker, *Battles*, 113-115; Washington to Hancock, December 27, 1776, Founders Online, accessed June 24, 2025, https://founders.archives.gov/documents/Washington/03-07-02-0355.

34. Joshua Slocum, *An Authentic Narrative of the Life of Joshua Slocum: Containing a Succinct Account of His Revolutionary Services* (Hartford, CT: Printed for the author, 1844), 85-86, HathiTrust, accessed June 7, 2025, https://catalog.hathitrust.org/Record/009596164.

35. Dwyer, *Day Is Ours,* 239, 246; Stryker, *Battles*, 138-139; Fischer, *Washington's Crossing*, 225.

36. Stryker, *Battles*, 195, states that local historians "tell us" that two soldiers froze to death but adds, "This statement cannot now be officially confirmed." Yet the *Freeman Journal*, January 21, 1777, in Stryker, *Battles*, 474, states that two soldiers did freeze to death. Greenwood, *Revolutionary Services,* 39, describes the frigid conditions, which show that freezing to death was not only possible but likely occurred.

37. Greenwood, *Revolutionary Services,* 39; Stryker, *Battles*, 143.

38. Jac Weller, "Guns of Destiny: Field Artillery in the Trenton-Princeton Campaign," *Military Affairs* (Spring 1956): 1-15. Weller states that Washington's ratio of artillery to infantry was greater than almost any general from Marlborough to World War II. Munchausen, *Diary*, 8, notes that Rall's troops were outnumbered three to one in artillery against Washington's army. Ironically, on December 22, just four days before the Battle of Trenton, a clueless Howe shipped ten guns from New York that reached Burlington on December 23, where they would be just ten miles away, tantalizingly close to the battle, but of no use.

39. Captain William Hull to Andrew Adams, January 1, 1777, in Stryker, *Battles*, 375.

40. Fischer, *Washington's Crossing*, 231. Fischer discusses this intriguing phenomenon in his book *Paul Revere's Ride* (Oxford University Press, 1994), 129-146.

CHAPTER TWENTY-FOUR: THE BATTLE OF TRENTON

1. Bardeleben, "Court Martial," 45-49; Stryker, *Battles,* 145-146.

2. Stryker, *Battles,* 146-147.

3. This story is well documented, but credit for leading Wallis's company is often mistakenly given to General Robert Anderson. For a good explanation of the mix up, see Harry Ward, *Major General Adam Stephen and the Cause of American Liberty* (University Press of Virginia, 1989), 151, 276n48. Also, Fischer, *Washington's Crossing*, 517n29, gives a detailed explanation.

4. Bardeleben, *Diary Bardeleben,* 83; Greenwood, *Revolutionary Services*, 41; William S. Powell, "A Connecticut Soldier Under Washington: Elisha Bostwick's Memoirs of the First Years of the Revolution," *William and Mary Quarterly*, 3rd ser., no. 6 (1949): 102.
5. Fischer, *Washington's Crossing*, 234-235.
6. Wiederhold, "Diary," 74; Wiederhold to Gilsa, April 15, 1777, in Gilsa, *War in America.*
7. Wiederhold to Gilsa, August 29-31, 1776, German History Intersections.
8. Wiederhold, "Diary," 74.
9. Captain William Hull to Andrew Adams, January 1, 1777, in Stryker, *Battles,* 375.
10. Wiederhold to Gilsa, April 15, 1777, in *Gilsa Private Letters.*
11. Washington to Hancock, December 27, 1776, Founders Online, accessed June 2, 2025, https://founders.archives.gov/documents/Washington/03-07-02-0355; von Donop in Huth, "Letters," 497.
12. Johnston to Leven Powell, December 29, 1776, Founders Online, accessed June 2, 2025.
13. Stryker, *Battles,* 151-152.
14. James Wilkinson, *Memoirs of My Own Time*, 129; Stryker, *Battles,* 151-152.
15. Hauptmann von Heister, *Hessian Court of Inquiry: The Affair at Trenton, December 26, 1776*, Lidgerwood Collection, Morristown Historical Park, microfiche 251-270, sec. ML, 95, 349.
16. Findings of Hessian Court Martial, January 5, 1782, in Stryker, *Battles,* 415. All but two of Gröthausen's Jägers fled across the bridge. The Hessian court-martial decided: "The Jäger company cannot be blamed because they had no bayonets and they all followed their commander Lieutenant von Grothausen now deceased, but how much he was blameworthy cannot now be decided because he cannot be examined, for he died of his wounds." The lieutenant's actions were cowardly, but likely because he was killed in battle a few days later, the court was lenient with his reputation. What is not mentioned in any of the Hessian records is that the British dragoons were not seen by anyone during the battle and most likely just took off at the first sign of trouble.
17. Findings of Hessian Court Martial, January 5, 1782, in Stryker, *Battles,* 421.
18. Stryker, *Battles,* 155.
19. Burgoyne, "Diary," 20.
20. Colonel Clement Biddle to unknown recipient, December 29, 1776, in Stryker, *Battles,* 365-366.
21. Stryker, *Battles,* 153; Wiederhold, "Diary," 74.
22. Washington to Hancock, December 27, 1776, Founders Online, accessed June 2, 2025.
23. Karl *Elsea and William Welsch.* "Artillery Engagements at the Battle of Trenton. Parts 1, 2, 3." Emerging Revolutionary War Era, December 26, 2020, accessed April 21, 2025, https://emergingrevolutionarywar.org/2020/12/26/the-first-of-three-artillery-engagements-at-the-battle-of-trenton-december-26-1776/.
24. Heister, *Hessian Court of Inquiry*, section ML, 93.
25. Stryker, *Battles,* 156.
26. Henry Knox to Lucy Knox, December 28, 1776, January 2, 1777, in Stryker, *Battles,* 371-372, 436.
27. Heister, *Hessian Court of Inquiry*, section ML, 511-515, 533-534; Stryker, *Battles,* 156-157.
28. Wiederhold, *Diary,* 74-76; Henry Knox to Lucy Knox, December 28, 1776, in Stryker, *Battles,* 371-372.
29. Washington to Congress, December 27, 1776, in Stryker, *Battles,* 218.
30. Reuber, *Diary,* Burgoyne translation, 24; Fischer, *Washington's Crossing*, 246.

31. Reuber, *Diary,* Burgoyne translation, 24; Captain William Hull to Andrew Adams, January 1, 1777, in Stryker, *Battles,* 375.
32. White, "Good Soldier," 77; Henry Knox to Lucy Knox, December 28, 1776, in Stryker, *Battles,* 371-372; Wilkinson, *Memoirs,* 130.
33. Reuber, *Diary,* Burgoyne translation, 24.
34. Heister, *Hessian Court of Inquiry,* section ML, 351.
35. Heister, *Hessian Court of Inquiry,* section ML, 351.
36. Stryker, *Battles,* 170. According to Stryker, the Knyphausen Regiment received orders from Rall to send one company to the bridge while the other four companies were fighting on 2nd Street and King Street. Fischer, in *Washington's Crossing,* states on page 251 that the Knyphausen Regiment was actually ordered to join the rest of the Rall Brigade for an attack back into town, but due to a miscommunication, Knyphausen separated from the other regiments and countermarched back to the southern end of town. Fischer likely based this on testimony (including Jacob Piel's) given at the Court of Inquiry in section ML, 117, 124-125. Based on a letter from Landgrave Friederick to General Knyphausen in section ML of the Court of Inquiry, even the landgrave was curious about this and requested that the question be pursued at the Court of Inquiry.
37. Stryker, *Battles,* 171.
38. Wilkinson, *Memoirs,* 130-131; Stryker, *Battles,* 168.
39. Wiederhold, "Diary," 75.
40. Stryker, *Battles,* 171.
41. Stryker, *Battles,* 176; Kidder, *Crossroads,* maps 7-9.
42. The surrender of the Knyphausen Regiment is well covered in Stryker, *Battles,* 176-186.
43. Knox to Lucy Knox, December 28, 1776, Founders Online, accessed June 2, 2025.
44. Reuber, *Diary,* Burgoyne translation, 24; Stryker, *Battles,* 170.
45. Stryker, *Battles,* 172-173; Heister, *Hessian Court of Inquiry,* section ML, 95.
46. Bardeleben, "Court Martial," 47-48; Heister, *Hessian Court of Inquiry,* section ML, 259; Stryker, *Battles,* 173-174.
47. Heister, *Hessian Court of Inquiry,* section ML, 103, 260, 272; Stryker, *Battles,* 174-176.
48. Stryker, *Battles,* 180-182.
49. Stryker, *Battles,* 176-178.
50. Wiederhold, "Diary," 76; Heister, *Hessian Court of Inquiry,* section ML, 117-118.
51. Stryker, *Battles,* 183.
52. Stryker, *Battles,* 184.

CHAPTER TWENTY-FIVE: VICTORY AND DEFEAT

1. Some prisoners were taken over by ferries, including Johnson's Ferry, the Trenton Ferry, and Beatty's Ferry. Joseph Reed, "General Reed's Narrative of the Movements of the American Army in the Neighborhood of Trenton in the Winter of 1776–1777," *Pennsylvania Magazine of History and Biography* 8 (1884): 391.
2. Stryker, *Battles,* 207. "[W]ade about 200 feet through the angry waters" is Stryker's description.
3. Stryker, *Battles,* 208.
4. Piel, "Diary," 20-21.
5. Wiederhold, "Diary," 76.
6. Wiederhold, "Diary," 77-78.
7. Piel, "Diary," 20.
8. Piel, "Diary," 20-22.

9. This section detailing Reuber's post-Trenton years is based on Reuber, *Diary,* Burgoyne translation, 24-52.
10. Piel, "Diary," 23-62.
11. Wiederhold, "Diary," 83, 100-101.
12. Wiederhold, "Diary," 113-134.
13. Wiederhold, "Diary," 87, 90.
14. Wiederhold to Gilsa, October 9, 1781, in *Gilsa Private Letters.*
15. Wiederhold to Gilsa, May 4, 1782, in *Gilsa Private Letters.* Wiederhold wrote about the electricity making machine: "During this time, one of his metrics [electricity machines] had to be kept ready at home so that he could once more in his life have his member, strengthened by the electricity [so it would not] fall into its previous inability to stand up with vigor. Think what you will about this."
16. Wiederhold to Gilsa, April 12, 1782, in *Gilsa Private Letters.*
17. Wiederhold to Gilsa, December 14, 1782, in *Gilsa Private Letters.*
18. Wiederhold, "Diary," 91.

CHAPTER TWENTY-SIX: REPERCUSSIONS

1. I have translated from German to English Wolf von Both and Hans Vogel's biography *Landgraf Friedrich II.* I have found it to be the best biography on Frederick II, capturing his personal life and his desire to be an enlightened prince. This section describing Frederick's 1777 antiquity shopping spree in Italy is based on pages 217-220.
2. Prince of Hesse to Lieutenant General Knyphausen, June 16, 1777, in Stryker, *Battles,* 403.
3. Frederick to Knyphausen, April 23, 1779, in Heister, *Hessian Court of Inquiry,* section ML.
4. Finding of Hessian court-martial, January 11, 1782, in Stryker, *Battles,* 417.
5. Finding of Hessian court-martial, January 11, 1782, in Stryker, *Battles,* 415.
6. Prince of Hesse to Lieutenant General Knyphausen, June 16, 1777, in Stryker, *Battles,* 403.
7. Nicholas Cresswell, *The Journal of Nicholas Cresswell, 1774–1777* (Dial, 1924), 179-180.
8. Greenwood, *Revolutionary Services*, 44-46.
9. Serle, *American Journal*, 163; Ellis, *His Excellency*, 274.
10. Howe to Germain, January 20, 1776, in Stryker, *Battles,* 482.
11. Both and Vogel, *Landgraf,* 145-147
12. Both and Vogel, *Landgraf,* 143, 146-147.
13. Both and Vogel, *Landgraf,* 122-123; Atwood, *Hessians*, 251-252; Ingrao, *Mercenary State*, 91-97.
14. Atwood, *Hessians*, 250-253. Casualties listed here represent all the Germanic states' casualties for the entire war.
15. Both and Vogel, *Landgraf,* 231.
16. Gregory Pedlow, "The Nobility of Hesse-Kassel" (PhD diss., Johns Hopkins University, 1979), 16; Ingrao, *Mercenary State*, 164, 188.
17. Ingrao, *Mercenary State*, 80-85; 164-167, 193.
18. Pedlow, "Nobility," 11; Ingrao, *Mercenary State*, 112, 189, 199, 201, 207.
19. Atwood, *Hessians*, 165, 231; Ingrao, *Mercenary State*, 203.
20. Niall Ferguson, *The House of Rothschild* (Penguin, 1999), ch. 2; Kapp, *Soldier Trade*, 238-239. Ferguson's book contains the most detailed analysis I have seen of the rise of the Rothschild banking business and of the relationship between William IX and Mayer Rothschild.

EPILOGUE: THE PAINTING

1. Worthington Whittredge and John Baur, "The Autobiography of Worthington Whittredge," *Brooklyn Museum Journal* (1942): 10-11; John Howat, "Washington Crosses the Delaware," *Bulletin of the Metropolitan Museum of Art* 26, no. 7 (March 1968): 289; Anne Hawkes Hutton, *Portrait of Patriotism* (Chilton, 1959), 108; Anne Hawkes Hutton, *The Year and the Spirit of '76* (Franklin Press, 1977).
2. John Baur, *An American Genre Painter: Eastman Johnson* (Brooklyn Institute of Arts and Sciences, 1940): 11-13.
3. Whittredge and Baur, "Autobiography," 22; Hutton, *Portrait*, 27, 39.
4. Baur, *American*, 13.
5. Hutton, *Portrait*, 112; Whittredge and Baur, "Autobiography," 22.
6. Hutton, *Portrait*, 111
7. Raymond Stehle, "Washington Crossing the Delaware," *Pennsylvania History* 31 (1964), 270-273; Baur, "American," 13.
8. Barbara Groseclose, *Emanuel Leutze* (Smithsonian Institute Press, 1975), 31-32.
9. Stehle, "Washington," 278; Hutton, *Portrait*, 4-5, 7-8; Groseclose, *Emanuel Leutze*, 32.
10. For descriptions of Leutze's dog, see Hutton, *Portrait*, 39, 114.
11. Whittredge and Baur "Autobiography," 23; Hutton, *Portrait*, 112.
12. The International Art Union was a French establishment engaged in selling works of art. Stehle, "Washington," 276; *New York Observer*, February 5, 1852, cited in Stehle, "Washington," 281; letter from Leutze in Dusseldorf to unknown recipient, November 10, 1850, cited in Hutton, *Portrait*, 113.
13. *New York Evening Mirror*, November 7, 1851, cited in Stehle, "Washington," 279.
14. *New York Daily Tribune*, February 28, 1852, cited in Stehle, "Washington," 281; *Literary World*, October 18, 1851, cited in Stehle, "Washington," 278-279.
15. *Home Journal of New York*, November 8, 1851, cited in Stehle, "Washington," 280; *New York Daily Tribune*, February 28, 1852, cited in Stehle, "Washington," 281; Groseclose, *Emanuel Leutze*, 37-40.
16. Groseclose, *Emanuel Leutze*, 40-43.
17. Groseclose, *Emanuel Leutze*, 88; Hutton, *Portrait*, 113.

Bibliography

Anderson, Enoch. *Personal Recollections of Captain Enoch Anderson*. Papers of the Historical Society of Virginia, 1896.

Anderson, Troyer. *The Command of the Howe Brothers*. Oxford University Press, 1936.

Andrews, Melodie. "Myrmidons from Abroad: The Role of the German Mercenary in the Coming of American Independence." PhD diss., University of Houston, 1986.

Anonymous officer of Lossberg Regiment. "Hessian Journal of December 18, 1776, Found at Trenton." *Evening Post* (Philadelphia), July 26, 1777. Reprinted in *New Jersey Archives*, 2nd ser., vol. 1, 432-433.

Anonymous. "Ferries." Vertical File of the David Library. Washington Crossing, Pennsylvania.

Atwood, Rodney. *The Hessians: Mercenaries from Hessen-Kassel in the American Revolution*. Cambridge University Press, 1980.

Azoy, A. C. M. "Merry Christmas 1776." *Infantry Journal* (November-December 1938): 483-494.

Baer, Friederike. *Hessians: German Soldiers in the American Revolutionary War*. Oxford University Press, 2022.

Balderston, Marion. *The Lost War: Letters from British Officers During the American Revolution*. Horizon Press, 1975.

Bardeleben, Johann Heinrich. *The Diary of Lieutenant von Bardeleben*. Translated by Bruce Burgoyne. Heritage Books, 2007.

Bardeleben, Johann. "Report of the Court Martial for the Trial of Hessian Officers Captured at Trenton." *Pennsylvania Magazine of History and Biography* 7, no. 3 (1883): 45-49. Accessed June 4, 2025. https://www.jstor.org/stable/20084591.

Bauer, Carl. *Journal of the Hochfuerstlichen Grenadier Battalion Platte from 16 February 1776 to 24 May 1784.* Journal of a Hessian Grenadier Battalion (Koehler), Hessian State Archives at Marburg, in Jones, George Fenwick. "Hessian Participation in the Attack on Fort Washington, 1776, and the Occupation of Northern New Jersey, 1777." *Report: A Journal of German-American History* 43 (1996): 81–90.

Baur, John I. H. "American Genre Painter: Eastman Johnson." *Brooklyn Institute of Arts and Sciences* (1940): 11-13.

Baurmeister, Baron Karl Leopold. *Revolution in America: Confidential Letters and Journals 1776 to 1784 of Adjutant General Major Baurmeister of the Hessian Forces.* Edited by Bernard Uhlendorf. Rutgers University Press, 1957.

Beatty, William. "Journal of Captain William Beatty." *Maryland Historical Magazine* 3, no. 2 (1908): 104-106.

Bergpark Wilhelmshöhe. UNESCO Application Documents. Accessed May 18, 2025 (https://whc.unesco.org/en/list/1413/documents/.

Bergpark Wilhelmshöhe. *Hercules.* Hessen Kassel Heritage. Accessed May 15, 2025. https://www.heritage-kassel.de/en/locations/herkules.

Bergpark Wilhelmshöhe. *UNESCO Application.* UNESCO.org. Accessed May 18, 2025. https://whc.unesco.org/uploads/nominations/1413.pdf.

Bill, Alfred. *The Campaign of Princeton, 1776–1777.* Princeton University Press, 1948.

Billias, George Athan. *General John Glover and His Marblehead Mariners.* Henry Holt, 1960.

Bliven, Bruce. *The Battle for Manhattan.* Henry Holt, 1955.

Bliven, Bruce. *Under the Guns: New York: 1775–1776.* Harper & Row, 1972.

Boking, Captain. "Letter from Captain Boking." Von Jungkenn Papers. Vol. 1, no. 26. William Clements Library, University of Michigan.

Bolton, Charles Knowles. *The Private Soldier Under Washington.* Charles Scribner's Sons, 1902.

Bolton, Reginald. *Fort Washington: An Account of the Identification of the Site.* Empire State Society of the Sons of the American Revolution, 1902.

Both, Wolf von, and Hans Vogel. *Landgraf Friedrich II.* Deutscher Kunstverlag, 1973.

Boyer, Charles. *Old Inns and Taverns in West Jersey.* Camden Historical Society, 1962.

Brewington, M. V. "Washington's Boats at the Delaware Crossing." *American Neptune* 2 (1942): 167-170.

British Public Record Office, Colonial Office, Class 5 Files: Part 5: The

American Revolution, 1772–1784. Edited by Randolph Boehm. University Publications of America, 1984.

Butterfield, L. H., ed. *Letters of Benjamin Rush.* Princeton University Press, 1951.

Callahan, North. *Henry Knox: General Washington's General.* A. S. Barnes, 1958.

Cecere, Michael. "The Army of Observation Forms: Spring 1775 in Massachusetts." *Journal of the American Revolution*, May 19, 2025. https://allthingsliberty.com/2025/05/the-army-of-observation-forms-spring-1775-in-massachusetts/.

Clinton, Henry. *The American Rebellion: Sir Henry Clinton's Narrative.* Yale University Press, 1954.

Coester, C. C. *The Diary of Chaplain C. C. Coester*. Giebel, Helwig, Krause, 1969.

Collins, Varnum. *A Brief Narrative of Ravages of the British and Hessians.* Princeton Historical Association, 1906.

"Colonel Johann Rall." Road to Freedom Biographies. Accessed April 4, 2025. https://id3491.securedata.net/imagecog/roadtofreedom/rall.html.

Cresswell, Nicholas. *The Journal of Nicholas Cresswell, 1774–1777.* Dial, 1924.

Delancey, Edward F. "The Capture of Mount Washington, November 16th, 1776: The Result of Treason." *Magazine of American History*, vol. 1, no. 2(February 1877): 66-90.

DeVillo, Stephen. *The Battle of White Plains.* History Press, 2022.

Dippel, Horst. *Germany and the American Revolution*. Steiner, 1977.

Dixon, Edward. *Scenes in the Practice of a New York Surgeon.* New York: DeWitt and Davenport, 1855.

Douglass, Elisa P. "German Intellectuals and the American Revolution." *William and Mary Quarterly* 17, no. 2 (April 1960): 200–218.

Dunkerly, Robert. "How Did They Communicate?" Emerging Revolutionary War Era. Accessed February 4, 2025. https://emergingrevolutionarywar.org/2016/02/16/how-did-they-communicate/.

Dunlap, William. *A History of the American Theater*. New York: J&J Harper, 1832.

Dwyer, William M. *The Day Is Ours.* Viking, 1983.

Eelking, Max von. *The German Allied Troops in the North American War of Independence, 1776–1783.* Translated by J. G. Rosengarten. Joel Munsell's Sons, 1893.

Ellis, Joseph J. *His Excellency: George Washington.* Knopf, 2004.

Elsea, Karl and William Welsch. "Artillery Engagements at the Battle of Trenton. Parts 1, 2, 3." Emerging Revolutionary War Era. Accessed April 21, 2025. https://emergingrevolutionarywar.org/2020/12/26/the-first-of-three-artillery-engagements-at-the-battle-of-trenton-december-26-1776/.

Engel, Jonathan. "The Force of Nature: The Impact of Weather on Armies During the American War of Independence, 1775–1781." Master's thesis, Florida State University, 2011.

Ferguson, Niall. *The House of Rothschild*. Penguin, 1999.

Fischer, David Hackett. *Washington's Crossing*. Oxford University Press, 2004.

Flexner, James. *Washington in the American Revolution*, Little & Brown, 1967.

Force, Peter. *American Archives.* Ser. 5, vol 3. M. St. Clair Clarke and Peter Force, 1848–1853.

Founders Online. National Archives. Accessed May 30, 2025. https://founders.archives.gov/.

Franko, Alfred. *Pelham Manor: The Forgotten Battle of the Revolution*. Pelham Manor Bicentennial Committee, 1966.

French, Allen. *The Siege of Boston*. Macmillan, 1911.

Galloway, Joseph. *Letters to a Nobleman, on the Conduct of the War in the Middle Colonies.* London: J. Wilkie, 1780.

Gilsa, Georg Ernst von und zu. "Wiederhold to Ernst von und zu Gilsa Aug 29–31, 1776." German History Intersections. Accessed May 20, 2025. https://germanhistory-intersections.org/.

Gilsa, Georg Ernst von und zu. *The War in America and Enlightenment in Hesse: The Private Letters of Georg Ernst von und of Gilsa (1772–1784)*. Edited by Holger Graf. Hessian State Office for Historical Regional Studies Marburg, 2010. The letters are viewable on DFG Viewer (https://dfg-viewer.de/en/), a browser web service for displaying digital representations from decentralized library repositories. The web service is also accessible from German History Intersections, which is listed above in this bibliography. Accessed May 20, 2025. https://dfg-viewer.de/en/show?tx_dlf%5Bdouble%5D=1&tx_dlf%5Bid%5D=https%3A%2F%2Farchiv.ub.uni-marburg.de%2Feb%2F2020%2F0443%2Fmets-9821.xml&tx_dlf%5Bpage%5D=1&tx_dlf%5Bpagegrid%5D=0&cHash=d9f74523adfb572191a1d7be94946f8f.

Glover, T. N. "The Retreat of '76 Across Bergen County." Paper presented at the Society of Hackensack, November 20, 1905.

Glyn, Thomas. *Ensign Glyn's Journal.* Manuscript. Firestone Library Special Collections, Princeton University.

Graydon, Alexander. *Memoirs of His Own Time.* Philadelphia: Lindsay and Blakiston, 1846.

Greene, Nathanael. *The Papers of Nathanael Greene.* Edited by Richard Showman. Chapel Hill: University of North Carolina Press, 1976.

Greenwood, John. *The Revolutionary Services of John Greenwood.* Edited by Isaac Greenwood. De Vinne Press, 1922. Reprinted as *The Wartime Services of John Greenwood: A Young Patriot in the American Revolution.* Westvaco, 1981.

Groseclose, Barbara. *Emanuel Leutze.* Smithsonian Institute Press, 1975.

Gruber, I. R. *The Howe Brothers and the American Revolution.* University of North Carolina Press, 1972.

Haarmann, Albert W. "Contemporary Observations on the Hesse-Cassel Troops Sent to North America, 1776 to 1781." *Journal of the Society for Army Historical Research* 54, no. 219 (Autumn 1976): 130–134.

Hadaway, William. *The McDonald Papers, Part 1.* Westchester County Historical Society, 1926.

Hall, John. *History of the Presbyterian Church in Trenton, New Jersey.* New York: Anson D. F. Randolph, 1859.

Haven, C. C. *Thirty Days in New Jersey Ninety Years Ago: An essay revealing new facts in connection with Washington and his army.* Trenton, State Gazette, 1867.

Heister, Hauptmann von. *Hessian Court of Inquiry: The Affair at Trenton, December 26, 1776.* Lidgerwood Collection, Morristown Historical Park. Microfiche 251-270, sec. ML.

Heister Regiment. *Account of the North American War.* Lidgerwood Collection, Morristown Historical Park. Microfiche 364, sec B.

Heister Regiment. *Journal of von Heister.* Lidgerwood Collection, Morristown Historical Park. Microfiche 364, sec. FZ.

Heister Regiment. *Journal of the first Brigade of the von Heister corps.* Lidgerwood Collection, Morristown Historical Park. Microfiche 364, sec. H.

Hill, Steven W. "Hessian Flags in the American War for Independence, 1776–1783." *Military Collector & Historian* (Winter 2003/2004): 226-231.

Hinrichs, Johann. "Extracts from the Letter Book of Captain Johann Hinrichs of the Hessian Jäger Corps." *Pennsylvania Magazine of History and Biography* 22, no. 2 (1898): 146-149.

Hoare, Richard. *Balby Beginnings: The Launching of Quakerism.* Sessions of York, 2002.

Hoffman, Elliot. "The German Soldiers in the American Revolution." PhD diss., University of New Hampshire, 1982.

Hofmeister, Andrea. "Elementary Education, Schools, and the Demands of Everyday Life: Northwest Germany in 1800." *Central European History* 31, no. 4 (1998): 329-384.

Howat, John. "Washington Crosses the Delaware." *Bulletin of the Metropolitan Museum of Art* 26, no. 7 (March 1968): 289.

Howe, William. Letters to Lord George Germain, November 30, 1776, and December 20, 1776. In *American Archives: Documents of the American Revolutionary Period, 1774–1776*, edited by Peter Force. Series 5, vol. 3, 921–927, 1316–1317. Washington, DC: Government Printing Office, 1837–1853.

Hubbs, V. C. *Hessian Journals*. Camden House, 1981.

Hunter, Andrew. *The Revolutionary War Diary of Chaplain Andrew Hunter, New Jersey Brigade, Continental Army*. Rare Book Library, Princeton University, Princeton, NJ. Accessed May 29, 2025. https://revwar75.com/library/bob/HunterDiaries2.htm.

Hunter, Martin. *The Journal of General Sir Martin Hunter.* Edinburgh Press, 1894.

Huth, Hans. "Letters from a Hessian Mercenary." *Pennsylvania Magazine of History and Biography* (October 1938): 488-501.

Hutton, Anne Hawkes. *Portrait of Patriotism.* Chilton, 1959.

Hutton, Anne Hawkes. *The Year and the Spirit of '76*. Franklin Press, 1977.

Ingrao, Charles. *The Hessian Mercenary State.* Cambridge University Press, 1987.

Jones, Kenneth. *Johannes Schwalm: The Hessian.* Johannes Schwalm Historical Association, 1976.

Kalm, Peter. *Travels into North America.* William Eyres, 1770.

Kapp, Friedrich. *The Soldier Trade of German Princes to America.* Reprint, Project Gutenberg ebook, guttenberg.org. Accessed June 18, 2025. https://www.gutenberg.org/cache/epub/47054/pg47054.txt.

Kemble, Stephen. "The Kemble Papers." *Collections of the New-York Historical Society for 1883.* Vols. 16 and 17. Published 1884.

Ketchum, Richard. *Decisive Day: The Battle for Bunker Hill.* Doubleday, 1974.

Ketchum, Richard. *The Winter Soldiers*. Doubleday, 1973.

Kidder, William. *Crossroads of the Revolution: Trenton 1774–1783.* Post Hill/Knox Press, 2019.

Kidder, William. *Ten Crucial Days: Washington's Vision of Victory Unfolds.* Post Hill/Knox Press, 2019.

Kipping, Ernst. *The Hessian View of America, 1776–1783*. Philip Freneau Press, 1971.

Knyphausen Regiment. *Journal of the Regular Corp Under the Command of His Excellency Lieutenant General Knyphausen*. Lidgerwood Collection, Morristown Historical Park. Microfiche, box P.

Krebs, Daniel. *A Generous and Merciful Enemy*. University of Oklahoma Press, 2013.

Lane, Wheaton. *From Indian Trail to Iron Horse*. Princeton University Press, 1939.

Lederer, Richard. *The Place Names of Westchester County*. Harbor Hill Books, 1978.

Lee, Francis. *History of Trenton, New Jersey*. State Gazette, 1895.

Lefkowitz, Arthur. *The Long Retreat*. Rutgers University Press, 1999.

Leiby, Adrian. *The Revolutionary War in the Hackensack Valley*. Rutgers University Press, 1962.

Lengel, Edward G. *General George Washington: A Military Life*. Random House, 2005.

Londahl-Smidt, Donald. "British and Hessian Accounts of the Invasion of Bergen County 1776." In *The Revolutionary War in Bergen County: The Times That Tried Men's Souls*, edited by Carol Karels. History Press, 2007.

Longmore, Paul K. *The Invention of George Washington*. University of Virginia Press, 1999.

Lossberg Regiment. *Journal of the Regular Corp Under the Command of His Excellency Lieutenant General Lossberg*. Lidgerwood Collection, Morristown Historical Park. Microfiche box M.

Lossing, Benson. *The Pictorial Field-Book of the Revolution*. Vols. 1 and 2. Harper & Brothers, 1852.

Lowell, Edward J. *The Hessians and the Other German Auxiliaries of Great Britain in the Revolutionary War*. New York: Harper & Brothers, 1884.

Ludlum, David. "The Weather of American Independence: The Loss of New York City and New Jersey." *Weatherwise* 28, no. 4 (August 1975): 172-176.

Ludlum, David. "The Weather of American Independence: Trenton and Princeton." *Weatherwise* 29, no. 2 (April 1976): 74-83.

Lundin, Leonard. *Cockpit of the Revolution*. Princeton: Princeton University Press, 1940.

MacKenzie, Frederick. *The Diary of Frederick MacKenzie*. Harvard University Press, 1930.

Mackesy, Piers. *The War for America*. Harvard University Press, 1964.

Martin, Joseph Plumb. *A Narrative of a Revolutionary Soldier*. Signet Classics, 2001.

Mayo Clinic staff. "Adult Attention-Deficit/Hyperactivity Disorder (ADHD)." Mayo Clinic. Accessed 4/2/25. https://mayoclinic.org/diseases-conditions/adult-adhd/symptoms-causes/syc-20350878.

McCarty, Thomas. "The Revolutionary War Journal of Thomas McCarty." *Proceedings of the New Jersey Historical Society* 82 (1964): 29-46.

McIntyre, James. *Johann Ewald: Jager Commander*. Knox Press, 2020.

McMichael, James. "The Diary of Lieutenant James McMichael of the Pennsylvania Line." *Pennsylvania Magazine of History and Biography* 16 (1892): 129-149.

McNealy, Terry. "The Durham Family and the Durham Boats." *Journal of the Bucks County Historical Society* 7, no. 1 (1990): 14-15.

Melsheimer, F. *Journal of The Voyage of the Brunswick Auxiliaries*. Pamphlets of American History. Morning Chronicle Steam Printing, 1891.

Mockler, Anthony. *The Mercenaries*. Macmillan, 1969.

Mollo, John. *Uniforms of the American Revolution*. Blandford Press, 1985.

Montross, Lynn. *Rag, Tag and Bobtail: The Story of the Continental Army, 1775–1783*. Harper & Brothers, 1952.

Morgan, William, ed. *Naval Documents of the American Revolution*. US Department of the Navy, 1976.

Münchhausen, Friedrich von. *At General Howe's Side*. Philip Freneau Press, 1974.

New York State Historical Association. "Diary of Voyage from Stade in Hanover to Quebec in America of the Second Division of Ducal Brunswick Mercenaries." *Quarterly Journal of the New York State Historical Association* 8, no. 4 (October 1927): 323-351.

Norris, David. "Halberds and Spontoons." *Warfare History Network*, May 2016. Accessed April 3, 2025. https://warfarehistorynetwork.com/article/halberds-and-spontoons/.

Paine, Thomas. *Collected Writings*. Edited by Eric Foner. Citadel Press, 1945.

Pausch, Georg. *Journal of Captain Pausch*. Albany: Joel Munsell's Sons, 1886.

Peale, Charles Wilson. "Autobiography, December 8, 1776, entry." Unpublished ms. American Philosophical Society, Philadelphia.

Peale, Charles Wilson. *The Selected Papers of Charles Wilson Peale*, vol 1, no 1. Yale University Press, 1983.

Pedlow, Gregory. "The Nobility of Hesse-Kassel." PhD diss., Johns Hopkins University, 1979.

Pemberton, Phineas. "The Phineas Pemberton Weather Diary, Philadelphia, 1776–1777." American Philosophical Society. In *American Philosophical Society Transactions*, n.s. 6 (1839), 395. Reproduced in *Washington's Crossing*, by David Fischer, appendix K, 399-403.

Pettengill, Ray, trans. *Letters from America, 1776 to 1779.* Houghton Mifflin, 1924.

Pfister, Albert, and Johann Gottfried Seume. *The Voyage of the First Hessian Army From Portsmouth to New York, 1776.* Charles Frederick Heartman, 1915.

Powell, Levan. George Johnston to Leven Powell, December 29, 1776. Leven Powell Papers. Library of Congress, Washington, D.C.

Powell, William S. "A Connecticut Soldier Under Washington: Elisha Bostwick's Memoirs of the First Years of the Revolution." *William and Mary Quarterly*, 3rd ser., no. 6 (1949): 94-107.

Proprietary House. "Royal Governor 1774-1776." Accessed April 18, 2025. https://www.theproprietaryhouse.org/royal-governor. theproprietaryhouse.org.

Raum, John. *History of the City of Trenton.* W. T. Nicholson, 1871.

Redlich, Fritz. *The German Military Enterpriser and His Workforce.* Franz Steiner Verlag, 1964.

Reed, Joseph. "General Reed's Narrative of the Movements of the American Army in the Neighborhood of Trenton in the Winter of 1776–1777." *Pennsylvania Magazine of History and Biography* 8 (1884): 391.

Retzer, Henry. "March Route from Hessen to America: Jeramias Kappes." *Johannes Schwan Historical Association* 7, no. 4 (2004): 7–14.

Reuber, Johannes. *Johannes Reuber Diary.* Translated and edited by Bruce Burgoyne. Editor's private copy and correspondence on April 7, 1991.

Robertson, Archibald. *Diaries and Sketches in America, 1762–1780.* New York Public Library, 1930.

Robson, Eric. *The American Revolution in Its Political and Military Aspects, 1763–1783.* Archon Books, 1965.

Romeyn, Theodore B. *Historical Discourse Delivered on Occasion of the Re-Opening and Dedication of the First Reformed [Dutch] Church, at Hackensack, N.J.: May 2, 1869.* New York: Board of Publication, Reformed Church in America, 1870.

Ross, David. "The Hessian Jägerkorps in New York and Pennsylvania, 1776–1777." *Journal of the American Revolution*, May 14, 2015. Accessed

May 30, 2025. https://allthingsliberty.com/2015/05/the-hessian-jagerkorps-in-new-york-and-pennsylvania-1776-1777/.

Rueffer, Karl. "Journal of Lieutenant Rueffer of Melsungen." In *The Hesse-Cassel Mirbach Regiment in the American Revolution.* Edited and translated by Bruce E. Burgoyne. Heritage Books, 2008.

Ruppert, Bob. "A Fast Ship from Salem: Carrying News of War." *Journal of the American Revolution*, April 17, 2015. Accessed April 17, 2025. https://allthingsliberty.com/2015/04/a-fast-ship-from-salem-carrying-news-of-war.

Ryden, George. *Letters to and from Caeser Rodney.* Da Capo Press, 1970.

Satterthwaite, Elizabeth. "Mahlon Stacy, Quaker Founder of Trenton." *Proceedings of the New Jersey Historical Society*, n.s., vol. 9, no. 2 (April 1924): 150-154.

Schenawolf, Harry. "A Hessian Soldier's Letter Home Describes Colonial America," contains letter from Johann von Hinrichs to Professor Schlozer, September 18, 1776, Revolutionary War Journal, September 19, 2013; accessed May 20, 2025. https://revolutionarywarjournal.com/hessian-soldiers-letter-home/

Schmidt, H. D. "The Hessian Mercenaries: The Career of a Political Cliché." *History* 43, no. 149 (1958): 207–212.

Schnitker, Anna. "Writing the Nation." PhD diss., University of Edinburgh, 2004.

Schwab, Johannes. *German Troops in the American Revolution.* Historical Society Press, 1965.

Schwalm, Mark. "The Hessian Auxiliaries to the British Crown: A Series of Four Lectures." Messiah College, 1984.

Serle, Ambrose. *The American Journal of Ambrose Serle.* Huntington Library, 1940.

Slagle, Robert. "The Von Lossberg Regiment." PhD diss., American University, 1965.

Slocum, Joshua. *An Authentic Narrative of the Life of Joshua Slocum: Containing a Succinct Account of His Revolutionary Services.* Hartford: Printed for the Author, 1844. Hathitrust.org. accessed June 7, 2025. https://catalog.hathitrust.org/Record/009596164.

Smith, Morton. *George Washington: A Profile.* Hill & Wang, 1969.

Smith, Paul. *Letters of the Delegates to Congress 1774 to 1789.* Library of Congress, 1976.

Smith, Samuel. *The Colonial History of New Jersey.* W. S. Sharp, 1890.

Snell, James. *History of Hunterdon and Somerset.* Philadelphia: Everts & Peck, 1881.

Spees, Everett. "The Erbprinz Fusilier Regiment at Staten Island." *Journal of the Johannes Schwalm Historical Association* 23 (2020): 26-47.

Spilman, Rick. "Update: Looking Back at When New York Harbor Froze." *Old Salt Blog*, January 4, 2018. Accessed June 7, 2025. https://www.oldsaltblog.com/2018/01/update-looking-back-new-york-harbor-froze/.

Stehle, Raymond. "Washington Crossing the Delaware." *Pennsylvania History* 31 (1964), 271-294.

Steuernagel, Philip. *A Memoir by Philip Steuernagel.* Collection of Bruce Burgoyne, Dover, DE.

Stirke, Henry. "A British Officer's Revolutionary War Journal." Edited by Sydney Bradford. *Maryland Historical Magazine* 56, no. 2 (June 1961): 150-176.

Stryker, William S. *The Battles of Trenton and Princeton.* Houghton, Mifflin, 1898.

Stryker, William S. *Trenton 100 Years Ago.* Library of Congress, 1878.

Toothman, Stephanie. "Trenton, New Jersey, 1719 to 1779." PhD diss., University of Pennsylvania, 1977.

Trevelyan, George Otto. *The American Revolution, Vol. 3.* Longmans, Green, 1905.

Ukers, William. *All About Coffee.* Tea and Coffee Trade Journal Co., 1922.

Urquhart, Frank J. *A History of the City of Newark, New Jersey: Embracing Practically Two and a Half Centuries, 1666–1913.* Lewis Historical Publishing, 1913.

Wade, Herbert, and Robert Lively. *The Adventures of Two Company Officers in Washington's Army*. Princeton University Press, 1958.

Waldeck, Philip. *Diary of Philip Waldeck.* Collection of Bruce Burgoyne, Dover, DE.

Walker, Edwin Robert. *A History of Trenton 1679 to 1929*. Trenton Historical Society, 1929. Accessed June 1, 2025. https://www.trentonhistory.org/His/colonial.html.

Ward, Christopher. *The War of the Revolution*. Macmillan, 1952.

Ward, Harry. *Major General Adam Stephen and the Cause of American Liberty.* University Press of Virginia, 1989.

Washington, George. *The Writings of George Washington*. Collected and edited by Worthington Chauncey Ford. Vol. 5, 1776–1777. G. P. Putnam's Sons, 1890.

Webb, Samuel Blachley. *Correspondence and Journals of Samuel Blachley Webb, 1772–1806*. Edited by Worthington Chauncey Ford. 3 vols. Wickersham Press, 1893.

Webster, Ian. "Value of 1776 British Pounds Today." UK Inflation Calculator. Accessed February 4, 2025. https://www.in2013dollars.com/uk/inflation/1776.

Weller, Jac. "Guns of Destiny: Field Artillery in the Trenton-Princeton Campaign." *Military Affairs* (Spring 1956): 1-15.

Westervelt, Frances, ed. *History of Bergen County, New Jersey, 1630–1923.* Vol. 1. Lewis Historical Publishing, 1923.

White, Joseph. "The Good Soldier White." *American Heritage,* vol. 7, no. 4 (June 1956): 74-79.

White, Matthew. "Statistics of Wars, Oppressions, and Atrocities of the Eighteenth Century." Necrometrics.com. Accessed April 2, 2025. https://necrometrics.com/wars18c.htm.

Whittredge, Worthington, and John Baur. "The Autobiography of Worthington Whittredge." *Brooklyn Museum Journal* (1942): 7-68.

Wickwire, Franklin B., and Mary B. Wickwire. *Cornwallis and the War of Independence.* Faber and Faber, 1971.

Wiederhold, Andreas. "Diary of the Hessian Lieutenant Andreas Wiederhold." In *Defeat, Disaster and Dedication.* Translated by Bruce Burgoyne. Heritage Books, 1996.

WikiTree. "Mahlon Stacey, Sr. (1638–1704)." Accessed June 1, 2025. https://www.wikitree.com/wiki/Stacy-192.

Wilkinson, James. *Memoirs of My Own Time.* Philadelphia: Abraham Small, 1816.

Woelfel, Margaret, trans. "Memoirs of a Hessian Conscript: J. G. Seume's Reluctant Voyage to America." *William and Mary Quarterly* 5, no. 4 (October 1948): 553-570.

Wright, Robert. "Side by Side: British, Germans and Loyalists." *Johannes Schwab Historical Society* 23 (2020): 3-25.

Wyss, Arthur. "Friedrich II: Landgrave of Hesse-Kassel." *Allgemeine Deutsche Biographie* 7 (1878): 524-528.

Zin, Johann. "Journal of the Hesse-Cassel von Donop Regiment." In *The Diary of Lieutenant von Bardeleben and Other von Donop Regiment Documents.* Translated by Bruce Burgoyne. Heritage Books, 2007.

Acknowledgments

My deepest gratitude to my great friend, English Professor Steve Streeter. I have lost count of how many times he critiqued and revised my writing. He changed my life when he ripped a speech from my hands and told me to talk to the audience, not read to them. As eleven-year-old boys, we were blessed to experience the golden age of New York basketball, watching Willis Reed's Knicks from front-row seats, courtesy of a Brooklyn mafioso. (Perhaps that real-life thriller will be my next book.)

Special thanks to author and professor of writing John Bowers, who brought infectious literary inspiration to every room he entered. Born in Tennessee during the Great Depression, John honed his craft writing under tremendous pressure at a pulp fiction publishing house where he was expected to produce at least two stories a week. He was essentially working in a literary version of a sweatshop, sharing a desk with another young writer trying to get published: Mario Puzo. When someone once described John as "a very wise, cosmopolitan country boy," he replied, "That's flattering, and I won't try to improve on it."

Thanks to the great novelist and screenwriter Scott Sommer, taken from us too soon. Scott despised commercialism and refused to watch television. His only indulgence with the "boob tube" was New York Giants football, though he swore he turned down the sound during commercials.

My gratitude to the late Bruce Burgoyne, who generously shared copies of unpublished translations of several Hessian diaries, and to the late Lieutenant Colonel Donald M. Londahl-Smidt for sharing his extraordinary knowledge of the American Revolution in New Jersey.

To writer, publisher, book agent, and tour guide extraordinaire Roger Williams, I give my deepest thanks for his continuous ability to push me to a higher level. Without Roger, this book would not exist.

To my parents, Marvin and Shirley Bier, whose rule was simple: as long as it wasn't a comic book, they would buy me any book that interested me. To my cousin Gail Franz, who opened up my world of reading with *Charlotte's Web*.

Finally, to Barbie, my dear, sweet, blushing bride of almost four decades. She has improved more lives than I could ever dream of doing. She carried our family when things were rough and propped us up when we felt down. Without Barbie, everything would have fallen apart.

Love ya, babe!

Index